MERLEAU-PONTY'S PHENOMENOLOGY OF LANGUAGE

MERLEAU-PONTY'S PHENOMENOLOGY OF LANGUAGE

Dimitris Apostolopoulos

ROWMAN &
LITTLEFIELD
———————INTERNATIONAL
London • New York

Published by Rowman & Littlefield International, Ltd.
6 Tinworth Street, London SE11 5AL
www.rowmaninternational.com

Rowman & Littlefield International, Ltd. is an affiliate of
Rowman & Littlefield
4501 Forbes Boulevard, Suite 200, Lanham, Maryland 20706, USA
With additional offices in Boulder, New York, Toronto (Canada), and London (UK)
www.rowman.com

Copyright © 2019 by Dimitris Apostolopoulos

All rights reserved. No part of this book may be reproduced in any form or by any electronic or mechanical means, including information storage and retrieval systems, without written permission from the publisher, except by a reviewer who may quote passages in a review.

British Library Cataloguing in Publication Information
A catalogue record for this book is available from the British Library

ISBN: HB 978-1-78661-199-4

Library of Congress Cataloging-in-Publication Data Is Available

ISBN 978-1-78661-199-4 (cloth)
ISBN 978-1-5381-4798-6 (pbk)
ISBN 978-1-78661-200-7 (electronic)

CONTENTS

Acknowledgements	ix
A Note on Abbreviations and Texts	xi
Introduction	1
Notes	10
Part I	13
1 Structure and Language	15
1. Behaviour, Meaning and Structure	16
2. Description, Sense and Signification	21
3. Structure and Expression	27
4. Unresolved Questions	31
Notes	36
2 Empirical Expression	39
1. Schneider's Linguistic Capacities	40
2. Merleau-Ponty's Hermeneutic Account of Linguistic Expression	46
2.1 Sedimentation	
2.2 Gesture	
2.3 Meaning and Interpretation	
3. Authentic Expression	57
4. Authentic Language and Freedom	59
Notes	64
3 Transcendental Expression	69
1. Objective Thought	71
2. Explanatory Openness	74

3. Transcendental Reflection	78
3.1 Circularity	
3.2 'Tacit' and 'Spoken' *Cogito*	
4. Language and Foundation	87
5. 'Transcendental or Authentic Speech'	97
6. Description or Creation?	100
Notes	105

Part II   113

4   Scientific and Literary Expression   115

1. 'Metaphysics' or 'Rationality' and 'Expression'   116
2. Formal Expression   120
3. Expression in Linguistics: Saussure   127
   - 3.1 *'Langue'* and *'Parole'*
   - 3.2 *'Parole'* and Dialogue
   - 3.3 'Diacritical' Meaning-Formation
   - 3.4 Institution, Rationality and History
4. 'Indirect' or 'Operant' Expression: Proust and Valéry   137
   - 4.1 On Painting and Literature
   - 4.2 Valéry and 'the Voice'
   - 4.3 Proust and Literary Description
5. Literature, Phenomenology and Metaphysics   147

Notes   150

5   The Linguistic Foundations of Ontology   153

1. Ontology, Sense and Intersubjectivity   155
2. The Implicit Ontological Implications of Dialogue   159
   - 2.1 Reversibility and Narcissism
   - 2.2 Activity and Passivity
   - 2.3 Intentional 'Transgression' and 'Encroachment'
3. The Explicit Ontological Implications of Dialogue   173
4. Ontological Expression in the Making   176

Notes   180

Part III   185

6   Language and World   187

1. Philosophical Predecessors and Potential Influences   190
   - 1.1 Humboldt's *'innere Sprachform'*
   - 1.2 Cassirer, Language and Representation

CONTENTS

    2. Meaning as Cohesion   196
        2.1 The '*Écart*'
        2.2 'Latent' Intentionality ('Flesh', 'Reversibility' and 'Narcissism')
        2.3 'Institution'
    3. Articulating the World   208
        3.1 The Intertwining of Speech, Thought and Perception
        3.2 'Inherent' and 'Spoken' Language
        3.3 Expression and World-Formation
    4. The Limits of Language and World   227
    Notes   231

7 Ontology and Language   237
    1. 'Hyper-Reflection'   240
    2. 'Interrogation'   246
    3. Creative Description   250
    4. Dialectical Expression   254
    5. Concept Invention   262
    6. Language and Essence   269
    7. Philosophy as 'Operative Language'   276
    Notes   280

Conclusion   287
    Notes   296
Bibliography   297
    1. Works by Merleau-Ponty   297
        Published Works
        Unpublished Works
    2. Works by Other Authors   298
Index   307
    Index Nominum   307
    Index Rerum   308
About the Author   313

ACKNOWLEDGEMENTS

I have accrued many debts in the course of this project. My greatest academic debt is owed to Steve Watson and Gary Gutting, who supervised the thesis that is the basis for this monograph. I have benefitted greatly from their perspicuous comments, advice, erudition and friendship. Gary tragically passed away as this book was nearing completion. I hope that its appearance will honour his memory.

Sara Heinämaa deserves special thanks for generously agreeing to lend her expertise and time to the initial project, and for taking an interest in it. I hope her efforts have not been in vain, and I thank her for her sustained support and scholarly inspiration. The philosophy department at the University of Notre Dame offered an intellectually stimulating research environment, and I have benefited from many discussions with departmental friends and colleagues. I have learned a great deal about European philosophy from Karl Ameriks and Fred Rush, who in addition to being excellent scholars, are also fine philosophical interlocutors. I thank the editorial team at Rowman & Littlefield International for their initial interest in the project, their professionalism, and their prompt help throughout the production process. I am grateful to reviewers who read the manuscript, suggested helpful improvements, and deemed it worthy of publication. I was fortunate to be nourished and supported by friends and loved ones while undertaking research for this project; you know who you are, and I thank you. Above all, my parents' unconditional love made all of this possible.

A number of institutions provided material support that made this research practically feasible. In particular, I am grateful for the generous financial support provided by the Social Sciences and Humanities Research Council of Canada, the Nanovic Institute for European Studies at the University of Notre Dame, the Department of Philosophy at the University of Notre Dame, and the Institute for Studies in the Liberal Arts.

Some parts of chapter 3 are informed by my contribution 'Merleau-Ponty, Hegel, and the Task of Phenomenological Explanation' in the 2018 issue of *Phänomenologische Forschungen*, published by Felix Meiner Verlag, Hamburg (https://meiner.de/phaef). Most of chapter 5 originally appeared as D. Apostolopoulos (2018), 'On the Motivations for Merleau-Ponty's Ontological Research', *British Journal for the History of Philosophy*, 26:2, 348–70; this is the copyright of BSHP and is reproduced with permission from Taylor & Francis. Some parts of chapter 4 and chapter 7 originally appeared in D. Apostolopoulos (2018), 'The Systematic Import of Merleau-Ponty's Philosophy of Literature', *Journal of the British Society for Phenomenology*, 49:1, 1–17. This is the copyright of the British Society for Phenomenology and is reproduced with permission from Taylor & Francis (http://www.tandfonline.com).

A NOTE ON ABBREVIATIONS AND TEXTS

The following abbreviations will be used to cite Merleau-Ponty's works in text:

AD: *Adventures of the Dialectic* (1973/1955)
CPP: *Child Psychology and Pedagogy* (2010)
HLP: *Husserl at the Limits of Phenomenology* (2001/1998)
IP: *Institution and Passivity* (2010/2003)
IPP: *In Praise of Philosophy* (1953)
MPR: *The Merleau-Ponty Reader* (2007)
MSME: *Le monde sensible et le monde de l'expression* (2011)
N: *Nature: Course Notes from the Collège de France* (2003/1995)
NC: *Notes de cours au Collège de France, 1958–1961* (1996)
OE: *L'Œil et l'Esprit* (2007/1964)
PD: *Parcours Deux* (2001)
PhP: *Phenomenology of Perception* (2012/2005)
PrP: *The Primacy of Perception* (1964/1996)
PW: *The Prose of the World* (1973/1969)
RULL: *Recherches sur l'usage littéraire du langage* (2013)
S: *Signs* (1964/1960)
SB: *The Structure of Behaviour* (1967/1967)
SNS: *Sense and Non-Sense* (1964/1948)
VI: *The Visible and the Invisible* (1968/1979)

Citations from published works refer to the most recent English translation and the French original, respectively. I have often modified existing translations. Where there is no translation, I supply my own. All translations of *La prose du monde* are my own. Citations from unpublished manuscripts refer to the manuscript volume and pagination of the Bibliothèque nationale de France (e.g., BNF Ms. Vol. XX *r/x*). When available, Merleau-Ponty's own pagination is also noted.

INTRODUCTION

Phenomenology studies the structures of conscious experience. It breaks with an ancient and enduring assumption of Western thought, according to which the essence of something cannot be known from its appearance.[1] Against this assumption, philosophers in the phenomenological tradition argue that appearances are primary access points to reality. These thinkers are chiefly interested in understanding the intentional structures associated with different modalities of consciousness. To have an experience is to be directed in some determinate way towards something: consciousness is always consciousness of some object or other. The objects of cognition, imagination, perception and of other modes of intentional experience are first and foremost *phenomena*: objects of experience show or 'give' themselves in some way.[2] Philosophical analysis of intentional states and their objects will turn up different structural and qualitative characteristics. But prior to analysis, we encounter a rich layer of meaningful appearances whenever we conceive, imagine or encounter some matter at hand. The people outside my window seem to be hurrying; a scent reminds me of a familiar place; an argument strikes me as weak. While each of these experiences has a different intentional structure, in each case I find myself directed to determinate meanings that come before the mind or the senses. The intentional structure of experience provides us with evidence about the world and helps us understand it. Phenomenology explores the intentional manifestation of meaning and details its conditions of possibility.

Phenomenological accounts of experience have chiefly analysed vision or visual intuition. Etymologically, this focus is unsurprising: a 'phenomenon' is something that shows itself, appears or comes into view. An emphasis on vision is fitting for a discipline that investigates lived experience and how objects are present to consciousness. Unsurprisingly, most phenomenologists have defined phenomena in visual terms. In *Ideas* I, Husserl's 'principle of all principles' identifies the evidence that nourishes phenomenological reflection with that given in visual intuition.[3] Husserl's call to return to the 'things themselves' is often interpreted as a return to the original givenness of objects in visual intuition.[4] Heidegger's *Being and Time* contends that the '[p]henomenon, the showing itself in itself, signifies a distinctive way in which something can be encountered'.[5] Despite his criticisms of Husserl, Heidegger agrees that phenomenology attempts 'to let that which shows itself be seen from itself in the very way in which it shows itself from itself'.[6] For Sartre, 'The phenomenon is what manifests itself' to consciousness.[7] Even Merleau-Ponty, who I will argue eventually departs from this assumption, often accepts a visual interpretation of the phenomenon (PhP lxx/7).

A focus on intuition has encouraged the view that questions pertaining to language and expression, while significant, are not of decisive importance for phenomenology's basic philosophical aims. Needless to say, phenomenologists have devoted significant attention to the philosophy of language. Husserl's *Logical Investigations*, a foundational phenomenological text, offers detailed analyses of expression, meaning and signs. Husserl argues that cognitive activity is always cloaked in language. However, while he worries about how phenomenological results might be translated into everyday language, the subsequent trajectory of his research suggests that he does not consider the philosophy of language to be a central problem-domain for phenomenology.

Subsequent developments in phenomenology brought increased interest in language. Fink, for example, focuses on an issue that Husserl highlights in the *Crisis* (though the problem has earlier origins).[8] Husserl suggests that natural language terms must be purified and transformed if the phenomenological reduction is to succeed. In the sphere of reduced perception, phenomenology must avail itself of a 'new sort of language'. Even if a recourse to 'ordinary language' is 'unavoidable', 'its meanings are also unavoidably transformed'.[9] Husserl does not say much about how this procedure is to unfold, however. In his *Sixth Cartesian Meditation*, Fink argues that phenomenological language must remain partially inadequate. Insofar as language is primarily intended to signify objects in the natural attitude, it 'rebels' when it is limited to expressing only transcendental meanings, which lack existential predication. The mismatch between these two realms should be curtailed as much as possible, but it is not possible to fully bridge the gap between natural and transcendental language.[10] An always, imperfect analogy obtains between phenomenological and everyday expression.

Heidegger's reflections on language are arguably the most well known and most influential phenomenological treatment of language-related issues, and have attracted scholarly and popular attention. In a 1924 to 1925 seminar on Plato's *Sophist*, he claims that phenomenology must devote as much attention to its modes of expression as it does to faithfully detailing phenomena.[11] Heidegger stresses that studied attention to phenomena and to language is needed to understand experience. In *Being and Time*, he argues that the *logos* is a fundamental element of phenomenological disclosure, and offers detailed analyses of everyday language use, its possibilities and its pitfalls.[12] Perhaps most famously, his later writings offer extended meditations on poetry and poetic expression, language and truth, and develop a distinctive mode of expression in their own right.

In light of some important phenomenological predecessors, Merleau-Ponty's interest in language may not strike an informed reader as particularly novel or noteworthy. A careful reading of his life's work will show that this conclusion is unwarranted. While the thinkers above have advanced our understanding of the phenomenology of language, I will argue that Merleau-Ponty goes further in his estimation of the philosophical importance that language has for phenomenology. More than most other phenomenological thinkers, Heidegger stresses the importance of language, but he also suggests that the phenomenon takes priority.[13] *Being and Time* contends that any study of language must be grounded 'on foundations which are ontologically more primordial' than those given by the parameters of post-Humboldtian 'philosophy of language'.[14] These foundations, however, are neither linguistic nor expressive; instead, they refer us to Dasein's ontology or its state of being, of which a capacity for discourse is but one modality. Heidegger's writings from the 1930s onwards place greater emphasis on the disclosive power of language, and arguably shift his earlier view; but while they offer one interpretation of how philosophy can profit from poetry and poetic modes of expression, the degree to which they are phenomenological is unclear and remains a matter of scholarly debate.

This book argues that on Merleau-Ponty's interpretation, phenomenology is essentially an expressive undertaking. More forcefully than his phenomenological predecessors, he ties the philosophical prospects of phenomenology to its expressive capabilities and their limits. On Merleau-Ponty's reading, phenomenology is a labour of language. Its fundamental task is to articulate the meaning of appearances. To meet its basic goals, phenomenology must attend to and entertain a broad range of methodological and conceptual questions. But insights from phenomenological reflections on language will guide every step. To a greater degree than other thinkers in the tradition, Merleau-Ponty probes the philosophical implications of an interpretation of phenomenology that takes seriously the claim that it is a descriptive enterprise with its own distinctive, expressive characteristics. Phenomenologists of different stripes subscribe to this basic commitment. One of Merleau-Ponty's most valuable philosophical contributions is to have highlighted and explored its full theoretical implications, which have been overshadowed by phenomenologists' abiding interest in intuition.

Phenomenology attempts to detail the meaning and structure of experience through description. If this effort is to prove successful, extended meditation on how appearances and objects can be articulated in language is required, for description is a linguistic activity. The phenomenological *logos* always responds to and takes direction from phenomena. Intuition is a primary and basic evidentiary source. But phenomenality is as much a result of articulation as it is a residue of perceptual experience. We encounter a range of different objects in experience, but by itself, experience has no philosophical weight. Perception alone does not translate into any particular philosophical position. To understand the intentional structure of an appearance, this structure must be described. But everything changes when we commit ourselves to articulating phenomena. Phenomena and intuitive evidence can be critically and thoroughly studied provided they are expressed in language. Phenomenology employs a reflective methodology when probing appearances. According to Merleau-Ponty, like all other cognitive activities, reflection unfolds in language. If language is the medium that brings appearances to philosophical scrutiny, this suggests that phenomena are co-constituted by the language in which they are articulated. For Merleau-Ponty, perceptual and linguistic meaning jointly constitute the meaning of objects and the structure of experience.

If this is right, then attending to the modes of expression that support the disclosure of intentional structures becomes a pressing demand. This is the work of a phenomenological philosophy of language. But if phenomenology remains through and through an account of perception, and is not perception itself, foundational questions in the philosophy of language will surface whenever phenomena are disclosed. The philosophy of language is not, then, of regional or ancillary interest to phenomenology; its implications touch any area of phenomenological research.

On the received view, Merleau-Ponty is a philosopher of perception *par excellence*. Many major commentaries on his work take a broadly visual approach.[15] This seems solidly justified by his interest in perception, already detectable in his earliest philosophical writings in the 1930s.[16] His first mature works focus on concepts like 'behaviour' and 'perception', terms that do not suggest any particular interest in questions pertaining to language.

Some recent studies have helpfully highlighted some of Merleau-Ponty's important contributions to the philosophy of language, and are a welcome addition to work from an earlier generation of scholars.[17] This book attempts to go one step further: it argues that Merleau-Ponty's phenomenology of language is essential for understanding the motivations and arguments behind some of his most important concepts and insights (including many that do not pertain to language); for properly understanding his complex philosophical development; and for appraising the distinctive view of phenomenology that he invites us to entertain. This book argues that the phenomenology of language is the interpretive key for understanding Merleau-Ponty's thought and his conceptual development. And it contends that for Merleau-Ponty, the philosophy of language is phenomenology's *prima philosophia*.

Before sketching the steps this study will take, some methodological notes are needed. The first concerns the terms 'philosophy' and 'phenomenology' of language. I will often use these terms interchangeably. The former is somewhat more general, and touches on issues that sometimes extend beyond the lived experience of language use, while the latter is often used to refer to the description of concrete acts of linguistic expression. For the purposes of this study, I will assume that there is no significant philosophical difference between the two terms.

Second, this book is focused on issues that are internal to Merleau-Ponty's thought. It attempts to defend a series of claims about Merleau-Ponty and about his standing in the phenomenological tradition. It also uses these results to draw some broader and tentative conclusions about the phenomenological enterprise. The texts, thinkers and terminology I rely on reflect this focus. It is not a goal of this book to draw connections with analytic or post-Kantian philosophy of language. Attentive readers will observe connections with and implications for debates in analytic philosophy of language, linguistics and cognitive science, and broader post-Kantian philosophical currents. Along the way, I note some of these connections, but it is not my intention to develop or explore them in detail. This would be a worthwhile and profitable undertaking, but it is beyond the scope of this study, which is focused on understanding the genesis, substance and philosophical implications of Merleau-Ponty's philosophy of language.

In chapter 1, I suggest that in Merleau-Ponty's research into the concept of 'behaviour', undertaken in a period whose intellectual pursuits seem far removed from concerns proper to the philosophy of language, the philosophical importance of language is nevertheless announced *in nuce*. *The Structure of Behaviour* avails itself of the concepts of 'structure' or 'form' with the promise that they will yield a nonreductive account of matter, life, perception and 'behaviour'. As it turns out, even if we encounter meaningful data in elementary vital and perceptual structures, their meaning, like that of 'structure', ultimately depends on the descriptive activity of consciousness. But description is a special kind of language use. As I argue, for Merleau-Ponty the clarification of perceptual, biological and physical structures is guided by an implicit linguistic criterion, which yields the unexpected result that language plays some non-negligible role in forming the meaning of perceptual structure. Merleau-Ponty does not address this directly in this work. But together with other suggestive concepts and distinctions first articulated in *Structure* (e.g., that between *sens* and *signification*, or 'ideal' and 'real' meaning), his subsequent writings can be understood as an extended attempt to work out its philosophical implications.

As I show in chapter 2, this effort continues more systematically in *Phenomenology of Perception*. This text offers more detailed accounts of everyday linguistic expression. Merleau-Ponty's interest in the full range of expressive and embodied phenomena leads him to articulate a tripartite, loosely hermeneutic view of expression, centred on the concepts of 'sedimentation', 'gesture' and ultimately on embodied acts of linguistic interpretation (sometimes referred to using the term 'transcendence'). Everyday linguistic expression attempts to articulate meanings encountered in experience, using tools whose familiarity hides a more complex structure. As I will show, key components of this view surface in his much-discussed analysis of Schneider, whose linguistic import has been overlooked. And their implications extend to Merleau-Ponty's account of existential freedom, which can clarify how it relates to Sartre's view.

Arguably, deeper philosophical insights accrue from the *Phenomenology*'s account of transcendental expression, which I consider in chapter 3. Merleau-Ponty's account of the phenomenological *cogito*'s rational or discursive activity demonstrates that, while always guided by perceptual meaning, transcendental phenomenological description is an instance of 'authentic' language use, a creative form of expression characteristic of art. The view of phenomenological rationality developed in this text leans heavily on linguistic criteria. Transcendental forms of expression are supported by the perceptual data on which linguistic meaning is 'founded', but also by the creative, explicative operations that appropriate and transform existing expressive and conceptual resources. These two conditions lead phenomenology's nominally descriptive goals to brush up against the creative transformations that reflection brings to perceptual experience. The tension between phenomenology's attempt to faithfully transcribe the 'text' of experience, and the inevitable modifications resulting from reflection, remains unresolved in the *Phenomenology*. The attempt to resolve this tension is an important influence on the trajectory of Merleau-Ponty's subsequent philosophical research.

Some themes from Merleau-Ponty's early work on perception and expression are explored in post-*Phenomenology* research, especially in texts from the early 1950s. This period presents difficulties for any interpreter of Merleau-Ponty. As I show in chapter 4, new professional posts and intellectual interests encouraged a wide-ranging exploration of culture, science and philosophy. Among the many lines of enquiry in this fertile, transitionary period, Merleau-Ponty's interest in the relation between different modes of expression, scientific rationality and 'metaphysics' is of particular importance. Science has its own metaphysical assumptions, which are reflected in its distinctive, formal mode of expression, which privileges precision and clarity. Phenomenology should take an interest in scientific accounts of experience, not only because it has much to gain from fields like linguistics, but also because a study of scientific or naturalistic worldviews sheds light on how deeper, metaphysical pictures or modes of intelligibility are formed. Merleau-Ponty profits from his study of formal modes of expression, and draws some important conclusions from Saussure. However, I will argue that Saussure's influence is relatively modest. Ultimately, Merleau-Ponty is more interested in 'indirect' modes of literary expression, and especially those developed by Proust and Valéry. These authors offer theoretical resources with which to develop a hybrid and sophisticated mode of phenomenological description, which Merleau-Ponty avails himself of in his later writings.

Merleau-Ponty's post-*Phenomenology* research is also significant for the all-important insights he draws from his study of dialogical expression, which I explore in chapter 5. More so than in his study of the broader metaphysical implications of literary or scientific expression, his interpretation of the structures of intersubjective communication marks the genesis of his later 'ontology'. At this stage of his career, the deep philosophical implications of the phenomenology of language are clearly identified. His overlooked analysis of dialogue leads him to conclude that in dialogical speech, speakers' and listeners' positions are interchangeable, that speaking subjects are active and passive in varying degrees, and that the intentional roles of subjects and objects are liable to shift or 'transgress' themselves. These observations develop early versions of the concepts of 'divergence', 'reversibility', intentional 'transgression' (*transgression*) or 'encroachment' (*empiétement*), of the reflexive or 'narcissistic' nature of perception, and offer a modified account of activity and passivity; these tenets are all central to Merleau-Ponty's later work. This result testifies to the continuity of Merleau-Ponty's philosophical development, and to the foundational role that the phenomenology of dialogue plays for his transition to the concerns of his later texts. Together with the results of his study of indirect literary expression, it solidifies the conclusion that a more suggestive and less categorical mode of expression is needed to do justice to the structure of intersubjective meaning-formation, the paradigm of constitution Merleau-Ponty increasingly favours.

In chapter 6 I explore Merleau-Ponty's later account of everyday or empirical expression. To do so, I first unpack some important new concepts that he uses to define perception and to detail the perception-language relation (e.g., the '*écart*', 'institution', 'the flesh', 'reversibility'). In a major shift from his earlier view, he no longer accepts that language is 'founded' on perception. Instead, linguistic meaning is a basic condition that secures the 'cohesion' or coherence of everyday experience. The new philosophical framework developed in his later writings entails that the integrity of perceptual experience depends equally on perceptual and linguistic meaning, and it suggests that concepts (which are linguistic unities, for Merleau-Ponty) play an important role in making experience coherent and meaningful. Merleau-Ponty contends that our perceptual frequenting of the world is informed by background linguistic commitments, and that everyday linguistic expression not only articulates but also forms and transforms the world. In doing so, he offers an original phenomenological interpretation of the view that language forms experience.

This strong claim about the role that language plays in everyday life is matched by an equally strong and idiosyncratic view of the expressive character of 'ontology'. As I argue in chapter 7, Merleau-Ponty's ontology is distinguished from that of his phenomenological and philosophical predecessors by the claim that ontology is an expressive or descriptive project. In this basic sense, phenomenology and ontology are continuous. But Merleau-Ponty's ontology overcomes the tension between description and creation that first arose in *Structure* by affirming that conceptual invention is needed to detail the structures of experience. Accordingly, the fundamental task of ontology is to articulate the meaning of experience using a conceptually inventive mode of philosophical expression that is both creative and descriptive. Expressive invention is needed because traditional philosophical categories and concepts are inadequate to capture the pre-theoretical qualitative character of experience, and to account for the full range of possible meaning-formations. By reading Merleau-Ponty's later work in light of his philosophy of language, his ontology can be read as a chiefly descriptive rather than a speculative project. It remains firmly focused on the domain of experience, and its essential insights into its structure are expressive products whose normative and explanatory force obtains within specific historical limits.

Throughout the wide-ranging philosophical concerns that surface in Merleau-Ponty's philosophical career, a deep interest in the philosophy of language remains constant. Merleau-Ponty offers us good reasons to think that language co-constitutes the structure of appearance. This challenges the tenability of the extra-linguistic, intuition-centric criteria that have hitherto guided phenomenological accounts of experience. Merleau-Ponty's engagement with the phenomenology of language offers a novel and fruitful interpretation of phenomenology, which moves the project beyond the limitations of classical metaphysical and epistemological categories and expands its philosophical scope. Instead of an epistemological project, another version of Kantian transcendental idealism, a neo-realist account of perception, or a taxonomy of mental activity, phenomenology is a labour of expression that articulates the sense of life.

NOTES

1. In the *Sophist*, Plato claims that a world full of falsity would be populated by 'copies, likenesses, and appearances' (Plato 1997, *Sophist* 260d; see also *Republic* 598a). Lambert's *Neues Organon*, which is thought to be the text that first invokes the term *phenomenology*, cautions us against taking direction from appearance (*Schein*), which we should not mistake for reality (Lambert 1764, Phänomenologie §1). Kant would first question this basic assumption (Kant 2004, chapter 4).
2. For an analysis of this concept see Patočka 2002, 32.
3. Husserl 2014, §24.
4. Husserl 2001, I.10.
5. Heidegger 1962, ¶7.

6. Heidegger 1962, ¶7. As the account of 'existential understanding' in ¶31 demonstrates, Heidegger's account of vision, intuition and the phenomenon is more complex. He claims that perception depends on prior interpretive conditions, which allow objects to be encountered as meaningful entities; this deprives 'pure intuition' of its philosophical 'priority'. This original insight does not, however, impinge on the definition of the phenomenon Heidegger gives earlier in *Being and Time*.

7. Sartre 1984, introduction 2.
8. Husserl 1973, 58.
9. Husserl 1973, part 3 B §59.
10. Fink 1995, 98.
11. Heidegger, 1997, §1 A.
12. Heidegger 1962, ¶7.
13. Heidegger 1962, ¶7. See also his 1924 to 1925 Marburg lecture course (Heidegger 1997, §1 A).
14. Heidegger 1962, ¶34, 209–10.
15. For some examples, see Madison 1981, Dillon 1988, Barbaras 2004.
16. See 'The Nature of Perception' (Geraets 1971, 188–99).
17. See Inkpin 2016, part 2; Noble 2014; Kristensen 2010; and Hass 2008, chapters 6–7. For earlier studies see Fontaine-de Visscher 1974; Thierry 1987; Edie 1987; and especially Dastur 2001; Watson 2009a, 2009b; and Heidsieck 1993.

Part I

1

STRUCTURE AND LANGUAGE

The Structure of Behaviour was Merleau-Ponty's first of two doctoral theses.[1] It is tasked with clarifying the relation between consciousness and nature (SB 3/1). Among other topics, it investigates the relation human subjectivity bears to the physical and perceptual world. Much like *Phenomenology of Perception*, its thematic focus does not suggest that the philosophy of language is important for answering the work's guiding questions. This view is widely held among commentators. Some even suggest that Merleau-Ponty deliberately ignores the topic of language in *Structure*.[2]

This chapter will explore how the philosophy of language informs some of Merleau-Ponty's more fundamental conclusions about the consciousness-world relation. Despite the incipient character of many of its claims and arguments, some key conclusions in *Structure* depend on nontrivial assumptions about language. As will become clear in subsequent chapters, this work also sketches the theoretical framework within which Merleau-Ponty's later reflections on language unfold. Undeniably, this text does not aim to provide extended discussions of language-related topics (e.g., analyses of first-order or empirical language use). But it would be a mistake to ignore its many consequential observations about language.

After reviewing its basic aims, and the important concepts of 'behaviour', 'meaning' and 'structure' (section 1), I turn to Merleau-Ponty's account of description (section 2). These remarks suggest that the question of how to best express the meaning of behaviour using a distinctive phenomenological terminology is already a pressing problem in this early work. The important role that language plays in the disclosure of behaviour and perceptual consciousness is confirmed in Merleau-Ponty's remarks about the concept of 'structure' (section 3). As it will turn out, the explanatory force of the structures of behaviour will depend in large part on how their meaning is taken up and expressed by human subjects. Despite leaving many questions unanswered, *Structure* establishes the general outline of Merleau-Ponty's phenomenological approach to the study of language, and anticipates some fundamental problems he will attempt to resolve in later writings (section 4).

1. BEHAVIOUR, MEANING AND STRUCTURE

Despite the overtones contemporary readers may hear, for Merleau-Ponty the concept of 'behaviour' (*le comportement*) offers a nonreductive way to probe the consciousness-world relation. The term *behaviour* describes how an organism lives in and engages with its environment or milieu. Merleau-Ponty is not, as this term might suggest, a behaviourist. He argues against behaviourism.[3] For him, a focus on behaviour is useful because the concept is not easily reduced to classical categories like the 'mental' or 'physiological', and thus, it does not foreclose on a more nuanced understanding of the relation between consciousness and world or mind and matter. In *Structure*, he attempts to work within the conceptual schemes and assumptions of contemporary psychology, biology and physics in order to evaluate the extent to which these sciences offer a persuasive explanation of behaviour in human and nonhuman life. An overview of his many intricate arguments is not possible here.[4] For our purposes, it will suffice to note some of his more general conclusions – in particular, those drawn in the important 'Human Order' chapter.

In a summary of his results, he claims that, with the help of 'the notion of structure [*structure*] or form [*forme*]', it has become clear that 'both mechanism and finalism should be rejected and that the "physical", the "vital" and the "mental" do not represent three powers of being, but three dialectics' (184/199). He also concludes that 'what we call nature is already consciousness [*conscience*] of nature, what we call life is already consciousness of life and what we call mental is still an object *vis-à-vis* consciousness'. According to this evaluation, physical, biological or psychological explanations of behaviour essentially miss that the subject they treat (e.g., matter, biological or mental life) in each case presupposes *consciousness* of the physical, the biological or the mental. By dividing their domains of enquiry from one another, these sciences overlook the fact that a human subject always experiences the phenomena in question, and that the investigation of these areas is also an experience had by consciousness. In effect, Merleau-Ponty is stressing the primacy and ineliminability of the first-personal perspective for understanding the meaning of scientific findings.

The first point above suggests that the concepts of 'structure' and 'form' play an important role in demonstrating this result (following Merleau-Ponty, I will use these terms interchangeably). For Merleau-Ponty, 'structure' (*la structure*) or 'form' (*la forme*) is a locally emergent unified whole that lends meaning to a particular experience. A structure demarcates possibilities for acting and engaging within an organic milieu, alternatively, for the behaviour of an organism. Structure is not ultimately analysable in terms of any set or subset of its constituent parts, including perceptual, mental, qualitative or physical facts that might figure in a given experience. Instead, '[f]orm, in the sense in which we have defined it, possesses original properties with regard to those of the parts which can be detached from it. Each moment in it is determined by the grouping of the other moments, and their respective value depends on a state of total equilibrium the formula of which is an intrinsic character of "form"' (91/101). On this view, form unifies the distinct features that make up an object, experience or event, and serves as its determining or organising principle. In contemporary parlance, we might say that form 'supervenes' on the physical, in the sense that any change in physical makeup will be reflected in form (without being reducible to such changes, in a causal, ontological or explanatory sense of reduction). According to the concept of form, higher forms are 'founded', in the Husserlian sense, on lower forms or activities.[5] For example, a factory produces its output most efficiently, or realises its most efficient form, when each of its workers performs their tasks at their most efficient rate. The factory's most efficient state depends on the individual activity of each of its workers, without being reducible to any particular worker's (or subset of workers') activity. When each worker satisfies this level of efficiency, the factory as a whole will realise its most efficient structure.

Structures are fundamentally qualitative entities, insofar as they reflect the 'value' (*la valeur*) of a given state or moment of experience. Early in *Structure*, Merleau-Ponty hints that a qualitative approach will eventually be needed to understand the concept of behaviour. He suggests that if the distinctions and terms of classical analyses (considered in parts 1 to 3 of *Structure*) are ultimately inadequate, then 'value and signification' will turn out to be 'intrinsic determinations of the organism', and will be accessible only with a 'new mode of "comprehension"' (10/8). This new method of analysis focuses on the value or meaning of behaviour. The meaning of behaviour is accounted for in terms of its 'signification' (*signification*). *Signification* is another term for 'meaning', a concept that is also designated using the term 'sens'. In *Structure* these two variants of 'meaning' are often used interchangeably. This decision ultimately leads to an important theoretical challenge for Merleau-Ponty, which I will return to. For now, the important point to note is that if form and structure are fundamentally significative or meaningful entities, then behaviour, especially that associated with human subjectivity, is ultimately explained by appeal to the category of meaning. This point has often been overlooked in analyses of Merleau-Ponty's account of structure.

A focus on the meaning of structure and behaviour requires a more holistic method of analysis. The meaningful character of form encourages us to consider behaviour '"in its unity" and in its human meaning' (182/197). If behaviour is not reducible to mental or physical facts, then a broader set of categories are required to understand it. For Merleau-Ponty, this entails that 'realism in general . . . must be called into question'. Philosophical realism is a difficult position to characterise, not least because it has multiple senses in *Structure*.[6] Most basically, Merleau-Ponty accepts a version of realism on which the objects or experiences subjects encounter already possess some meaningful characteristics prior to analysis. On this view, meaning in the broadest sense already inheres in the world, and is not a product of human consciousness. Merleau-Ponty seems to endorse this admittedly thin view of realism because he is committed to the claim that there are immanent structures in perception that are not produced by subjective activity.[7]

However, there is a more robust version of realism that Merleau-Ponty rejects. This version holds that the features, properties or meanings of objects exist and can be understood independently of their experience by human consciousness. This view denies that objects' properties or meanings are mediated in any significant way by human subjectivity. Merleau-Ponty identifies two corollaries of this view; namely, that objects in an organism's milieu affect it only in constant, regular and predictable ways, and that an organism's stance in relation to an object has no bearing on the object's causal powers (or its structure). But if the meaning of behaviour is not reducible to causal forces, and if it can vary, then a classical realist view is inconsistent with the holistic approach needed to grasp the meaningful structures of behaviour.

An example of Merleau-Ponty's aversion to this brand of realism can be found in his reading of Gelb and Goldstein's analyses of brain disorders.[8] Their research supports the conclusion that behaviour must be analysed in terms of signification, even in the scientific domain, an insight that Merleau-Ponty relies on in his evaluation of biology (161/ 174–75). Using Gestalt-psychological methods, Gelb and Goldstein's analyses of subjects suffering from aphasia (the inability to use language, especially symbolically) or apraxia (the inability to express or understand speech) do not isolate the specific location of brain lesions to explain why subjects lack certain linguistic capabilities. Instead, they appeal to a broader context of action and behaviour (63–64/68–69). Their studies support the conclusion that to be understood in its full human dimension, 'a specific disorder should always be put back into the context of total behaviour', and demonstrate that the 'behaviour of the patient adheres much more closely to the concrete and immediate relations of the milieu'. Once our focus is broadened to include facts about a patient's milieu, including how patients practically engage with objects in their environment, then their disorders require a different set of explanatory concepts. Taking direction from this approach, a disorder could be defined, for example, 'as "the impairment of the capacity to comprehend the essential features of an event" or, finally, as the incapacity of clearly disengaging a perceived, conceived or exercised grouping, as a *figure*, from a *ground* treated as indifferent'. Explanations of this sort are neither causal nor reductive; they are formulated by attending to how subjects act in and engage with their milieu and practical context. Of course, a Gestalt-psychological approach need not deny that significant differences in the brains of patients suffering from apraxia or aphasia may be observed. Still, it holds that facts about the brain are inadequate to explain the pathologies in question.

By describing language pathologies in terms of an inability to 'comprehend . . . an event', or by appeal to the figure-ground structure of Gestalt perception theory, Gelb and Goldstein introduce fundamentally qualitative terms into their analyses. A consequence of their studies is that an adequate understanding of brain disorders cannot be attained solely at the level of physiology. They demonstrate that behaviour is central to explaining differences in these patients' linguistic capacities, and that it is conceptually irreducible. Patients' behaviour must ultimately be explained by appeal to their perceptual life or experience, which become central terms in an analysis of the 'total' meaning of their disorders. According to this 'new' form of analysis,

> Sickness is no longer, according to the common representation, like a thing or a power from which certain effects follow; nor is pathological functioning, according to a too wide-spread idea, homogeneous with normal functioning. It is a new *signification* of behaviour, common to the multitude of symptoms; and the relation of the essential disorder to the symptoms is no longer that of cause to effect but rather the logical relation of principle to consequence or of signification to sign. (65/70)

A key virtue of this new approach is that it takes account of a wider range of facts, which classical analyses consider irrelevant. This is particularly important for understanding complex cases like Schneider, who Gelb and Goldstein argue cannot be properly diagnosed (even at the physiological level) without adopting a more holistic approach than that offered by causal or reductive methodology.[9] In their analysis of Schneider, Gelb and Goldstein develop a methodology centred on the meaning of disorders, which departs from the dominant causal paradigm.

While he praises Gelb and Goldstein, Merleau-Ponty has deeper motivations for privileging scientific accounts that emphasise a holistic analysis focussed on the meaning of disorders. Recall that in his estimation of the limitations of mechanistic or deterministic explanations, he noted that these approaches ignore the fundamental fact that human consciousness always lies behind physical, biological or psychological phenomena. He is chiefly interested in understanding human subjectivity. For him, the subject is a 'significative' being: it comes to grips with the qualitative character or meaning of experience. In *Structure*, the latter is given a perceptual interpretation: perception is the privileged avenue through which we engage with the world. That his interpretations of physical, biological or psychological phenomena rely on concepts like 'form', 'figure' or 'ground', which are more qualitative than physiological, leads him to question the extent to which the relevant objects of analysis 'are still physiological'. The likelihood that they are not leads him to take a different approach when detailing 'what is ordinarily called "consciousness"' (92/101).

2. DESCRIPTION, SENSE AND SIGNIFICATION

Merleau-Ponty employs a descriptive method to understand consciousness. Instead of constructing the structure of perceptual consciousness a priori, locating its explanatory ground in intellectual activities like judgement, or reducing it to the physical or to causal forces, he begins from the 'descriptive characteristics' of consciousness – that is, from data encountered in everyday perceptual experience – and takes direction from them in his analysis of behaviour (166/179). As he claims, a descriptive method is consonant with *Structure*'s basic aims: 'The descriptive dimension of incipient [*commençante*] perception demands a reformulation of the notion of consciousness' (169/183).

Description is a linguistic undertaking. A description of experience requires deliberate and considered decisions about what sort of expressions can best capture the meaning of a particular perceptual experience or object. On this score, Merleau-Ponty's approach in *Structure* is firmly within the confines of classical phenomenology. For him, a description of experience provides a linguistic translation or transcription of the meaning of its object (183/198). Assuming that appearances are access points to the world, there is no sense in asking if we really reach the object in question when we describe its appearance. To suggest otherwise would be to succumb to a realistic assumption about perception (namely, that we can grasp the features of perceptual objects in their totality) or to a precritical naïveté about metaphysical knowledge of things in themselves. Descriptions give us the meaning of objects, which are always accessed according to a particular, limited and partial perspective.

An interest in description leads Merleau-Ponty to make an additional distinction between 'verbalised perception' (*la perception parlée*) and 'lived perception' (*la perception vécue*). The first refers to 'common sense, [and] the manner in which it verbally accounts for [*rend compte verbalement*] perception', while the latter refers to 'the perceptual experiences themselves' (185/200).[10] While we perceive and experience the world without accounting for what we see, we are also usually able to explain it, most often by appeal to the conventional meanings of readily available expressions or concepts. While I can perceive a tree without reflecting on its particular features, I can also describe them by invoking concepts – for example, those of shape, colour, thickness and more. In doing so, I assume that the meaning of the word 'brown', for example, is adequate for describing this particular brownish bark before me (and that what I see and describe can be understood by others).

For Merleau-Ponty, the distinction between verbalised and nonverbalised perception ultimately boils down to a distinction between 'sense' (*sens*) and 'signification' (*signification*). A focus on consciousness leads Merleau-Ponty to claim that 'the only way for a thing to act on a mind [*esprit*] is to offer [*offrir*] it a meaning [*sens*], to manifest itself to it, to constitute itself [*se constituer*] before the mind in its intelligible articulations' (199/215). Perceptual consciousness engages objects that are already meaningful, and this is not a result of our sense-making activity. This meaning is captured by the term 'sens', and includes, for example, the colours, shapes, tones, hue or contours of intended objects; also the sense of sounds, smells, landscapes, persons and of any other entity encountered in perceptual experience. *Sens* refers to the meanings we encounter in perception.

Signification refers to more abstract or conceptual meanings. Signification is closer to what philosophers sometimes refer to as 'propositional' meaning. In addition to recognising a particular object as a tree, we also possess the concept 'tree'. The counterpart to the embodied meaning of this particular tree (e.g., this oak) is the ideal *signification* 'tree'. A tree's signification is a general term that is not defined by reference to its instances (i.e., the old, thick branches of this particular oak). Merleau-Ponty sometimes describes ideal signification as an unchanging, static, abstract conceptual entity, something akin to an 'idea':

> The signification which I find in a sensible whole was already adherent in it. When I 'see' a triangle, my experience would be very poorly described by saying that I conceive or comprehend the triangle with respect to certain sensible givens. The signification is embodied [*incarnée*]. It is here and now that I perceive this triangle as such, while the conception gives it to me as an eternal being whose meaning and properties, as Descartes said, owe nothing to the fact that I perceive it. (211/228)

When we see a triangular shape in the world, we do not perceive its ideal signification. As the remark suggests, the latter takes on a corresponding embodied form. Still, these two orders of meaning are closely linked. While the triangular object I see may not be fully accounted for in terms of its significative counterpart, the latter can still be used to analyse the former. Ideal or abstract signification is like the concept or essence (in the Husserlian sense) of the triangle. As the passage above suggests, this category of meaning is insufficient to account for its embodied, perceived version.

Some ideal significations are never encountered in perception. For example, assuming that objects are perceived from a particular perspective, and are only ever given in profiles, the concept of a cube has a nonempirical origin or counterpart: we never see all sides of a cube perfectly when we look at it, and must supplement one view of the cube by taking up different perspectives. (Merleau-Ponty does not suggest that the signification of the complete cube, with all its sides, can be constructed out of different perceptual experiences.) Accordingly, the signification of the cube is its nonperceptual, abstract meaning: 'It is the cube as signification or geometrical idea which is made of six equal sides' (213/230). The perceived cube is always partially given, whereas the significative version is thought according to its ideal properties. Merleau-Ponty accepts that there can be significant differences between *signification* and *sens*.

Which category of meaning, if any, should be privileged in a description of perceptual consciousness? In his early work, Merleau-Ponty is unequivocal that *sens* is more basic than *signification*. The tree that 'my consciousness wordlessly intends . . . is not a signification or an idea'. Instead, it is chiefly encountered as a meaningful perceptual unity (e.g., as this old oak) that can be subsequently analysed using the concepts 'tree' or 'oak'. But our 'acts of expression or reflection intend an original text [*une texte originaire*] which cannot be deprived of meaning [*sens*]' (211/228).[11] When we interpret experience using the concept 'tree', we bring a derivative unity of meaning to bear on a primary perceptual experience. Perceptual sense, which is the primary 'text' that our concepts refer to and in terms of which they are analysable, takes priority in the attempt to describe consciousness.

The decision to privilege *sens* over *signification* is not only motivated by a desire to capture the true meaning of the consciousness-nature relation. Recall that Merleau-Ponty claimed that 'verbalised' or 'spoken' perception, which relies on predefined significations, provides a 'common sense' account of conscious experience. Commonsense views, he thinks, typically impede a proper understanding of perceptual consciousness, for they embed realist assumptions in the language and the concepts used to account for perception. Accordingly, the decision to privilege *sens* is also informed by a deeper interest in evacuating unhelpful assumptions from philosophical language. Together with an emphasis on linguistic description, this suggests that language plays an important role in *Structure*'s broader philosophical goals.

Most basically, a realist or commonsense view of perception defines consciousness as an entity subject to causal (or lawlike) determination by objects in its milieu. On this view, objects leave their mark on the mind (e.g., through impressions on the retina) and reliably transfer the true sense of the world to a passive subject. According to Merleau-Ponty, however, if we suspend our everyday realist assumptions and attend to perceptual experience, the evidence we garner does not support realist views of consciousness or perception. If we focus on what 'immediate consciousness' tells us, perceptual objects like a table, a chair or a tree 'do not appear to me to be causes of the perception which I have of them, . . . which would impress their mark on me and produce an image of themselves' (185/200). By describing perceptual *sens* in terms that are more faithful to it, its pre-theoretical meaning (hidden behind commonsense assumptions) becomes clearer. This paves the way for a more accurate account of the consciousness-world relation.

However, Merleau-Ponty's project in *Structure* is not definitional. Realism or finalism are not inadequate chiefly because they define perception poorly. Still, he accepts that a proper description of consciousness requires that we disassemble the conceptual commitments of philosophical and scientific accounts that construe perceptual consciousness in realist terms – that is, as an entity subject to causal determination. Realism is also limited, then, by the fact that it employs a terminology that is not supported by the meaning of first-order experience. This is a subtle and often overlooked point in Merleau-Ponty's argument: a failure to adequately describe perceptual consciousness is a significant strike against realism.

This observation helps to bring the linguistic commitments of *Structure* into further relief. A basic concern in Merleau-Ponty's analysis of the consciousness-world relation is to properly account for the connection between *sens* and *signification* (215/232). He aims to specify how the concept 'rectangle', for example, refers or relates to this particular rectangular shape before me. As I have suggested, this relation is construed as one between linguistic (or conceptual) and perceptual sense. A basic goal of *Structure*, then, is the formulation of an adequate set of philosophical concepts (*significations*) with which to describe the sense of perceptual experience. In fact, this goal is paramount for phenomenology and phenomenological description, as Merleau-Ponty understands them at this point in his career. To 'return to perception' or to 'original experience' is 'to impose upon oneself an inversion of the natural movement of consciousness', in which the goal is to understand 'the lived relation of the "profiles" to the "things" which they present, of the perspectives to the ideal significations which are intended through them' (220/236–37). A note to the text clarifies that with the expression 'inversion of the natural movement of consciousness', '[w]e are defining here the "phenomenological reduction" in the sense which is given to it in Husserl's final philosophy'.[12] For Merleau-Ponty, the phenomenological reduction, which suspends the truth claims and adequacy of everyday assumptions associated with the 'natural attitude', amounts to an investigation of the relation between perceptual sense and the linguistic *significations* or concepts used to account for it. This suggests that for him, the phenomenological reduction is undertaken for the sake of developing a better linguistic description of experience.

Together with the failures of realist accounts, this aim leads Merleau-Ponty to an outline of a principle that he will refine and develop over the course of his career. This principle holds that 'the properties of the phenomenal field are not expressible in a language that would owe nothing to them' (193/208). Alternatively, experience can only be understood using a philosophical terminology that closely tracks the modes of perceptual givenness. It is therefore of key consequence for the success and broader argumentative goals of *Structure* that a philosophical language that properly defines the consciousness-nature relation be developed. Merleau-Ponty gestures towards this goal, at an admittedly high level of abstraction, when he claims that it is better to define objects as 'phenomena' instead of mere appearances (199/215). The term 'phenomenon', he thinks, better captures the mode in which material objects are given, and by extension, discloses their perceptual meaning. This sort of terminological refinement contributes to phenomenology's attempt to understand the 'inventory of consciousness as milieu of the universe'.

Broader theoretical questions about this view of philosophical expression, chief among them, how one can formulate a language adequate to perceptual objects, are not tackled in *Structure*. However, a suggestive discussion is found in one of Merleau-Ponty's descriptions of material objects. This example also disambiguates structural features of our perception of objects in space and time. Given that we only ever see 'profiles' of a cube from a particular perspective, our experience suggests that a cube is a 'perspectival' object, which reveals itself 'only gradually and never completely' (187–88/202). Its perspectival nature leads to a definition of the cube as '[a] transcendence which is nevertheless open to my knowledge – this is the very definition of a thing as it is intended [*visée*] by naive consciousness'. A cube (like other material objects) is a transcendent entity because its total perceptual features are not instantaneously accessible to our gaze. A complete view of the cube always escapes us, even if additional features are discovered when we take up different views of it. Merleau-Ponty concludes that this analysis demonstrates that 'the thing seen in profiles' is 'an original structure' that cannot be fully explained by a 'real psychological or physiological process' (194/209). Instead, it is better described using the language of 'transcendence'. We are led to assume that similar processes will generate phenomenological definitions of other experiences (perceptual or otherwise).

Like some other descriptions in *Structure*, this example is suggestive and leaves something to be desired. But the upshot is clear: to properly account for our experience of perceptual *sens*, phenomenological description must adopt a different set of philosophical terms than those on offer in realist or commonsense views. This attempt amounts to a search for an adequate mode of expression. This suggests that the philosophy of language is anything but peripheral to *Structure*'s deeper goals.

3. STRUCTURE AND EXPRESSION

Thus far, I have suggested that the task of developing a philosophical terminology that adequately describes perceptual experience is an important precondition for offering a persuasive account of the consciousness-world relation. The broader implications of this claim are not probed further in *Structure*. However, Merleau-Ponty's interest in expression can also be detected in his account of the key concept of 'structure' (or 'form'). While commentators have noted its 'founded' character, its reliance on a whole-part relation, its mixture of 'formal' and 'embodied' features, and its nonreductive characteristics, another important feature of the term has been overlooked.[13] A structure derives part of its explanatory force from human subjects' 'expressive activity': whereas elementary perceptual structures 'constitute themselves' prior to analysis, they only serve as explanations of behaviour when they are linguistically expressed by human consciousness.

Merleau-Ponty's many stated and working descriptions of structure lend themselves to a schematic or formal definition of the term. There are, for example, behavioural, perceptual, vital and mental structures, and he offers different accounts of how each version is constituted. As I noted above, structures are localised unities of meaning. A structure is 'the contingent arrangement by which the materials placed before us begin to have a sense [*les matériaux se mettent devant nous à avoir un sens*], intelligibility in a nascent state' (206–7/223). Consider the important class of perceptual structures. The distinctive character of a perceptual experience is made possible by a meaningful, embodied unity whose constituent parts include bodily position and posture, the physical characteristics of objects (size, colour, shape, etc.), lighting conditions and so on. In other words, a particular experience is dependent on a mixture of qualitative and nonqualitative conditions, which jointly lend an experience its coherence and distinct character. Perceptual structures supervene on lower elements 'according to laws of equilibrium which are neither those of a physical system nor those of the body considered as such' (206/222).[14] This suggests that structure is located between the physical and the nonphysical, and unites them without being reducible to either category.

This characteristic makes a general analysis of structure difficult: by definition, structures are local entities, whose particular features are organised by general and formal categories (e.g., that structures are qualitative unities, which supervene on their parts and unify disparate elements of experience). An additional theoretical consideration requires that structures be highly specific – namely, the view that structures become more determinate when their features are expressed by human consciousness. While other organisms rely on structures when engaging with their milieu, human subjects can actively take up and analyse the meaning-formation at work in a given structure, and use it to reflect on their experience:

> When we were describing the structures of behaviour it was indeed to show that they are irreducible to the dialectic of physical stimulus and muscular contraction and that in this sense behaviour, far from being a thing which exists in-itself [*en soi*], is a whole significative for a consciousness which considers it; but it was at the same time and reciprocally to make manifest in 'expressive conduct' the *spectacle* [*le spectacle*] *of a consciousness* under our eyes, to show a mind [*un esprit*] that *comes into the world*. (209/225)

Here the claim that behavioural structures are nonreductive is closely tied to their significative status. Behaviour is meaningful, and meaning is ultimately evaluated by human consciousness (Merleau-Ponty allows that nonhuman animals meaningfully engage with their milieu, but he does not suggest here that they can take anything like a reflective stance on the conditions that make this engagement possible). This passage makes an additional point: if a perceptual structure is not meaningful 'in itself', but only for consciousness (or for an organism), this suggests that the structures of behaviour take on a more determinate meaning when they are evaluated by subjects. By attempting to understand a given perceptual structure, we further clarify how it guides behaviour, and in doing so, become aware of ourselves as meaning-comprehending and meaning-forming beings. The passage above describes this as an 'expressive' process, which suggests that the clarification of a structure's meaning is a linguistic activity.[15]

The process of meaning-formation is briefly discussed in Merleau-Ponty's analysis of the important topic of soul (or mind) and body relations, a distinction that he claims is central for understanding behaviour. In this chapter, meaning formation is characterised using the familiar phenomenological concept of a 'constituting operation' (210/227). Broadly understood, constitution is the process by which meaning is formed in experience.[16] However, Merleau-Ponty's understanding of constitution reserves an uncharacteristically important role for language. For instance, the meaningful formation of soul body-relations (as we understand them) is said to be a result of 'living *speech* [*la parole vivante*] . . . in which meaning [*le sens*] is formulated for the first time as meaning [*sens*] and thus becomes available [*devient disponible*] for later operations' (210/227). This form of constituting language (or 'speech') is contrasted with the expression characteristic of 'empirical languages', which he standardly associates with well-formulated formal meanings or commonsense views.[17]

This observation is doubly important. First, it shows that features of the structuring relation between soul and body, like those obtaining other domains of conscious experience, are not invented by human subjects. As I noted, structures emerge from embodied meanings (*sens*) encountered in everyday experience. However, the observation also tells us that on their own, these meanings are insufficient to explain how a particular structure works. To explain or understand structure, a 'constituting operation' is needed, in which the meanings encountered in perception are further scrutinised. In the passages following this claim, Merleau-Ponty does not say much more about the constituting operation of 'living speech'. Still, constitution clearly involves language use, and engages meanings that are not mere copies of givens encountered in lived experience. Further, this operation does not rely only on extant or available concepts (*significations*). And it seems that the meaning of soul-body relations, like that of any other structure, is only fully understood after it is expressed by a language-using subject, who can identify and appraise its own relation to both *sens* and *signification*.[18]

An example from Chapter IV, in which Merleau-Ponty analyses the perception of material objects, can clarify how structure is constituted by *sens* and *signification*. This case also suggests how language might partially constitute structure. The example finds Merleau-Ponty arguing against the familiar targets of realism and naturalism. While I cannot consider his argument in full here, he concludes that the projection of objects upon the retina (the desired realist account of vision) is insufficient to explain how a cube is perceived from the perspective of lived experience. This leads him to ask:

> Indeed, what are 'my eyes', 'my retina', 'the external cube' in itself, and 'the objects which I do not see'? They are logical significations which are bound up with my actual perception on valid 'grounds' and which explicate [*explicitent*] its meaning [*le sens*], but which get the index of real existence from it. These significations do not have in themselves therefore the means to explain the actual existence of my perception. The language [*le langage*] which one habitually uses is nevertheless understandable: my perception of the cube presents it to me as a complete and real cube, my perception of space, as a space which is complete and real beyond the aspects which are given to me. Thus it is natural that I have a tendency to detach the space and the cube from the concrete perspectives and to posit them in-themselves [*en soi*]. (217–18/234–35)

The first point is familiar: even if my retina projects three sides of the cube, the terms 'retina', 'projection' and 'image' are too abstract and too divorced from lived experience to serve as genuine explanations of the underlying perceptual processes. These terms are not adequately sensitive to the meaning implicit in our conscious perception of the cube, which Merleau-Ponty thinks is the ultimate arbiter in an analysis of perceptual structure. Nevertheless, concepts like 'retina' still figure in analyses of perception; we cannot but appeal to existing linguistic conventions or 'empirical language' when offering an explanation of perception. But the terms of empirical language must be modified so that they better reflect the meaning and structure of this particular perceptual experience. As Merleau-Ponty claims, logical or abstract significations 'make sense explicit' (*explicitent le sens*). That is, they help us work out the meaning of perception, even if we must guard against reifying the largely abstract picture of perception they might otherwise encourage us to adopt.[19]

These considerations bear directly on how we should understand the concept of structure. On the interpretation I have offered, structure depends on both *sens* and *signification*. While *sens* is primary, it is further clarified by abstract concepts, which are used to understand the *sens* of a particular structure. Since the abstract concepts used to interpret a particular structure ultimately get their meaning from perception, their 'common sense' interpretations must be revised so that they adequately reflect the local character of a particular experience (224/240–41). Merleau-Ponty's remarks elsewhere suggest that this activity amounts to a 'constituting' or expressive operation. Expressive constitution plays an important role in forming a structure's meaning: by attempting to further clarify the meaning implicit in experience, subjects supplement and refine the meanings initially encountered in perception. This effectively changes the meaning of structure; by extension, it refines our understanding of how structure organises experience and makes it intelligible. Linguistic or expressive activity, then, plays a central role in clarifying the meaning of experience and the structures obtaining in it.

4. UNRESOLVED QUESTIONS

Having reviewed the accounts of structure, sense and description on offer in *The Structure of Behaviour*, I would now like to consider some broader implications and questions. It is often thought that Merleau-Ponty's treatment of the physical, vital and human orders leads him to a somewhat ambiguous idealist position. He endorses the view that the perceiving human body, a central term in his analysis of behaviour, has an 'ideal' status (210/227). The account of structure and description given above can help us better understand this claim and *Structure*'s idealist conclusions.

Merleau-Ponty is obviously not an idealist in the spirit of Berkeley. He does not hold that the ontological status of material objects depends on the mind. Despite his focus on perception and appearance, he is not a Kantian transcendental idealist either. Merleau-Ponty thinks that we really are in contact with objects in the world (rather than representations). He accepts that the being of objects is not separate from their appearance. He does not hold that the conditions for the possibility of perception, and our receptivity to objects in space and time, are chiefly grounded in subjectivity (as per Kant's account of inner and outer sense). The evidence above suggests that the idealism of *Structure* ultimately concerns the category of meaning: the 'natural "thing", the organism, the behaviour of others and my own behaviour exist only by their meaning' (224/241). While 'this meaning which springs forth in them is not yet a Kantian object', and while 'the intentional life which constitutes them is not yet a representation', the meaning of behaviour is ultimately intelligible given the reflective activities of human consciousness. The meaning of behaviour is individuated by structure. But structure ultimately crystallises in conscious, expressive activity. Consciousness clarifies, explicates or constitutes meanings it finds in the world. To do so, it relies on elementary structures of perception, but it transforms their original meaning when studying natural life or consciousness. By no means do subjects invent the meaning of structure, nature or world. But at its higher levels, sense-making necessarily depends on subjective human activity.

Consider what Merleau-Ponty says about the division between soul and body. This distinction does not originate in our meaning-comprehending activity: soul or mind and body exist independently of any particular view one might form about these terms and about how one relates to the other. That mind or body are independent from one another is not a philosophically salient observation, however. For Merleau-Ponty, this distinction must not ultimately be worked out in ontological or metaphysical terms, but according to the 'relations of consciousness as flux of individual events, of concrete and resistant structures, and that of consciousness as tissue of ideal significations' (215/232). Put differently, the division between soul and body should be worked out in terms of a more fundamental division within the category of meaning – namely, between *sens* (which pertains to the body) and *signification* (which pertains to the mind). The distinction between these two orders of meaning originates in consciousness. Merleau-Ponty thinks that any significative distinction ultimately depends on an entity capable of making distinctions of this sort. Consciousness is par excellence an entity of this order.

A focus on the subjective standpoint also helps to resolve *Structure*'s guiding question; namely, how we should understand the consciousness-nature relation: '[t]he antinomy of which we are speaking disappears along with its realistic thesis at the level of reflective thought [*la pensée réfléchie*]; it is in perceptual knowledge that it has its proper location' (215–16/232–33). Deterministic or physicalist explanations of this relation, and classical idealist or subjectivist accounts, incline in different directions; but both explanations fail because they misconstrue how subjective sense-making activities unfold. 'Determination of consciousness by nature' or 'determination of nature by consciousness' are two rival explanations whose persuasiveness is ultimately measured by sense-making subjects. A critical idealist or subjectivist view fails because it ignores the fact that consciousness finds meaning already in the world when it begins reflecting (this view places too much emphasis on the subject). But realist and naturalist approaches fail to grasp that consciousness is essential for maintaining the distinction between uniform active causes and passive effects (this view ignores the ineliminable role of subjectivity). Both accounts, therefore, misunderstand how meaning is encountered and transformed by consciousness. As Merleau-Ponty has argued, this process begins at the perceptual level, and is in turn transformed by the concepts used to analyse it. By appealing to the category of meaning, which is explored in the reflective (phenomenological or transcendental) domain, he takes himself to have resolved the dilemma above, which is 'the philosophical truth of naturalism and realism' and critical idealism (224/241).

While the outlines of his solution can be sketched, important questions remain unanswered. Recall that perceptual structures require clarification by language-using subjects. By clarifying perceptual *sens* using conceptual *signification*, the structures of experience can be better understood. This has important consequences for the form of expression that discloses the structures of behaviour:

> It has seemed to us that matter, life, and mind could not be defined as three orders of reality or three sorts of beings, but as three planes of signification or three forms of unity. [. . .] In a living being, bodily movements and moments of behaviour can be described and understood only in a language made to measure [*dans un langage fait sur mesure*], according to the categories of an original experience. (201–2/217)

This confirms the important role accorded to language in the description of experience and behaviour. But how is the special, tailor-made language required for understanding the structures of behaviour formulated? Clearly, conceptual *significations* are needed, and should be adjusted to reflect perceptual sense. Beyond this minimal condition, and the suggestion that 'the existent thing is [not] reducible to the signification by which we express it', Merleau-Ponty provides no indication of what norm(s) or procedure(s) should guide the formulation of this special language (221/237). Given the important transformations that result from expressive activity, this is a pressing demand.

A closer look at Merleau-Ponty's understanding of the reflective activity needed to express structures raises additional questions. The clarification of perceptual meaning, he claims, necessarily 'transcends' it. 'Transcendence' is the transformation of existing conditions or states of affairs. Following Hegel's account in *Phenomenology of Spirit*, Merleau-Ponty calls our self- and other-transcending capacity 'work' (162–63/175–76).[20] Work 'designates the ensemble of activities by which man transforms physical and living nature'. But this transformative capacity is not directed solely to tools or material objects. Work is also understood as 'the capacity of going beyond created structures in order to create others' (175/190). Transcendent or transformative activity is also directed to structure and meaning. For Merleau-Ponty, human subjects are destined to 'reject' and 'surpass' existing explanations of experience (176/191). In chapter 2, I show that 'transcendence' plays an important role in Merleau-Ponty's account of expression.

The claim above about work or transcendence suggests, first, that the clarificatory or constitutive work of reflection will necessarily transform the initial meaning of behaviour. If subjects transcend structures, then the meaning implicit in experience will undergo significant modifications in reflection. Second, this result suggests that a direct description of behaviour will be difficult to obtain. This directly challenges the basic phenomenological goal Merleau-Ponty is otherwise committed to, which presupposes the possibility of a faithful description of experience. He is not unaware of this tension: he claims that the tension between what lies outside consciousness, and consciousness' internal descriptive work, is definitive for his project (176/191). But at this point in his career, he does not take this to be a pressing enough theoretical problem, and he is happy to evade the problem by asserting that there is nothing 'inexpressible' in experience; alternatively, that there is no meaning that cannot be adequately accounted for (214/231). As I show in chapter 3, this problem persists in *Phenomenology of Perception*, and eventually motivates a new interpretation of phenomenological description.

An additional challenge looms large. As we saw, while perceptual *sens* is primary, *signification* is also needed to clarify meanings implicit in behaviour. But if expressive and constitutive processes transform elementary *sens*, and rely on terms that are not clearly traceable to perception, then the hitherto well-defined relations of priority between *sens* and *signification* become blurred. Despite Merleau-Ponty's stated view that perceptual meaning is prime, his arguments in *Structure* challenge this primacy. As will become clear, while he attempts to refine the grounding relation between ideal and perceptual meaning, the limitations of this picture lead him to reject it in later writings (see chapter 6).

Correlatively, Merleau-Ponty poses but leaves unanswered another fundamental problem that will guide his subsequent research: namely, what relation 'common sense' or everyday language bears to its philosophical or phenomenological counterpart. Clearly, the language used to clarify the structures of experience is not identical to natural language. But Merleau-Ponty says little more about its other characteristics, for example, if it is coextensive with the conceptual language of *signification*, if the phenomenological reduction transforms the meaning of natural language terms (as Fink argues), or if a genuinely new form of expression is required to understand behaviour.[21] Given that Merleau-Ponty claims, following Cassirer, that language has a 'guiding role . . . in the constitution of the perceived world', addressing these questions seems to be of some importance for the phenomenological enterprise (169/184).

While these questions remain unresolved, that we have been led to pose them testifies to the theoretical and methodological importance of language for *Structure*'s overall philosophical goals. A number of its key concepts and argumentative junctures are closely linked to problems and questions in the philosophy of language. Despite the incipient character of his arguments and conclusions, the basic concerns of Merleau-Ponty's phenomenology of language, and the fundamental challenges he will attempt to resolve, are already sketched in this early treatise.

NOTES

1. For background on Merleau-Ponty's intellectual formation and research in the 1930s, see Geraets 1971, 4–30, and Noble 2011.
2. See, for example, Silverman 1980, 123–24; cf. Noble 2014, 46–52.
3. Merleau-Ponty rejects J. B. Watson's definition of behaviour, and claims he gives it 'insufficient philosophical articulation' (225/2–3 n.2). The main failure of Watson's account is that it reduces behaviour to a sum of atomistic reflexes divided from one another (4/1–2).
4. For an overview of *Structure* see Gendlin and Spiegelberg 1964; Low 2004; Thompson 2007, chapter 4; and Toadvine 2009.
5. For the concept of *Fundierung* see Husserl 2001, Investigation 3 §21.
6. For Merleau-Ponty's criticisms of realist views of science see Rouse 2005, 280–88.
7. Merleau-Ponty sometimes uses the expression 'to constitute itself' or 'is constituted' (*se constituer*) to describe the formation of meanings that are not products of consciousness (e.g., 199/215).
8. See Noble 2014, 16–31 for a detailed discussion of Goldstein's influence on Merleau-Ponty, which also discusses Kant's influence on *Structure*.
9. As I argue in chapter 2, Merleau-Ponty's analysis of Schneider's pathologies also bears directly on his philosophy of language.
10. Talk of 'common sense' should not be understood along the lines of Reid or Moore. Instead, the term refers to widely held assumptions about experience, and is broadly continuous with Husserl's concept of the 'natural attitude'.
11. For later remarks about the 'primary text' of experience, see PhP lxxxii/18, 50/75, 353/394.
12. Despite many critical remarks (e.g., VI 107–12/142–49, 114–17/150–55, 121–22/159–60, 127–28/166–67, 186/237), Merleau-Ponty has a nuanced understanding of Husserl's reduction. Whilst he denies its adequacy and suffi-

ciency (PhP lxxvii/14), he sees it as a useful methodological tool, and even claims that his later work aims to develop a version of the reduction (VI 47–48/69, 178/229–30). For more see the relevant discussion in chapter 7.

13. For some helpful accounts of structure see Waldenfels 1980, 22–24, and Edie 1980, 45–46.

14. As Thompson has argued, this account of meaning-formation anticipates enactivist accounts of meaning and 'information' (2007, 51–60, 70).

15. It has been argued that Merleau-Ponty's account of structure is beholden to a matter-form dichotomy, insofar as it separates the immaterial (*la signification*) from the material (*le sens*) (Schenck 1984). Merleau-Ponty occasionally speaks in these terms (see Sanders 1994). However, it would be wrong to conclude that these occasionally imprecise formulations signal a commitment to a matter-form dichotomy. As this account suggests, the supposedly 'material' domain of perception is further refined by the ostensibly 'immaterial' level of structure, *signification*, and language, and *vice versa*. This shows that Merleau-Ponty does not accept a rigid matter-form distinction.

16. For more on constitution see Sokolowski 1964 and Zahavi 2002, chapter 5.

17. In subsequent work (especially in *The Prose of the World*), Merleau-Ponty returns to the topic of 'empirical' or 'scientific' expression (see chapter 4).

18. See Noble 2014, 50.

19. As subsequent chapters will show, *explicitation* is an important element of transcendental phenomenology (see PhP lxxx/16–17, 59/85–86).

20. See Hegel 1977 ¶¶190–96.

21. See Fink 1995, 89. Merleau-Ponty refers to Fink by name only once in *Structure*, when arguing that his interpretation of causal explanations points to the need for a transcendental method of analysis (206/222).

2

EMPIRICAL EXPRESSION

In contemporary philosophy of language, it is customary to distinguish semantics from pragmatics. This distinction is often used to separate the study of a sentence or word's meaning from that of its context of use. For Merleau-Ponty, linguistic meaning and usage cannot be clearly separated. Everyday language use aims to express the meaning of first-personal experience. This attempt is often complicated, sometimes confused, and its conditions of possibility resist transparent clarification. Still, a philosophically rich meditation on language must attempt to describe our firsthand experience of linguistic expression and understanding. For the meaning of any expression, Merleau-Ponty thinks, is best explained in light of the conditions in which it is uttered and understood by language users. *Phenomenology of Perception* contends that these conditions can ultimately be analysed in terms of the structure of perceptual experiences. Even if perceptual meaning must be consulted to explain linguistic meaning, attention to linguistic usage reveals that instead of merely representing the meaning of experience, language use also intervenes in and can even transform it.

This chapter provides an overview of the *Phenomenology*'s analyses of everyday ('empirical' or 'first-order') linguistic expression.[1] Some important assumptions guiding Merleau-Ponty's approach to empirical expression show up in his analysis of Schneider, and I will begin with a look at this case (section 1). In his interpretation of Schneider's pathologies, Merleau-Ponty makes a number of observations that directly inform the account of linguistic meaning and expression advanced in subsequent sections of the *Phenomenology*. They are also of importance for understanding his much-discussed interpretation and diagnosis of Schneider.

Merleau-Ponty develops a philosophical approach to first-order language use on which empirical expression depends on 'sedimented' linguistic meaning, takes the form of an embodied gesture and is a fundamentally interpretive activity (section 2). On this account, interpretation is a driving force behind the attempt to express ourselves, understand others and articulate lived experience. The recurring importance of interpretive activity suggests that Merleau-Ponty advances a 'hermeneutic' account of empirical language use, in which interpretive activity is understood in a non-cognitive and phenomenological vein. While he offers sustained observations about the structure of everyday linguistic expression, he is more interested in cases of 'authentic' or meaning-transforming expression, of the sort found in original aesthetic productions (section 3). After describing this mode of expression, I conclude by suggesting that it can serve as a site of existential freedom (section 4).

1. SCHNEIDER'S LINGUISTIC CAPACITIES

A study of Schneider's intentional and linguistic capacities is triply helpful. First, according to Merleau-Ponty, a proper grasp of Schneider's linguistic capabilities helps us understand his pathologies. Some of the insights of this account directly support his broader diagnosis of Schneider. By extension, given the role that this case plays in Merleau-Ponty's broader analysis of perception, insights from Schneider's pathological use of language can shed light on 'normal' or non-pathological modes of expression. Third, the case also highlights an important topic treated in the *Phenomenology*; namely, the extent to which scientific and empirical research can assist phenomenological analyses of perception. Like *Structure*, the *Phenomenology* is informed by scientific studies. It contends that science is a form of perception that has 'forgotten' its origins (PhP 54/80, 57/83–84). The chief failure of scientific accounts is that they define perception in overly 'objective' terms, which suppress lived meanings. This failure is instructive, insofar as it helps to highlight concepts that may prove more productive for developing a first-personal, consciousness-centric analysis of perception. By studying the inadequacies of scientistic arguments and terminology, we 'are led back to the very experiences that these words designate in order to define them anew' (10/33). This process realises a version of the phenomenological reduction, which as we saw in chapter 1, suspends our commonssense and philosophical assumptions about the being of objects and the world (53/79). Following Husserl, Merleau-Ponty thinks that these assumptions often take on a naturalistic or scientific character.

Merleau-Ponty's interpretation of Schneider has received much attention in the literature.[2] I do not intend to offer an exhaustive reconstruction of the case and its many intricacies. Instead, I will highlight its linguistic import, a dimension of the discussion that is often overlooked in most commentaries.

Merleau-Ponty's analysis unfolds in a chapter focused on the topic of bodily spatiality. One of its immediate goals is to work out the important concept of the 'body schema'.[3] According to Merleau-Ponty, this term details how 'my body is in and toward the world' (103/130). The *Phenomenology* assumes that subjects are chiefly embodied agents, capable of integrating immediate practical tasks and sketching possibilities for future action in a non-cognitive, pre-reflective, or 'unthematic' manner. For Merleau-Ponty, Schneider offers a good case study for understanding the relations between embodiment and space. In particular, his case clarifies the structure of motor intentional activity, which explains how embodied subjects are directed to their environment, material objects and other subjects.

Schneider suffered a brain injury while serving in World War I. According to Gelb and Goldstein, whose interpretation Merleau-Ponty heavily relies on, he suffered from visual agnosia (an inability to recognise objects in one's visual field).[4] Researchers continue to debate the exact nature of Schneider's agnosia. For Merleau-Ponty, the key feature of Schneider's pathology lies in his differing capacities for engaging in practical or habitual movements, on the one hand, and more abstract movements, on the other. Schneider can perform simple habitual actions, like searching for a handkerchief, and more complex habitual activities, like making a wallet. However, when blindfolded and explicitly asked to perform these tasks, he cannot do so with the same ease and degree of success. Instead, he must engage in a complex series of movements and steps, gradually eliminating a range of possible activities, before finally identifying a limited set of options that allow him to successfully realise the task he has been asked to perform.

Goldstein's observations lead him to draw a distinction between Schneider's 'concrete' and 'abstract' movements.[5] Subjects enact concrete movements whenever they unreflectively identify the steps needed to attain a given practical goal, and seamlessly succeed in reaching it. Abstract movement is explicitly goal directed. In abstract movement, subjects explicitly identify a specific course of action and attempt to see it through. Goldstein contends that in each form of movement, which could appear identical to an observer, two distinct attitudes are obtained: concrete movement exemplifies 'grasping' (*Greifen*) attitudes, whereas abstract movement exemplifies 'pointing' (*Zeigen*) attitudes. In non-pathological cases, these two attitudes are not usually separated. Subjects can, for the most part, identify different tasks and perform the movements necessary to realise them in seamless succession. On the basis of these observations, Merleau-Ponty concludes that whereas 'concrete movement . . . takes place within being or within the actual', abstract movement 'itself sets up its own background' (114/142). Schneider's action lacks a harmonious unity between the grasping and pointing attitudes.

While he mainly relies on secondary interpretations of Schneider's ailments, Merleau-Ponty offers a distinctively phenomenological interpretation of his differential capacities for action. Unlike Gelb and Goldstein, he claims that Schneider's behaviour is best explained by an intentional analysis focussed on how he meaningfully comprehends instructions and performs habitual actions. Schneider is lacking neither motricity (the ability to engage in embodied intentional movement) nor cognitive capacities or the use of abstract concepts. Instead, he is unable to integrate and unify them in goal-directed activity (112–13/140). Schneider lacks normal motor-intentional powers, which allow subjects to evaluate possible (or virtual) and actual actions without conflating the two.[6] Instead, he must link possible actions he is asked to perform with occurrent ones 'through an explicit deduction' (112/140).

The precise nature of Schneider's 'explicit deduction' and his deliberate attempt to connect a conceptual possibility with concrete action has been debated at length. This debate has largely focused on the extent to which, on Merleau-Ponty's premises, abstract thought can motivate concrete action. Some commentators (e.g., Hubert Dreyfus) suggest that the motivation of action occurs at a largely unthematic and tacit level, whereas others (e.g., Komarine Romdenh-Romluc) argue that if this interpretation is correct, it effectively deprives subjects of any sort of deliberate, conscious or explicitly goal-directed capacities.[7]

The terms of this debate have shifted focus away from the important question of how Schneider's thought can generate action, to the question of whether it can at all. But Merleau-Ponty is clear that an account of Schneider's pathology must be given at 'the junction of sensitivity and signification' (132/164). That is, it must take account of how his embodied pre-reflective activity intersects with his capacities for abstract thought (the range of capacities referred to using the term *signification*). Whatever those might be, it is clear that non-conceptual or unthematic and conscious or thought-directed conditions will figure in the final explanation. Once this important feature is recognised, the deeper nature of Schneider's 'explicit deduction' can come into greater relief.

Textual evidence suggests that Schneider surmounts obstacles to motor-intentional activity through a deliberate use of linguistic expression:

> The pen is then brought closer to the patient and the clip is turned toward him. He continues: 'it must be a pencil or a fountain pen'. (He touches his vest pocket). This is where it goes, for writing something down. Language clearly intervenes in each phase of the recognition by providing possible significations for what is actually seen, and the recognition clearly progresses by following the connections of language, from 'oblong' to 'the form of a stick', from 'stick' to 'instrument', then to 'instrument for writing something down', and finally to 'fountain pen'. (132–33/164)

By identifying objects and uttering the linguistic names associated with them, Schneider deduces their meaning (*signification*), the actions they might be associated with and what context these actions could be realised in. For him, commands and objects do not have a definitive meaning before they are interpreted. The passage suggests that this interpretive activity is linguistic. Schneider can generate possible courses of action by importing conceptual (*viz.* linguistic) significations into his lived experience, through an 'explicit subsumption' (129/160).

For Schneider, '[t]he translation of the perceived into movement passes through the express significations of language, whereas the normal subject penetrates the object through perception and assimilates its structure, the object directly regulates his movements through his body' (134/165).[8] In addition to confirming that abstract thought can motivate action, these observations also show that language plays an essential role in Merleau-Ponty's account of how Schneider overcomes his motor-intentional deficiencies. While it has been noted that Schneider has difficulty using 'speaking speech', a more seamless and unthematic form of linguistic expression, and that he relies instead on 'spoken' speech, a more circumscribed and rudimentary form of expression, it has yet to be noted that Schneider's ability to 'reckon with the possible' is also supported by his distinctive use of language, and not only by abstract thought or reflection.[9] His abstract, reflective capacities consist in a deliberate use of language that associates words or concepts with things and actions.

Assuming that Schneider does not represent a normal version of motor intentionality, this case helps us better understand what role language might play in standard intentional activity. Merleau-Ponty cautions against inferring directly from Schneider's case to normal functioning; but his descriptions nevertheless suggest that standard cases of motor intentionality do not depend on explicit or implicit language use. Schneider draws on 'constituted language', whose meanings are already well formed (recall the discussion of 'common sense' language in *Structure*) (130/161). But this process must be contrasted with what Merleau-Ponty calls 'living thought', which does not rely on concepts or *significations* to understand perceived structures, perform actions and engage objects in the world. At this stage in his career, Merleau-Ponty would reject the view that perceptual experience is mediated by concepts or contains conceptual content.[10] Instead, 'living thought' directly grasps the 'silent language' of perception, which is meaningful prior to conceptual analysis or any appeal to language (50/75).

Having offered an interpretation of Schneider, Merleau-Ponty draws further conclusions about the language-perception relation. Some of these conclusions are worked out later in the *Phenomenology*. Perhaps most importantly, he claims that linguistic meaning is 'founded' on perceptual meaning (131/162–63). I will consider this important position in more detail in chapter 3. For now, the claim that language is founded on perception can be understood as the view that perceptual *sens* must ultimately be invoked to explain the content of any linguistic unit, concept or *signification*. This claim is consistent with a basic premise of the *Phenomenology*: that perception is prime. On this view, the meaning of the concept 'cat' can be specified by reference to experiences of seeing or observing cats. Perception supplies meanings that are subsequently converted to a conceptual and linguistic form. If someone never happened to come across a cat, they would be unable to make sense of the furry, four-legged being that appears before them. If this person were part of a linguistic community that counts 'cat' among its concepts, they could appeal to their peers for assistance. In either case, the meaning of this concept would at some point be linked to an intentional experience of perceiving cats, even if a particular subject happens to lack this specific intuitive experience and the evidence associated with it (but acquires it, for example, through testimony or from peers). If I do have such an experience, the sight of a furry, four-legged being supplies the semantic content of the word 'cat'.

Merleau-Ponty is notoriously vague when advancing his version of the claim that language is founded on perception. It is clear, however, that this view is not a cousin of empiricism: for him concepts are not products of sense impressions. Rather, he uses the concept of founding to make an ontological and an explanatory point about meaning and our experience of it. Perception is the primary medium through which we engage the world, whereas language is secondary. Given this priority, linguistic meaning can be understood as a translation of perceptual meaning. The latter enjoys explanatory priority, insofar as it can be used to explain the former. This is also the case, as Merleau-Ponty often suggests, because perceptual meaning is a more fundamental or more ontologically basic kind of meaning. Recall that the relation of priority between *sens* and *signification* was sometimes conflated in *Structure*. The *Phenomenology* is clear that *sens* and *signification* are two distinct types of meaning, and that the former grounds, explains or 'projects' the meaning of the latter (147–48/182).[11] Even if we do not have any first-personal experience of appealing to perception to explain the meaning of a given concept, Merleau-Ponty maintains that perceptual meaning always remains in the background, and that it serves as the foundation for any non-perceptual meaning.

In addition to the point about founding, the Schneider analysis draws an important connection between language and 'situation'. Whereas Schneider must use language to escape the boundaries of his immediate, actual experience, normal subjects have recourse to a 'fundamental function' that permits them to 'orient [themselves] toward anything' (137/169). The fundamental function allows subjects to place themselves in a given situation, and act according to the possibilities it supports. A 'situation' is best understood as an embodied set of conditions allowing for or motivating certain courses of action, and is made up by cultural, (inter-) personal, perceptual, significative and embodied features. Schneider 'lacks the concrete freedom that consists in the general power of placing oneself in a situation' (137/169). By extension, language can create a situation for normal subjects, by establishing a field of possible expressive activity. In Schneider's case it does so nonstandardly; but language use can also establish a situation through non-pathological means.

2. MERLEAU-PONTY'S HERMENEUTIC ACCOUNT OF LINGUISTIC EXPRESSION

The Schneider analysis demonstrates that Merleau-Ponty is chiefly interested in the pragmatics of language. This is also clear from his frequent references to the term 'speech' (*parole*), which he sometimes uses to describe language *tout court*.[12] While he is no speech-act theorist, he shares Austin's view that context (or 'situation') is essential for understanding everyday language use.[13] Like Husserl, he takes the pragmatic side of language to consist in expression.[14] However, for Merleau-Ponty, this is chiefly an embodied and not a mental-significative activity: expression is a 'gesture' (*un geste*) (189/223). For him, the structures that enable and explain language use can be understood by detailing the contextual, local conditions of expression. This orientation places Merleau-Ponty somewhat far from semantic or truth-conditional theories of meaning influenced by Frege or Tarski. For him, language is not a tool, and it does not chiefly serve to represent reality. Through language use, human beings give voice to their experience and articulate the sense of their world.

EMPIRICAL EXPRESSION

In this section, I unfold three basic features of his account of empirical expression: sedimentation, gesture and interpretation. These tenets show that empirical expression involves a taking-up and a transformation of existing linguistic conventions; both require some minimal interpretive activity. Merleau-Ponty can be understood to advance a hermeneutic account of empirical language use because he accepts that some form of interpretation (sometimes designated using the term 'transcendence') is the deeper condition for the possibility of articulating and understanding speech. This account does not directly engage with or borrow from thinkers like Schleiermacher, Dilthey, or Heidegger, even if it is consistent with some of their teachings.

2.1 Sedimentation

According to Merleau-Ponty, linguistic expression depends on already existing word-meanings, grammar and syntactical rules. A focus on how a subject 'handles' or modifies this existing store of meanings and conventions must be a mainstay of any analysis of empirical expression (192/227). Following Husserl, he uses the term 'sedimentation' to describe the process by which word-meanings, grammar, and other features of natural language gradually crystallise over time, take on a more determinate form and become available for use in a linguistic tradition.[15] For example, the meaning of the English word 'awesome', once associated with fear-inspiring phenomena, has gradually shifted its meaning through modulations in usage, and currently enjoys a largely positive valence. Shifts in expressive acts have in this case sedimented a new meaning associated with the term. Given the view that language is founded on perception, this sedimented linguistic meaning is ultimately a version of perceptual experiences associated with this term.

The important role that sedimentation plays for expression leads Merleau-Ponty to make a distinction between 'spoken speech' (*parole parlée*) and 'speaking speech' (*parole parlante*) (202/238).[16] In *Phenomenology*, spoken speech refers to the sum of previous acts of expression, grammatical rules, and more, all of which circumscribe subjects' opportunities for expression in the present. Spoken speech is the stuff of many everyday expressive engagements (such as small talk, formulaic greetings or techno-bureaucratic jargon). But this repository of semantic contents and formal features must be taken up, or 'acquired', by language-using subjects. It supports particular 'acts of speech' in the present, which are partly captured by the term 'speaking speech'. Speaking speech is an active and in some cases transformative use of existing linguistic meanings. In elementary cases of language use, speaking speech activates or actualises existing conventions and applies them in a particular context of use. In special cases, it can create new modes of expression (I will return to this point below).

As the analysis of Schneider indicated, Merleau-Ponty is chiefly interested in linguistic expression as it unfolds here and now. Speaking and spoken speech are co-present, insofar as subjects take up existing meanings, which support but are insufficient to explain their particular linguistic expressions (189/224; S 86/140).[17] Already in *Structure*, Merleau-Ponty shows that he is keenly interested in how existing conventions or 'structures' are transformed. Linguistic expression offers a prime example of this transformative activity (269/307). Most linguistic transformations occur in mundane, everyday life. For example, I might decide to start using a particular word in a certain way (e.g., 'awesome') in response to my friend's increasingly standard refrain ('that's awesome'!). According to Merleau-Ponty, these changes in linguistic usage contribute something nontrivial to linguistic meaning, and we must attempt to understand them if we want to grasp how everyday linguistic expression functions (409/449).

An example from a later section in the *Phenomenology* helps to clarify the relationship between sedimentation and expression:

> The word 'sleet', when I know it, is not an object that I recognise through a synthesis of identification; it is a certain use of my phonatory apparatus and a certain modulation of my body as being in the world; its generality is not the generality of an idea, but rather that of a style of behaviour that my body 'understands' insofar as my body is a power of producing behaviours and, in particular, of producing phonemes. (425/451)

While the word 'sleet' has a general *signification*, it is also uttered by subjects at a particular time and place. The former captures the 'spoken' dimension of this term, while the latter refers to its active, 'speaking' use in the present. When invoking the word 'sleet', a subject particularises a general linguistic meaning. She applies this word to a given context for the sake of making some point or expressing some view. The case of 'sleet' is obviously a mundane example. But Merleau-Ponty thinks that a subject's expressive characteristics (e.g., how our body or 'phonatory apparatus' pronounces the word 'sleet') are important for understanding the word's meaning, which is not encountered in a propositional but in a lived form, as a sound uttered and heard by an embodied agent. This description also suggests that Merleau-Ponty is keenly interested in how a particular meaning is produced at a given time and place. This points to the important gestural dimension of expression.

2.2 Gesture

The *Phenomenology* argues at length against 'empiricist' and 'intellectualist' interpretations of perceptual experience. Its account of empirical expression also serves this goal. The account of gestural expression deliberately aims to undermine intellectualist accounts, on which '[t]hought has a sense and the word remains an empty envelope', and empiricist views, which reduce linguistic meaning to verbal 'images' produced by particular phonemes (181–82/214–16).[18] Instead of rehearsing these arguments here, it will suffice to note that whatever their more specific failures might be, Merleau-Ponty ultimately rejects these approaches because they are inadequately attuned to lived expression, in which language use chiefly gives voice to our experience and particular expressive needs.[19] On these grounds, he would also reject as insufficient a philosophy of language centred on propositional or sentential analysis, which indexes meaning to truth conditions.[20] While these analyses offer helpful information, they overlook our first-personal experience of linguistic meaning, which offers the most salient evidence (according to Merleau-Ponty) for philosophical meditations on language.

A gestural view of language denies that language use can be adequately understood according to intentionalist, representational or mentalistic theories. Attention to lived expression shows that even if subjects can make a mental sketch of speech before uttering it, the activity of speaking does not involve the translation of a pre-existing mental text into a verbalised form (183/218). If we attend to expression in dialogue or communication, for example, we do not encounter something akin to a 'representation' of a mental linguistic project: 'for the speaking subject, thought is not a representation; that is, thought does not explicitly posit objects or relations. The orator does not think prior to speaking, nor even while speaking; his speech is his thought' (185/ 219; see also S 89/145). Expression is better understood as an unguided, pre-reflective and non-cognitive search for the right combination of words. Everyday experience testifies that this process is sometimes fraught with difficulties. But given its lived character, it cannot be adequately characterised as the application of a representation or a mental content to a set of terms that bear a particular meaning. Instead, it is an existential or lived activity that is on a continuum with other forms of embodied expression (e.g., facial gestures, sighs, hand movements and more); that is, with the embodied tools we use to state and externalise the meaning of what we feel and experience. If this description of language use points in the right direction, it suggests that linguistic meaning is located in embodied acts of linguistic expression. Speech is itself a vehicle of meaning (*sens*): '[sense and speech] are enveloped in each other; sense is caught in speech, and speech is the external existence of sense' (187/222).

According to Merleau-Ponty, speech is a 'gesture'. If representation is inadequate, the meaning of language can be located in subjects' embodied articulative attempts. While representationalist or intentionalist theories tend to identify some mental entity as the bearer of linguistic meaning, Merleau-Ponty's gestural theory aims to show that linguistic meaning is given as an embodied whole, in which distinctively semantic and pragmatic elements cannot be separated. Most basically, speech is a gesture because expression always has some physical or bodily support: while speaking we project sound, move our bodies, indicate with our hands and more. But this is not the embodied dimension of gesture that most interests Merleau-Ponty. Unlike Cassirer, he does not define linguistic gestures as lower-order, physical preconditions.[21] For Merleau-Ponty, linguistic gestures are genuine vehicles of meaning that are not supplemented by higher-order symbolic or mental activities. Sound, intonation, and bodily posture directly support a distinctively linguistic project that is usually seamlessly understood without drawing on additional conceptual resources (189/224). Perceived and ostensibly non-linguistic conditions are important features of linguistic expression, and contribute something essential to the meaning of what is said. Speech can be characterised as a gesture because the meaning of the words we pronounce or hear cannot be separated from the auditory, visual or embodied conditions that enable these experiences. These conditions jointly support the articulation of linguistic meaning.

As the frequent references to 'style' suggest, linguistic meaning is also a function of how a given gesture is enacted or performed. Particular words may be associated with rote gestural performances, but they take a specific form. Expressions come in the form of a distinctive 'sonorous and articulatory style' (186/220). If Merleau-Ponty is right that expression is not a process whereby minds exchange mental content or representations, then speakers' intentions and linguistic meaning will be explained in terms of how a given word or sentence is expressed (and, as we will see below, how it is received by others). The concept of 'style' captures this dimension of language use. For Merleau-Ponty, gestural style helps to circumscribe the sense of speech. Style is pervasive in all forms of expression. It is the 'how' of speech. In written language, style is legible in diction, sentence length, use of syntax or punctuation. In spoken language, style is encountered in tone, volume, bodily position, pronunciation and accentuation, the pace of expression and so on. Some approaches to the philosophy of language assume that these features are ancillary to linguistic meaning, properly understood. But it makes a world of difference if I blurt out 'come on!' curtly and with a contorted facial expression, or if I do so by drawing out each word, with a smile and a soft voice. Merleau-Ponty stresses that 'speech or words carry a primary layer of signification that adheres to them and that gives the thought as a style, as an affective value, or as an existential mimicry, rather than as a conceptual statement' (188/222).

Writing in the wake of Merleau-Ponty, and influenced by philosophers who stress the active and embodied dimensions of language, Charles Taylor provides a helpful summary of what such a view entails:

> Let us say I am trying to formulate how I feel, or how something looks, or how she behaved. I struggle to find an adequate expression, and then I get it. What have I achieved? To start with, I can now focus properly on the matter in question. When I still do not know how to describe how I feel, or how it looks, and so on, the objects concerned lack definite contours; I do not quite know what to focus on in focussing on them. Finding an adequate articulation for what I

want to say about these matters brings them in focus. To find a description in this case is to identify a feature of the matter at hand and thereby to grasp its contour, to get a proper view of it.[22]

As this description suggests, language use is a search for resources adequately suited to a particular expressive goal. The feeling that a word or expression is 'adequate' is largely a matter of context; no formula or cut-and-dried criterion can explain what makes a particular expression adequate to its expressive goals. Language-users search for this implicit and local criterion of adequacy through their linguistic gestures. Linguistic gestures are the non-conceptual, embodied vehicles through which we attempt to articulate ourselves in a way fitting to the context and matter at hand. When articulating how we feel, what we see, or what we hope for, we place ourselves in a linguistic situation with a familiar set of expressive resources, and adapt them to our expressive intentions. Our attempt to do so, in turn, circumscribes the meaning of existing linguistic conventions, and gives our speech its style.

To put the point differently, in gestural expression 'sign' and 'signification' cannot be clearly separated (184/219; see also CPP 11–12).[23] This distinction roughly corresponds to the medium through which a particular word or sentence is expressed (its material manifestation, e.g., writing or sound), and what the word or sentence expresses (i.e., the meanings given by a *signification* or a gesture). If speech is a gesture with a specific style, it makes little sense to distinguish the meaning one intends from the particular means employed to express it. The latter includes the 'how' of expression; that is, the manner in which our expressive aims are executed. Insofar as dialogue or communication are concerned (the cases of expression that most interest Merleau-Ponty), a subject's gestural style helps to fix the meaning of what she is attempting to convey. For example, a solicitous tone of voice helps us understand if a subject's consoling words are really genuine. Their meaning is not simply that of consolation, in general, but rather that of this particular consoling attempt, in response to some specific matter at hand. Absent this 'how' of expression, the same words take on a different meaning. On these grounds, it makes little sense to divide what we mean from how we intend it, and what we refer to from what we mean.[24]

These descriptions are obviously geared towards a limited subset of linguistic activities. They do not address other questions one might expect to encounter in standard philosophical analyses of language. Readers with different methodological and conceptual commitments might be inclined to see this as a failure, or as evidence of an incomplete account of expression. I have suggested that this focus reflects Merleau-Ponty's fundamental interest in our lived experience of language. Like his analyses of perception and mind, which break from mentalistic or computational assumptions, he sees linguistic usage as an embodied undertaking. Guided by a focus on this lived dimension, he opts for description over speculation, and attempts to develop a philosophy of language consistent with experience, as he understands it.

2.3 Meaning and Interpretation

In addition to escaping the ills of intentionalist or representational theories, a gestural view also highlights the centrality of interpretation in everyday expression. According to Merleau-Ponty's account, interpretive activity is at work on two interrelated levels of empirical language use: in a speaker's attempt to express herself, and in a listener's attempt to understand a speaker. Both conditions are fundamental for defining the meaning of a particular expression. The hermeneutic or interpretive dimensions of Merleau-Ponty's account of empirical language use have yet to be fully appreciated.[25]

While sedimentation is a basic condition for expression, existing meanings and conventions must be brought to bear on experience here and now. Recall that meaning-transformation, which Merleau-Ponty sometimes called 'transcendence' in *Structure*, is a basic condition of linguistic expression. The account of sedimentation above indicated that a process of appropriation and particularisation supports empirical expression (one that is reminiscent of the hermeneutical circle). Transcendence is the 'movement by which existence takes up for itself [*reprend à son compte*] and transforms a *de facto* situation' (PhP 173/ 208). Transcendence can take different forms. With respect to language, it consists in a 'reorganisation' of existing linguistic meaning, and produces new combinations of linguistic units.[26] As Merleau-Ponty notes, Schneider lacks the capacity to seamlessly transcend existing meanings and generate new ones, but transcendence is a feature of standard linguistic expression (202/238).

Transcendence in language is best understood as a form of interpretation. In using the term 'interpretation', I do not want to suggest that transcendence requires deliberate cognitive activity, as in the interpretation of a poem. The account of gesture above shows that expressive interpretation is more akin to a probing search for the right linguistic resources with which to articulate a given meaning. Interpretation tacitly explores and isolates expressions that appear fitting or appropriate for a given expressive task, from those that are available. While speaking, we get the sense that a particular term serves as an adequate means of expressing some meaning. Even in the most mundane cases, subjects are called to reinterpret the meaning of a word in order to suitably apply it to their expressive aims. We take *this* word and apply it to *that* context, that is, we see both 'as' appropriately geared in with one another. This is a fundamental background condition for the account of gesture just considered. Like tools, words are 'part of my equipment' and can be variously deployed in different linguistic situations (186/220).[27] As in our use of tools, we do not usually think expressly or deductively about how to cut this piece of wood, adjust this screw or dig this hole; our existing facility with saws, screwdrivers or hoes leads us to the best means of doing so, even if we must make adjustments along the way. Certainly, language use might require not just tacit but also explicit reflection on one's linguistic resources; it is sometimes difficult to find the right word. But in either case, expression results from an interpretive or deciphering activity that combines words into a meaningful whole or sentence (the basic structural unit of language) (408/449).[28] When searching for a word or expression, we often do not know where we will be led. The indefinite and open feeling we have when doing so, as if we were waiting for the right term or expression to appear before us, describes the kind of non-cognitive interpretive activity at work here.

Recall that an important conclusion in Merleau-Ponty's analysis of Schneider was that language can establish a situation. For interpretation to play a fundamental role in expression, a linguistic situation must offer possibilities for modifying and producing new meanings in a language. Another important feature of the linguistic situation is tied to interpretation: language is situated because expression is usually directed to or unfolds in proximity to others. Our gestures are not ours alone; they are also perceived by other language-using subjects, who attempt to understand them. The essentially public or intersubjective character of language entails that other subjects will interpret our gestures, and that linguistic meaning is 'given with words for those who have ears to hear' (VI 155/201).[29]

Merleau-Ponty claims that 'the sense of a sentence is its aim or its intention, which again assumes a point of departure and a point of arrival, an intended thing [*un visée*], and a point of view' (PhP 454/493). While speaking, we might intend to make a particular point (this would be our expressive 'intention'). But our individual view of the particular expressive matter at hand is only one part of the gesture's total meaning. For the 'sense of gestures is not given but rather understood, which is to say taken up by an act of the spectator. The entire difficulty is to conceive of this act properly and not to confuse it with an epistemic operation' (190/225). Language is *par excellence* a public entity; there is no private language. Instead of being contained in a speaker's mental acts, linguistic meaning is supported by modulations of embodied motor-intentional capacities. While subjectively experienced, embodied linguistic meaning is also heard by others. Gestures are understood when they are 'caught and taken up by a speaking power [*puissance parlante*]' (425/464). This is another way of stating that gestures are understood when they are interpreted by fellow language-using subjects.

Embodied intentionality integrates meanings it encounters in its milieu in a largely unthematic manner, without deliberate deductions. For example, in a familiar neighbourhood, we turn the corner and can immediately navigate. Similarly, access to the store of sedimented meanings is a background condition that makes most cases of linguistic interpretation seamless. It helps us comprehend familiar words and allows us to contrast them with unfamiliar expressions (e.g., terms in foreign languages). The 'body is not merely one object among all others, not a complex of sensible qualities among others. It is an object sensitive to all others, which resonates for all sounds, vibrates for all colours, and that provides words with their primordial signification through the manner in which it receives them' (245/283). While this remark confirms that the intuitive reception of a gesture is important for circumscribing its meaning, Merleau-Ponty says little more about how the body's intentional capacities handle linguistic sense. It is safe to say, however, that in addition to presupposing first-personal interpretive activity, gestures are standardly interpreted by an external point of view (PhP 190–91/225; PW 29/41). It would seem that embodied language-users receive the meaning of a gesture in a way consistent with the interpretive activity described above. When hearing another subject's speech, our existing linguistic capacities allow us to integrate their expressions, and incline us towards a meaning consistent with what we hear and see. According to Merleau-Ponty, this process cannot be understood in physicalistic terms. His emphasis on its interpretive character (he likens expressions to symbols, whose meaning must be interpreted) should not, then, be read in a 'naturalistic' vein.[30] The interpretation of gestural style is not construed as a physical or biological response to sound, but as an embodied and non-cognitive transformation of a meaningful linguistic project (189/224).[31]

For Merleau-Ponty, interpretation pervades our experience of language use 'all the way down'. The character of this interpretive activity varies, and comes in degrees, but the expressive attitudes described above remain fundamentally interpretive. For this reason, I have suggested that Merleau-Ponty offers a 'hermeneutic' view of language use. Like Heidegger, he accepts that linguistic meaning is not inert and that it requires interpretation by speakers and listeners for it to take on an existential or lived value.[32] Like earlier hermeneutical philosophers, he also accepts that linguistic interpretation has a broadly circular and reintegrative structure. Merleau-Ponty's account of expression seems to have even greater affinities with Gadamer's emphasis on the intersubjective or dialogical dimension of language, and with his claim that interpretive intentions (or 'thought') is coextensive with language use.[33] Considering these connections in greater detail would take us too far afield. Like his possible affinities with tenets advanced by analytic philosophers of language, Merleau-Ponty's proximity to hermeneutical philosophers only goes so far. His account of linguistic interpretation responds to and is better understood in terms of his own philosophical concerns.

3. AUTHENTIC EXPRESSION

Merleau-Ponty offers some descriptions of everyday language use, but he is especially interested in a distinctive form of expression that he variously calls 'authentic', 'originary' and 'speaking' speech (*parole parlante*). The use of the term 'authentic' might suggest a proximity to Heidegger's concept of authenticity (*die Eigentlichkeit*), but the two accounts differ in their details and basic aims.[34] Some basic characteristics of authentic expression are similar to those of everyday empirical expression. However, authentic expression differs in one important respect: it transforms conventional meanings to a more profound degree than the cases considered so far, which generally presuppose 'that the decisive step of expression has been accomplished' (189–90/224).

His account of authentic expression aims to answer the primordial question of why human beings speak at all. Unfortunately, this guiding concern is occasionally obscured by remarks about the possible conventional or natural origin of linguistic meaning (193–95/227–30). The interpretive character of expression suggests that both explanations are insufficient. Despite differences in the expressive resources of existing natural languages, at bottom human beings speak in order to express the 'emotional essence' of the world (193/228). This sounds like a naturalistic claim, but it is not. Language articulates the lived texture of experience, a process that promises to transform 'the given world', which includes nature (194/299).[35] Authentic language, Merleau-Ponty thinks, is a privileged means of bringing about such transformations.

Like other forms of first-order expression, authentic expression relies on sedimented meaning, is a form of gesture and unfolds according to a logic of transcendence (323/365). It is distinguished from standard modes of empirical expression by the degree to which it transforms existing linguistic conventions, and by the novelty of its expressive products. If authentic, 'speech gives rise to a new sense, just as the gesture – if it is an initiating gesture – gives a human sense to the object for the first time'. Insofar as authentic expression is concerned, 'significations now acquired must surely have been new significations' (200/236). The interpretation and creativity at work in authentic expression offers subjects genuinely novel cores of meaning that are not mere modifications of existing conventions (e.g., in the 'sleet' case above). While everyday language use might transform conventions by using a word in a new context, authentic expression offers subjects a perspective that can articulate the world in a new light. This 'opens a new field' or adds 'a new dimension to our experience' (188/222–23). Authentic expression is distinguished by its experience-transforming possibilities.

As these characterisations suggest, authentic expression has broader cultural value. A 'construction' of this sort 'constitutes a linguistic and cultural world' (203/239; see also S 92/115). Acts of 'speaking speech' develop cultural and intellectual resources that allow us to reinterpret everyday life. Proust's writing is a good example of authentic expression (I will return to Merleau-Ponty's reading of Proust in parts 2 and 3). As Proust notes, in 'authentic' forms of expression 'the world around us (which was not created once and for all, but is created afresh as often as an original artist is born) appears to us entirely different from the old world, but perfectly clear'.[36]

Like other linguistic gestures, authentic expression does not observe the sign/signification dichotomy (169/204). However, given that many of Merleau-Ponty's remarks about authentic expression refer to literature or poetry (and also to expression in painting), arguments for the sign/signification unity do not in this case chiefly serve anti-intellectualist and anti-representationalist aims. The point here is that the novel content of authentic expression is inseparable from its form. Alternatively, how an artist expresses her view of experience is key to understanding the new insights her view offers. For example, Proust's long, sinuous sentences and his sensitive, detailed descriptions establish a certain conscious flow in the minds of his readers. This effect is a key component of Proust's unique take on our experience of time and place, and on our relation to objects and other people. Similar observations could be made about literary genres (e.g., realism) or schools of painting (e.g., impressionism), whose formal features are ineliminable from the meaning and basic point their works attempt to convey.

The unity of form and content in authentic expression entails that when we encounter authentic expression, we often struggle to understand it. In this basic sense, it is unlike everyday expression. However, by attempting to understand how the formal features of an artist or philosopher's language support deeper insights, we acquire intellectual and cultural resources of real value. By probing the meaning of an authentic expression, subjects enact a kind of interpretive training, honing their discriminatory and evaluative skills. This teaches us to attend to features of an artwork or idea, and to situate them within the broader claims of a work or argument. By engaging with authentic expression, we develop an interpretive attitude that can be applied more liberally, and can be directed to non-literary or non-linguistic objects (e.g., places or persons). According to Merleau-Ponty, this promises to disclose new features of our world.

Ultimately, these observations about authentic language or 'speaking' speech attempt to shed some light on a form of expression that Merleau-Ponty finds deeply enigmatic. Expression is a 'miracle' (333/375). From a philosophical perspective, it remains fundamentally 'obscure' (423/463). Merleau-Ponty ultimately aims to sensitise readers to dimensions of linguistic usage that may be easily overlooked or dismissed. Some tenets of authentic expression are developed in other discussions in the *Phenomenology*, and in subsequent writings. I will consider two important examples in chapters 3 and 4.

4. AUTHENTIC LANGUAGE AND FREEDOM

Before turning to his account of transcendental expression, I would like to consider an overlooked consequence of Merleau-Ponty's view of authentic expression. According to his premises, the structure of authentic linguistic expression realises the basic conditions for 'concrete' freedom. While he does not explicitly draw this conclusion in the *Phenomenology*, authentic language use can be understood as a paradigmatic exercise of human freedom. This result helps to clarify Merleau-Ponty's understanding of freedom and language, and brings together two topics that are seldom linked.

Merleau-Ponty adopts some basic premises from Sartre's interpretation of existential freedom in *Being and Nothingness*.[37] For Sartre, freedom is only possible given certain 'factical' conditions. These conditions are individuated by our situation, a claim Merleau-Ponty also accepts (BN 78, 347, 623–27; PhP 467/506). A 'situation', for Sartre, can be understood as an ensemble of meanings and conditions that enable us to make decisions about which courses of action to take up or reject. The sort of conditions that constitute a situation include our occupation, language, nationality, gender and the historical period in which one lives. A situation is also constituted by the more local spatio-temporal relations that subjects encounter when engaging in the world (707–8). Merleau-Ponty has these sorts of embodied conditions in mind when he claims that language use is 'situated'.

For Sartre, Merleau-Ponty and Beauvoir, free actions modify existing factical conditions and situations (BN 59–60; PhP 476/514, 481–82/518–19). By taking up the already existing lifestyle of a student, for example, and living it according to my own particular understanding of what makes for a good student life, I transform what it means to 'be a student', and instantiate a particular form of student life. In doing so, I revise the received or situated meaning of what it is to be a student. By making a general structure and set of historical circumstances particular, I infuse the world with new meaning (or, in Sartre's terms, I 'negate' the given). Sartre, Merleau-Ponty and Beauvoir think that this amounts to an act of existential freedom.

Another way of putting this point is that existential freedom is an act of transcendence. While these thinkers would agree with this claim, their respective accounts of transcendence differ. A central disagreement touches on the temporal structure underlying transcendence.[38] For Sartre, even if an act of freedom begins from existing conditions and meanings, free action fundamentally transforms the past and present. The subject 'nihilates' its past and its present situation, giving each a fundamentally new meaning: the past takes on a sense only in light of my current projects and future-directed goals (BN 64, 707). By contrast, Merleau-Ponty does not index the sense of situations, including past, present and future states, to a subject's activities or projects. For him, freedom requires that we integrate past meanings into the present. But we cannot cast the past or present in a wholly new light: even if a subject modifies her past, she continues to be conditioned by meanings that are not wholly up to her to determine (PhP 479/517; see also 437–44/476–84). For Sartre, we are free to interrupt and refigure the temporal sequence that freedom depends on; an act of transcendence is an explicit posit. For Merleau-Ponty, freedom remains a largely implicit and unthematic activity. We only come to fully understand the meaning of a free act (and recognise it as such) after it is realised, and once its meaning has become more determinate (472/510). Like their underlying temporal structure, the meaning of free acts remains ambiguous *ex ante*. They have the 'appearance' of clearly demarcated goals only retrospectively.

These differences manifest themselves in Sartre and Merleau-Ponty's respective views of linguistic expression. We saw above that for Merleau-Ponty linguistic expression depends on sedimented meanings. For the most part, in everyday life expression operates within the strictures of sedimented and 'spoken' speech. But language users also transcend sedimented meanings. When they do, they establish a new situation, in which linguistic usage becomes reconfigured (189/223). In describing a child's experience of hearing a story, Merleau-Ponty suggests that language creates a situation when it discloses new expressive possibilities. For the child, who makes no distinction between the sound of a word or a sentence and its meaning, hearing a story triggers new questions, possibilities and expectations. The child has a largely immediate relation to language: for her, words are meaningful gestures, not bearers or representations of propositional meanings. Words immediately 'induce' their sense. To listen to a story is to enter into a world whose future possibilities depend on the progress of a narrative. While the child might be familiar with some of the terms in the story, an author's imaginative reinterpretation of familiar meanings transforms the child's understanding of what she can expect from the plot. Her lived experience is situated in light of the structure of the story. Authentic language manifests its deeper situation-creating power in cases of this sort. By creating a new linguistic situation, authentic expression transforms the limits of possible experience, including those of existing linguistic expression (423/462).

In addition to its situation-generating possibilities, authentic expression also mirrors the structure of temporality and transcendence at work in freedom. Both mundane and genuinely new language use requires 'the subject's taking up of a position in the world of his significations' (199/235). In authentic expression, subjects draw on the expressive efforts of their linguistic predecessors, but also imbue them with new life. This suggests that the cyclical temporal structure underlying acts of freedom is also a feature of linguistic expression. This is especially clear in cases of authentic expression, which distinguishes itself from other versions of linguistic transcendence by the degree to which it modifies sedimented meanings. Not any novelty will do, however. I might be the first English speaker to utter the word 'swan' in Siberia, but this does not afford speakers of my language any experience-transforming perspectives. Still, when it is authentic, linguistic expression will manage to 'incorporate the past into the present and to weld this present to a future, to open an entire cycle of time where the "acquired" thought will remain present as a dimension without our needing to ever again summon it or reproduce it' (413/453). This temporal structure allows authentic acts of expression to become part of our broader cultural and linguistic heritage. Persons or groups who invent genuinely new ways of expressing human experience succeed in meeting this goal. This kind of creation differs from mundane modifications of meaning in that it establishes new and general categories of expression, instead of mere instances of expressive novelty. While they initially depart from existing conventions, acts of authentic expression eventually become sedimented and available for subsequent generalised use (the latter can, in turn, be authentic or mundane).

Unlike Sartre, then, for Merleau-Ponty linguistic expression depends on a situation whose meanings can be modified without being wholly reinvented. The situated character of authentic expression also qualifies it as an existential act of freedom. The linguistic project that leads me to pronounce or use a word in a new way is guided by existing rules and meanings. These conditions incline a particular word to '[appear] as something "to be pronounced"' in a given way (425/464). By contrast, even if Sartre accepts that there is a linguistic situation (e.g., a sentence), he thinks it originates in a subject's projective activity, which breaks with its situation and its past (BN 660–62). He goes as far as to suggest that '[i]t is by speaking that I make grammar', and concludes that 'freedom is the only possible foundation for the laws of language'. Even if Sartre is not making a temporal claim (grammar or syntactical rules exist before a particular subject speaks), the account in *Being and Nothingness* seems to entail that the negating activity of the For-Itself is the ontological foundation for freedom.

Merleau-Ponty denies this claim largely because he holds that the transcendent use of authentic language must genuinely modify a particular situation. Artists or philosophers rely on a given set of conventions and meanings, against which the novelty of their expressive contributions come to light. These meanings are a feature of an artist or a philosopher's world, and cannot be simply invented or posited away. We take an interest in art (and in authentic expression more generally) because it promises to disclose new perspectives on a world we share in common with an artist, or because it shows us a genuinely new world that we can make some sense of. To transform this world beyond recognition would undermine the expressive power of authentic expression, as Merleau-Ponty understands it.

Authentic expression is a free act in large part because an artist may not realise that she is engaged in an activity of this sort. The question of which expressive operations are genuinely authentic cannot be settled in advance. Like other cultural products, expression is identified as authentic in retrospect. The work of authentic expression is characterised by 'ambiguity', which in this case is highly productive. A poet or writer is led by a creative impulse that is not experienced as clearly structured or goal-directed from the first-personal standpoint. To express oneself is to 'crystallise a collection of indefinite motives' that 'enter back into the implicit, that is, into the equivocal and the play of the world' (PhP 309/348–49). Authentic expression is a

> paradoxical operation in which – by means of words whose sense is given and by means of already available significations – we attempt to catch up with [*nous tentons de rejoindre*] an intention that in principle goes beyond them and modifies them in the final analysis, itself establishing the sense of the words by which it expresses itself [*se traduire*]. (408–9/449)

Like standard empirical expression, authentic gestures do not separate sign from signification. However, even if we initially rely on well-defined meanings, and posit some vague expressive goal(s), in authentic expression subjects cannot anticipate how, when or why these goals might yield novel results. As Merleau-Ponty will later claim, authentic expression 'gropes around' (S 44/71). Pure creation is not subject to lawlike guidance, even if it appears highly structured to observers or critics. This too is a key part of existential freedom: authentic expression transforms the given without relying on a pre-determined plan, and without submitting to existing conceptual constraints.[39] In such cases, subjects are geared into a creative activity that is only ever constrained by the bounds of sense, which it nevertheless manages to reimagine.

Merleau-Ponty's remarks about authentic expression often highlight its ability to disclose and refigure our experience. This characteristic suggests wider-ranging implications. The preface to the *Phenomenology* contends that '[p]henomenology is as painstaking as the works of Balzac, Proust, Valéry, or Cézanne', and holds that it exhibits 'the same will to grasp the sense of the world or of history in its nascent state' (lxxxv/22). This remark identifies a fundamental similarity between the work of phenomenology and that of artistic or aesthetic expression: both articulate the meaning of the world. But what about phenomenology's descriptive goals? If phenomenology is akin to or on a par with creative expression, in what sense does it describe the meaning of experience and the structures of perception? This worry is only strengthened by Merleau-Ponty's view that 'transcendental' or phenomenological expression instantiates a version of authentic expression. I will consider this claim and its implications in greater detail in chapter 3. On the whole, this question remains unresolved in the *Phenomenology*. But it motivates new lines of inquiry that lead Merleau-Ponty to the philosophical concerns of his later writings. As we will see in part 2, Merleau-Ponty builds on his account of authentic speech when criticising formal modes of expression and developing his account of literary expression.

NOTES

1. I use the terms 'empirical' and 'first-order' to distinguish modes of expression treated in this chapter from those that figure in philosophical analysis or phenomenological description, which I sometimes describe using the term 'higher-order'. Merleau-Ponty sometimes suggests that a distinction between these two domains cannot be maintained. The decision to separate empirical from transcendental expression might accordingly raise a methodological red flag for some readers, who might take seriously Merleau-Ponty's claim to have moved beyond this distinction (PhP 130/162; 230/266–67). Doubtless, Merleau-Ponty attempts to weaken the transcendental/empirical distinction. However, the claim that this distinction is immaterial to his analysis of language is difficult to maintain in the face of textual evidence. While many of his arguments in the *Phenomenology* do not depend on it, he observes the distinction in practice – for example, by identifying a distinctly transcendental field for phenomenology (60–65/87–91) or a 'true transcendental' (382/423), a position he even seems to maintain in later writings (for example, VI 175–76/227). Perhaps most clearly, the *Cogito* chapter distinguishes 'empirical speech' from 'transcendental speech' (411/451). While many features of empirical expression are also found in transcendental expression, a rough distinction between the transcendental and the empirical will prove helpful for tracking the *Phenomenology*'s organisational structure, its argumentative moves, and for understanding Merleau-Ponty's analyses of different modes of linguistic expression.

2. For discussion see Jensen 2009, Romdenh-Romluc 2007, Dreyfus 2005, 2007, and Kelly 2002.

3. The concept was developed by the Austrian psychologist Paul Schilder (see Schilder 2013).

4. See Gelb and Goldstein 1920 and Goldstein 1923. Notes to the text show that Merleau-Ponty draws liberally on Cassirer's interpretation of Gelb and Goldstein's findings in his *Philosophy of Symbolic Forms*, Volume 3 (Cassirer 1965, 205–77).

5. See Goldstein 1931.

6. Scholars question the extent to which Schneider exhibits normal, seminormal or pathological versions of constitution, motor intentionality and the body schema. Kelly argues that Schneider enjoys normal motor intentional capacities (2002, 75), which Dreyfus 2005 and Jensen 2009 deny. On the whole, I believe that textual evidence better supports the latter interpretation. Merleau-Ponty cautions against deducing normal functions from pathological cases (PhP 110/138), and claims that Schneider's intentional abilities approximate normal capacities to a limited degree (126/157). This suggests that Schneider's case is not a standard version of motor intentionality.

7. See, for example, Dreyfus 2007, 69; *cf.* Romdenh-Romluc 2007, 57 (see also 53 ff.).

8. Already in *Structure*, Merleau-Ponty recognised that patients must 'improvise' where their physiology is lacking (SB 88/97). In that text he aimed to undercut the adequacy of physiological explanations: 'Function has a positive and proper reality; it is not a simple consequence of the existence of organs or substrate'.

9. See Baldwin 2007, 96–98. Despite offering a far more persuasive account of Schneider's ability to 'reckon with the possible', Romdenh-Romluc does not touch on this feature (2007, 52–53). It is also unaddressed in Dreyfus's account of 'maximal' or 'general' grip (2007, 62–63).

10. For this view see, for example, McDowell 1996.

11. While 'sens' standardly refers to perceptual meaning, and 'signification' standardly refers to abstract meaning, there are passages in which Merleau-Ponty seems to conflate these two categories (e.g., 239/276). On the whole, however, the distinction is more clearly marked than it was in *Structure*.

12. The two terms are often used interchangeably, however, as I note below, there are important exceptions to this rule.

13. See, for example, Austin 1962, 100 (see also Dillon 1988, 190).

14. Husserl 2001, I §4.

15. Husserl 1970, 365–66; 371. In writings after the *Phenomenology*, Merleau-Ponty adopts Husserl's account of written sedimentation (S 95/156).

16. While Merleau-Ponty claims that this division tracks the 'famous distinction' between *langue* and *parole*, he does not explicitly cite or invoke Saussure here, or anywhere else in the *Phenomenology*. See chapter 4 for more on Merleau-Ponty's reading of Saussure (see also Watson 2009a, 47–68).

17. The choice to refer to texts that postdate the *Phenomenology* may be objected to, given non-negligible differences in the topics treated in Merleau-Ponty's later research. Important theoretical shifts may even be detected in work from his Sorbonne period (1949–1952). In this chapter, I refer only to later claims or texts that are unambiguously consistent with the *Phenomenology*'s orientation and assumptions.

18. Merleau-Ponty also seeks to undermine naturalistic views of language, of the sort offered by Condillac.

19. See Priest 1998, 166–69 for more on this.

20. See Davidson 1984, 24.

21. See Cassirer 1953, 178–85 for his analysis of gesture.

22. Taylor 1985, 257.

23. While he emphasises the expressive character of linguistic acts, Husserl seems at odds with this view in *Formal and Transcendental Logic*: 'the speaker's practical intention is obviously not directed ultimately to the mere words, but is directed "through" them to their signification . . . words carry significative intentions; they serve as bridges leading over to significations, to what the speaker means "by" them' (Husserl 1969, §3, 20).

24. Like Husserl, Merleau-Ponty does not observe a clear distinction between meaning and reference (Husserl 2001, I §13). He does not seem to be interested in the problem of reference in its own right. Husserl rejects the view that there are two sides to expressive acts (one that expresses its meaning and another that establishes a reference relation). Similarly, for Merleau-Ponty, to mean or to intend something is also to refer to that object or state of affairs. Expression establishes a reference relation to what is intended, since the idea comes before our mind or that of others.

25. See Gallagher 1992 on hermeneutic elements in Merleau-Ponty's thought.

26. In later writings, Merleau-Ponty occasionally describes this process as one of 'coherent deformation', adopting a phrase from André Malraux (S 91/149).

27. Despite focusing on linguistic usage, Merleau-Ponty would not straightforwardly accept Wittgenstein's view that meaning is use. Studying linguistic usage is a basic condition for understanding linguistic meaning, but interpretation cannot be reduced to or explained by current usage. Interpretation in first-order expression modifies existing linguistic norms and meanings, and can produce unique ones. Still, Merleau-Ponty concedes that meaning can 'initial-

ly' be analysed in terms of its 'configuration in current usage' (PW 36/51–52), and that our 'use of words ... ends up assigning them a new and characteristic signification' (S 91/149). But these are necessary and not sufficient conditions for an analysis of meaning.

28. Merleau-Ponty follows Beneviste, Cassirer and Sartre in holding that the sentence is the most important individual unit of linguistic meaning. See Cassirer 1953, 303; Sartre 1984, 660 and Beneviste 1971. In writings that postdate the *Phenomenology*, Merleau-Ponty suggests that the process of sorting and combining linguistic terms into a whole can be understood as a process of differentiation, *pace* Saussure: meaning is fundamentally interdependent and holistic, and the meaning of a particular sentence is a function of the differences between the terms it contains (PW 28/40–41, 31/44–45, 102–3/145). But he transforms this Saussurean point into a phenomenological observation that attempts to explain how the combinations at work in a linguistic unit produce meaning. Prior to being differentiated, particular words are recognised as salient or appropriate for a particular expressive goal, and interpretation guides this process. Crucially, his emphasis on interpretation suggests that Merleau-Ponty is not a conventionalist like Saussure: meaning cannot be defined by convention because it is interpreted in ways that fundamentally diverge from existing conventions of use (even if it is informed by them).

29. While his focus on conversation or communication shares some affinities with Gricean views (e.g., Grice 1989, 90–91), Merleau-Ponty's anti-intentionalist strain would lead him to deny that 'speaker's meaning' should guide an analysis of linguistic meaning. A conversational context allows that a speaker's statement will be subjected to interpretation by others, and he takes this to be an important consideration for understanding its total meaning.

30. For this view see Barbaras 2004, 47/65, who claims that Merleau-Ponty's account of expression results in a 'naturalistic conception of the body' (cf. CPP 8, and Madison 1981, 118). That Merleau-Ponty draws on Cassirer's account of 'symbolic pregnance' in *The Philosophy of Symbolic Forms*, on which matter and form are inseparable from one another, suggests that he does not believe that linguistic sound can be separated from sense, or that it affects us in a way captured by naturalistic accounts (see Cassirer 1965, 202). See Masuda 1993 for an analysis of Merleau-Ponty's views on the symbolic.

31. See chapter 5 for more on this.

32. Heidegger 1962, ¶¶32–34.

33. Gadamer 2004, 388–89.

34. Dillon claims that 'Merleau-Ponty's distinction between originating or creative expression and secondary or institutionalised language owes as much (or more) to Heidegger's distinction between authentic and inauthentic speech as it does to Saussure's distinction between *la parole* and *la langue*' (1988, 190).

In light of the textual evidence above, Merleau-Ponty's use of the term 'authentic' suggests significantly different aims. He invokes it to describe a form of expression that is far more prevalent than the sorts of activities or life-plans associated with Heidegger's concept of authenticity. Unlike for Heidegger, for Merleau-Ponty the term usually has an aesthetic and creative dimension. What is more, Merleau-Ponty does not contrast authentic speech with 'inauthentic' expression (as Heidegger does with *das Gerede*).

35. For more on this concept see Cassirer 1953, chapter 1, section 4 (see also Scheler 1970).

36. Proust 1998, 445.

37. Sartre's *Being and Nothingness* will be referred to in text using the convention BN.

38. For more on this, and for an excellent summary of the debate on existentialist freedom between Sartre, Beauvoir and Merleau-Ponty, see Wilkerson 2010, 214–34.

39. Landes helpfully notes that the theme of expression is at work in Merleau-Ponty's account of freedom, but the link between the structure of authentic expression and freedom in the *Phenomenology* is not a focus of his account (2013, 98–102).

3

TRANSCENDENTAL EXPRESSION

This chapter explores *Phenomenology of Perception*'s account of transcendental expression. Transcendental expression is a higher-order philosophical mode of language use. According to Merleau-Ponty, phenomenology will profit from softening the transcendental-empirical distinction. Accordingly, some features of empirical expression encountered in chapter 2 also characterise transcendental expression. This commitment, like others considered below, puts significant distance between Merleau-Ponty's nominally transcendental view and more standard interpretations of the transcendental that follow Kant. On more than one occasion, his interpretation of transcendental phenomenology breaks with basic tenets developed by Kant and later reformulated by Husserl.

In addition to offering a unique interpretation of transcendental phenomenology, the *Phenomenology*'s *Cogito* chapter, which is the focus here, is pivotal for Merleau-Ponty's broader philosophical goals. The latter parts of the *Phenomenology* broach the all-important language-perception relation. While ostensibly of limited scope, this issue touches the heart of the phenomenological framework Merleau-Ponty has been developing since *Structure*. Phenomenology is continuous with the transcendental tradition insofar as it attempts to identify and explain the conditions for the possibility and intelligibility of experience. Phenomenology accounts for or explains experience (in a non-reductive sense) by describing it. Merleau-Ponty's approach to this classical transcendental goal is unique in part because he stresses the linguistic characteristics of description, that philosophical categories are products of reflective and expressive activity, and that the task of identifying conditions for the possibility of experience is limited by the expressive conditions that support such an endeavour.

I begin with a brief look at Merleau-Ponty's criticisms of 'objectivist' approaches to reason (section 1). This will introduce his general approach to transcendental philosophy, and will show why he rejects views of cognitive activity that privilege judgement or synthesis. He argues that our basic relation to the world is pre-reflective and pre-thematic, and that sense-making is more open-ended than these views allow for. Objectivist approaches and classical transcendental accounts assume that a complete explanation of sense and of the conditions for the possibility of experience can be given. By contrast, for Merleau-Ponty transcendental phenomenology must first consider if such a goal really is attainable (section 2). His considered view is that it is not, and that phenomenology must instead adopt an ideal of explanatory openness. His understanding of how phenomenology discloses experience through reflection brings this position into further relief (section 3). As it turns out, reflection unfolds in language, and always transforms empirical meaning; this raises significant doubts about the extent to which description can present an objective and definitive account of perceptual experience, and requires that reflection adopt a circular (and not merely a genetic) model.

This approach to phenomenological description puts some distance between Merleau-Ponty and standard transcendental attempts to identify conditions for the possibility of experience. His argument that the continuity between the transcendental and empirical dimensions of human experience is supported by the expressive activity of the reflecting or 'spoken' *cogito* only strengthens the relevant differences (section 4). The subject engaging in transcendental description is a language-user, and its clarificatory work relies on existing linguistic conventions. As I suggest, together with other features of his account of transcendental phenomenology, the view that 'thought' or cognitive activity is linguistic challenges the assumption that perception is prime, and commits Merleau-Ponty to the conclusion that language is as important a foundation for phenomenological disclosure. The suspicion that language plays a fundamental role in Merleau-Ponty's account of the transcendental is strengthened by his claim that transcendental language is 'authentic' (section 5). This further weakens the view that perception is the primary ground of thought, language and meaning, since it accepts that description produces new meanings that are semantically untethered from pre-predicative intuitive evidence. To conclude, I note that these commitments show that Merleau-Ponty entertains two divergent ideals of phenomenological description: he claims that transcendental language should faithfully articulate the meaning of perception and nothing more, but his premises force the result that reflection inevitably transforms it (section 6). As I will argue in parts 2 and 3, the attempt to move beyond the disjunction between description and creation animates much of his subsequent philosophical research.

1. OBJECTIVE THOUGHT

Merleau-Ponty argues against a theoretical attitude he calls 'objective thought'. He constructs his interpretation of transcendental phenomenology against it. Accordingly, it will be helpful to consider two important strains of objective thought. *Structure* already identified basic affinities between empiricism or realism and intellectualism (SB 187/202; cf. PhP 41–42/65). Similarly, the *Phenomenology* claims that '[t]he naturalism of science and the spiritualism of the universal constituting subject, to which reflection upon science leads, share in a certain levelling out of experience' (PhP 56/82).

Empiricism or realism is one version of objective thought. In *Structure*, Merleau-Ponty argued that empiricist or realist accounts of perception mask the qualitative or significative dimensions of experience (SB 122/133). In that text, he embraced a version of what he called 'reflective thought' (*la pensée réfléchie*).[1] Reflection was defined as an introspective activity that investigates the constitution of meaning. It was opposed to causal or deterministic modes of explanation. As the Schneider case shows, similar considerations are developed in the *Phenomenology*.[2]

In addition to misinterpreting the findings of scientific studies, empiricist or realist analyses develop a highly suspect picture of cognitive activity. By accepting that sensations affect subjects in a lawlike fashion, these accounts suggest that reflection is a closed mental circuit, without any autonomy (PhP 24/46–47). Once mental activity is defined in empirical or physiological terms, we are left with a picture of the mind on which human reason is trapped within a network of effects that it is subject to and cannot exercise any agency over. In effect, this precludes the possibility of an active role for reflection. Reflection can merely clarify the effects it is subject to. Given the important role of reflective activity for phenomenology, Merleau-Ponty finds this account untenable.[3]

'Intellectualism' is the more important strain of objective thought. An analysis of this theoretical attitude is complicated by the fact that Merleau-Ponty associates many positions with intellectualism.[4] A key characteristic of intellectualism is its emphasis on judgement. At this abstract level, intellectualism is compatible with empiricism or realism. Empiricist versions of objective thought privilege causal determination by the physical. This invites accounts of cognition and reflection that privilege judgement. Judgement is a mental activity that synthesises the givens of experience, and its categorical operations (e.g., logical inferences) assign meanings to meaningless pre-judgemental givens; this promises to explain how the mind unifies disparate causes or sensations into a coherent whole. However, when discussing intellectualist accounts of judgement, Merleau-Ponty usually refers to the 'Cartesian' view (the connections to Descartes are often tenuous). For Descartes, judgement delivers us to the truths of reason, and the veracity of judgement is guaranteed by God. This basic Cartesian view partly explains Merleau-Ponty's frequent association of intellectualism with an ostensibly Cartesian account of judgement.[5] That he has Descartes in mind is also suggested by his decision to title the first chapter of Part 3 '*Le cogito*'.

But a closer look suggests a different target. Although this chapter begins by referring to Descartes, and liberally invokes the Cartesian *cogito*, Merleau-Ponty seldom refers to Descartes in any detail.[6] Instead, the heart of the intellectualist account is drawn from the work of the neo-Kantian Pierre Lachièze-Rey.[7] Views that Merleau-Ponty attributes to Descartes can be traced to Lachièze-Rey. For example, he criticises Descartes for claiming that the meaning of the world is 'constructed' or 'constituted' *in toto* by the subject, but refers to a 1933 article by Lachièze-Rey (388/428).[8] He also claims that Descartes's *cogito* is a self-sufficient thinker who finds in the world only what it has put into it, is eternal, and 'owes nothing to time'; Lachièze-Rey's reading of Descartes makes similar observations (390–91/430).[9] Lachièze-Rey argues that the Cartesian *cogito* leads 'above all an idealism of the eternal' [*surtout un idéalisme de l'éternel*].[10] He also argues that the Cartesian *cogito* 'leads me to coincide with God' (392/432).[11] Merleau-Ponty's portrayal of the intellectualist *cogito* owes as much to this neo-Kantian interpretation as it does to Descartes.

One might conclude that because Merleau-Ponty relies on Lachièze-Rey when identifying an untenable view of the *cogito*, he thereby endorses the latter's own neo-Kantian view, or indeed a Kantian account of the subject.[12] But Merleau-Ponty does not go in this direction. In addition to some ostensibly Cartesian commitments, key Kantian tenets also support an intellectualist view of the mind, as does Husserl's approach to act-constitution. In addition to emphasising judgement, for him views that rely heavily on act-constitution or synthesis are generally untenable, since both prioritise deliberate mental acts (407/447). According to Merleau-Ponty, affectivity and passivity play an important role in cognitive activity.[13] Embodied subjects are essentially temporal beings that are affected by their spatio-temporal milieu in ways they cannot regulate or control. Lachièze-Rey's account of the subject emphasises synthetic activity, and overlooks this feature of experience. According to Merleau-Ponty, on his view the subject 'affirms its activity at the moment in which it seems to hold itself back; if it is the mind that places itself in the world, then that mind is not in the world and self-positing is an illusion. It is unclear how Lachièze-Rey, for example, could avoid this consequence' (391/431). On the intellectualist proposal, to cognise an object is to unify representations in a way that clearly determines the object's possible meanings (391/431).[14] Merleau-Ponty certainly finds much of value in Lachièze-Rey's reading of Kant's schematism, but he recoils from his broader reading of Kant, which privileges acts, synthesis and emphasises the subject's role in constituting worldly meaning.[15] The extent to which this reading does justice to Kant is up for debate; but Merleau-Ponty does not find it congenial to his own views.

As these remarks suggest, the basic problem with Cartesian, Kantian or 'Husserlian' 'objectivist' views of mental life is their assumption that the sense of the world or experience is delivered by means of synthetic or judgemental activity. By contrast, Merleau-Ponty (influenced by Fink's reading of Husserl) develops an account of 'operative intentionality' (*fungierende Intentionalität*), on which directedness to objects is understood as an unthematic, pre-reflective, embodied relation (lxxxii/18, 453/492).[16] This account of intentionality is worked out in detail in Parts 1 and 2 of the *Phenomenology*. Assuming that this view provides a more faithful description of our relation to the world, a corresponding account of reflection and reason must be developed. Merleau-Ponty maintains that the empirical and transcendental registers share key points in common, and contends that they cannot be clearly separated from one another. Pre-reflective intentional directedness has its transcendental counterpart: 'There is a sort of operative reason, or a *raison d'être* that directs the flow of phenomena without being explicitly posited in any of one of them' (51/76).

2. EXPLANATORY OPENNESS

The choice to use the term 'transcendental' to characterise the later sections in the *Phenomenology* suggests at least a terminological allegiance to the tradition inaugurated by Kant and canonised in phenomenology by Husserl. Some commentators have argued that Merleau-Ponty advances a version of transcendental phenomenology in this vein. While not wholly Kantian or Husserlian in its details, they suggest that his view still attempts to identify necessary conditions that explain the meaning and structure of conscious experience.[17] More strongly, it has been argued that the *Phenomenology* is Kantian, not only in spirit but also in its substantive commitments to explanatory necessity, the a priori, and to other classical transcendental tenets.[18]

Sorting out Merleau-Ponty's allegiances to classical transcendental views is difficult given the textual evidence, which underdetermines the success of diverging interpretive strategies. Merleau-Ponty occasionally pledges his allegiance to the transcendental tradition. But when doing so, he also qualifies the basic meaning of transcendental tenets; this puts significant distance between him and recognisably classical transcendental views. The suggestion that Merleau-Ponty adheres to a Kantian or Husserlian view of necessity, transcendental conditions, the phenomenological reduction, or related tenets, is difficult to maintain (without significantly modifying the meaning of these terms) in the face of numerous remarks to the effect that the *Phenomenology* does not aim to advance a standard transcendental account.[19] I cannot directly defend this claim here; but if this interpretive stance is *prima facie* justified by a body of indeterminate textual evidence, it allows for a different line of enquiry, which can serve as an indirect argument that Merleau-Ponty adopts a different approach. A focus on his more immediate stated aims in advancing his version of transcendental phenomenology will isolate the distinctive features of his view, and will permit readers to evaluate the extent to which it might modify or break from the transcendental tradition.

The possibility of what can be called 'explanatory completeness' looms large in Merleau-Ponty's account of transcendental phenomenology. A philosophical explanation is complete when it identifies the totality of relevant facts or conditions needed to account for a given object or phenomenon. Kant and Husserl accept versions of the claim that transcendental accounts enumerate the necessary and sufficient conditions that will offer a comprehensive and conceptually closed explanation of experience (e.g., categories, essences).[20]

For Merleau-Ponty, any transcendental account (*a fortiori* a phenomenological one) aims 'to make explicit [*expliciter*] our primordial knowledge of the "real" and to describe the perception of the world as what establishes, once and for all, our idea of the truth' (PhP lxxx/16–17; see also 61/87–88). While it has been noted in passing, the basic explanatory import underlying Merleau-Ponty's approach to the transcendental has yet to be considered in detail.[21] Here, 'explanation' should be understood in non-reductive and non-causal terms. Merleau-Ponty accepts a weaker view of explanation, which is not simply opposed to description. Instead of causal-reductive or cognitive-intellectualist modes of explanation (which he rejects), phenomenology attempts a 'making-explicit', a 'clarification' or an 'explicitation' (*explicitation*) (a term we encountered in chapter 1). For Merleau-Ponty, perceptual meaning (*sens*) is the object of phenomenological clarification or explanation. Perceptual experience is explained or made explicit when it is expressed using a philosophical vocabulary that disambiguates its meaning and structure. This occurs through description. The *Phenomenology* holds that description is a characteristic feature of transcendental approaches.[22] This sense of 'explanation' is obviously unlike that in deductive-nomological, causal or naturalistic models. But insofar as a description sheds light on and clarifies how an object or experience is given to a subject, it also accounts or explains the relevant objects in question.

However, unlike Kant or Husserl, for Merleau-Ponty 'philosophy becomes transcendental' once it entertains the possibility of a 'total making-explicit of knowledge' (64/90). Phenomenology does not assume that explanatory completeness is in fact attainable. Instead, it sees 'this presumption of reason as the fundamental philosophical problem'. In Merleau-Ponty's estimation, 'It is striking to see that classical transcendental philosophies never question the possibility of carrying out the complete making-explicit [*explicitation*] that they always assume is completed somewhere' (62/89). By contrast, this suggests that transcendental descriptions remain provisional and are subject to modification (62/89). On Merleau-Ponty's proposal, a distinguishing characteristic of the phenomenological approach is that it does not assume the last word has been said about a particular object or experience, irrespective of how thorough or plausible a given description might be.

The end of Part 2 identifies possible motivations for this interpretation. For Merleau-Ponty, the 'true transcendental' is a supplementary reflection on 'direct description'; that is, it is a critical evaluation of the plausibility or success of existing descriptive attempts (382/424). Transcendental accounts require multiple stages of reflection. Invoking a phrase from Fink, he claims that the *Phenomenology*'s analyses of embodiment lead to a view of 'reflection more radical than objective thought', and license 'a phenomenology of phenomenology'. I will return to the claim that transcendental accounts encourage reflection on the adequacy of existing descriptions. For now, the key point to note is that phenomenological descriptions should be supplemented by further critical and methodological reflections.

In addition to arguments against objective thought, and the suggestive claim that transcendental philosophy investigates the possibility of complete explanations, Merleau-Ponty's attempt to develop a new approach to rationality also helps to clarify his view of the transcendental.[23] This topic was a key focus in the November 1946 session of the Société française de philosophie, which was dedicated to the recently published the *Phenomenology*. Merleau-Ponty defended the view that rationality must be defined by recourse to lived experience, a key claim of his doctoral thesis (PrP 11/43, 17/50). On his approach, 'rationality' does not issue in timeless explanatory conditions, concepts or categories. Reason explores the intelligibility or coherence of experience: objects, claims or ideas appear as intelligible wholes with a meaningful structure subject to further analysis.

At the end of the *Cogito* chapter, Merleau-Ponty defines 'the problem of rationality' as the question of how the various objects, events, or subjects we encounter in the world are formed into meaningful and determinate unities (PhP 431/470; see also lxxxiv/20–21). Alternatively, an account of rationality attempts to understand how 'perspectives intersect, perceptions confirm each other, and [how] a sense appears' (lxxxiv/20).[24] Unlike more classical approaches, Merleau-Ponty thinks that rational or intelligible structures are formed at the intersection of the objective and the subjective standpoints. Experience implicates a world and a perceiver that encounters it. Rationality is formed 'through an initiative that does not have a guarantee in being'. To be understood, rational forms must be brought to expression.

Doubtless, if one has rationalist, empiricist or naturalistic inclinations, these remarks might seem senseless, relativistic or worse. They were not well received by Émile Bréhier, Merleau-Ponty's doctoral supervisor. He argued that his student 'changes and inverts the ordinary meaning of what we call philosophy' (PrP 28/73). For Bréhier, like the concept of truth, rationality cannot be explained by appeal to subjective grounds. Terms like 'rational', 'true' or 'real' have force only if they are defined according to an extra-subjective or objective criterion. On Bréhier's view, anything else amounts to relativism. By contrast, Merleau-Ponty contends that there is no single foundation of rationality: rational or intelligible forms instantiate themselves according to the varying conditions of lived experience.

Bréhier's evaluation might ring true for some contemporary readers (including phenomenologically inclined philosophers). As Merleau-Ponty sees it, however, an objectivist approach to rationality overlooks much that is of real philosophical value. It misses what he thinks amounts to our experience of coming to grips with the truth or reason behind perceptual experience. To investigate how and why subjects encounter coherent, intelligible and meaningful perceptual structures, and how they proceed to elucidate them, is to work towards the 'aggrandisement' of reason (PrP 30/77–78). This activity is understood as a form of reflection, and is directed to experience.

3. TRANSCENDENTAL REFLECTION

The concept of 'genesis' plays an important role in Merleau-Ponty's account of transcendental phenomenology and reflection (PhP lxxxii/18–19).[25] A genetic mode of phenomenological enquiry attempts to identify the 'total intention' or meaning of the conditions that support an object's mode of givenness (lxxxii/18–19).[26] Genetic reflection traces the steps by which objects are formed or constituted in experience (156/191). This approach assumes that objects do not have fixed meanings, or that closed sets of necessary and sufficient conditions can account for their givenness. The meaning of an object or experience is understood and given gradually, across the temporal flow of conscious life. Focusing on a given time-slice might produce a uniform snapshot of some object; but from a more extended temporal perspective, the object is given in different modalities and is subject to alternative interpretations.

Reflection begins from the givens of first-order phenomena (meanings encountered in everyday perceptual experience) and regressively probes their conditions of possibility in higher-order analyses. A regressive reflective *modus operandi* is a widely acknowledged feature of transcendental accounts. According to Charles Taylor, transcendental views take departure from secure observations about experience, and identify the conditions enabling them.[27] Kant and Husserl are thought to endorse a regressive view of explanation.[28] Like Kant, Husserl holds that reflection maintains an essential correlation with empirical objects, even if it is purified from their 'mundane' (i.e., empirical) features.[29] Merleau-Ponty's emphasis on the genetic character of reflection, a commitment that owes much to Husserl, suggests a fidelity to the transcendental tradition. However, a closer look shows that his understanding of genesis is more complex. I will focus on two interrelated tenets that are of particular importance.

3.1 Circularity

Regression is a common characteristic of transcendental views, but it is only one part of Merleau-Ponty's account of reflection.[30] The early sections of the *Phenomenology* identify another stage of reflective activity (63/89). Phenomenological reflection is an artificial undertaking, which intervenes in the natural flow of conscious life. By introducing new concepts that attempt to capture lived meaning, reflection transforms everyday life. In doing so, it also runs the risk of 'objectifying' and distorting it (302/341). This possibility, according to Merleau-Ponty, is seldom addressed in sufficient detail in Kantian, neo-Kantian and German idealist models of reflection. Even if Husserl is keenly aware of the possibility that phenomenological thematisation can distort experience, Merleau-Ponty thinks his own account offers a more sophisticated treatment of this issue.

As in *Structure*, he argues against the assumption that phenomenological reflection presents the structure of objects without significant transformations. This view 'is a naïvete, or, if one prefers, an incomplete reflection that loses an awareness of its own beginning. I began to reflect, my reflection is a reflection upon an unreflected; it cannot be unaware of itself as an event; henceforth it appears as a genuine creation, as a change in the structure of consciousness' (lxxiii/10). Reflection is always liable to change the givens of experience. Like other currents of thought that employ a reflective or introspective methodology, phenomenology must keep this possibility in the foreground of its investigations. The possibility that reflection will distort experience leads Merleau-Ponty to argue that phenomenological reflection must reconsider meanings initially encountered in perception (insofar as this is possible) and check descriptions against them. Methodological reflection on the contents of phenomenological descriptions should be understood as a return to and a reevaluation of primary perceptual evidence. A return to first-order perceptual meaning is just the sort of secondary reflective movement that distinguishes Merleau-Ponty's view of reflection from alternative transcendental or neo-Kantian views (this is also how he interprets Fink's suggestion above about phenomenological methodology).

The claim that recursion to primary experience is needed has important implications for the *Phenomenology*'s view of reflection. Despite its ostensibly genetic or regressive characteristics, on Merleau-Ponty's considered view, reflection has a circular structure. Its circularity is not due to the fact that it reconsiders the same contents or presupposes what it claims to show. Phenomenological reflection is circular because in order to develop a persuasive account of experience, reflecting subjects must retrace the steps they took when developing a description of a particular object. Regression to the *cogito* is supplemented by a return to experience. Any description could idealise perceptual content, transform the meaning of objects, or offer descriptions that significantly diverge from other subjects' experiences. Accordingly, meditating subjects cannot avail themselves of a single account of an object or experience (416/456). To offer a faithful *explicitation* of experience, they must continually and critically scrutinise the results of reflection against perceptual evidence (lxxxv/21).[31]

The claim that reflection has a recursive structure brings together the themes of genesis and explanatory openness. Genetic reflection charts the formation and transformation of perceptual meaning, and assumes that constitution is an open-ended process. But because perceptual meaning can be transformed whenever reflection unfolds, even highly refined descriptions with strong evidentiary bases can distort their objects. Accordingly, phenomenological clarification is defined by an openness to revision. The methodological requirement that reflection return to experience suggests the possibility of a better or more refined account. By extension, it precludes the possibility of a final or definitive one.

The tight relation between these two tenets comes out in the following passage:

> it will be necessary that philosophy direct toward itself the very same interrogation that it directs toward all forms of knowledge. It will thus be indefinitely doubled [*se redoublera donc indéfiniment*]; it will be, as Husserl says, an infinite dialogue or meditation, and, to the very extent that it remains loyal to its intention, it will never know just where it is going. The unfinished nature of phenomenology and its inchoate appearance are not the sign of failure; they were inevitable because phenomenology's task was to reveal the mystery of the world and the mystery of reason. (lxxxv/21–22)

To understand the rational or meaningful structure of appearances, phenomenological descriptions must continually return to and reevaluate first-order experience. Intelligible structures are difficult to disambiguate, and even a persuasive account of experience remains an approximation (even if it is plausible or compelling) that must be critically evaluated. Descriptions are continually 'doubled' because they are refined in light of data supplied by the phenomenologist's return to experience. The latter attempts to bring to light other possible layers of meaning that could have been overlooked or ignored in earlier stages of reflection. This helps to measure the persuasiveness of existing descriptions.

Given the *Phenomenology*'s ostensible allegiance to extant interpretations of genetic and transcendental phenomenology, its circular reflective structure is not explicitly stressed. But a suggestive discussion of the *cogito*'s attempt to understand (or 'interrogate') experience is instructive:

> a word [*un mot*], an idea, considered as events in my history, only have a sense for me if I take up this sense from within. The intending of a transcendent term and the view of myself intending it, or the consciousness of the connected [*du lié*] and the consciousness of the connecting [*du liant*] are in a circular relation [*dans une relation circulaire*] (421/461).

The 'transcendent term' refers to the object of reflective analysis. This term stands in a recursive relation to the subject analysing it. The possibility that descriptions offer a partial view of an object, 'word' or 'idea', encourages reflecting subjects to reconsider objects' conditions of reception in light of meanings given in primary experience. These two terms stand in a reciprocal relation with one another (see also PrP 30/77–78).[32]

As commentators have noted, a distinctively phenomenological view of the transcendental need not deny that explanations should incorporate new evidence.[33] Even if Kant would likely not accept this, Husserl does not cut the transcendental ego off from the natural attitude. Scholars have argued that for Husserl, the natural attitude continues to inform the work of transcendental clarification. The 'fluid' or 'productive' features of genesis that are important for Merleau-Ponty can be found in Husserl's texts.[34]

Merleau-Ponty surely agrees with these points, but he goes one step further. That reflection 'participates in the facticity of the unreflected' also entails that there is no clear relation of explanatory priority between the transcendental and the empirical (PhP 62/89). If analyses of objects' meaning and the genetic processes disclosing them are reciprocal, then meanings from the natural attitude enjoy explanatory import in transcendental clarification. Husserl seems firm in his view that explanatory priority falls to the transcendental.[35] Even if the transcendental stance is a gradual achievement generated out of the natural attitude, the former ultimately explains empirical phenomena, whose meaning is essentially 'rooted' in transcendental subjectivity.[36] For Merleau-Ponty, the continuity between the empirical and transcendental licenses the conclusion that the 'word [transcendental] signifies that reflection never has the entire world and the plurality of monads spread out and objectified before its gaze, that it only ever has a partial view and a limited power' (62/89). Once again, his approach to transcendental philosophy shows that he does not assume the possibility of a complete accounting of experience. When Husserl argues that phenomenology is an infinite task, he has something different in mind. Phenomenological explications are progressive, but for him they aim for a 'universal', 'essential' or 'absolutely grounded' foundation.[37]

Merleau-Ponty alleges that his view of reflection can better account for the ambiguity and indeterminacy of lived experience than classical accounts. Despite their differences, Husserl and Kant are identified as proponents of a classical view of reflection (539 n.2/290 n.1).[38] Transcendental analyses of perception 'would have to go on indefinitely', for the meaning of perception is 'inexhaustible' (378–79/419–20). This is not only a thesis about the givenness of perceptual objects; it also applies to the structure of transcendental reflection. Unless one takes Merleau-Ponty's idiosyncratic reading of the transcendental at face value, he seems to have strayed from the parameters of Kantian or Husserlian approaches. This has motivated the suggestion that his choice to invoke the term is misleading, and that he is a transcendental philosopher of a mitigated kind, if one at all.[39]

3.2 'Tacit' and 'Spoken' *Cogito*

I have suggested that for Merleau-Ponty, transcendental explanations are open-ended. The need to track the transformative effects of reflection is a key motivation for this position. Explanatory openness can be understood as the requirement that phenomenological descriptions be continually refined in light of a reevaluation of empirical *explananda* and transcendental *explanans*. If reflection does not follow a linear and regressive path that moves from one explanatory condition to another, but instead reevaluates the relations obtaining between descriptions and facts, then phenomenology can become more sensitive to lived experience. An advantage of a circular view of reflection is that it elevates the revision and refinement of descriptions to a methodological principle. This promises to resist its potentially 'idealising' effects.

This brings us to a second distinctive feature of Merleau-Ponty's understanding of transcendental phenomenology: his view that transcendental reflection is essentially linguistic. Since he assumes that thought presupposes language, it is unsurprising that he would also hold that phenomenological reflection unfolds in language. But he goes beyond this minimal claim. The linguistic character of transcendental reflection also rests on a new distinction introduced in the final part of the *Phenomenology*.

As we saw in chapter 2, Merleau-Ponty argues that human thought always unfolds in language. Having considered part of his account of transcendental reflection, we can better understand the claims from the 'Expression' chapter that '[t]here is a privileged place for Reason' in linguistic expression (196/231), and that the 'supposed silence' of mental life turns out to be 'buzzing with words – this inner life is an inner language' (188–89/223).[40] The attempt to unfold the meaningful structure of experience in transcendental reflection is an expressive undertaking.

Transcendental expression can be better understood by focusing on an important conceptual distinction introduced in the *Cogito* chapter. While he has invoked the empirical/transcendental and unreflected/reflected distinctions, Merleau-Ponty now claims that these two realms can be redefined by considering the extent to which each relies on linguistic meaning. The subject of first-order experience, we now learn, is the 'tacit *cogito*' (*le cogito tacite*). Perceiving subjects need not have recourse to language to intelligibly experience the world. For example, I see the pencil on my desk and recognise it without searching for the linguistic units or concepts 'pencil' or 'desk'. This experience makes sense without them. This is not to say that everyday experience does not feature language use. On the contrary: the descriptions from chapter 2 show that empirical expression helps subjects come to grips with experience. But the point is that linguistic meaning is not intrinsic to perceptual experience. Pathological cases like that of Schneider are an exception that proves the rule. Embodied subjects do not standardly rely on or presuppose linguistic concepts to access and understand perceptual meanings encountered in the phenomenal field, or to intelligibly experience the world (422/461).

The transcendental or reflective subject, in turn, is redefined as the 'spoken *cogito*' (*le cogito parlée*). This characterisation seems to draw an identity between language and transcendentality: if the subject of transcendental experience is a spoken *cogito*, then the transcendental is an expressive domain. The reflecting subject can only engage in the work of transcendental analysis by appealing to linguistic meaning. Unlike the tacit *cogito*, the transcendental subject is a language-user *par excellence*.

Curiously, the distinction between spoken and tacit *cogito* is invoked as an 'example' of how subjectivity is both constituting and constituted, that is, how it is formed by its world but still able to contribute to the meaning of experience. The tacit or empirical *cogito* is in contact with the full range of perceptual sense in the phenomenal field. By drawing on available concepts and distinctions, the spoken *cogito* filters and refines perceptual sense. The spoken *cogito* engages in explicative phenomenological clarification. This suggests that the distinction is surely more than a mere example: it effectively redefines the empirical-transcendental relation. The distinction suggests that language is ultimately inessential in the realm of perceptual experience. By contrast, it shows that language is a fundamental condition for the possibility of phenomenological reflection, that reflection is a linguistic activity, and that the transcendental is a *sui generis* linguistic domain.

The division between spoken and tacit *cogito* further clarifies Merleau-Ponty's understanding of transcendental subjectivity. It follows from this distinction that the spoken *cogito* also shapes perceptual meaning. This occurs in two interrelated ways. The first is linked to worries about the transformation of empirical meanings considered earlier. This concerns the mechanics or semantics of transcendental expression, and I will return to it below. A second source of transformation can be traced to the spoken *cogito*'s use of philosophical concepts. Recall that already in *Structure*, Merleau-Ponty argued that existing conceptual commitments (the views of 'common sense' or the 'natural attitude') are a double-edged sword. They help us initiate and proceed with an interpretation of experience, but they also hide unexamined assumptions that can obscure it. For example, to resolve a dispute about the status of matter, a philosopher in the thirteenth century would likely resort to concepts that owe a debt to hylomorphism. These concepts are philosophical 'second nature', and stand ready for application to philosophical problems. On this score, Merleau-Ponty has profited from Husserl's reflections on ideality and traditionality.[41] For Husserl, conceptual assumptions are preserved in the language subjects inherit. For a thirteenth-century philosopher, the matter-form distinction lends material objects an immediate intelligibility and allows them to be categorised. The conceptual horizons of philosophical language and concepts also exclude other definitions of material objects. In this and similar ways, existing assumptions delineate philosophical investigations, help us formulate questions and preclude or encourage possible answers.

Earlier versions of this worry were not clear about the extent to which existing conceptual commitments (those handed-down by cultural, religious or intellectual traditions) will impede the attempt to understand experience and resolve philosophical questions. This worry is now openly acknowledged and taken seriously. This marks an important development from *Structure*. It is especially clear in Merleau-Ponty's reading of Descartes's *cogito*. As I have already noted, this interpretation is more focused on the spirit rather than the letter of Descartes's texts.

As Merleau-Ponty sees it, the *cogito* of the *Meditations* draws on sedimented and inherited conceptual assumptions. Descartes's meditator implicitly relies on them in his analysis of experience, and is a good example of the spoken *cogito*: 'Descartes and, *a fortiori*, his reader begin meditating within a universe that is already speaking [*parlant*]. Language has, in fact, installed in us this certainty that we have of reaching, beyond its expression, a truth separable from that expression, and of which this expression is only the clothing and the contingent manifestation' (422/462). Two claims can be delineated here. First, the meditator or reader of the *Meditations* relies on some existing conceptual assumptions (or, on a world that is 'already speaking'). Second, existing conceptual commitments cultivate a certainty that philosophical language or terminology is a vehicle that grants access to 'universal' and 'indubitable' grounds, which do not essentially depend on the particular language or terminology in question. Despite the methodology of doubt, Descartes does not question basic presuppositions that undergird the meditator's reflective activity. For example, the meditator relies on the assumption that geometry and mathematics study the most general objects, are apodictically true and obtained irrespective of time and place, and cannot be doubted; these assumptions in turn tacitly support a geometrical definition of material objects using the category of 'extension'. Assumptions like these may remain undetected even by a radical scepticism. Despite attempting to rid himself of all preconceived notions, Cartesian reflection remains 'impure', and relies on thick conceptual assumptions. These assumptions are reflected in the language of the *Meditations*.

The fact that Merleau-Ponty takes exception to the second assumption suggests that for him, language is not a mere vehicle of thought, which delivers us to necessary propositions or unshakeable truths. Philosophical assumptions preserved in language always shape reflective processes and introduce new contingencies. This entails that philosophical language must be carefully scrutinised. As Descartes shows, even the most pared-down view of philosophical language is already 'constituted' and relies on nontrivial conceptual assumptions (indeed, the view that a 'pure' philosophical language is possible is itself a nontrivial assumption). These prejudices anticipate the concepts and categories needed to understand experience. The concept of 'extension' circumscribes the range of features that could be invoked to explain the material world. These limits might engender a certainty about material objects, but this certainty is an effect of prior conceptual assumptions that may be untenable in a different conceptual framework. To grasp the plausibility of any philosophical account, seemingly intuitive, transparent or innocuous conceptual assumptions preserved in philosophical expression must be carefully dissected.

Another important element of Merleau-Ponty's reading of Descartes's 'spoken' *cogito* should be noted. As we saw in chapter 2, Merleau-Ponty argues that expressive acts 'activate' and interpret sedimented meanings, which continue to be shaped by speakers in the present. However, like proponents of 'intellectualist' views, Descartes ignores the important role that expression plays in reflection.[42] If reflection is linguistic, then the truths of reason owe something important to expressive activity. This is not to say that consciousness is separated from experience and trapped within a universe of propositions or word-meanings (which Merleau-Ponty refers to using the term '*Wortbedeu-*

tungen'), or that rational reflection is beholden to one theoretical language or another (lxxix/16). Phenomenological descriptions ultimately refer to perceptual and not to linguistic content. Still, these considerations suggest that language is an animating force behind phenomenological disclosure. In particular, Merleau-Ponty's reading of Descartes's spoken *cogito* suggests that transcendental expressive activity is more creative or inventive than a phenomenological emphasis on 'description' might suggest. If transcendental clarification can be inhibited by linguistic commitments (a claim that follows from the reading above), then a critique or even a dismantling of existing conceptual (viz. linguistic) assumptions is a key condition for the possibility of a faithful description of experience. But if some concepts are unsatisfactory, others must take their place. By extension, conceptual invention becomes important. Merleau-Ponty does not draw these conclusions just yet. Still, as I show below, the issue of conceptual 'construction' or invention resurfaces in the *Phenomenology*'s account of the transcendental. In chapter 7, I argue that Merleau-Ponty eventually concludes that linguistic concept-invention is a fundamental precondition for phenomenological description.

4. LANGUAGE AND FOUNDATION

One year after the publication of the *Phenomenology*, Merleau-Ponty maintains that perception 'is the always presupposed foundation of all rationality, all value and all existence' (PrP 11/43). This is closely connected to one of the text's more striking claims: that phenomenology 'founds itself' (PhP lxxxv/21). These claims unambiguously identify perception as the basic point of departure and legitimating ground of phenomenological enquiry, a point stressed by commentators.[43] However, even if phenomenological findings are nourished by perceptual evidence, they are not, as is often assumed, solely legitimated by it. Phenomenology expresses and does not merely study intuitive evidence. For Merleau-Ponty, the meditating *cogito*'s expressive activity helps to establish the rational unity of perceptual experience and to identify the conditions that secure the intelligibility of perception. Ultimately, the reflective activity of a language-using subject undergirds phenomenological disclosure.

To see why, let us return to the view that linguistic meaning is 'founded' on perceptual meaning, which is adopted from Husserl (414/454).[44] This claim admits of multiple readings. On the one hand, it captures one of the *Phenomenology*'s guiding assumptions about experience; namely, that perception is prime. If one considers what it is like to have an experience, some perceptual engagement typically comes to mind (e.g., seeing, feeling, hearing, smelling or touching some thing). Perceptual experiences are immediate, familiar and enjoy a certain integrity and self-sufficiency. When I look towards a lake surrounded by a forest, I do not worry about perceptual illusions or deception, nor do I need to translate visual data using conceptual constructs. In this and similar experiences, there is no reason to doubt basic perceptual evidence, or the fact that I see a lake and trees before me. Even if subjects make mistakes, entertain doubts or observe ambiguities in perceptual experiences (e.g., how many or what kind of tree I might see), perception and especially vision is generally characterised by a high degree of subjective security and empirical success. To be sure, Merleau-Ponty is interested in a range of embodied behaviours and experiences, and does not overlook or exclude cases where perception is compromised or inhibited. As the Schneider case shows, supposedly 'non-standard' experiences offer important insights. Still, perception is foundational because it serves as the anchor of sense experience.

Correlatively, the foundational role of perception can also be interpreted as a suggestion that the philosophy of perception is a privileged method of analysis. First and foremost, perceptual data must be invoked to resolve philosophical questions about experience. The silent 'perceptual syntax' of the phenomenal field, or the structure of the appearance of space, time and empirical objects, are ultimate grounds of experience and therefore of phenomenological disclosure (38/61). If experience is primarily a perceptual engagement, and if the concepts used to account for it ultimately refer us to perceived experiences, then phenomenology should chiefly analyse perception.

Together with the claim above, this methodological assumption also rests on the view that perception is semantically prior to language. This entails that perceptual meaning can disambiguate linguistic and conceptual meaning (*la signification*), and is another dimension of the founding claim. Merleau-Ponty holds that there is 'a silence of consciousness that envelops the speaking world, a silence in which words first receive their configuration and their sense' (425/465).[45] This suggests that perceptual meaning is more basic than linguistic meaning.

Now because Merleau-Ponty does not standardly separate questions of meaning from questions of being in the *Phenomenology*, the semantic priority claim can also be read ontologically (lxxxiv/20–21; 418–19/458). He often suggests that to define what something is, one should give an account of what it means. Questions about the meaning of an entity are typically addressed by appeal to appearance or perceptual experience. Like Husserl, Merleau-Ponty assumes that ontological questions can be approached from the perspective of the meaning of phenomena (even though, unlike Husserl, he does not clearly divide ontological and semantic enquiries, nor does he assume that the suspension of ontological claims could help us better grasp the meaning of an object).[46] In the *Phenomenology*, then, references to 'being' can plausibly be understood to refer to meaningful appearance. A semantic (or ontological) reading of the foundation claim also assumes that perceptual being or meaning can be clearly distinguished from other kinds of meaning; for example, from linguistic meaning, or from what Merleau-Ponty calls 'thought'. As I noted, he does not think that (linguistic) concepts mediate or make perceptual experience possible. If being is broadly coextensive with meaning, and if meaning is given as an appearance, then the most fundamental entity, kind of being and category of meaning is perceptual. In this respect, the *Phenomenology* is more precise than *Structure* about the ontological or semantic priority of perceptual *sens* over linguistic *signification*.

The claim that linguistic meaning derives from perceptual meaning should not be read in an empiricist vein. It means that to define terms like 'chair', 'tree' or 'book', one should enlist evidence from one's perceptual experience of these entities. Merleau-Ponty would reject the view that these objects produce uniform impressions in subjects, from which concepts derive. Perceptual meaning solicits responses from subjects without determining how they will respond. This applies *a fortiori* to the transcendental level, where it is clear that perceptual meaning, while primary, must still be interpreted.

One may readily invoke examples challenging the view that concepts or linguistic meanings *tout court* can be defined by appeal to perception. It is hard to see how a square root, for example, could be defined in this way. Merleau-Ponty would accept that in such cases, abstract *significations* do more explanatory work. Following Husserl's account in the 'Origin of Geometry', he could claim that whereas subjects here and now relate to these terms using language or abstract concepts, at some point the meanings in question were generated out of intuition or lived experience.[47] Some concepts are inherited as pure *significations* (i.e., as purely linguistic entities), and their link to perceptual experience is severed or hard to trace. Still, at some point, like any other concept, they were formulated in response to experience.

One might still find this response wanting. In practice, Merleau-Ponty's approach to abstract concepts suggests he might accept a more mitigated view of the founding claim. It might require that perceptual meaning always be consulted, even in cases where it seems to fall short as an explanation of what something means. While perceptual meaning is needed to disambiguate non-perceptual meaning, it need not be sufficient. All things considered, and given other arguments for the primacy of perception, when abstract terms like 'square root' are concerned, one could readily concede that formal *significations* are more philosophically relevant. Merleau-Ponty's commitments are not inconsistent with this more tempered view. Nevertheless, the *Phenomenology* holds firm to the view that perception founds linguistic meaning, and that (as Husserl believes) ideal entities are generated in experience by subjects and inherited through linguistic traditions.

With these clarifications in place, we can return to the broader question of what sort of foundation phenomenology requires. The *Phenomenology* and subsequent writings unambiguously identify perception as the foundation of meaning or being, and by extension, of phenomenology itself (PrP 11/43). What has yet to be appreciated, however, is that Merleau-Ponty's premises commit him to the conclusion that language also serves as an equally important transcendental foundation. This claim may at first seem to be a mere entailment of the phenomenological doctrine of founding. For founding is a two-way relation, in which founding and founded terms (respectively, perception and language) are clarified by and sometimes depend on one another. However, Merleau-Ponty does not directly draw this conclusion, and typically stresses the foundational role of perceptual consciousness. Instead, he is committed to the conclusion I have identified for a different and arguably more interesting reason.

As we saw, the view of the transcendental that Merleau-Ponty adheres to differs from that of Kant or Husserl. The important role he identifies for transcendental expression marks another important difference from these approaches. At the transcendental level, language is a founding term because the unity of the empirical and transcendental realms is established by means of philosophical expression. By making the meaning of experience explicit, phenomenological reflection allows conditions for the possibility of perceptual experience to show themselves. Linguistic expression links the experience of the tacit *cogito* with its transcendental counterpart. Phenomenological description has an active and formative role, and is inventive; this is the sense in which phenomenology 'founds itself'.

Despite claims to its temporally, ontologically or explanatorily foundational status, the primacy of the perceptual subject ultimately also depends on the expressive activity of the reflecting transcendental subject:

> This first perspective waits to be reconquered, fixed, and made explicit through perceptual exploration and through speech. Silent consciousness only grasps itself as 'I think' in general in the face of a confused world that is 'to be thought'. Every particular grasp, and philosophy's recovery of this general project, requires that the subject deploy powers of which the subject himself does not hold the secret and, in particular, that he turns himself into a speaking subject [*qu'il se fasse sujet parlant*]. The tacit *cogito* is only a *cogito* when it has expressed itself. (426/465–66)

Merleau-Ponty does not claim that the spoken *cogito* invents the meanings encountered by the tacit *cogito*. The point is that even if perception is prime and prior to language, its primacy is possible provided that the 'spoken' *cogito* (the language-using reflective subject) articulates the meaning of first-order experience, and identifies the tacit *cogito* (the 'first perspective') *as* primary. According to Merleau-Ponty, everyday perceptual experience is 'mute'. It must be expressed and made explicit if the meanings we encounter are to be understood. But *explicitation* or phenomenological description is a linguistic and not a perceptual activity. Doubtless, the subject does not 'hold the secret' to this newly emergent condition: reflecting subjects do not invent the language they use to explicate perception. Nevertheless, the passage is clear that without recourse to expression, the pre-linguistic meaning of experience, and its foundational role, cannot be studied or understood.

More strongly, the passage suggests that the 'tacit *cogito*' is a fiction; it is an invention or product of transcendental reflection. Once again, the claim is not that first-order perceptual meaning is created *ad hoc* by reflecting subjects. Still, first-order experience is 'reconquered' in phenomenological description or 'speech'. This is to say that the meaning of first-order experience is reconfigured and reinterpreted. Most immediately, it is reinterpreted according to the distinction between the 'empirical' or 'unreflected' and the 'transcendental' or 'reflection'. In the latter, reflecting subjects associate everyday perceptual experience with the former. Natural or pre-reflective experience does not recognise such a distinction. In the transcendental domain, we learn that perceptual experience is had by an 'empirical' subject or a 'tacit *cogito*', two posits supposedly important for understanding the structure of appearances. But these issue from transcendental reflection, which is inaugurated and sustained by linguistic expression (recall that thinking is linguistic). On this point, Merleau-Ponty is proximate to a current of thought originating in early German idealism, which emphasises the importance of transcendental activity, though he does not suggest that the world is a product of the I.[48]

In attempting to make experience explicit, the transcendental subject objectifies its empirical counterpart by turning it into an object of study. In doing so, transcendental subjectivity also establishes a continuity between its perceptual and reflective modalities. It recognises itself in both guises, and transcendental expression unifies these two moments of subjectivity. However, this unity is

> not a series of psychical acts, nor for that matter a central I who gathers them together in a synthetic unity, but rather a single experience that is inseparable from itself, a single 'cohesion of life', a single temporality that makes itself explicit [*s'explicite*] from its birth and confirms this birth in each present. It is this advent or rather this transcendental event that the *cogito* recovers. (430/469)

Clearly, transcendental *explicitation* is not a form of intellectual synthesis. Its activity is not akin to an act or a judgement. Still, by identifying and expressing the meaning of lived experience and connecting it

TRANSCENDENTAL EXPRESSION

with the broader structures of perceptual life, reflective activity weaves a unifying thread that ties empirical and transcendental together. In this sense, transcendental *explicitation* is productive: it shows that the empirical and transcendental modes of subjectivity cohere with one another.

But is the empirical/transcendental unity not, as the passage above also suggests, ultimately explained by the deeper structure of temporality? This thought is motivated by the observation that the *Phenomenology* gives analytical and explanatory priority to the subject's experience of time. Indeed, temporality and perception are tightly linked (450/489). The 'Temporality' chapter, which follows the remark quoted above, defines subjectivity as temporality. This definition is thought to work out the more fundamental meaning of the results of the *Cogito* chapter. Ultimately, the problem of sense is explained by temporality (this even applies to the discussion of freedom, which follows the penultimate chapter on temporality) (454/494). Unsurprisingly, commentators have stressed the importance of the *Phenomenology*'s account of temporality for understanding its broader philosophical positions.

Temporality plays a fundamental role in Merleau-Ponty's account of experience, and it is of central importance for phenomenological analysis. But even if the articulated structure of time is a key condition for experience and is lived prior to analysis, like all other meaningful structures it too must be disclosed if its conditioning role is to be understood. As with other conditions, reflective and expressive activity will ultimately demonstrate how temporal conditions underwrite experience and transcendental clarification. As the passage above intimates, even if experience has a fundamentally temporal dimension, the latter must be made explicit by a subject. Once again, language surfaces as the concomitant condition of a putatively temporal foundation.

This indicates that temporality and perception require expression for their conditioning roles to become clear. But even if phenomenological expression unfolds according to a temporal structure, and is guided by intuitive evidence, it is ultimately just as basic. Like perception or temporality, language is prime. This holds in spite of Merleau-Ponty's assertion that no form of human expression (e.g., bodily or gestural) is privileged; his premises suggest that this cannot be the case (411/452). If description ultimately demonstrates that, and how the tacit *cogito* is continuous with the spoken *cogito*, then time, subject and language are all necessary and equally fundamental conditions for the possibility of transcendental subjectivity, for the analysis of an empirical perceptual subject, and for the establishment of a phenomenological foundation. Time, subject, and language form the triptych of Merleau-Ponty's canvas of phenomenological reflection.

The following remark brings this conclusion to the fore:

> It is true that we would speak of nothing if it were necessary to speak only of that with which we coincide, since speech is already a separation. Moreover, there is no experience without speech [*il n'y a pas d'expérience sans parole*], the purely lived [*le pur vécu*] is not even found within [our] speaking life. But the primary sense of speech is, nevertheless, in this text of experience that it attempts to utter. (353/394)

Once again, the point is not that perception is impossible without recourse to language (Merleau-Ponty will move closer to this position in his later work). Still, in the full phenomenological sense, the meaning of 'experience' depends on language. Perceivers have experiences, but understanding them requires that subjects commit themselves to describing their contents. Whatever we have to say about experience will necessarily be mediated by language. Even if transcendental descriptions always attempt to detail the lived meaning of experience, the 'pure' content of lived experience cannot be captured. Every translation of perceptual experience converts it into a linguistic form and thereby changes it. A purely perceptual experience can only be posited as an ideal limit that never becomes a theme of phenomenological disclosure.

This seems to brush up against the claim that perception is the sole foundation of meaning, being, or philosophical reflection. Merleau-Ponty's remarks in the *Phenomenology*'s preface do not foreclose on this possibility, even if he elsewhere stresses the foundational sufficiency of perception: 'The phenomenological world is not the making explicit [*l'explicitation*] of a prior being, but rather the founding of being; philosophy is not the reflection of a prior truth, but rather, like art, the realisation of a truth' (lxxxiv/20–21). He later notes that '[w]hat is new in phenomenology is not that it denies the unity of experience, but that it establishes it differently than classical rationalism' (307/347). A distinguishing feature of his view of transcendental phenomenology is that, in addition to perception or intuition, he recognises that language is basic to phenomenological foundations. Thus, even the essential insights that phenomenology delivers owe something significant to language: '[s]eparated essences are the essences of language'. Any separation from the empirical realm, however, 'is merely apparent, since through language they still rely upon the pre-predicative life of consciousness' (lxxix/16). This view is developed in Merleau-Ponty's later work (see the account of essence in chapter 7). The point is that even on a definition of perception on which its meaning is pre-predicative and primary, transcendental expression links reflective activity with pre-linguistic meaning. It unites the empirical and transcendental self, and makes a foundation for the analysis of experience possible.

The phenomenological foundation Merleau-Ponty favours remains 'a synthesis that [is] *in the making* [se faisait]' (400/439). Insights acquired through reflection are provisional. They require continuing evaluation of experience and its possible transformations by reflective activity (401–2/441–42).[49] Hence, phenomenology is not founded on a fixed ground. In this account of the transcendental, '[t]he *a priori* is the fact as understood, made explicit [*explicité*], and followed through into all of the consequences of its tacit logic [*logique tacite*]; the *a posteriori* is the isolated and implicit fact' (230/256). These definitions would surely give Kant and Husserl pause. They reinterpret the a priori and the a posteriori as two moments of phenomenological clarification. The a priori is not the pre-existing foundation or explanation of the a posteriori. The former is but a more developed *explicitation* of the latter. To unfold the 'tacit logic' of a priori is to explore the possible permutations (or 'consequences') of lived experience; namely, its meaning and how it could be otherwise. But if the continuity between lived experience and its explicated counterpart depends on explicating activity, any ground of phenomenological clarification remains open and undetermined: 'self-coincidence with myself, such as is accomplished in the *cogito*, must never be a real coincidence, and must merely be an intentional and presumptive coincidence' (360/402).

This approach to the transcendental can address the criticism that the *Phenomenology* succumbs to a version of idealism or intellectualism, two of its intended targets. This criticism was first articulated by Beaufret in Merleau-Ponty's public defence of the *Phenomenology*, and has been taken up by Renaud Barbaras. Barbaras argues that this text ultimately leads to the conclusion that sense depends on consciousness.

As he sees it, 'Merleau-Ponty remains a prisoner of the duality between reflection and the unreflective; dominated by the presupposition of the primacy of an autonomous, reflective order, he can characterise the phenomenal only as the unreflective itself, in the sense of a negation of all reflection'.[50] In his later texts, Merleau-Ponty will overcome this duality; but the *Phenomenology* succumbs to it, and by extension, comes closer to the subject-centrism it denounces. By privileging the reflective order, and by opposing it to the unreflected, Merleau-Ponty's premises entail that perceptual sense (or the 'unreflective') is subject to the determination of reflective consciousness.

The account above suggests an alternative reading. Even if the *Phenomenology* undoubtedly favours subjectivity as an explanatory ground, Merleau-Ponty does not posit or argue for the autonomy of reflection. First, phenomenological foundations (developed by means of reflection) only obtain in light of a continuing revaluation of experience. As I have suggested, reflection is a circular process that necessarily revises itself. Experience is more fully elucidated when its meaning is reinterpreted. But to recognise the possible transformation of pre-reflective experience is not to define experience as the 'negation' of the reflective domain. A reevaluation of experience may turn up new layers of sense; but these can be discovered provided transcendental reflection retains its contact with experience. Any new insights discovered here are not (Merleau-Ponty maintains) invented by us. Instead, reflective activity takes direction from first-order experience, and is not severed from it. The extent to which Merleau-Ponty can sustain this position is another matter; but his view is that an opposition or strict relation of priority between these two realms does not obtain. On this reading, the role of subjectivity seems less idealist in the intellectualist sense of the term, which is relevant for the criticism above. However, the *Phenomenology*'s idealism may not be fully exhausted by intellectualist readings. Merleau-Ponty rejects both critical and transcendental idealism, but his emphasis on the dialectical relation between reflection and unreflected arguably brings him closer to a more Hegelian version of philosophical idealism.[51] This is a more difficult matter to settle, and I cannot consider it here.

Second, the important linguistic conditions of phenomenological disclosure also push back against the suggestion that the *cogito* is the sovereign arbitrator of unreflected experience. Expression depends on sedimented, ideal meanings handed down by linguistic or cultural traditions (420/460). Consciousness is not sovereign over the meaning of its language or the historical conditions it encounters. Attempts to elucidate the structure of experience are circumscribed by existing conventions and sedimented meanings (424–25/464–65). If consciousness depends on prior linguistic conditions that it does not fully control, it cannot be the *sine qua non* of perceptual meaning. Even if natural languages sediment expressive acts performed by language-using subjects, shifts in linguistic meaning occur gradually, and individual subjects are not standardly aware of the transformations they bring to existing linguistic conventions (recall that products of authentic expression, for example, are not deliberate results).

That existing linguistic conventions are a precondition for reflective activity raises a question about their philosophical adequacy. Merleau-Ponty does not explicitly address this issue in the *Phenomenology*. However, he resists the view that philosophical expression is beholden to linguistic conventions. He leaves open the possibility that subjects will creatively modify them, without specifying how much leeway they enjoy. This leads to a tension with his stated and modest descriptive goals, which is important for understanding his position in the *Phenomenology*.

5. 'TRANSCENDENTAL OR AUTHENTIC SPEECH'

Two conflicting ideals of transcendental description seem to be at work in the *Phenomenology*. On the one hand, the text suggests that it is possible to describe experience without transforming its meaning. For example, the *Cogito* chapter claims that '[t]he whole issue is to properly understand the tacit *cogito*, to only put into it what is really there, and to not turn language into a product of consciousness on the pretext that consciousness is not a product of language' (424/464). Versions of this ideal are articulated already in *Structure*, and some other remarks in the *Phenomenology* strike a similar chord.[52] They point to a norm for descriptive work, on which descriptions are strictly held to the meanings given in perceptual experience. Any claims or conclusions that cannot be traced to first-order experience should be discarded or replaced. If taken to its logical conclusion, this ideal could yield an account of 'the essence of the world': guided by demands of strict fidelity to primary experience, phenomenology would be in a position to disclose the essential structure of experience as 'it in fact [*en fait*] is for us, prior to every thematisation' (lxxix/16).[53] Were Merleau-Ponty to fully embrace such a view, he would move even closer to Husserl.

However, Merleau-Ponty's hesitations about immutable foundations, together with his account of reflection, also place him closer to a different ideal of phenomenological description. The position sketched in the paragraph above is consistent with the classical transcendental goal of explanatory completeness, which I have suggested he rejects. In some other passages, he claims that reflection is 'a creative operation that itself participates in the facticity of the unreflected' (62/89). This evaluation is at odds with any supposed opposition between 'construction' (or 'constitution') and 'description' (lxxiii/10). It suggests that reflection and description are consistent with creation or construction, and it allows that description not aim only to transcribe the meaning of perception without transforming it.

Together with the evidence considered in earlier sections, these remarks suggest that Merleau-Ponty entertains and is committed to two incompatible ideals of phenomenological explanation. He advances the view that description can yield the 'truth' or meaning of experience 'just as it is' (lxxix–lxxx/16–17). But he also advances a circular account of reflection, which does not observe a tension between fidelity and transformation, and which accepts that description always transforms the original text of experience.

This tension is sharpened by Merleau-Ponty's understanding of the semantics of transcendental expression. Transcendental language, he claims, is a form of 'authentic speech' (411/451). This issues a fundamental challenge to the possibility of describing objects as they really are, and to the goal of offering a complete explanation of their meaning and structure. As we saw in chapter 2, expression is authentic when it fundamentally transforms existing conventions or meanings. Authentic expression draws on sedimented conventions, but it modifies them to a degree that produces genuinely novel meanings, beyond the typical modifications encountered in standard linguistic usage (323/365).[54] As I noted earlier, literature or poetry are examples of authentic expression (203/239). Merleau-Ponty draws a link between transcendental and authentic expression, but he does not isolate special features of authentic expression that are distinctively transcendental. We may assume, then, that basic tenets of authentic expression also apply to phenomenological expression.[55]

If transcendental expression is authentic, this entails, first, that descriptions will necessarily transform the meaning of perceptual experience. Merleau-Ponty is clear that this mode of 'expression is everywhere creative' (411/451). An account of perception 'does not merely discover the sense [objects] have, but rather, sees to it that they have a sense [*fait qu'elles aient un sens*]' (38/61). While phenomenological description clarifies meanings encountered in experience, it also alters their meaning, just as a new metaphor shifts the meaning of an existing term.[56] Second, this view entails that transcendental expressions have novel semantic content: authentic 'speech gives rise to a new sense, ... for the first time' (200/236). In authentic expression, 'the expressed does not exist apart from the expression' (recall the sign/signification unity discussed in chapter 2) (169/204). Further, in transcendental expression 'an idea begins to exist' (411/451). Like authentic expressions, phenomenological descriptions promise to show experience in a new light by offering us a new perspective on the world. Despite endorsing the position that language is founded on perception, the view that transcendental expression yields genuinely new expressive products means that descriptions are not a simple copy or translation of a perceptual text.

These remarks lend more credence to the claim that reflection should have a circular structure. If phenomenological expression transforms perceptual meaning, there is good reason to critically compare descriptions with first-order experience. Further, this possibility requires that the relation between transcendental *explanans* and empirical *explanandum* remains open to modification (229–30/266–65; cf. IP 59/99). More strongly, Merleau-Ponty concludes that the 'word [transcendental] signifies that reflection never has the entire world and the plurality of monads spread out and objectified before its gaze, that it only ever has a partial view and a limited power' (PhP 62/89). Due in large part to the means by which it expresses its insights, reflection retains a limited grasp of sense, and a reappraisal of experience seems justified.

These commitments are of consequence for how we should approach the view of phenomenology on offer in *Phenomenology of Perception*. If it is true that for phenomenology 'the whole issue' stands or falls on the demand to put only as much into the tacit *cogito* as is really there, then the view that transcendental expression is authentic requires a revision in Merleau-Ponty's understanding of the basic task of phenomenological research, and the abiding tension between transcendental description and creation must be resolved in favour of the former. However, while he sometimes gestures in this direction, textual evidence in the *Phenomenology* and in subsequent writings suggests that a shift in his understanding of the basic aims of phenomenology is more likely. As I will show in chapter 4, after the publication of the *Phenomenology*, Merleau-Ponty searched for the conceptual resources with which to articulate a new understanding of phenomenological expression. He would eventually reject the claim that descriptions should aim to put into the tacit *cogito* just those meanings that are originally given in perception. This shift is supported by a reformulated approach to experience and by a new account of the perception-language relation.

In the *Phenomenology*, Merleau-Ponty largely embraces the tensions above. He affirms that phenomenology should not only record the meaning of experience but also disclose new ways of understanding the world (lxxxv/21). Given that 'ambiguity' is an ineliminable feature of everyday experience, it is unsurprising that it would also characterise the transcendental domain and subjects' attempts to describe experience.[57] To observe a tension between description and creation is tantamount to a humble recognition of our finitude *qua* reflecting subjects: 'The power language has of bringing the expressed into existence, and of opening routes, new dimensions, and new landscapes to thought, is ultimately just as obscure for the adult as it is for the child' (421/463).

6. DESCRIPTION OR CREATION?

The possibility that descriptions can transform the original structure of experience has been noted.[58] But less attention has been directed to related challenges stemming from Merleau-Ponty's account of transcendental expression and from his view of the circular and incomplete nature of transcendental clarification. These issues touch the heart of his view of the perception-language relation. The account of transcendental phenomenology sketched above offers an opportunity to pose deeper questions about what form of expression is best suited to articulate the sense of experience. Some are firmly grounded in the *Phenomenology*'s theoretical framework, while others point to its limits, and anticipate future developments in Merleau-Ponty's phenomenology and philosophy of language.

Most immediately, if descriptions transform the meaning of phenomena, in what sense does the account above promise to yield a genuine *description* of experience? While we may not be able to fully understand how this unfolds, we know that phenomenological description will always transform perceptual meaning. The extent to which this poses a serious methodological problem remains an open question. On this score, the *Phenomenology*'s methodologically sophisticated view of reflection and description cuts in two directions. On the one hand, the structure of phenomenological expression requires some necessary (but perhaps innocuous) divergence between the meaning of phenomena and their explicated, linguistic counterparts. On the other hand, the circular structure of reflection encourages subjects to revisit descriptions. This presents the opportunity to revise descriptions in light of aberrations from experience, thereby limiting (or perhaps eliminating) discrepancies introduced by descriptive activities. This is not an explicit *desideratum* of the *Phenomenology*, but it is a virtue of the text that it has the resources to meet challenges of this sort. Still, the question of what degree of transformation phenomenology should allow, if any at all, remains unresolved.

In large part, the tensions identified above are motivated by two closely linked assumptions: that transcendental expression is partly continuous with empirical expression insofar as it preserves some of its features (while maintaining a degree of semantic and expressive uniqueness); and that phenomenology can either describe or reinterpret the meaning of perception, but not both. These assumptions set up a degreed relationship between transcendental and empirical and embed a division between literal and creative modes of expression. First consider the view that transcendental and empirical expression share key features in common. While he rarely addressed it directly, Husserl's *Crisis* offers a brief but suggestive observation on this point:

> All the new sorts of apperceptions that are exclusively tied to the phenomenological reduction, together with the new sort of language (new even if I use ordinary language, as is unavoidable, though its meanings are also unavoidably transformed) – all this, which before was completely hidden and inexpressible, now flows into the self-objectification, into my psychic life, and becomes apperceived as its newly revealed intentional background of constitutive accomplishments.[59]

This text is clear that phenomenological language is not coextensive with natural language. After the reduction, natural language meanings are inevitably 'transformed'. A study of these transformations, the text claims, is an important task of constitutive analysis. Despite identifying its theoretical importance, Husserl says little about how this transformation unfolds and should be understood. In particular, it is unclear how we should refashion natural language to meet the demands of phenomenological explication. Still, some special mode of phenomenological signification must be developed.

Fink did address these issues, and his interest in transcendental language follows from an extant but underexplored concern already present in Husserl's work.[60] For Fink, language-related issues pose special challenges for phenomenology (and especially for a broadly Husserlian framework) that should not be ignored (Heidegger's reflections on language in this period are of an altogether different order). As far as our aims are concerned, evidence shows that Fink was an important influence on Merleau-Ponty's early work, and especially on the *Phenomenology*.[61] While he does not cite or quote Fink in the *Cogito* chapter, it is safe to say that Merleau-Ponty was familiar with Fink's treatment of the issues above when he was writing the *Phenomenology*. Given that Fink was one of the first phenomenologists to broach them, it will be helpful to briefly consider some of his observations about the relation between empirical and transcendental language (a detailed treatment of Fink's account of transcendental language is not possible here).

Fink expresses the view that a fundamental tension obtains between natural (or empirical) and phenomenological (or transcendental) language. For him, phenomenological expression is not coextensive with empirical expression. Most immediately, the former does not predicate existence of its objects, whereas expression in natural language typically presupposes a basic belief in the existence of the objects that expressions quantify over. Transcendental language is 'reduced' and therefore free of ontological commitments.[62] But because phenomenology cannot simply invent a language of its own for its descriptive work, it must draw on meanings from natural language.[63] Transcendental language 'rebels' against this association with empirical language, but the limitation just noted entails that this tension must be sustained. It remains a necessary feature of transcendental expression. For Fink, this also entails that the results of phenomenological reflection will be imperfectly communicated, since they mix elements from the natural attitude. Ultimately, phenomenological results can only be understood from within the phenomenological attitude; that is, after performing the reduction.

Fink proposes that the relation between these two kinds of expression be understood as an 'analogy to the analogy'.[64] The *Sixth Cartesian Meditation* does not develop this position in much detail, but the view seems to be that the meanings of transcendental language are similar to those of natural language, without relying on the existence-predication that occurs in the latter. Thus, for example, in natural language we use the term 'tree' to refer to that particular tree over there. In transcendental explication, the term 'tree' refers to this tree understood as a unity of meaning, or 'sense', without referring to any actually existing tree. Transcendental discourse details the features of trees, and their essential structure, in a way analogous but not identical to empirical expression. In effect, transcendental expression indicates its objects by separating meaning from being. Still, because phenomenological language is analogous to empirical language, some natural meanings cannot be purged from the transcendental domain. It is therefore necessary to continually scrutinise transcendental meanings in light of their mundane counterparts, to ensure that they are free of existence predication and other assumptions proper to the natural attitude. Still, Fink notes that this effort remains imperfect. Phenomenological expression is analogous to natural expression, and its meaning thereby remains '*fluid* and open'.[65]

Fink is led to these conclusions because he assumes that natural language terms are also subject to the reduction. This motivates him to define the empirical-transcendental relation according to the category of analogy. The account of Merleau-Ponty's view of the transcendental in this chapter shows that the reduction does not occupy the same importance for him. This is not to say that he rejects the need for the reduction.⁶⁶ Still, the reduction never attains the status of an absolutely necessary methodological step. By extension, the need to clearly demarcate the boundaries of natural and phenomenological predication is not a pressing concern for Merleau-Ponty. That independent philosophical considerations lead him to conclude that the empirical/transcendental distinction should be further weakened lends more evidence to the view that transcendental and empirical expression fundamentally overlap, a position also occupied by Fink, albeit for different reasons.

Merleau-Ponty's choice to not rigidly define the boundaries of transcendental and empirical predication leads to an important question: Do the transformative effects of phenomenological expression also apply to the being, and not only the meaning, of empirical objects? The answer seems to be 'yes', since for him phenomenological expression is not reduced and therefore does not necessarily surrender existence-predication. From the perspective of Merleau-Ponty's thought, this question may seem ill formed: after all, since they rest on intentional experiences, do ontological claims not also, in general, concern the meaning of various object-domains? Even if he often uses 'meaning' to refer to 'being' (and vice versa), the question stands, most immediately because he has yet to directly consider the broader ontological implications of a phenomenology of perception (the link between being and meaning is an implicit and unexamined assumption).⁶⁷ And because language seems to play a formative role in circumscribing the meaning of perceptual experience, one may still wonder what relation language and perception bear to ontology; or, to put the point differently, one may wonder if language has ontological import.

As I will show in parts 2 to 3, this problem, together with unresolved questions about the extent to which transcendental descriptions can embrace the interpretive and creative characteristics of authentic expression, while also remaining true to the basic descriptive goals of phenomenology, are tackled in tandem. The first is addressed after a protracted engagement with literary expression; I explore the origins of this in chapter 4. The latter will be clarified when Merleau-Ponty returns to the topic of philosophical expression in his later work, after having concluded that language does indeed have ontological import; I consider this in chapter 7. The issues motivating the basic problems above require a significant modification of the boundaries of phenomenology first sketched in *Structure* and refined in the *Phenomenology*. To anticipate the findings of subsequent chapters: Merleau-Ponty will argue that description and creation are both part and parcel of the attempt to capture the meaning of experience, and that phenomenological clarification amplifies and even forms it. An important observation from his discussion of Descartes's *cogito* anticipates the substance of his response. Recall that for him, Descartes's *cogito* remains hidden under 'the entire thickness of cultural acquisitions' (424/463). Alternatively, it is insufficiently sensitive to the conceptual assumptions preserved in philosophical language. By contrast, to surmount this problem, phenomenology must attend to and refine the meaning of the concepts and natural language terms it relies on. This is a creative and expressive activity, but it is undertaken for the sake of improving descriptions. Merleau-Ponty resolves some of the dilemmas above by offering an inclusive interpretation of the disjunction between description and creation: phenomenological description can best capture the meaning of experience if it is sufficiently creative and inventive. However, the creative dimensions of phenomenological expression are not construed as analogies or metaphors, but as indirect statements of how sense is given to consciousness. A hybrid view of phenomenological expression, Merleau-Ponty will maintain, can best express the sense of experience, and can realise the basic aims of the phenomenological research program.

NOTES

1. Since *Structure*, this term is typically associated with Brunschvicg's thought. The *Phenomenology* offers a less sympathetic take on the merits of critical idealism (PhP 206 n.41/223 n.1).

2. See PhP 138/170 for the claim that Schneider's case undermines intellectualist and empiricist modes of explanation.

3. However, Merleau-Ponty admits that empiricism can, in principle, offer a more sophisticated view of reason. For example, he claims that nineteenth-century French positivist accounts offer more promising empiricist approaches to the mental. Following Husserl's sympathetic reading, he accepts that Hume has 'taken radical reflection further than anyone', by attempting 'to take us back to the phenomena of which we have an experience beneath every ideology', and by recognising (unlike Kant) that thought 'must produce its genealogy

beginning from our actual experience' (229/265). This suggestive reading of empiricism is not further developed. On the whole, he does not think an empirically oriented approach to the mind is compelling.

4. See Behnke 2002 for an overview.

5. See the introduction, chapter 3 ('Attention and Judgment'), and PhP 210/246, 268/306, 318–19/359. Merleau-Ponty sometimes attributes views to Descartes that are much closer to his own (see e.g., 44/68, 205/241).

6. The chapter contains only one reference to the *Rules for Direction of the Mind* (405/445).

7. Merleau-Ponty also has Brunschvicg in mind when criticising intellectualism. (See PD 249–50 for the observation that during his philosophical development '[t]he most important philosophical thought of the time in France was that of Léon Brunschvicg'.) See de Saint Aubert 2005, 60–70 for an overview of Merleau-Ponty's relation to Brunschvicg. Brunschvicg openly accepts the term 'intellectualism' (Brunschvicg 1905, chapter 4). See Gutting 2001, 40–48 for an overview of Brunschvicg's thought and its influence in France.

8. Lachièze-Rey 1933–1934.

9. Lachièze-Rey 1950.

10. Lachièze-Rey 1950, 25.

11. Lachièze-Rey 1938.

12. See Matherne 2016 for the view that Merleau-Ponty adopted Lachièze-Rey's reading of Kant's schematism and applied some of its basic insights to his analysis of geometrical construction in the *Cogito* chapter (PhP 403–8/443–48).

13. Lachièze-Rey stresses that Kant's theory of perception requires a sensible, embodied support. He finds this in the schematism, which he claims is an embodied and not simply an intellectual activity: 'La perception, comme structure realisée, renvoie necessairement à une structure realisante et à des principes spirituels de constitution. Or ces intentions organisatrices fondamentales ne peuvent être regardées comme purement elles sont inevitablement solidaires d'une realisation intuitive formelle, dans laquelle elles doivent se traduire et s'incarner avant de s'incorporer les données sensibles; et c'est ainsi qu'il ne paraît y avoir d'édification possible de la perception que conformement au schématisme kantien' (Lachièze-Rey 1937, 31; see also Lachièze-Rey 1933–1934, 142–43). Matherne 2016 is right to stress Merleau-Ponty's sympathy to Lachièze-Rey on this point, but it would be too strong to suggest that this attitude applies, in general, to Merleau-Ponty's reading of Lachièze-Rey.

14. Lachièze-Rey 1937, 145.

15. For an example, consider the following interpretation of Kant's 'conscience originaire': 'Il est certain que le 'je', étant le principe suprême de tous les rapports, étant l'essence même de ces rapports dans la mesure où ils sont

conçus sous un forme dynamique, ne saurait être séparé de lui-même. Mais cette séparation n'existe jamais que par suite d'une illusion. Les différentes opérations sont des actes, et ces actes [. . .]. En elles-mêmes, les opérations sont tout autre chose que des événements et se rattachent directement au pouvoir originaire de la pensée, sans considération de l'interruption temporelle qui, en fait, ne les affecte pas intrinsèquement' (Lachièze-Rey 1937, 145).

16. Fink took this view of intentionality to be one of Husserl's fundamental contributions. For him, the question of how sense-giving in latent or operative intentionality functions 'appears to be answered by the possibility of *reflection*', which is an observation that Merleau-Ponty takes seriously (Fink 1981, 52).

17. See Geraets 1971 for a positive interpretation of Merleau-Ponty's transcendental commitments. See also Pollard 2014.

18. See Gardner 2015, 2017 (cf. Inkpin 2017).

19. See PhP lxxv/11–12, lxxix/15–16, lxxx/17, 56/82–83, 64/90–91, 215/252, 228–29/265, 394/434.

20. Despite a subjective inability to cognise it, for Kant it is still necessary to seek 'the unconditioned whereby cognition's unity is completed' (Kant 1998, A307–8/B363–65). The 'Transcendental Doctrine of Method' also stresses the need for systematic completeness. The standing of any part of the critical system to any other must be fixed a priori: the 'absence of any part [will] be noticed in our knowledge of the rest, and there can be no contingent addition or undetermined magnitude of perfection that does not have its boundaries determined *a priori*' (Kant 1998 B860–B861). Husserl develops this basic Kantian insight, and maintains that phenomenology's systematic goals require that it account for 'all possibilities of being (and impossibilities of being)' according to 'absolutely fixed essential laws' (Husserl 2014, 177). Transcendental conditions 'leave no further room for any conceivable questionableness' (Husserl 1960, 181).

21. See, for example, Geraets 1971, 171 and Gardner 2015, 306 (see also Gardner 2017, 5, and Pollard 2014, 123, 129).

22. See, for example, 382/423–24, 174/210, 415/455 ff., 498 fn. 8/29 n.1., 509–10 fn. 60/77–78 n.1. Rockmore 2011, 192 notes the importance of description but contrasts it with explanation *tout court*. Merleau-Ponty certainly criticises a narrow causal or reductive view of explanation (see, e.g., lxx/7, 34/56, 452/491). However, on the weaker reading I have outlined, phenomenological descriptions make some object or phenomenon explicit, and in this sense they give a qualitative explanation of how the object is given, perceived and understood.

23. Madison argues that '[t]he main object of phenomenology as a reflective philosophy is rationality itself' (Madison 1981 137; see also 150 ff.). See also Noble 2014, 80–81, and Bimbenet 2004, 295–96 for a helpful discussion of Merleau-Ponty's later view of rationality.

24. In later writings, Merleau-Ponty will define meaning as 'cohesion'. I return to this view in chapter 6.

25. See lxxxii–lxxxiii/18–20, 156/191 on the genesis of sense; see 127–28/158–60 on the need for genetic phenomenology.

26. A regressive or genetic mode of explanation is also evidenced by the *Phenomenology*'s structure, which moves from first-order analyses of perception to their deeper explanatory conditions (viz. the 'return' to the *cogito* and its deeper temporal structure).

27. Taylor 1978, 151–52.

28. See, for example, Kant 1998, B197/A158. For this theme in Husserl see Husserl 1973, 87, 108, 114; Husserl 2012; Husserl 1970, 158.

29. See, for example, Husserl 2014 §89, §30 and Husserl 1969, 160.

30. Merleau-Ponty claims that reflection does not 'work backward along a pathway already travelled in the opposite direction by constitution' (253/290). This is to say that reflection does not merely reproduce the results of constitution; it also adds new layers of meaning. Still, reflection follows a broadly regressive movement, and is likened to a 'return' to a more fundamental ground of sense (382/424). The point is that it does not return or regress only to already constituted meanings.

31. The aims of this chapter do not allow me to explore this issue, but circularity is also a feature of Merleau-Ponty's later account of phenomenological reflection and philosophical methodology (see VI 35/55–56, 87/119, 119–20/158, 166/218, 177–78/229–30).

32. Compare the view that the 'pre-objective being of perception . . . makes it possible for a subject to be presented with an articulated realm of objects' (Gardner 2015, 301–2). This passage suggests that the distinction between the 'pre-objective' and the 'objective' is hard to maintain. If the 'pre-objective' can be transformed, it is hard to see how it could serve as a determining transcendental condition.

33. See Romano 2010, 431–39, 443.

34. Loidolt 2014, 204.

35. See, for example, Husserl 1969, 245–46; Husserl 1960, 21, 85, 137.

36. Moran 2008, 418.

37. See Husserl 1979, 264–65 and 259.

38. Merleau-Ponty traces this 'Kantian' view of reflection to Lachièze-Rey's *L'Idéalisme kantien*, but also to Husserl, 'in the second period of his philosophy (the period of the *Ideen*)' (539 n.2/290 n.1). See Husserl's claim in *Ideas I* that Kant's transcendental deduction operates 'within the realm' of transcendental phenomenology (Husserl 2014 §62).

39. See, for example, Pollard 2014, Inkpin 2017.

40. For another version of this see Consciousness and Language Acquisition, where Merleau-Ponty holds, against Descartes and Kant, that consciousness is essentially linguistic (a claim advanced in the context of a discussion of child development) (CPP 3; see also 67).

41. See Husserl 1970.

42. Merleau-Ponty also makes this point against Brunschvicg (415/455).

43. See, for example, Dillon 1988.

44. For a good account of the relation between pre-predicative and linguistic meaning in Husserl, see Romano 2010, 134–74.

45. The distinction between language and 'silence' was developed by Brice Parain in his *Recherches sur la nature et les fonctions du langage* (1942, 10–20, 183–84). Merleau-Ponty claims that Parain is an intellectualist insofar as he allegedly believes that 'language . . . is nothing but the other side of an infinite Thought' (PhP 412/252). He points to chapter 11 of Parain's *Recherches* to substantiate this view (1942, 556 n.35/452 n.1). Parain agrees that thought is linguistic, and defines thinking chiefly as a species of reasoning (Parain 1943, 11). But the charge of intellectualism is less well founded than it might seem. Parain defines silence as 'sensation', a term seemingly proximate to perception (167–68), develops the view that 'silence' or pre-linguistic meaning stands in a dialectical relation with language, and claims that human language cannot possess silence (184). For Parain, speaking subjects are defined by an interchange of 'silent' and 'garrulous' (*loquace*) states (182), and he suggests that poetry is our highest form of expression as embodied and free agents (184). Both issues will occupy Merleau-Ponty in his later work, and suggest that the intellectualist label is somewhat unwarranted (see also Merleau-Ponty's remarks against Sartre's reading of Parain in a 1953 Collège de France seminar [RULL 229–35]).

46. See Husserl 2014, §55. Merleau-Ponty's ontological commitments are considered in more detail in part 3.

47. For more on this topic in Husserl, see Tieszen 1984, and Derrida 1978. In the *Phenomenology*, Merleau-Ponty seems to adopt a loosely intuitionist approach to geometrical, mathematical and formal entities. He stresses the intuitive construction of the formal and claims that geometrical or mathematical proofs are reached by means of abstract performances of motor-intentional capacities (PhP 403–8/443–48).

48. This view also tracks Fink's claim that transcendental subjectivity is essentially a product of its own self-constitution: 'Constituting subjectivity always constitutes itself' (Fink 1995, 107 fn. 374; see also 97).

49. On this point, see also 308–9/348, where Merleau-Ponty contends that we can recognise perceptual illusions because we maintain a link to truth.

50. Barbaras 2004, 16/35.

51. See Hegel 2010, 124/21.142.

52. See for example, lxxix/16, 52–53/78–80.

53. See Geraets 1971, 162, for the connection between transcendentality and fidelity.

54. See PhP 195–96/231, 202/238, 406/505, for more on sedimentation.

55. However, it would be too strong to draw a strict identity between all forms of transcendental and authentic expression (cf. Baldwin 2007, 90). This would dilute the properly phenomenological domain, and would entail that all authentic aesthetic productions (irrespective of their philosophical commitments, if any) are also transcendental. Merleau-Ponty does not seem to want to go this far.

56. A later statement clarifies this point: 'Perception opens us onto a world already constituted, and cannot but reconstitute it. [. . .] Already, the meaning [*sens*] of the perceived is the shadow brought by the operations that we prepare to execute on the things; it is nothing else than our view and situation towards things' (PW 124–25/174–75).

57. For more on 'ambiguity' see 87/114, 172/207, 347/387, 360/402, 401/441, 471/509, and de Waelhens 1967.

58. See, for example, Watson 2009b, 31–32; Rockmore 2011, 193; and Kristensen 2010, 74.

59. Husserl 1973, 58.

60. For the Husserl-Fink relation, see Bruzina 2004.

61. See references to Fink's 'disinterested onlooker' from the *Sixth Cartesian Meditation* (lxxxiv/20–21; Fink 1995, 86), to 'fluid' concepts (553 n.14/423 n.1; Fink 1995, 93), to the 'phenomenology of phenomenology' (PhP 382–83/423–24), and to Fink's view of the reduction (547 n.95/348 n.2). Merleau-Ponty learned about Fink's then-unpublished text through Gaston Berger.

62. Fink 1995, 93.

63. Ibid., 1995, 89.

64. Ibid., 1995, 91.

65. Ibid., 93.

66. Merleau-Ponty occasionally suggests that his analyses of perception and embodiment can be understood as phenomenological reductions, and serve a similar methodological role (see, e.g., 48/74, 53/79).

67. This problem was first identified by Jean Hyppolite during Merleau-Ponty's doctoral defence (PrP 39/97–99).

Part II

4

SCIENTIFIC AND LITERARY EXPRESSION

A review of Merleau-Ponty's post-*Phenomenology* research turns up a wide range of new intellectual pursuits. Some are connected to new professional engagements. After publishing the *Phenomenology*, Merleau-Ponty taught at the Université de Lyon until 1949, where he also served as chair of psychology.[1] He subsequently became chair of child psychology at the Sorbonne. These posts encouraged a deeper engagement with research in empirical psychology and linguistics. During this period, he also pursued a budding research interest in literature and literary expression. In 1952, Merleau-Ponty became chair of philosophy at the Collège de France, a position he would hold until the end of his life. While some thematic interests from his previous positions continued to occupy him, this new appointment coincides with a deeper focus on issues that are now acknowledged to be definitive for his later work.

At the risk of artificially streamlining a fertile and conceptually variegated period of research, two interrelated concerns repeatedly surface in his writings from the late 1940s and early 1950s. Texts from this period demonstrate sustained interest in understanding the phenomenon of 'expression' and in developing a new account of 'metaphysics' or 'rationality' (two terms often used interchangeably). In this chapter, I will clarify some key motivations behind Merleau-Ponty's increasing interest in metaphysics, rationality, scientific and literary modes of expression. I will also sketch some of the provisional conclusions he draws during this transitional period. An exhaustive accounting of the many threads and themes in this period is not possible, but a look at his engagement with empirical psychology, linguistics and the philosophy of literature will clarify what insights he might have adopted from these areas of study. This will help us appreciate why he is more sympathetic to the philosophical implications of literary rather than scientific expression, and will lay the groundwork for the claims of subsequent chapters.

Merleau-Ponty's increasing interest in expression unfolds in the context of a broader attempt to appraise 'metaphysical' thought; that is, systematic pictures or accounts of the structure of reality. Accordingly, I begin with a look at the relation between metaphysics and expression (section 1). While this link is incipiently articulated in this period, it will eventually occupy Merleau-Ponty at length. In his estimation, scientific research has its own expressive ideals, which motivate broader philosophical assumptions about experience (section 2). Saussure's linguistics offers one of the more sophisticated versions of scientific expression, and points to a scientific worldview that remains sensitive to lived experience (section 3). On the whole, however, insights from linguistics and other empirical domains are eclipsed by the philosophical implications of literary expression, as Merleau-Ponty understands them. On this score, Proust and Valéry are particularly important figures (section 4). While Merleau-Ponty's enquiries into expression, science, literature and metaphysics tend towards unification in this period, their deeper links will become clearer in part 3.

1. 'METAPHYSICS' OR 'RATIONALITY' AND 'EXPRESSION'

Merleau-Ponty's reflections on his research at the time of his candidature for the Collège de France (1951–1952) mark some of the most important junctures in his post-*Phenomenology* work. He claims that this research led him to discover a

> 'good ambiguity' in the phenomenon of expression, a spontaneity which accomplishes what appeared to be impossible when we observed only the separate elements, a spontaneity which gathers together the plurality of monads, the past and the present, nature and culture into a single whole. To establish this wonder would be metaphysics itself and would at the same time give us the principle of an ethics. (PrP 11/PD 48)

Some of these allegedly newer findings repeat the *Phenomenology*'s observations about the logic of creative expression (recall that an ability to unify disparate elements into a whole was captured using the concept of 'form' or 'structure' in *Structure*). But unlike in previous work, the ability to 'gather' different elements is thought to have deeper metaphysical implications. Insights from this unificatory logic carry over to the practical realm. We know that Merleau-Ponty did not develop the practical project he refers to in this text (though he makes written interventions about contemporary politics, and offers reflections on Marxism, political theory and the philosophy of history in the mid-1950s).

Merleau-Ponty's decision to invoke the term 'metaphysics' above may appear strange for some readers. The description above suggests that by 'metaphysics' he has in mind a higher-order structure that unifies a series of disparate parts, or a 'plurality of monads'. That these 'monads' include natural, cultural and historical meanings suggests that this higher-order structure is qualitative; that is, that it is on the order of *significations*. A metaphysical structure of this sort contains something like the principle of unity (or what he will later call 'coherence') of a range of phenomena or lived facts. But its unifying, coherence-making characteristics suggest that it has a broader cultural status, and that this somehow governs possible experience. This evaluation is also borne out by his prediction that studies of literature, painting and child expression will lead

> to a reflection on this *transcendental man*, or this 'natural light' common to all, which appears through the movement of history – to a reflection on this Logos which gives us the task of vocalising a hitherto mute world. Finally, they should lead us to a study of the Logos of the perceived world which we encountered in our earliest studies in the evidence of things. Here we rejoin the classical questions of metaphysics, but by following a route which removes from them their character as *problems* – that is to say, as difficulties which could be solved cheaply through the use of a few metaphysical entities constructed for this purpose. (10/47)

Here too, the view of metaphysics referred to is best understood as the study of an intelligible or rational principle, or a 'Logos', which pervades the perceptual and cultural world (these domains will be subsequently explored in tandem). Metaphysics must explain or 'vocalise' this principle, a goal consistent with 'transcendental' analysis, according to Merleau-Ponty's distinctive understanding of the term. On this proposal, metaphysical enquiry overlaps with the study of the rationality or intelligibility of experience – that is, with an attempt to disambiguate the grounds that orient subjective meaning-making in the world. While this thread is not developed at this stage of his career, evidence considered in part 3 will show that this view is developed in a somewhat deflationary direction: metaphysics (or 'ontology') can be understood as a descriptive undertaking, not a speculative or systematic exploration of timeless categories. Like classical metaphysics, phenomenological metaphysics aims to elucidate the structure of the world. But unlike classical metaphysics, to do so, phenomenology chiefly focuses on the structures of conscious experience. These structures are lived phenomena that change and can evolve. Accordingly, this mode of enquiry takes the form of a continual disclosure, rather than a reduction to a set of core principles (e.g., 'atoms', 'void', 'spirit', or 'elementary particles'). On this proposal, metaphysical thinking does not inherit and concern itself with puzzles that admit of conclusive, once-and-for-all solutions.

The philosophical consequences of this approach to metaphysical or rational enquiry are developed in Merleau-Ponty's later projects, but some are already evident in the late 1940s and early 1950s. First, 'metaphysics' (in the sense described above) is tightly linked to everyday life. In the article 'Metaphysics and the Novel', he accepts Péguy's evaluation that '[e]veryone has a metaphysics – explicit or implicit – or he does not exist' (SNS 27/53). Metaphysical assumptions mark the limits of the world's intelligibility; that is, the boundaries of sense and non-sense. For example, common sense or colloquial expressions like 'mind over matter' harbour latent metaphysical assumptions (e.g., that these two categories designate the basic 'stuff' of the world, or that the mind can 'direct' the body). A distinctively phenomenological view of metaphysics is tasked with

> formulating an experience of the world, a contact with the world which precedes all thought *about* the world. Henceforth, whatever is metaphysical in man cannot be linked to something outside his empirical being – to God, to Consciousness; it is in his very being, his loves, hates, in his individual and collective history, that man is meta-

physical, and metaphysics is no longer, as Descartes said, an engagement [*l'affaire*] of a few hours per month; it is present, as Pascal thought, in the least movement of the heart. (28/54–55)

To understand the metaphysical assumptions governing everyday life (e.g., a tacit acceptance of naturalism, or faith in scientific findings), it is necessary to express the sense of lived experience. For experience is the unacknowledged ground from which metaphysical assumptions are nourished.

This points to a second important consequence. If expression is an important feature of metaphysical consciousness, then metaphysics and the philosophy of language are closely related. The details of this relation are not explored in depth in this period. Still, the preface to *Sense and Non-Sense* claims that the goal of forging 'a new idea of reason' is bound up with metaphysics and with the problem of expression (SNS 3/ 8). Rational or metaphysical principles are 'inseparable' from their 'embodiment' or conditions of enunciation: a *logos* is at once a rational principle and an expressive principle (4/9). A metaphysics must articulate the rational principles pervading and unifying the disparate elements of experience. But if metaphysics is inseparable from expression, reflection on the nature of expression is also necessary: metaphysical pursuits require a sophisticated philosophy of language.

The chapter 'The Metaphysical in Man' also draws a link between metaphysics and language. A footnote in this chapter signals that, in this period, Merleau-Ponty has already started to conceive of a new, decidedly metaphysical project. Entitled 'The Origin of Truth', it promises 'a precise description of the passage of perceptual faith into explicit truth as we encounter it on the level of language, concept, and the cultural world' (SNS 94 n.13/188 n.1). In chapter 5 I trace the genesis of this project, and I explore its details in chapter 7. As we will see, the phenomenology of dialogue provided Merleau-Ponty with important paradigms of what would later become central theses of his 'ontological' projects. This confirms the hypothesis that the phenomenology of language is of utmost importance for the development of his later work. This result is already anticipated by the 1951 paper 'On the Phenomenology of Language', given at the first Colloque International de Phénoménologie in Brussels. Scientific and philosophical reflections on language lead Merleau-Ponty to conclude that 'more clearly than any other, this problem requires us to make a decision concerning the relationships between phenomenology and philosophy or metaphysics. For more clearly than any other it takes the form of both a special problem and a problem which contains all the others, including the problem of philosophy' (S 93/151). The philosophy of language is no mere 'regional' domain of enquiry: it concerns nothing less than 'our conception of being' (94/153). For Merleau-Ponty, it is 'absolutely necessary to underline the *philosophical* meaning [*sens*] of the return to speech' (93/151). Key motivations for these conclusions will be explored in the next chapter.

A third important consequence of this broadened view of metaphysics concerns its possible systematic commitments. In 'The Metaphysical in Man', Merleau-Ponty holds that '[u]nderstood in this way, metaphysics is the opposite of system' (94/189). This claim is partly motivated by the view that '[m]etaphysical consciousness has no other objects than those of experience: this world, other people, human history, truth, culture. But instead of taking them as all settled, as consequences with no premises, as if they were self-evident, it rediscovers their fundamental strangeness to me and the miracle of their appearing'. The continuity between metaphysics, experience and expression requires that metaphysical reflection remain open-ended. If experience does not admit of rigidly defined boundaries, and if careful reflection can uncover new layers of lived experience, then metaphysical pictures must follow suit, and systematicity must take a back seat. We will also have occasion to clarify this view in subsequent chapters.

2. FORMAL EXPRESSION

In the *Phenomenology*, Merleau-Ponty argued that science is a mode of perception that has 'forgotten itself'. By studying it, we can better understand interpretations of perceptual experience supported by scientific developments (which may or may not be borne out by the first-personal perspective). This remains an important task in the late 1940s and early 1950s. But he now makes the stronger claim that scientific assumptions also carve out zones of sense-making that implicate our view of 'being'; that is, our understanding of the broader metaphysical principles underlying experience. Importantly, scientific and naturalistic approaches are not strictly equivalent: 'The sciences of man are metaphysical or transnatural in that they cause us to rediscover, along with structure and the understanding of structure, a dimension of being and a type of knowledge which man forgets in the natural attitude' (SNS 92/185). Scientific assumptions support a particular 'dimension of being', or a view of reality, which is more sophisticated and powerful than merely unacknowledged naturalistic assumptions. The term 'dimension' recurs often in Merleau-Ponty's middle and late writings. It partly refers to the meaningful connections obtaining between occurrent and possible experience. An analysis of a particular 'dimension of being' helps us understand how subjects make sense of their world. Attention to a scientific dimension of being isolates the empirically informed conditions that underlie or encourage a scientific worldview, and a related set of expressive operations.

Merleau-Ponty's inquiries into child psychology, linguistics and the human sciences in the late 1940s and early 1950s are too extensive to do justice here.[2] I would like to focus on his more basic aims in claiming that there are distinctive scientific modes of expression. Merleau-Ponty's deeper interest in the sciences (especially linguistics and psychology, but also sociology and anthropology) is motivated in large part by his belief that scientific research (including mathematics) instantiates versions of a formal mode of expression. Like other modes of expression, formal expression attempts to capture the meaning of experience. The first chapter of *The Prose of the World* claims that

> science is not devoted to another world but to our own; in the end it refers to the same things that we live. Science constructs these things by combining pure ideas that it defines, as Galileo constructed the fall of a body on an inclined plane from the ideal case of free fall. But in the end, ideas are always subject to the condition of illuminating the opacity of facts, and the theory of language must become a path to the experience of speaking subjects. The idea of a possible language forms and supports itself on the actual language that we speak, that we are, and linguistics is nothing other than a methodical and intermediary [*médiate*] way of clarifying, through all the other facts of language, this speech that pronounces itself in us, and which, in the very milieu of our scientific work, we remain attached to like an umbilical cord. (PW 15/23–34)

This remark develops a point from the *Phenomenology* by suggesting that scientific findings result not only in a specific attitude to the world, but more narrowly in a view of how 'facts' about the world are best expressed. Despite their non-negligible differences, various domains of scientific enquiry coalesce on a 'formal' approach to articulating the meaning of facts. A core assumption of this approach is that scientific findings should be expressed in an exact and precise language. While this assumption often remains implicit in the specific research programs proper to, for example, mathematics, physics, or linguistics, different scientific domains share the goal of developing a clear, universal and formal language. A governing assumption of scientific enquiry is that indeterminate empirical data are best understood when they are depicted by formal symbols that enjoy universal validity. A formal apparatus is thought to secure the degree of precision needed to understand the structure of the empirical world.

According to Merleau-Ponty, the assumptions governing a formal model of expression are succinctly captured by the algorithm. Every term in an algorithm can be defined with precision. Its rules identify specific and unambiguous methods or steps to resolve a particular problem. Science issues in an 'algorithmic' view of expression. This view sees language as a formal system whose constituent symbols or numbers clearly correspond to distinct objects in the world. Here, *significations* are well defined and contain no ambiguity. The sciences attempt to attach clear and unambiguous meanings to their findings, and establish rigorous relationships between the signs that represent the data in their respective domains of enquiry. Apparently, for Merleau-Ponty this also holds true (but perhaps to a lesser degree) for psychology and linguistics.

Since they take direction from empirical results, the meaning of formal terms may change to reflect new findings. But this is not a concession that meanings in a formal system are ambiguous or indeterminate. Rather, it is consistent with the view that formal terms are defined by convention. Stipulation prevents possible confusion or loss of sense, and a formal system only profits from more exact definitions (an algorithmic view of expression permits this kind of updating). By extension, the component parts of the algorithm 'in themselves say nothing, that therefore they will never say more than what one has made them say by convention [*par convenu*]' (PW 4/9).

One could certainly take exception to this characterisation of science, which might seem unsophisticated or inaccurate. Positivism and conventionalism in logic no longer reign; historically inflected philosophers of science have emphasised the contingency and the historicity of scientific practice and ideals of scientificity. One might also wonder if the relevant object of scientific enquiry is comparable or proximate to anything like perceptual 'meaning' (*le sens*). If science aims to understand matters of fact, some of which we have no determinate experience of (even if we have determinate experience of enquiry into matters of fact), why assume that scientists should take an interest in meaningful categories like expression, or that their research has implications for such questions? Scientific terminology, one might think, is necessarily formal given the nature of the objects of scientific enquiry.

These criticisms may call the tenability of some of Merleau-Ponty's views about science into question, but it is less important for our purposes if his remarks about scientific enquiry or expression are consistent with scientific practice. The key is to understand why he focuses on and ultimately rejects the idea that we should avail ourselves of formal methods of expression when analysing experience. One reason for this is clear enough. The view that symbols or scientific terms get their meaning solely from convention, or that formal terms may be substituted for one another without loss of meaning, brushes up against the assumption that meaning is sedimented. Of course, sedimentation may itself be understood as an expanded account of the conventional constitution of linguistic meaning. But sedimented sense is also thought to genuinely track the meaning of perception: linguistic usage may modify sedimented meanings (in this sense it is conventional), but acts of expression, like linguistic conventions, once took direction from perceptual meanings that were prior to any convention. If linguistic meaning is ultimately a translation of perceptual sense, then formal expressions also depend on it, even if this dependence remains unacknowledged, and even if sedimented (or currently conventional) meanings may be privileged for pragmatic purposes.

The account of empirical expression reviewed in chapter 2 offers more reasons to suspect that an algorithmic or formal account of expression is ill suited for analysing the phenomenon of lived expression. Formal expression ostensibly resolves the ambiguities and indeterminacies of everyday language use. In doing so, however, it suppresses one of its more important features: 'The algorithm, the project of a universal language, is a revolt against language in its existing state and a refusal to depend upon the confusions of everyday language'. The algorithm leaves us with the impression that conventionally or formally defined terms are sufficient and self-standing (and by extension, that the meanings or objects they represent are similarly transparent). A formal language does not seem to depend on any creative or inventive effort on the part of scientists: algorithmic expression trades on the idea that it holds true for everyone and belongs to no one in particular. This is especially evident in mathematics, which 'shows itself to have the character of a construction after the fact, of a reconquest' (124/173).[3] But formal expression gets the order of expressive priority backwards. The conceptual precision found in formal modes of expression (or even in precisely formulated everyday speech) depends on a prior indeterminate and imprecise interpretive activity. Merleau-Ponty's gestural account of expression holds that this is a necessary condition of any expressive modality. This important element of expression remains unacknowledged in scientific practice. It suggests that formal expression is ultimately a derivative mode of expression.

Against its better intentions, 'science directs us more securely to the speaking subject' (20–21/30). At this stage of his career, Merleau-Ponty maintains that formal modes of expression ignore their dependence on primary perceptual experience: 'Nothing limits our power to formalise, that is to say to construct ever more general expressions of the same fact, but, as far as one takes the formalisation, its signification [*signification*] remains as if in delay [*en sursis*]. It has nothing really to say and no truth at all unless we build its superstructures on a visible thing' (106/150–51). The fact that language (as I argued in chapter 3) is a co-constitutive condition of a perceptual foundation further strengthens the claim that formal modes of expression depend on a more fundamental, non-formal ground. This understanding of the relation between formal and non-formal modes of expression is nicely summarised by the following passage:

> In the formula $n/2\,(n+1)$, only terms borrowed from the hypothesis, related through algebraic operations, enter. The new signification [*signification*] is represented by the given signs and significations, without being diverted from their initial meaning [*sens*], as in language [*le langage*]. The algorithmic expression is *exact* on account of

the exact equivalence it establishes between the given relations and those that follow from them. But the new formula is not a formula *of* the new signification; the formula does not truly express it except on the condition that we give, for example, to the term *n* first its ordinal meaning and then its cardinal meaning; but this is possible only if we refer to the configuration of the number series under the new aspect that our interrogation gives it. Now, the restructuring *shift [le bougé]* characteristic of our language appears here. We forget [it] in due course, once we have succeeded in finding the formula, and we then believe in the preexistence of truth. But the shift is always there, and only it gives meaning to the formula. The algorithmic expression is therefore secondary. It is a peculiar instance of speech. (128/180)

This example is supposed to show that there is a deeper creative element at work in ostensibly self-sufficient formal modes of expression. An identity relation between two terms is supported by a subject's ability to recognise those terms as similar or dissimilar. For Merleau-Ponty, qualities like 'similarity' or 'dissimilarity' are not intrinsic to the terms in question; they depend on a subjective standpoint, namely on an expressive or interpretive activity that searches for and draws equivalences and relations between symbols in a formula. But this process only seems clean, precise and exact when it is completed. This is where formal expression begins. As the *Phenomenology* contends, thought has a linguistic structure, and rational reflection is fraught with uncertainties and ambiguities that characterise expressive processes, and which only recede when relations between given terms become clear. Only after a thought process meets its putative goal will such indeterminacies appear superfluous; but they are a necessary precondition. Formal languages overlook their dependence on this deeper expressive ground.

While Merleau-Ponty thinks that formal modes of expression depend on non-formal (or 'creative') conditions, he does not dismiss their value. Formal expression is an interesting site for philosophical exploration in its own right. Despite his criticisms of formal expression, he embraces a position occupied by Parain and Cavaillès – namely, that non-formal or intuitive modes of experience play an important role in formal expression.[4] Indeed, while he does not develop this point in subsequent writings (it may, in fact, conflict with other claims in *The Prose of the World*), he notes that '[w]e are not trying to show that mathematical thought rests upon the sensible but that it is creative'.

(127/177). Mathematics and non-Euclidean geometry are even identified as instances of 'authentic' expression (120–21/168–69, 127–28/178). Non-Euclidean geometry develops a new means of understanding spatial dimensions, and for this reason is a distinctive case of creative expression. Unfortunately, Merleau-Ponty interrupted his work on this project, and he only leaves us with suggestions for how this position might be further developed.[5]

What is more, formal approaches teach us something important about the broader modalities of expression: 'The phenomenon of expression, as it appears in literary speech, is no curiosity or introspective fantasy marginal to the philosophy or science of language, . . . the objective study of language comes across it as well as literary experience, and that these two areas of research are concentric' (15/23). By studying expression using formal or 'objective' methods, we can better understand the distinctive features of literary expression. At the time of his candidature to the Collège de France, he claims that

> an examination of the domain of algorithm would show there too, I believe, the same strange function which is at work in the so-called inexact forms of language. Especially when it is a question of conquering a new domain for exact thought, the most formal thought is always referred to some qualitatively defined mental situation from which it extracts a meaning only by applying itself to the configuration of the problem. The transformation is never a simple analysis, and thought is never more than relatively formal. (PrP 8/44)

This intimates that creative scientific expression presupposes a logic that properly belongs to non-formal, creative modes of expression. Even if this remark suggests some uncertainty about the relations of priority at work here (I will return to this point below), it is clear that studying formal modes of expression is of value in its own right, and that it helps us better understand the distinctive structure of properly creative modes of expression.

3. EXPRESSION IN LINGUISTICS: SAUSSURE

After the publication of the *Phenomenology*, Merleau-Ponty's interest in linguistics increases.[6] At Lyon he taught a course entitled Communication et Langage (1947–1948).[7] A significant part of the course was devoted to arguing for the limits of positivistic and reductionist approaches to language promoted by some theorists in linguistics. Still, findings from linguistics present a special case. Although linguistics adopts basic features of formal expression, it also offers insights that phenomenology can profit from. In his Lyon course, Merleau-Ponty is clear that he does not reject formal methods outright. Instead, he claims that they must be supplemented with reflections from lived experience.

Merleau-Ponty's engagement with linguistics is extensive and cannot be considered in full here, but some of his more important conclusions should be noted. In the Lyon course, he contends that the close relation between language and thought (argued for using independent premises in the *Phenomenology*) finds empirical confirmation in linguistic research. This theme was subsequently taken up in a 1949 to 1950 Sorbonne seminar entitled Consciousness and Language Acquisition. This course also explores the relation between linguistics and philosophy. In contrast to positivist accounts, Merleau-Ponty attempts to approach the problem of language acquisition and expression with help from reflections on intersubjectivity, by appeal to linguistics (especially the work of Jakobson, Guillaume and Saussure), and with reference to literature. These fields, he thinks, confirm his own phenomenological conclusions (CPP 4–5).

This course also examines theories of language acquisition in children. Merleau-Ponty argues that it makes little sense to adhere to rigid stages of progressive language development (13–14). Here is a summary of some of his more important conclusions:

> From the beginning, it appears that all possibilities are inscribed in the child's expressive manifestations. There is nothing absolutely new; instead there are anticipations, regressions, the permanence of archaic elements in new forms. This development where, on the one hand, everything is sketched out in advance and, on the other, it proceeds by a series of discontinuous progressions, denies both intellectualist and empiricist theories. The Gestaltists have helped us

understand the problem better by explaining how in decisive periods of development, the child appropriates linguistic 'Gestalten', general structures, not through an intellectual effort or by an immediate imitation. (13–14)

These insights motivate further analyses of phoneme acquisition and language-use imitation by children. Jakobson's account of phoneme acquisition must be rejected on the grounds that it relies too heavily on representation. Language use might appeal to representative structures, but it is also 'self-expression' and 'an appeal to others', two features that are better addressed using phenomenological methodology (20). With respect to the important question of imitation in expression, Merleau-Ponty finds Guillaume's account superior to alternatives, insofar as it too does not rely on the category of representation, and because it is informed by reflections on intentional directedness to objects (21–22). During childhood we are primarily directed towards others and not towards ourselves, a conclusion that the phenomenon of pronoun confusion seems to confirm (24). On the whole, Merleau-Ponty thinks that these problems, which implicate basic philosophical questions of intersubjectivity, are better addressed from the phenomenological perspectives of Husserl and Scheler (in this course he favours Husserl) (26–35). Other parts of the 1949 course are dedicated to analyses of language acquisition at later stages of childhood (35–40), to language pathologies like aphasia (40–50), to an overview of the concepts of sound, grammar and semantics in linguistics (50–62), to Saussure's account of signs (64–66), and the course concludes with brief reflections on its consequences for the philosophy of history (66–67).

The claim that phenomenological methods should be favoured in the study of language use in child development is also stressed in the 1951 to 1952 course Method in Child Psychology:

> A child psychology chiefly concerned with the child's understanding would be extremely artificial. For example, when considering the child's acquisition of language, we must recognize that the child's understanding of language is not in question; instead we must analyse the practice of language – a practice that can lead to some very striking modes of expression (since they do not belong to 'objective' language). (386)

As in the *Phenomenology*, notes from this course contend that a study of language use by children encourages us to revise overly conceptual or 'objective' formal models of communication (cf. PhP 182–83/216–18). That there are distinctive practices of expression exhibited by children, a special kind of dependence on others, and an intimate, non-representational relation between language and thought is suggested by phenomenological and empirical observations. Non-formal methods, however, are better able to decode the properly lived nature of the phenomena in question.

Nevertheless, Merleau-Ponty maintains (following an approach already sketched in *Structure*) that scientific findings, especially in linguistics and psychology, have direct philosophical bearing: 'The progress of psychology and linguistics holds precisely insofar as, by revealing the *speaking subject* and speech in the present, they find a way to ignore the alternatives of the occurrent and the possible, the constituted and the constituting, of facts and conditions of possibility, of contingency and reason, of science and philosophy' (PW 37–38/54). In psychology, concepts like 'field' and 'behaviour', and a new focus on the phenomenal (in Koffka and Guillaume, for example), have also dulled the classic opposition between psychology and philosophy (CPP 337–42). These scientific developments blur the distinction between the conceptual and the natural, because they revise the antinomies of the 'subjective and the object', 'of the body and consciousness', 'of individuality and generality', and 'of the simple and the complex' (341–42).

Above all, Merleau-Ponty singles out Saussure's findings, which he thinks have distinct philosophical import. Saussure demonstrates

> that one can renounce an eternal philosophy without falling into irrationalism. Saussure shows admirably that if words and, more generally, language [*la langue*] considered across time – or, as he says, according to diachronically – in effect offer an example of all semantic slippages, this is not because the history of the word or of language [*la langue*] make up their current meaning [*sens*]. (PW 22/33)

Unlike the formality characteristic of mathematics or the sciences, Saussure's emphasis on speech points to a logic of semantic invention and a transformation of meaning that is more sophisticated than standard versions of formal substitution or equivalence. Saussure demonstrates that expression can be creative without sacrificing its inner coherence, and without disfiguring the meanings of the individual terms out of which new expressions are generated.

Remarks to this effect are not uncommon in Merleau-Ponty's writings in the late 1940s and early 1950s. Saussure comes in for high praise. These remarks have justifiably attracted commentators' attention.[8] Some scholars contend that Merleau-Ponty's reading of Saussure fundamentally transformed the trajectory of his career. It is argued, for example, that 'the flesh' and related later concepts originate in Merleau-Ponty's reading of Saussure, and are effectively philosophical (or 'ontological') translations of Saussurean positions.[9]

Undeniably, Merleau-Ponty's engagement with Saussure (which effectively introduced Saussure to the French intellectual scene) led him to adopt some of Saussure's distinctive insights. Still, in my estimation, the conclusion that the motivations behind Merleau-Ponty's later work can be adequately explained in light of his reading of Saussure is too strong, especially when the full range of textual evidence is considered. My reconstruction of the genesis of Merleau-Ponty's later ontology in chapter 5 is the strongest argument I can offer in support of this claim. While I do not think that Saussure is the key catalyst for Merleau-Ponty's later projects, it is still important to carefully consider what positions he might have adopted from Saussure. Below, I review four points of Saussurean influence, and offer an estimation of their significance for understanding Merleau-Ponty's philosophy of language.

3.1 'Langue' and 'Parole'

While he does not directly name Saussure in the *Phenomenology*, Merleau-Ponty calls attention to his important and 'famous' distinction between *'langue'* and *'parole'* (PhP 202/238). For Saussure, *'langue'* refers to the diachronical and enduring structural features of language, which make particular acts of speech (*parole*) possible.[10] As Merleau-Ponty reads him in *The Prose of the World*, 'Saussure inaugurates next to the linguistics of language [*langue*], which makes it seem, at the limit, that language is a series of chaotic events, a linguistics of speech [*parole*], which must show in it, at each moment an order, a system, [and] a totality without which communication and the linguistic community would be impossible' (PW 23/33).

As we saw in chapter 2, Merleau-Ponty seemed to accept Saussure's position that semantic content in a language is a function of differences between terms (alternatively, that linguistic units 'mean nothing by themselves'), and that it takes on a more determinate meaning in a context of use (PhP 408/448). He transformed this into a phenomenological argument for a kind of semantic holism (with the sentence as a basic unit), in which meaning is formed through a complex of embodied and sedimented meaning (PW 28/40–41; PhP 408/449). The distinction between *langue* and *parole* is also important for his gestural account, insofar as it divides conventional meaning (*la signification*) from its uttered spatio-temporal instances (*parole*). Both layers must be taken into account in a holistic, gestural theory of expression and speech. While the distinction between *langue* and *parole* is itself a significant discovery that should be adopted, it paves the way for other important claims.

3.2 '*Parole*' and Dialogue

According to Merleau-Ponty, Saussure's distinction between the diachronic and the synchronic allows one to separate these different levels of language, and to study each on its own (PW 22/33). Saussure's distinction encourages the study of speech, conversation and linguistic usage, and is therefore praiseworthy. That dialogue or *parole* can become its own proper area of study is particularly important for Merleau-Ponty. He builds on this insight by offering his own distinctive interpretation of dialogue. Some remarks seem to suggest that Merleau-Ponty did not think this was possible before the advent of Saussure's structural linguistics, or, at the very least, that henceforth any study of speech will presuppose its findings. Of central importance is the fact that Saussure's account of speech does not rely solely on historical or formal features of language. By encouraging an analysis of synchronic structures or *parole*, Saussure's linguistics lay the groundwork for a phenomenology of speech and dialogue.

3.3 'Diacritical' Meaning-Formation

The Consciousness and Language Acquisition course devotes significant attention to Saussure's theory of signs (CPP 64–66). It credits him with discovering the 'diacritical' nature of signs. According to Merleau-Ponty, a diacritical view holds that signs get their meaning by being differentiated from other signs. This may occur phonetically (e.g., through sound) or graphically (e.g., by placing an accent above a word). The 1953 article 'Indirect Language and the Voices of Silence' (the sole excerpt from *The Prose of the World* published in Merleau-Ponty's lifetime) identifies the source of this discovery: 'What we have learned from Saussure is that, taken singly, signs do not signify anything, and that each one of them does not so much express a meaning as mark a divergence of meaning between itself and other signs' (S 39/63).

Some subsequent writings suggest that Saussure's view that linguistic differentiation is a source of meaning, directly informs Merleau-Ponty's account of perceptual meaning, and inspires some important tenets of his later work. For example, the 1953 lecture course *Le monde sensible et le monde de l'expression* makes the strong claim that 'Every sign is diacritical' (MSME 206; see also NC 127). *The Visible and the Invisible* holds that the *Gestalt* is 'a diacritical, oppositional, relative system whose pivot is the *Etwas*, the thing, the world' (VI 206/256), claims to 'describe perception as a diacritical, relative, oppositional system' (213/263, 233/282), announces an intention to offer a 'critique of the positive signification (differences between significations)', and claims that it will define 'signification as a separation [*écart*], theory of predication – founded on this diacritical conception' (224/273). These remarks suggest that Saussure's view of meaning-formation informs a number of Merleau-Ponty's later claims about the structure of the world, meaning and perception.

3.4 Institution, Rationality and History

Merleau-Ponty also credits Saussure with developing an incipient view of rationality, capable of integrating historical, perceptual and contextual data. Recall that these tenets make up the outline of the view of 'metaphysics' favoured in texts from the late 1940s. Saussure's linguistics inform Merleau-Ponty's search for a new account of reason and meaning by attesting to the possibility of a phenomenology of speech suitably sensitive to its historical presuppositions: 'With Saussure, the envelopment of language by language is just that which saves rationality, because it is no longer comparable to the objective movement of the observer, who compromises his observation of other movements; on the contrary, it attests to a permanent unity between the I that speaks and the language [*le langage*] that I speak' (PW 24/35). Saussure advances a view of semantic regimentation that takes account of the local, contingent activity of subjects speaking in the present, while recognising that speech acts depend on an inherited linguistic system. For Merleau-Ponty, this suggests a way to define rational structures or conditions for the possibility of experience that does not sacrifice perceivers' or speakers' freedom and creativity. It points to one interpretation of how contingency may still be present in structure. Recall that a key benefit of linguistics is that it ignores 'the alternatives of the existing and possible, of the constituted and the constituting, of facts and the conditions of possibility, of contingency and reason' (37–38/54).

In his 'Inaugural Lecture' to the Collège de France, Merleau-Ponty repeats the claim from the Consciousness and Language Acquisition course that one 'could have sketched a new philosophy of history' by taking direction from Saussure's linguistics (IPP 55/64). Saussurean tenets also point towards an account of institution, a concept that plays an important role in Merleau-Ponty's transition to his later work (see chapter 6). His engagement with Saussure overlaps with the early stages of his research into the concept of institution, which informed Merleau-Ponty's view of how diachronic or instituted meaning is instantiated in the present. As early as 1949, he claimed that

> linguistics is the most rigorous examination of language as an institution; we cannot conceive of a philosophy of language that is not obligated to collect and articulate on the basis of its own truths the truths that linguistics establishes. If we consider philosophy to be the elucidation of human experience, and science as an essential moment of that experience, the dilemma disappears. (CPP 53)

While Merleau-Ponty's renewed reflections on Husserl's account of institution or *Stiftung* would arguably play a more important role for his later account, Saussure's thought (and linguistics, more generally) also aided this effort, by offering one take on how instituted or diachronic meanings are acquired and modified by speaking subjects in the present.

The evidence above leaves no doubt that Merleau-Ponty profited from his engagement with Saussure. However, it does not lead to the conclusion that Saussure is the central figure behind his account of phenomenological expression and sense-making in post-*Phenomenology* research. While Merleau-Ponty praises Saussure for defending the possibility of studying dialogue in its own right, he also credits this to Husserl (whose concept of the 'living present' is of particular importance), and to the Dutch linguist Hendrik Pos (PW 25/37). Of course, his own account of expression in the *Phenomenology* (which does not rely on Saussure's premises) also paves the way for a more sophisticated account of *parole*. The account he eventually advances is consistent with his reading of Saussure, but none of its premises reflect Saussurean tenets. Different intellectual progenitors of a phenomenology of dialogue are identified in this period. At this level of abstraction, emphasis is largely a matter of philosophical preference. Detailed analysis of the substance of Merleau-Ponty's account of dialogue and speech, however, is a surer guide, and casts some doubt on its alleged Saussurean origins (see chapter 5).

What is more, as with other philosophical, literary or scientific figures, it is often difficult to reconcile the spirit of Merleau-Ponty's interpretation with the letter of Saussure's texts. Like his readings of other figures, Merleau-Ponty sometimes imputes to Saussure more than can be found in him. For example, he stresses the importance of the *langue-parole* distinction, but the account of communication and language use in the *Phenomenology* is not guided by it in practice. His use of the concept of the 'diacritical' is also instructive. Merleau-Ponty claims that it informs key positions of his later work, but by my count, it surfaces once in Saussure's *Course*, and in an unrelated context.[11] This is not to deny that Saussure's account of meaning and difference was not important for Merleau-Ponty, but it does put some stress on the idea that there is a worked-out account of the diacritical in Saussure (*versus* an account of linguistic differentiation). Merleau-Ponty does not quote from other texts to substantiate his interpretation of this concept. In what sense, then, could Saussure's doctrine of the diacritical nature of signs be said to have influenced Merleau-Ponty? His broad application of the term to domains that have little to do with its original usage (e.g., the claim that the perceptual *écart* is diacritical) suggests an inventive, original and selective reading on Merleau-Ponty's part, with faint links to Saussure.

A broader methodological point should also give us pause. Since his early work, Merleau-Ponty has attempted to bridge the gap between philosophy and empirical science. As far as linguistics is concerned, notes in Consciousness and Language Acquisition contend that 'linguistics, in principle, studies language objectively; in other words, it considers language as it is, "behind the backs" (Hegel) of the subjects who speak it. But we will see that in fact the objective method converges with a direct reflection on language' (CPP 53). Despite this 'objective' mode of enquiry, linguistics should inform the phenomenology of language. The former is but a 'rigorous' way of clarifying experiences treated by the latter (PW 15/23–24). This is an instance of the view that formal and phenomenological modes of enquiry are 'concentric'.

But even if (Saussure's) linguistics should inform phenomenology, this will necessarily encounter nontrivial limits. In the 1951 to 1952 Sorbonne course The Problem of Others, Merleau-Ponty is said to have stated that he 'will use the so-called structuralist conceptions of language insofar as they implicitly contribute to the philosophical intuitions that concern our subject' (CPP 457). Remarks from the 1954 course *Le problème de la parole*, which also engages with Saussure and repeats many of the points considered above, feature a similarly cautious approach: 'The role of linguistics is not to give us a philosophy, but to prepare us to see a philosophy in it, by showing us the partiality (*Einseitigkeit*) of those that we do have' (BNF Ms. Vol. XII 13/13r).[12] While Merleau-Ponty again praises Saussure for his observations about speech, he also notes that there are 'naturally' clear limitations to his account (22v).

These remarks suggest a more tempered approach to Saussure. Even with a creative interpretation of the diacritical, there is no question of assimilating Saussure's linguistics and phenomenology. Each domain has its proper methodology and its own presuppositions. Saussure does not help us develop the basic building blocks upon which to construct an analysis of language, even if he paves the way for a study of linguistic usage. Amidst the praise, this deeper methodological point is easy to overlook. Some textual evidence suggests that Saussure's findings are secondary to a properly phenomenological account (indirect textual evidence strengthens this point). A note from *The Visible and the Invisible* claims that

> the Saussurean analysis of the relations between signifiers and the relations from signifier to signified and between significations (as differences between significations) confirms and rediscovers the idea of perception as a divergence [*écart*] by relation to a level, that is, the idea of primordial Being, of the Convention of conventions, of the speech before speech. (VI 201/252)

Hindsight may have led Merleau-Ponty to be more cautious than he was during the writing of *The Prose of the World*. The implication here is that Saussure's discoveries corroborate findings uncovered by phenomenological analyses of speech. Saussure's account of signs, and his view that meaning is a function of differences between terms, are the empirical-linguistic confirmation or 'rediscovery' of independent philosophical observations. Above, the '*écart*' of perception (sometimes read as a direct translation of Saussure's claim about difference) is not clearly linked to findings from linguistics. In fact, Merleau-Ponty claims that lived speech constitutes the putatively intersubjective diacritical system, not the other way around (175/227). Saussure's point about linguistic differentiation is a secondary and not a guiding thread for a phenomenological account of speech, even if the latter undoubtedly benefits from his observations about *parole*. Further, the text above challenges the basic Saussurean claim (though one not limited to him) that linguistic meaning can be defined by appeal to convention. Merleau-Ponty observes elsewhere that there are 'non-language significations' in perception, which points to a non-conventional basis to linguistic (and perceptual) meaning, further distancing him from an account that relies on convention (171/223).

4. 'INDIRECT' OR 'OPERANT' EXPRESSION: PROUST AND VALÉRY

While formal and scientific reflections on expression offer important insights that phenomenology can profit from, non-formal modes of expression have more direct philosophical import. Literature is the most important mode of non-formal expression examined in writings after the *Phenomenology*. Merleau-Ponty is clear that he wants to bridge and not eliminate the important differences between philosophy and literature (SNS 26/53). Like his engagements with empirical science and formal expression, the goal is not to assimilate the two fields. Still, while formal expression shares the goal of clarifying experience, literature goes further:

> When one is concerned with giving voice to the experience of the world and showing how consciousness escapes into the world, one can no longer credit oneself with attaining a perfect transparence of expression. Philosophical expression assumes the same ambiguities as literary expression, if the world is such that it cannot be expressed except in 'stories' and, as it were, pointed at. (28/55)

Literary language is characterised by non-categorical modes of expression. More often than not, insights into experience must be suggested, and cannot be transparently stated. A non-categorical or suggestive mode of expression is thought to reflect the structure of experience. Since *Structure*, Merleau-Ponty has claimed that experience is characterised by ambiguity: its meaning is often difficult to decode and can be construed otherwise. Formal modes of expression introduce artificial degrees of precision not obtained in perpetual experience. As we will see in subsequent chapters, the view that literary and philosophical expression are proximate to one another in this respect encourages Merleau-Ponty to embrace more creative modes of philosophical expression. Émile Bréhier derisively suggested that this feature already characterises the *Phenomenology*, when he claimed that '[Merleau-Ponty's] philosophy results in a novel' (PrP 30/78).

Merleau-Ponty's evaluation of some basic similarities between philosophy and literature leads to heightened interest in literary modes of expression. Of particular importance is the relationship between author, reader and world created by a literary work. Remarks during his candidature to the Collège de France note that when studying literature,

> it is easier to show that language is never the mere clothing of a thought which otherwise possesses itself in fully clarity. The meaning of a book is given, in the first instance, not so much by its ideas as by a systematic and unexpected variation of the modes of language, of narrative, or of existing literary forms. [T]his particular modulation of speech — if the expression is successful – is assimilated little by little by the reader, and it gives him access to a thought to which he was until then indifferent or even opposed. Communication in literature is not the simple appeal on the part of the writer to meanings which would be part of an *a priori* of the mind; rather, communication arouses these meanings in the mind through enticement and a kind of oblique action. [. . .] the writer is himself a kind of new idiom, constructing itself, inventing ways of expression, and diversifying itself according to its own meaning. Perhaps poetry is only that part of literature where this autonomy is ostentatiously displayed. (PrP 8/44)

In this period Merleau-Ponty often approaches language use *tout court* from the perspective of dialogue (literature is initially understood as a mode of 'communication'). The passage claims that literary language is a distinctive mode of expression because it manages to create its own universe of meaning, and inaugurates readers into it. It also confirms a view encountered in chapter 2, namely that language use is poorly understood if it is ultimately defined as a mere translation of mental content. Instead, literary language invents an imaginary structure in a work, which has its own internal logic and hermeneutical resources. A writer invents a 'new idiom', a remark reminiscent of the account of 'authentic' expression advanced in the *Phenomenology*. But this description also suggests that the transformations effected by literary works enjoy some degree of 'autonomy'. By contrast, authentic expression was thought to be continuous with perpetual experience. But literary expression seems to feature a special or distinctive transformation of a writer's or reader's world, which can be understood separately from perceptual meaning.

The concept of 'indirect' or 'operant' expression is of central importance for understanding the distinctive features of literary expression identified here. This concept is often associated with the terms 'tacit' (*tacite*) 'lateral' (*latéral*) and 'speaking' (*parlant*). In effect, it is a development of the *Phenomenology*'s account of *parole parlante*. Insofar as literature is concerned, expression is indirect because it is non-categorical, nonanalytical, and non-thetic. The meanings found in literary texts cannot be reduced to expressions of the form 'S is p', or to equivalent, categorical uses of language. Instead, literary language 'gropes around': it employs suggestive and implicative modes of signification (MPR 79/36). To say that artistic expression is indirect is not to say that it is wholly indeterminate. It is to accept that a painting or a novel's meaning cannot be discovered by searching for authorial intention, by focusing on its received meaning, or by isolating some specific meanings or facts about the work. These features are important, but as the passage above suggests, indirect expression also invites readers or viewers to take up and develop the meanings they initially find in a work, a process supported by its distinctive structure. In contrast to the indicative or 'thetic' expression characteristic of science (and some philosophy), literary '[l]anguage speaks peremptorily when it gives up trying to express the thing itself'; that is, when it does not aim for a level of clarity and precision that would terminate further interpretive or expressive efforts (S 44/71). If works of art also require our interpretive efforts, their meaning remains open or 'incomplete'. Accordingly, what 'is proper to expression is to never be more than approximate' (233/380). To better understand how indirect expression functions in literature, it will help to first consider related instances of indirect expression in visual art, and then turn to the versions developed by Valéry and Proust.[13]

4.1 On Painting and Literature

In this period, Merleau-Ponty often likens expression in literature to that in painting. Already in 1945, he compares Cézanne's attempts to express the perceived world to the attempt to capture and render its meaning in language:

> Just as words name – that is, grasp in its nature and place before us as a recognisable object what appears in a confused way – the painter, said Gasquet, 'objectifies', 'projects', and 'fixes'. Just as words do not resemble what they designate, a picture is not a *trompe l'oeil*. Cézanne, in his own words, 'writes in painting what is not yet painted, and turns it into painting absolutely'. We forget the viscous, equivocal appearances, and by means of them we go straight to the things they present. (MPR 77/32–33)

Like writers, painters attempt to convert lived experience into a more permanent form, without sacrificing its richer meaning (78/35; see also PhP 203/239). To do so, visual artists produce new meanings out of well-established or 'sedimented' sense. Much like a writer, 'Cézanne's difficulties are those of the first word' (MPR 79/36).[14]

In 'Cézanne's Doubt', Merleau-Ponty claims that the painter (here, Cézanne) engages in an attempt to express the world or 'what exists'. Cézanne attempts to remain faithful to our lived perspective. His paintings do so by suspending the typical assumptions we rely on to understand it in natural and theoretical attitudes (e.g., scientific assumptions, an account of perspective, art-critical assumptions). This is why some of Cézanne's depictions of human subjects appear strange or unfamiliar. According to Merleau-Ponty, these depictions aim to capture the emergence or birth of landscapes, objects and people, at the intersection of vision, tradition, science and nature. On the canvas, painters attempt to express the nascent emergence of lived meaning we first encounter in perception, which we may have been unable to fully grasp or understand.[15] Merleau-Ponty is of the view that art, in general, serves this basic function.

The connection between painting and language is further explored in work from the early 1950s (PW 88/124, 99/140). Like literary language, poetry 'melts' or takes apart ordinary conventions. Similarly, Modern painters (the focus of Merleau-Ponty's remarks in these texts) 'rearrange the prosaic world' (63/89).[16] Given the dynamism and incompleteness of perceptual life, with its ability to open us to new perspectives, 'a world which announces itself in lightning signs as a spoken word or as an arabesque, why should the expression of the world be subjected to the prose of the *senses* or of the concept? It must be poetry; that is, it must completely awaken and recall our sheer power of expressing beyond things already said or seen' (S 52/83–84). Here, 'poetry' is understood more literally as *poiesis* or 'invention', and, in particular, as an ability to invent modes of expression that reveal the world in a new light. The painter's creative act is similar to the writer's in that both develop a 'tacit', 'lateral or oblique' form of expression that is built out of already existing forms of expression (46/75).

Paintings and literary works also develop a distinctive 'style'. Artistic style is the crystallisation of a particular perspective or a way of seeing the world. An artistic style shapes 'hollows' in the world, or norms for viewers and readers (PW 63/89). Borrowing an expression from André Malraux that often surfaces in texts of this period, style amounts to a 'coherent deformation' of existing meaning.[17] An artist's perspective, and our reflections on her work, trains us to begin seeing the world anew (89–90/126–27; cf. S 77/124–25). By forming a new interpretation of a literary work or a painting, we can acquire a new understanding of experience (S 53/85).

The fundamental similarities between painting and literature allow us to speak of a 'language of painting' (S 55/88, 75–76/122). When noting this connection, many commentators have stressed the importance of visual art.[18] But evidence suggests that the structural logic of indirect expression is properly a linguistic phenomenon. Some commentators have reversed this more fundamental priority.[19] But Merleau-Ponty is clear that 'painting as a whole gives itself as an aborted effort to say something that always remains to be said. Here one sees what is proper to language' (PW 99/140); that 'the arts of language go much farther toward true creation' (S 79/128); and that insofar as the all-important question of sense-transformation in aesthetic expression is concerned, nothing equals the 'ductility' of speech (80–81/129–30).

In chapter 5 and in part 3, Merleau-Ponty's deeper motivations for prioritising language will become clearer. But two reasons for this priority can already be adduced. First, for Merleau-Ponty painting is 'mute' (PW 110/156). In this context, this means that more effort on our part (or guidance from others, in the form of historical or critical instruction) is required to understand the novelty of painting. Even if understanding the novelty of literature is by no means easy, literary works are more accessible to us because they are built out of a 'material' we are already familiar with; namely, human language (S 110/156). This increases the likelihood that readers will grasp a writer's novel contributions, and the new perspectives that issue from them. Comparatively, it is harder to grasp the novelty of painting.

Second, indirect expression in literature better supports Merleau-Ponty's underlying goal of describing our experience of the world. The *Phenomenology* held that phenomenology is a transformative enterprise (PhP lxxxv/21). It discloses the world anew by articulating descriptions that grant us access to meanings we might have overlooked. The concepts and vocabulary that enter into phenomenological descriptions are therefore of utmost importance. As we saw in Merleau-Ponty's reflections on formal expression, a choice of terminology can open or occlude possible 'dimensions' of being. While the reasons for this shift will become clearer in chapter 6, he increasingly argues that perceptual experience can be better accounted for using a more poetic, allusive, suggestive and ultimately an indirect mode of expression. This position leads him to adopt the view that description must rely on creative resources. As we saw in chapter 3, this view was only implicitly articulated in the *Phenomenology*, and led to a fundamental tension with phenomenology's more literal descriptive aims. His choice to openly embrace the creative elements of description signals the increasing importance of the philosophy of literature (a domain of the philosophy of language) for phenomenology. With a look at his reading of Proust and Valéry, we can begin to get a better understand of the motivations that occasioned this important shift in Merleau-Ponty's view of expression and ultimately of phenomenology itself.

4.2 Valéry and 'the Voice'

For Merleau-Ponty, Valéry's writing is a paradigmatic case of indirect expression. Valéry's distinctive account of literary expression is sometimes offered in the guise of an explicitly 'poetic' form. But he is clear that this should be understood on a continuum with indirect literary expression (as I noted above, 'poetry' is used in the more basic sense of 'invention') (S 234/382). The 1953 Collège de France course *Recherches sur l'usage littéraire du langage* develops Merleau-Ponty's account of indirect expression, with particular focus on Valéry (and Stendhal).[20] Of special importance is Valéry's concept of 'the voice' (*la voix*). In *Tel Quel*, he claims that objects become accessible to us through their linguistic expression, and especially through the poetic voice.[21] *La Pythie* concludes with an ode to Saint Language, its 'Wisdom' and 'august Voice'. As Merleau-Ponty reads it, 'The voice of poetry is a voice of things, the pronunciation of what they want to say' (RULL 138). It is a 'manner of deciphering [*déchiffrer*] the object so as to be with it' (140).

Of central interest is how literary language is to go about documenting experience, especially the meanings of material objects. According to Merleau-Ponty, Valéry thinks that the literary and poetic registers do not aim to record correct or factual statements about experience (as formal modes of expression might), even if they succeed in doing so. Instead, they seek to 'let language live. To let it live in itself' (76). Literary expression assumes a freer form, since the body, the spirit and other themes of literary writing amount to a domain of 'non-things' (106). Unlike a 'mere' thing, the non-things of literature do not have fixed properties that can be captured in a precise, formal language, and whose truth conditions can be rigorously enumerated. On this view, the writer's task is to develop a mode of articulating 'the silence of the world of non-things'.

'The voice' is Valéry's proposal for how this should unfold. The voice attempts to return to the world of pre-linguistic expression, before a turn to the 'universal', or to the more regimented domain of theoretical reflection (121). To do so, the voice must not become overly abstract or conceptual (75, 106). It is necessary to suspend 'belief' (*croyance*) if literary language is to faithfully describe objects (108). As Merleau-Ponty reads him, for Valéry '[p]oetry is voice, creating [*faire*], not saying [*dire*]' (137). While literary expression is inventive, it still aims to express an object's properties. But a literary account of objects is not a one-to-one translation of perceptual qualities into a determinate linguistic form. The meaning of everyday material objects can only be understood if the language in which they are stated is sufficiently creative and allusive.

This entails that a writer must develop a new literary vocabulary, which she shares with her readers. By employing newfangled expressions, the poetic voice promises to bring unrecognised features of objects into relief, without categorically stating them (149). To do so, a writer draws on and modifies existing linguistic conventions.[22] Even if the voice is the result of a writer's creative efforts, it still expresses meanings that are thought to be obtained in experience, whose contours readers could have encountered. The poetic saying of things, 'the cries, the tears, the kisses, the sighs' of everyday life, is undertaken for the sake of communicating or sharing a writer's point of view with others (109, 112, 114).[23] The work establishes a direct relation between reader and writer, even if Valéry's poet does not attempt to describe or recreate the internal mental life that supported her poetic composition.[24] Instead, the voice encourages readers to interpret its view of objects, or to take up the 'musicalisation' heard when reading a poem or literary work aloud (149).[25] The 1951 article 'Man and Adversity' contends that for Valéry, 'the essence of poetic language' is that it can produce meanings not by means of 'words as a result of the lexical significations assigned to them in language', but by establishing seemingly contingent or accidental connections with objects, which underdetermine the structure and claims of a work, inviting readers to bring their own interpretations to bear on its account of experience (S 234/ 382). This is made possible by the non-rigid, indirect expressive form that characterises the literary voice.

4.3 Proust and Literary Description

Merleau-Ponty's reading of Valéry stresses that indirect literary invention fashions a creative vocabulary that can state the meaning of objects in unexpected ways. The written text allows other subjects to corroborate, criticise or inhabit the distinctive view of experience articulated by a writer. This suggests that there might be a distinctive kind of literary or poetic truth or objectivity that literary works establish, which is unlike more standard definitions (e.g., correspondence) (RULL 187, 210, 213). But this result also leads him to wonder: if 'by definition literature goes beyond verified truth [*la vérité vérifiée*], does it not risk being simply subjectivity, [a] phantasmagory of real relations, their sublimation? How to distinguish the sur-rational [*le surrationnel*] from the irrational'? (153). While the articulations of the voice may surmount some of the limitations of indicative modes of expression, and can reveal new and publicly accessible meanings, an account of literary expression whose insights are subject to greater intersubjective evaluation is welcome.

For Merleau-Ponty, Proust offers just such an account. Like Valéry (or Stendhal), Proust holds that things or objects 'call' or invite subjects to articulate them using definite modes of expression: 'the inside of things is speech' (BNF Ms. Vol. XII 95r/6).[26] As he notes in the 1953–1954 course *Le problème de la parole*, in this respect Proust goes further than other writers. Proust shows how creative literary expression can become a genuine description of experience, which becomes accessible to a wider range of perspectives.[27] Merleau-Ponty reserves high praise for Proust: 'No one has gone further than Proust in fixing the relations between the visible and the invisible, in describing an idea that is not the contrary of the sensible, that is its lining and its depth' (VI 149/193).

As Merleau-Ponty reads him, Proust attempts to understand 'the transcendence of things', or the appearance of objects in the world (BNF Ms. Vol. XII 94v/5). While we encounter objects with a determinate meaning in everyday experience, reflective activity is required to understand just what it is that we see or hear. For Proust, '[t]he world is not given as if already there', and deliberate interpretive activity is needed to understand it (97r/8). Proust's literature attempts to fix 'this medium where things are born – for us, where we live, and which knowledge surveys' (99r/1). He takes 'the appearance of the world in transcendence as a theme, the structure perspective-reality'.

Indeed, while creation is part and parcel of any literary work, Proust is equally interested in description, to a greater degree than Valéry. Proust's literature aims to 'constitute a languagely ensemble [*un ensemble langagier*] of the same sort as the pre-logical unity of our life' (115r/3). Fidelity, then, is a more pressing concern for Proust. His novels construct a structure (or 'ensemble') that reflects the meanings encountered in everyday experience, and the modes of conscious experience that characterise our relation to the world. For him, literature is 'a commentary on the world that precedes the written, [or] objectification (that which occurs "in the head")' (99r/1). In contrast to more objective or formal forms of writing, literature describes the emergence and appearance of things in a way that does not sacrifice their deeper qualitative character: 'The need to write, to speak, is the need to fix this medium where things are born – for us, where we live, and which knowledge surveys – speech will have the function of taking the appearance of the world in transcendence as a theme, this structure perspective-reality' (99r/1). The task of literature is to 'reveal the lived world [*le monde vécu*]' and the 'mute contact' with things that we experience with and among others (119/7). Put differently, it aims '[t]o constitute a quasi-science of the lived world, that would allow us to see it as others see it, [*i.e.*] insofar as it is lived'.

In notes associated with *The Prose of the World* project, Merleau-Ponty suggests that Proust's novels exhibit a 'transmutation by which the lived [*le vécu*] becomes a book that we do not cease to continue living' (BNF Ms. Vol. III 262r). A novel like *In Search of Lost Time* establishes a permanent record of a subject's experience, which allows readers 'to obtain a presentation of the thing across *Erscheinungsweisen* [modes of appearance] that are not constituted by nature, not given, but which nevertheless render the thing all the more masterfully, since the transposition is more free' (BNF Ms. Vol. XII 106/7; cf. 113/1). In Proust, literary accounts of a character's expectations or desires, of places, people and the objects they encounter, present a more unified version of their first-personal experience of these phenomena. While literary accounts might transform the meaning of objects, places or persons, they still offer a perspective from which readers can evaluate or appraise these transformations. The text serves as a second-order structure that we can use to interpret characters' experiences, and by extension, better understand our own. In this sense, literary works establish a common ground that supports a critical intersubjective evaluation, which is a precondition for a phenomenological account of objectivity.

The ability to order phenomena into a more permanent form is captured well by the painter Elstir in *In Search of Lost Time*. Elstir invents aesthetic forms that reflect his own understanding of objects; the meaning of things themselves takes shape in his paintings. Elstir's paintings (like Vinteuil's music, or Proust's writing) create a 'language of things' that present a coherent view of one lived perspective, which becomes a key that others can use to interpret their own experiences (105v). An interest in and pursuit of this quality distinguishes Proust from Valéry. Proust's version of indirect expression details experience and reveals new perspectives in a way that is more proximate and accessible to others. His literary descriptions resonate more with experiences that others may have undergone. This quality allows subjects to better evaluate the claims, insights and reflections about the structure of conscious experience at work in Proust's literature:

> Literary speech makes a universe exist for a reader, it becomes expression in the sense of testimony, expression in the sense of creation, and, precisely for this reason, namely, that it does not refer back to empirical life. [. . .] Literary speech will be this originary speech awakened and creating an intersubjectivity to the second power, or a super-objectivity [*surobjectivité*]. (102/4)

Proust aims to record the meaning of experience in a creative expressive modality that is not merely identical with the 'empirical'. This mode of expression transcends the standard boundaries of objective linguistic representation. But the recurring tropes or structures we find in his novels (e.g., his accounts of memory, habit, the intending of material objects, the perception of smells, etc.), and importantly the language through which these structures are articulated, leaves readers with a more permanent interpretive framework that they can explore and apply to their own experience. By 'super-objectivity', Merleau-Ponty has in mind more stable structures that remain subject to further interpretation. Still, while it is the work of an author's imagination, the content expressed by Proust's novels transcends a limited perspective, since it describes structures that are obtained for more than one subject. This form of literary writing manages to marry imagination and testimony, fidelity and invention, and creation with description.

5. LITERATURE, PHENOMENOLOGY AND METAPHYSICS

Merleau-Ponty's growing interest in metaphysics and expression leads him to incipiently articulate two positions that, while independently formulated, are eventually brought together: that phenomenology is well served by an indirect mode of expression that is descriptive and creative; and that 'metaphysical' thought, understood as an enquiry into the *logos*, rational structure or intelligibility of experience, requires keen attention to linguistic expression. As I show in part 3, these lines of thought converge in his later work: on his view, 'ontology' amounts to a description of the structures of conscious experience, which requires a significant degree of creative conceptual invention.

Before turning to that account (by way of a detour through Merleau-Ponty's important analysis of dialogue), I would like to address a potential challenge to this reading of the insights that Merleau-Ponty gleaned from reflections on formal and literary modes of expression in the late 1940s and early 1950s. I have suggested that creative, indirect or non-categorical modes of expression in writers like Proust and Valéry are proto-phenomenological: they offer a distinctive take on how we are to describe conscious experience, and their interpretation of the relation between literary invention and the description of material objects did not go unnoticed by Merleau-Ponty. However, one might think that Merleau-Ponty's gradual embracing of aesthetic modes of expression is evidence of a move away from decidedly phenomenological concerns. Claude Imbert, for example, contends that '[l]iterature [takes on] the role of a "philosophy of the sensible" and Merleau-Ponty reevaluates the concept of *phenomenology*. [. . .] This was the answer to the deepest intentions of phenomenology. But in order to conceive of a genealogy of disjointed regimes of expression, it was necessary to reject the words of order, ontological naïvetés and transcendental premises'.[28] Instead of serving a broadly Husserlian or Heideggerian phenomenological heritage, Merleau-Ponty's engagement with literature breaks with it. The apparent paucity of references to the conceptual machinery of classical phenomenology, and the seemingly tenuous link between classical phenomenology and the poetic expressions characteristic of Merleau-Ponty's later enquiries, seem to only confirm this evaluation.

Undeniably, Merleau-Ponty does reformulate his understanding of phenomenology. However, he attempts to bring literary expression closer to phenomenology, without sacrificing the latter's deeper intentions. In *Le problème de la parole*, on the basis of his appraisal of literary expression in Proust and other writers, he concludes that '[o]ne will now define literature as fundamental speech, *i.e.* which not only takes up the task of communicating only what is impersonal, but what is most individual, like a realism founded on a quasi-scientific and exhaustive analysis of the "impression", i.e., of the world insofar as it is lived – like phenomenology' (BNF Ms. Vol. XII 111v). On this reading, the goals of a descriptive and indirect view of literary expression, and those of phenomenology, or of a piece. In Proust, Merleau-Ponty discovers a mode of literary expression capable of articulating a given character's experience, but in a way that resonates with his readers. While most writers do not aim to articulate eidetic insights valid for all possible subjects, or necessarily accept transcendental premises, some of them still engage in the more basic task of articulating the recurring and structural features of conscious experience. Proust is a special case: he engages in a form of 'explicitation', a term that standardly refers to phenomenological description (121/9).

It is certainly correct that, at this stage, Merleau-Ponty is gradually developing a markedly different terminology with which to describe perceptual experience. But as will become clear in part 3, the new terms that emerge in his later texts are formulated for the sake of providing a description of experience. And as I will argue, a creative mode of philosophical expression still serves the goals of a descriptive phenomenological project. The tight connection between indirect literary expression and phenomenological themes is noted in a number of later remarks. For example, Merleau-Ponty claims that 'the language of the artist (as indirect and unconscious) is the means of achieving our common participation in this Being' (NC 196); that 'literature is the disclosure [*le dévoilement*] of the visible, speech [about] things' (187); that philosophical expression 'is inseparable from literary expression, *i.e.* from *indirect* expression' (391); and he announces his intention to '[make] an analysis of literature in this sense: as inscription of Being' (VI 197/247–48). These remarks stress the continuity between Merleau-Ponty's philosophy of literature, his later account of expression, and a classical phenomenological goal. Doubtless, the relation between indirect expression and philosophy still needs to be made more precise. As I will show in chapter 7, he stops short of identifying philosophy and literature, in part because he thinks that ontology should take direction from intuitive evidence (NC 217–18; VI 6/2). What is more, description cannot be sacrificed for creation. Instead, these two poles, which have remained in tension with one another since *Structure*, must be brought closer together.

NOTES

1. Among other professional engagements, Merleau-Ponty was also invited to teach at the University of Chicago. See Noble 2014, 125–26, for a summary of Merleau-Ponty's scholarly activities during this period.
2. See Welsh 2013 for a good account of Merleau-Ponty's engagement with these fields.
3. For an earlier version of this criticism, see the account of formal intuition in geometry (PhP 403–8/443–48).
4. See Parain 1943, 14, for the suggestion that the use of mathematical symbols is always subject to revision, a position he credits to Cavaillès's *Sur la logique et la théorie de la science* (Cavaillès 1997; see also Hyppolite 1997/1953, 52 n.6). See Watson 2016 for more on Merleau-Ponty's relation to Cavaillès and formal thought.
5. The *Phenomenology* adopted a broadly intuitionistic approach to formal entities (see the discussion of geometry in the *Cogito* chapter). Merleau-Ponty stressed that formalisation requires invention, and likened this to an abstract application of motor intentional activity. *The Prose of the World* does not further develop this account.
6. Merleau-Ponty invokes Saussure's distinction between *langue* and *parole* in *Phenomenology*, but Saussure is not cited in the text or in the bibliography, and findings from linguistics do not seem to guide his analysis. I will return to Merleau-Ponty's reading of Saussure later in this chapter.
7. See Silverman 1979, 95–107 for a summary of the course (student notes are not currently accessible).
8. For discussions of Merleau-Ponty's relation to Saussure, see Lagueux 1965; Watson 2009a; Carbone 1993; Bonan 2001, 252; Bimbenet 2004, 222–31; Landes 2013, 132–36; Kaushik 2013. For a phenomenological reading of Saussure's work, see Stawarska 2015.
9. See especially Alloa 2009, Kearney 2013, Stawarska 2013.
10. de Saussure 2006, 85 ff.
11. de Saussure 2006, 76.
12. I am grateful to Stefan Kristensen for sharing a copy of his transcription of this course with me.
13. The remarks in this section should not be taken in the spirit of a critical study of Merleau-Ponty's reading of Valéry, Proust, other artists, or art theorists, since my focus is their more specific philosophical import. A comprehensive critical study of his engagement with literature would be a tall task: in Merleau-Ponty's published and unpublished writings one finds studies of Beauvoir ('Metaphysics and the Novel'), Malraux (*Prose of the World*, chapter 3; 'Indirect Language and the Voices of Silence'), Valéry ('Man and Adversity';

RULL Part I), Proust (*Le problème de la parole*, Part II; *Institution and Passivity*), Stendhal (*The Prose of the World; Recherches sur l'usage littéraire du langage*, Part II), Claudel ('On Claudel'; NC 191-94), Sartre ('A Scandalous Author'; BNF Ms. Vol. III 240-61;), planned studies of Breton (BNF Ms. Vol. III 190), as well as scattered remarks about other literary figures (see, for example, 'Five Notes on Claude Simon', NC 204–20, and remarks about Gide in *The Prose of the World* and *Signs*).

14. While textual evidence shows that Merleau-Ponty had already developed this view of the relationship between painting and writing before the publication of Sartre's *What Is Literature?* (1947), Sartre's separation of the two art forms likely motivated Merleau-Ponty's arguments to the contrary in his later treatments of the topic.

15. For more on Merleau-Ponty's account of painting, see Johnson 1993, Mercury 2000, Foti 2013, 1996.

16. By his own admission, Merleau-Ponty is more interested in Cézanne or Klee than he is in earlier modern painters or schools (like Impressionism). This interest is partly polemical, since he aims to counter Malraux's claim that these painters were comfortable with incompleteness (PW 99/140). While he focuses on modern painters, Merleau-Ponty recognises that classical painting is also creative, despite the fact that (in his estimation) it aims to merely 'represent' reality (54/76). Still, the novelty of modern painting can only be understood against the background of classical painting, and it makes little sense to draw an artificial distinction between them.

17. For other uses of this term, see PW 91/128, 104/147, 113/160; S 78/126, 91/149.

18. See, for example, Kaelin 1962; Levine 1969, 441; Grene 1970, 217–19; Burch 1993, 360; Crowther 1982, 141. Note the relative absence of attention to the philosophy of literature in Johnson 1993.

19. See Smith 1993, 202–5, and Grene 1970, 229–30, who argue for a different order of priority between painting and language.

20. For an overview of this course see Zaccarello 2012 and Kristensen 2010.

21. Valéry 1944, 147.

22. As Crow notes, while the poetic voice is purified from mundane language, 'it is still to the conventions of ordinary language that Valéry will attend for his action of poetic purification, and it is still to the expressive action of speech itself – *la voix en action* – that he will look for stylistic inspiration as that purification takes place' (1982, 49).

23. In stressing this point, Merleau-Ponty obliquely responds with Valéryean premises to a question posed by Sartre's *What Is Literature?*; namely, 'For whom does one write'? (see also RULL 149–50). For Sartre's view see Sartre 1988, 70 ff.

24. Crow 1982, 48.

25. For Merleau-Ponty, Valéry establishes a line of communication between writer and reader: 'knowledge of self passes through knowledge of another: the *chiasma*' (RULL 114). This remark suggests that the concept of the '*chiasma*' (a term that will be run together with 'reversibility' and 'narcissism' in later texts) is directly influenced by his engagement with Valéry's work (see de Saint Aubert 2005, chapter 6). In 'Man and Adversity', Merleau-Ponty writes that Valéry is keenly aware of 'the body as a double-edged being', and that 'for Valéry too consciousness of the body is inevitably obsession with others'. He quotes remarks from *Tel Quel* to the effect that when 'glances meet, we are no longer wholly two, and it is hard to remain alone. This exchange realises in a very short time a transposition or metathesis – a chiasma of two 'destines', two points of view. Thereby a sort of simultaneous reciprocal limitation occurs. You capture my image, my appearance; I capture yours' (S 231/377–78). This account of the *chiasma* is quite proximate to Merleau-Ponty's theory of narcissistic perception (even if he here claims that 'I do not see myself'). It should also be noted, however, that Merleau-Ponty's view of the intersubjective dimension of the *chaisma* and its attendant account of 'narcissism' unfolds in roughly the same period that he develops his account of dialogue (in which the account of narcissism is worked out in more detail).

26. See the text entitled 'Mute Experience and Speech' (1959): 'Fundamental speech is (to be that which is called by the sensible *cf.* Proust) a sort of second silence' (Heisdeck 1993, 14–15).

27. For an overview of this course see Kristensen 2010, chapter 4. For Merleau-Ponty's reading of Proust, see Simon 1998 and Robert 2003.

28. Imbert 1998, 74–75.

5

THE LINGUISTIC FOUNDATIONS OF ONTOLOGY

In the previous chapter, we saw that Merleau-Ponty's research in the late 1940s and early 1950s led him to take up a wide range of new intellectual pursuits. Some focussed on linguistics and the phenomenology of language, while others were explicitly 'metaphysical' in nature. In this chapter, I will argue that these two tendencies coalesce in his analysis of dialogue. In particular, I will argue that what is known as Merleau-Ponty's 'ontology' can be understood as a response to a set of problems originating in reflections on the intersubjective use of language in dialogue, undertaken in the early 1950s. Some of the more specific claims below will be considered in greater detail in part 3, but their implications for Merleau-Ponty's transition to the concerns of his later writings will already become clear. A study of dialogue disclosed a structure of meaning-formation and pointed towards a theory of truth, both recurring ontological topics, that his post-*Phenomenology* premises could not account for. While Merleau-Ponty's early writings relied on a broadly subject-centric account of perception, meaning, and intentionality, the nature of expression and linguistic understanding in dialogue sharpened the need to adopt an intersubjective approach, which is a definitive feature of his later work.

I begin with an overview of the basic aims of Merleau-Ponty's later projects, which reveals a consistent focus on the topics of sense, truth and being (section 1). Evidence shows that this research was motivated by considerations originating in reflections on intersubjectivity. The structure of meaning-formation in dialogue brings this intersubjective focus into further relief. As I show, attention to the structure of dialogue reveals that speakers' positions are interchangeable; that speaking subjects are active and passive in varying degrees; and that the intentional roles of subjects and objects are liable to shift or 'transgress' themselves (section 2). These observations require a revision in Merleau-Ponty's existing premises, and anticipate, respectively, the concepts of 'reversibility' and 'narcissism', his later view of activity and passivity and his final view of intentionality. Despite the still implicit ontological import of this research, it seems that Merleau-Ponty was already aware of its broader implications in the early to mid-1950s (section 3). These implications lead directly to a new understanding of expression that he would continue to refine until his untimely death in 1961 (section 4).

Before considering this account, a brief methodological observation is needed. As is well known, the texts associated with Merleau-Ponty's ontological projects pose significant interpretive difficulties.[1] They introduce many new concepts and propose different theoretical points of departure. The indeterminate character of his final work has motivated a wide range of scholarly interpretations of its key terms, especially 'the flesh' (*la chair*), a central tenet. Some scholars argue that Husserl's account of double-sensations in *Ideen II* exercised a decisive influence on Merleau-Ponty's turn to ontology.[2] As I noted in the previous chapter, others emphasise the importance of Saussure's diacritical view of linguistic meaning.[3] For some, his later ontology is anticipated by *Phenomenology of Perception*; but it is also argued that it is a genuinely new development.[4] Heidegger, for example, has been identified as a positive and a negative influence on Merleau-Ponty's later work.[5]

To complicate matters further, Merleau-Ponty's philosophical *modus operandi* calls into question the explanatory adequacy of any interpretation that emphasises a single argument, concept, philosophical or literary interlocutor. His often fragmentary remarks, suggestive arguments and tentative plans support multiple and sometimes conflicting interpretations of his ontology, making even its basic motivations difficult to discern. For example, he often defines the flesh in terms of the double sensations felt in the experience of one hand touching the other.[6] But he also claims that the flesh (and its characteristic 'reversibility') is not material, denying that the term can be understood in any literal sense.[7] He also claims that the flesh and the structure of perception are 'diacritical', pointing to the influence of Saussure.[8] But he also identifies affinities and dissimilarities between his project and Heidegger's thought.[9] These remarks only complicate matters by equally supporting mutually incompatible lines of interpretation.

I do not intend to defend a strong view about the meaning of the concepts central to Merleau-Ponty's ontology (e.g., the 'flesh', the '*chiasma*', 'reversibility') in this chapter. I am chiefly interested in advancing a genetic account and in providing a philosophical aetiology of why Merleau-Ponty was motivated to shift his research towards topics that he claimed were more 'metaphysical' or 'ontological' in nature. The observations below do suggest, however, that intersubjectivity and language will be key elements of any account of the commitments and aims of Merleau-Ponty's ontology. In part 3, I defend this view, and offer a more detailed positive interpretation of Merleau-Ponty's ontology and the concepts that comprise it.

1. ONTOLOGY, SENSE AND INTERSUBJECTIVITY

Early in *The Visible and the Invisible*, the general goal of Merleau-Ponty's later research is clearly identified: 'We want to know precisely what the meaning [*le sens*] of the world's being is' (VI 6/2; see also 96/129).[10] His 'point of departure' is the observation that 'there is being, there is a world, there is *something*; . . . there is cohesion, there is meaning [*sens*]' (88/119). On the final page of the incomplete manuscript, he claims that philosophy aims to facilitate the 'birth of meaning' (155/201). At a highest level of generality, ontology attempts to understand our meaningful experience of the world.

The goal of an enquiry into sense is a consistent theme running throughout the projects associated with *The Visible and the Invisible*. These projects often connect investigations into sense with 'truth' or 'brute' (pre-theoretical and unthematised) being.[11] This connection is perhaps most evident in remarks about *Origine de la vérité*, the project Merleau-Ponty began drafting shortly after the publication of the *Phenomenology*. It sought 'to give a precise description of the passage of perceptual faith into explicit truth as we encounter it on the level of language, concept, and cultural world' (SNS 94 n.13/188 n.1).[12] Research notes from 1955 to 1956, associated with 'The Origin of Truth', also identify the need for a 'study of perceptual meaning as tacit meaning, by distance, constitution of existentials or "pivots", identity of consciousness and non-consciousness – (I know and I do not know the true)' (BNF Ms. Vol. VIII 126). In what will later become a standard formulation, this remark defines meaning across the 'distance' (*écart*) between perceivers. Instead of a reliance on 'consciousness', or overly theoretical, subject-centric accounts, meaningful phenomena must be analysed with reference to conditions that do not depend on the subject, or which the subject may be unaware of (hence the claim about 'tacit' meaning and 'unconsciousness'). Proposed studies of topics like the body, movement, nature, history and animality (all central concepts treated in his later ontology) will all be 'founded on [. . .] perceptual consciousness and perceptual signification, signification by difference [*écart*], tacit, consciousness of investment, consciousness of "pivots" or "hinges"' (124). To clarify this understanding of consciousness, Merleau-Ponty claims he will 'take up again the question of speech to expression, [. . .] to language as an institution, field, *Stiftung*, the concept as a difference of significations' (124).

While these formulations populate Merleau-Ponty's later texts, a similar observation in the 1955 passivity course at the Collège de France sheds light on their original motivations. These lectures offer one of the earliest explicit formulations of the goals of his ontological research. Here, he makes familiar refrains against the supposedly reigning 'objectivist ontology' of Western thought – that is, the underlying assumption that exclusive categories (e.g., 'being' *versus* 'non-being') are necessary and sufficient to clarify the meaning of experience and perceptual objects (IP 133/178). Instead, it is necessary to develop an 'expanded ontology', whose categories will be more varied. This will better clarify central ontological concerns like truth, subjectivity and freedom (133–34/179).

Of key consequence are the success conditions for this research. To understand truth or the '*logos* of the perceived world' (a term that, we saw in the last chapter, designates the metaphysical underpinnings of everyday experience), subjectivity must be at the heart of sense-making and understanding ('that the subject be that without which nothing has sense'). However, this condition must be combined with a 'lateral relation' that 'relativises [the subject's] *Sinngebung*' (135/181).[13] In other words, a subject's explicit, active sense-making capacities are no longer sufficient for an analysis of sense. As Merleau-Ponty claims, 'We live in intersubjectivity', there is 'no absolute privilege of the I' and 'we are one for others' (134/179). Was this not partly what Merleau-Ponty credited himself with demonstrating in the *Phenomenology*? Evidently, these remarks indicate that he thought he had not gone far enough.[14] In remarks from the 1953 Collège de France seminar *Le monde sensible et le monde de l'expression*, Merleau-Ponty holds that the analysis of perception undertaken in the *Phenomenology*

> remains all the same ordered to classical concepts such as: perception (in the sense of a position of an isolable, determinable object, considered as a canonical form of our relations with the world), consciousness (a centrifugal power of *Sinngebung* that finds in things what it put into it), synthesis (which presupposes elements to be unified) . . . , matter and form of knowledge. (MSME 45–46)

Commentators have noted the *Phenomenology*'s theoretical dependence on subjectivity, and it has even been argued that it leads to an idealistic point of view.[15] Even if one hesitates to accept this evaluation, or Merleau-Ponty's estimation that his descriptions of perception presuppose anything like the account of sense-giving found in Husserl, it is difficult to ignore passages arguing that subjectivity is the ultimate explanatory term of any meaningful phenomenon, for example, the preface claims that 'I am the absolute source' (PhP lxxii/9). Even if this claim is not intended in a reductive sense (Merleau-Ponty has just argued against reductive-scientific accounts of perception), the *Phenomenology*'s structure nevertheless suggests a heavy explanatory dependence on subjectivity. Its analyses culminate in an account of temporality, which is invoked to explain the meaning of preceding findings and the structures of perception. But it turns out that temporality is coextensive with subjectivity itself (444–45/483–84).

As Merleau-Ponty now stresses, a single subject only ever partially constitutes an object. Constitution always presupposes the efforts of others.[16] This observation leads to a key condition – namely, that sense is

> divergence [*écart*] between two or more perspectives [. . .]. If sense is this, not positive, but an interval between . . . , then whether it is 'natural' (from perception) or 'cultural' (from thought), 'passive' or 'active', in any case it is never a pure act of the subject; [it is] inconceivable without the perspectives between which it is outlined, belonging to the things as much as to me, taken up but not created by me – Sense [is] like determinate negation, a certain divergence [*écart*]; it is incomplete in me, and it is determined in others. The thing, the sensible world, are only ever completed in others' perception. (IP 136/182)

Put differently, perceptual meaning is formed across the views of multiple perceivers; it is not the domain of any single subject. For ontological analysis, meaning must be defined intersubjectively. As I noted, this does not obviate the role of subjective activity. It requires that the perspectives of other subjects are always part of an account of sense constitution. By extension, if 'the object is not only the correlate of my *acts*, but also provided with a double horizon by means of which it can become the object for others and not for me alone', then 'Being [is not] what is in itself or for someone, but what, being for someone, is ready to be developed according to another becoming of knowledge' (61/103). Like 'sense' and 'truth', 'being' must also be worked out in terms of intersubjectivity. For its meaning can be understood differently, according to different perspectives.[17] According to the reformulated view of perceptual consciousness described in texts of this period, we do not intend objects properly speaking through vision or grasp them through an essence. Perceptual consciousness is 'tacit' and receptive, in touch with a latent sense in objects (48–50), 'indirect' and 'reversed' [*inversée*] (MSME 60).

Merleau-Ponty's remarks during his candidature for the Collège de France also identify the central role of intersubjectivity for ontology. By extension, they also state the need to move beyond a subject-centric model. The investigations into truth he was pursuing in *L'Origine de la vérité* were approached 'less directly', he claimed, in *The Prose of the World* (PrP 8/PD 44). While his 'first two works sought to restore the world of perception', those 'in preparation aim to show how communication with others, and thought, take up and go beyond the realm of perception that initiated us to the truth' (3/37). This evidence indicates that intersubjective communication is especially important for an analysis of truth, and that it cannot be reduced to earlier analyses of perception. It also signals the importance of *The Prose of the World*'s account of intersubjectivity, which I will now turn to.

2. THE IMPLICIT ONTOLOGICAL IMPLICATIONS OF DIALOGUE

In this section, I argue that Merleau-Ponty's guiding assumption that sense must be analysed in light of intersubjectivity was motivated by his research into the structure of dialogue. This research provided an early testing ground for concepts that would become central for his ontology. I call attention to three claims in particular: that speakers' positions in a dialogue are reversible (2.1); that dialogue requires a reformulated account of activity and passivity (2.2); and that dialogue supports a relation of intentional 'encroachment' or 'transgression' (2.3).

While the topic of intersubjective communication was partly discussed in the *Phenomenology*, Merleau-Ponty devotes increasing attention to it in subsequent writings and lecture courses.[18] The most sustained philosophical analysis of dialogue in this period, which also integrates conclusions from other discussions, is found in chapter 5 of *The Prose of the World*. At the beginning of this chapter, Merleau-Ponty repeats earlier arguments against the plausibility of formal languages (see chapter 4), and reconsiders the expressive power of literary language (PW 3/7 ff.). Non-formal modes of expression claim to reveal the true nature of objects. But the transformation of meaning they effect can be fully grasped 'only when we understand it as the trespass of oneself upon the other and of the other upon me' (133/185).

It has been noted that there is a 'nascent ontology' and an 'ontological weight' in communication.[19] However, these claims are often interpreted as 'paradigmatic' instances of the kind of embodied 'performances' described since *Structure*.[20] In other words, the ontological import of speech is usually understood as a product or version of the broader ontological implications of embodiment. Correlatively, the distinctively linguistic characteristics of dialogue are often traced to Merleau-Ponty's reading of Saussure.[21] As I will argue, however, dialogue has an ontological import of its own, which extends beyond the framework of embodiment. Further, the ontological implications of speech considered below are not informed by Saussurean tenets.[22] Textual evidence suggests that we must ultimately look elsewhere to explain the development of Merleau-Ponty's ontology. Even if artists and linguists (including Saussure) demonstrate that language teaches us something new about the world, the meaning-transformation at work in dialogue is ultimately of greater philosophical consequence.

2.1 Reversibility and Narcissism

The claim that perception is 'narcissistic', and the view that the relation between subjects and objects is 'reversible', are key tenets of Merleau-Ponty's later work.[23] Both are anticipated in his reflections on dialogue.

Merleau-Ponty claims that dialogue is not, upon reflection, a 'face to face' exchange (133/185). He does not mean that we do not see another person before us in dialogue. We perceive others' gestures, hear someone's voice, see the spatial position of their body, and more. His deeper point is that dialogue is not structured according to an alternating correspondence between two isolable, self-reliant terms. Instead, dialogue establishes a relation with another person that makes it difficult to say that 'I' am 'here' and 'my interlocutor' is 'there'.

This claim is motivated by the observation that attempts to understand another speaker often leave us at a loss as to what they are claiming or suggesting. For Merleau-Ponty, this experience is not a mere failure of understanding, which could be explained by inopportune expressions, argumentative uncertainty or lack of clarity. It shows instead that dialogical experience is an 'alliance' that establishes a shared relation between two (or more) participants (134/186). In this relation, a particular speaker's position is under continuous revision: we give and take, moving from one claim to another, and our positions continually shift. A shift in our stance can lead to a corresponding change in another subject's view. This entails that we do not confront an isolable speaker in an immutable place (unless, of course, one defines speakers and listeners solely in perceptual or physical terms; Merleau-Ponty rejects this approach). The fact that speakers presuppose historically transmitted or 'sedimented' background meanings (syntax, word-meaning, concepts) that they do not invent further suggests that dialogue cannot be understood as an exchange between two self-sufficient subjects.[24]

These observations have important consequences for the philosophical status of subjectivity. If another subject also establishes and sustains the dialogical relation, the content of our contributions will also be formulated by our dialogical peer(s). Here, expression is only possible if another subject is present. Our expressions are responses to others, and often take direction from a peer's contributions. Merleau-Ponty provides a striking account of this experience:

> How can the '*I think*' emigrate beyond me, since it is me? The looks with which I scan the world, like a blind man tapping objects with his cane, are seized by someone at the other end and sent back to touch me in turn. It is no longer enough for me to feel: I feel that someone feels me, that he feels me while I feel, while I feel the very fact that he feels me. . . . It is not enough simply to say that henceforth I inhabit another body: that would only make a second me, a second dwelling for me. But *there is a myself which is other*, which lies elsewhere and deprives me of my central location, though, by all accounts, he cannot draw on this capacity except through his filiation with me. The roles of the subject and of what it sees are exchanged and reversed [*s'échangent et s'inversant*]: I thought I gave to what I see its meaning as a thing seen, and then one of these things suddenly slips out of this condition; the spectacle comes to itself establish a spectator who is not I but who is reproduced from me. How is that possible? How can I see something that begins to see? (134–35/187)

A basic conclusion in this passage is that dialogical speech undermines the hitherto central role of subjectivity. Dialogical expression shows that an ostensible spectator actually exercises significant demands on us, which we must respond to. The passage works out these demands in a perceptual, rather than a linguistic, register. But Merleau-Ponty's conclusion that the adequacy and self-sufficiency of a constituting subject is upset follows from the distinctively linguistic character of dialogue. In dialogue, the subject cannot be the sole arbitrator of sense, since the objects of experience (here, a conversational partner) eventually codetermine the meaning of what is said or seen. And because the meaning we express in a discussion soon becomes the object of another subject's evaluations, dialogue shows that subjects can take on the status of objects or things seen.

These observations anticipate two fundamental claims in Merleau-Ponty's ontology: the 'reversibility' of subject-object relations, and the claim that perception is 'narcissistic'. Consider the concept of 'reversibility' first. While he does not use the term *'réversibilité'*, Merleau-Ponty suggests that dialogue establishes a structural relation of reversibility between subject and object. A speaker can guide the flow of conversation, but they can also pass to the status of object while receiving the contributions of others. Speaker and listener exchange and effectively substitute their roles. In a contemporaneous article, he notes that speech is a prime example of engagements that 'reverse [*renversent*] my ordinary relation to objects and give some of them the value of subjects' (S 94/153).

Even if this is not quite the mature account of reversibility, the basic position is nevertheless offered in outline. In later texts, he will claim that a reversibility between seeing and object seen, touching and object touched, and so on, defines 'the flesh', a term used to describe the basic structure of experience. This relation generalises to a wide range of objects and domains of experience (VI 144/187). In *The Visible and the Invisible*, Merleau-Ponty will claim that there is a 'reflexivity' in speech of the same order as that in touch and sight (144/187–88). In a note from December 1959, he reproduces an earlier description of speech: 'The others' words make me speak and think because they create within me an other than myself, a divergence [*écart*] by relation to . . . what I see' (224/273). He continues to retain a link between reversibility and dialogue in later works, and uses the important term '*écart*' to describe the 'second self' that emerges in a dialogue. Even if this view is maintained in later works, the key point is that *The Prose of the World* first advanced an account of reversibility that is not antedated by other texts in Merleau-Ponty's corpus, at least until ca. 1952.

In addition to reversibility, the remarks above also anticipate the claim that perception is 'narcissistic', a related tenet. In *The Visible and the Invisible*, this term is used to describe the seamless contact between subjects and perceptual objects. As he puts it, 'Since the seer is caught up in what he sees, it is still himself he sees: there is a fundamental narcissism of all vision' (139/181). His point is not that perception is always reflexive, as if we only ever saw ourselves. Rather, he claims that subjects are so bound up with objects in everyday experience, and make seamless contact with meanings in their world, that it seems as if the meanings and objects encountered are tailored specially to them; alternatively, that perceivers' positions are reflected back to them by perceptual objects.

The term 'narcissism' also has a psychoanalytic dimension, and suggests the influence of psychoanalytic research on Merleau-Ponty's account. In the 1953 to 1954 course *Le problème de la parole*, he discusses dialogical relations in the context of psychoanalytic accounts, with particular reference to the concepts of 'projection' and 'introjection'. He had drawn on these concepts as early as the Consciousness and Language Acquisition course, and they are also referred to in *The Prose of the World* (see, for example, PW n.1 19–20/29). Already in the early stages of child development, maternal language can be understood according to 'introjection and projection and not by intellectual analysis' (BNF Ms. Vol. XII 16/65). Even in our earliest experience of language use, we observe a phenomenon in which 'I place myself in another to understand myself speaking when I speak, and I install another in myself as a speaker when I listen'. Descriptions of this sort, Merleau-Ponty claims, are better positioned to capture the nature of intersubjective language use than those offered in the spirit of Husserl's account of *Einfühlung*, which he claims is too intellectualistic. An important insight from psychological and psychoanalytic studies is that narcissism characterises relations to others and to the world, and is not merely one limited stage of child development (20/75). At more developed stages of language use, we continue to see something of ourselves in our interactions with others. These observations suggest that for Merleau-Ponty, the narcissistic features at work in dialogical relations ultimately generalise beyond the context of communication (though this is not a focus of his analyses in this course).

Despite appearances, the account of perceptual narcissism does not lead to a solipsistic, introspective account of perception (VI 141/183). In pre-theoretical experience, subjects do not standardly oppose themselves to a world of determinable objects. Our frequenting of the world in everyday experience makes it seem as if objects themselves offer meanings to us. Perception is an intimate connection to the world, which teaches us something about our intentional stance towards it. For Merleau-Ponty, perception is less of a deliberate engagement, and more like a passive openness to ourselves through our relation to objects. This is a key feature of his account of dialogue, and it is reflected in the claim that a dialogical partner is also a quasi-self, rather than an inert, determinable object. While it might seem that we speak to an inert object, who simply receives the meaning of our speech, we soon learn that this object can also exercise demands on us, modifying our contributions to a conversation. Accordingly, at the end of the account of dialogue quoted above, Merleau-Ponty asks: 'How can I see something that begins to see'? (PW 135/187).

As in the later account of narcissism, his point is not that I speak to and see a mere copy of myself. The long passage quoted above shows that a relation in which I begin to see another subject as myself is only possible if another speaker mitigates the centrality of my own position. We encounter a being similar to us, which reflects our stance, insofar as we detect conversational demands that are a response to our interventions, and insofar as we read the effects of our contributions in the responses issuing from our partner. The claim that perception is narcissistic aims to make just this point: we see ourselves in perceptual objects because we recognise a structure of perceptual solicitation that is a response to our highly particular intentional stance.[25]

Importantly, this account moves beyond some key tenets of the *Phenomenology*'s account of sense-giving and understanding. The analysis of dialogue discloses an 'I speak' significantly different from the 'I can' of the *Phenomenology* (17/26). While Merleau-Ponty draws on earlier analyses of embodiment, gesture and linguistic expression, the 'I speak' of dialogue is more passive and receptive to determination by objects in its milieu than the 'I can' is. The 'I speak' ultimately provides a different interpretation of the concept of 'motivation' developed in the *Phenomenology*: in dialogue, we are solicited by a meaning that only partially depends on us, and which is sustained by the contributions of others. The reversal of roles at work in dialogue leads Merleau-Ponty to more radically question the subject's central role in the analysis of meaningful phenomena (a basic assumption of the *Phenomenology*). This results in incipient versions of tenets that will become key parts of his later account of meaning-comprehension.

2.2 Activity and Passivity

The interpretation of dialogue also points towards a revised account of the concepts of 'activity' and 'passivity', widely acknowledged to be central for his transition to ontological research.[26] The 1955 course on passivity is often identified as a key turning point for this account. However, *The Prose of the World* already anticipates basic features of this view.

A closer look shows that the *Phenomenology*'s discussion of activity and passivity cuts in two directions. Some descriptions of passivity suggest a continuity with active or goal-directed behaviour. Consider its remarks about sleep. To fall asleep is to pass into an 'anonymous' sphere, no longer subject to the purview of motor intentional direction. Nevertheless, 'the sleeper is never completely enclosed in himself, never fully asleep' (PhP 167/202). The passive sleep state retains a link with activity because, as embodied agents, we can 'withdraw' from and resume active engagements according to certain situational conditions. More broadly, in waking life activity and passivity are 'geared into' one another: the subject passively accepts worldly conditions while actively responding to and shaping them (261/298). These descriptions suggest that activity and passivity are on a continuum, and that neither term is strictly speaking privileged.

But other remarks complicate this picture. First, Merleau-Ponty suggests that activity and passivity can also be understood in parallel to one another. The 'Temporality' chapter claims that the subject is 'simultaneously' active and passive because it is 'the sudden upsurge of time' (452/491). In addition to sleep or worldly motivation, passivity figures in temporal experience because subjects always bring their past into the present whenever they act in the world. Embodied habits are effectively acquired modes of behaviour, and habit always tacitly guides activity. However, Merleau-Ponty demurs on how subjects can be passive and active simultaneously. He acknowledges this while noting that even if contact with the past or future is not achieved by intellectual activity, and is effected through habituation, the 'passive synthesis of time [is] a term that is clearly not a solution, but merely a sign for designating a problem' (442/481). Whatever his solution to this problem is, it allows that activity and passivity are parallel to one another. This entails that they need not be continuous, but separate in kind, even if always co-present.

Second, Merleau-Ponty sometimes privileges activity over passivity, further undermining the claim that they are continuous, or equally important for experience. While temporal experience requires both terms, the tacit guidance of habit (or other passive modalities) is possible provided we actively take up some specific practical goal in the present.[27] Further, the view that activity and passivity are 'simultaneous' rests on the assumption that subjectivity is an 'upsurge'. And even in sleep, memory or aphonia, cases that ostensibly provide good evidence for parity between these two terms, any continuity underlying them is supported by bodily activity: a passive state is shown to maintain a connection to activity whenever the body 'signifies (in the active sense) beyond itself' (168/203). A passive sleep state is transformed into an active waking state through bodily 'transcendence', a paradigmatic instance of activity.

The discussion of dialogue helpfully clarifies these points. It rejects the view that activity and passivity are simultaneous (or parallel), and develops the implicit claim that they are continuous, affording equal weight to both. If speaker (subject) and listener (object) are in principle reversible, if each can lead and be led by the other, and if meaning in dialogue is formulated through openness to a conversational partner who co-constitutes our speech, then subjects cannot be active and passive at once. In addition to speakers' and listeners' positions, a reversal of activity and passivity is also required:

> Between myself as speech and the other as speech, or more generally myself as expression and the other as expression, there is no longer that alternative that makes a rivalry of the relation between minds. I am not active only when speaking, but precede my thought in the listener; I am not passive while I listening, but speak according to . . . what the other is saying. Speaking is not just my own initiative, listening is not submitting to the initiative of the other. (PW 143–44/ 199–200)

While activity and passivity might be equally important in dialogical experience, they do not unfold parallel to one another. An ostensibly active engagement like speaking also presupposes elements of passivity within it. When speaking to another subject, I might also anticipate a possible response, which a focus on my speech will not detect. Similarly, listening to a speaker (a seemingly passive engagement) requires keen attention to what is being said, and counts as a distinctive kind of activity.

The *Phenomenology* held that active and passive elements could be found in various embodied engagements, but it required that they be different in kind. The text above, by contrast, suggests that activity and passivity are not separate in kind. In another text, Merleau-Ponty claims that 'strictly speaking . . . [there is] an impossibility in maintaining the distinction between the active and the passive, between self and other' (18/27). A marginal note to the text adds that whereas 'listening and speaking' seem to be 'simple modalities of perception and movement', the phenomenology of dialogue shows that activity and passivity cannot be reduced to earlier analyses of embodiment or perception. Dialogue requires 'recognition of the passive by the active and of the active by the passive, of the hearer by the speaker' (n.1 19–20/29). This mutual recognition guides subjects' expressions and requires a more nuanced account of their active and passive behaviours. For example, a disapproving look from a listener usually results in a significant modification of a speaker's remarks. This often occurs with minimal awareness of the subtle modifications at work in a speaker's gestures and expressions, which remain active engagements, despite the passive elements discovered upon closer scrutiny. For these reasons, Merleau-Ponty maintains that activity in dialogue presupposes significant support from passivity, and that passivity is not mere submission to another's direction.

Activity and passivity, then, are now defined as 'degreed' concepts. Subjects are not either wholly active or passive (or both) when taking up roles in dialogue, which could support the earlier claim of simultaneity. On the whole, a listener remains in a largely passive modality, but also actively prepares the groundwork for a future reply. And even if a speaker actively expresses a view, she also passively anticipates possible responses from her conversational partner, and might begin modifying her claims accordingly. Listeners and speakers are not active and passive at once: instead, some activities contain passive elements, and vice versa.

The view that speakers cannot be active and passive simultaneously, together with the claim that subjects and objects in dialogue exchange positions, might suggest that dialogical experience (as Merleau-Ponty describes it) consists in a formulaic or mechanistic substitution of roles. Despite his reliance on binary categories (e.g., subject-object, active-passive), the view above points to a different model. Dialogue establishes a shared structure that effectively undermines the rigidity of circumscribed subject/object or active/passive relations. That there are degrees of activity and passivity, for example, entails that speakers or listeners are never merely subjects or objects in the classical sense. Speech supports conditions whereby active modalities are checked by more passive behaviours in others. Traditional categories like an actively determining subject, or a passively receptive object, quickly break down here, since participants in dialogue do not straightforwardly fall into or take turns occupying either category. To be sure, Merleau-Ponty is in the midst of reformulating his views, and continues to rely on classical divisions that occasionally hide the deeper upshot of his claims. While he uses terms like 'subject' or 'activity' to describe this multidirectional and shared model of meaning formation, speaking or listening have a novel expressive, intentional and behavioural status that is not fully captured by more standard labels.

By all accounts, Merleau-Ponty has moved closer to his later view of activity and passivity, often thought to originate in his later 1954 to 1955 lectures.[28] On this view, there is passivity 'in' and 'of' activity (VI 221/270, 264–65/312). While one can distinguish between more and less active or passive engagements, in either case it is necessary to posit a degree of passivity in what appear to be largely active engagements. Forgetting is one of Merleau-Ponty's most recurring examples of this relationship. Forgetting is understood as an activity 'in' passivity, since it is largely passive and is not directly undertaken by a subject. Nevertheless (following Husserl), forgetting actively forms or constitutes a determinate content that can be accessed later. Hence, seemingly passive forgetfulness still actively preserves the past (IP 197/256).[29]

The evidence above suggests that an activity 'in' passivity is at work in dialogue. Even if Merleau-Ponty does not define activity and passivity in these terms in *The Prose of the World*, his account clearly moves beyond the claims that activity and passivity are distinct in kind and unfold parallel to one another. Instead, he holds that there are degrees of activity in passivity, a claim that is worked out in subsequent lecture courses.

2.3 Intentional 'Transgression' and 'Encroachment'

Merleau-Ponty's descriptions of the reversal of roles that occurs in dialogue also hint at an underlying account of intentionality that enables this shift in stance (S 94/153). In later work, he develops a distinctive view of intentionality that extends the account of 'operative intentionality' (*fungierende Intentionalität*) offered in the *Phenomenology*.[30] While he sometimes claims to be uninterested in articulating such a view, a suggestion some commentators have picked up on, a number of texts show that he intends to offer a refined account of intentionality (and constitution), which he variously calls 'latent' or 'operative' intentionality.[31] As I suggest below, the phenomenology of dialogue was particularly important for the development of this view.

I cannot consider this view of intentionality in detail here, but two key features should be noted.[32] Merleau-Ponty claims that 'transgression' (*la transgression*) and 'encroachment' (*l' empiétement*) are central to the account of intentionality modelled after the flesh.[33] The subject 'encroaches' on objects or other subjects when it passes into the sphere of what it can be directed to, alternatively, when it itself becomes an intentional object. The reversibility between seer and seen is a characteristic example of encroachment. 'Transgression' is a closely related concept that describes a similar result.[34] This concept takes up Husserl's term *Überschreitung*, which Merleau-Ponty uses to describe his reformulated account of the relation between subject and object (likening it to intentional encroachment) (200/250).[35] In a note from May 1960, he claims that the subject (or 'the flesh of the body') can extend beyond its circumscribed role as intentional pole, taking that of its object ('the flesh of the world') (248/297). This shift produces a relation of intentional transgression.

The importance of these terms for Merleau-Ponty's later account of intentionality has been noted, but the central role that analyses of dialogue played for its development remains unexamined.[36] Early in the chapter on dialogue, he claims that 'speech accomplishes the anticipation, encroachment [*empiétement*], transgression [*transgression*], the violent operation by which I build within the figure' (PW 131–32/183). This claim suggests that the transgression or shifting of roles in speech is liable to generate novel meanings. At the end of the chapter, having offered his description of dialogue, he claims that 'we encroach [*nous empiétons*] upon one another insofar as we belong to the same cultural world, and first of all to the same language, and my acts of expression and those of the other bud [*relèvent*] from the same institution' (139/194). This remark suggests that encroachment in language is a special version of a broader relation, structure or 'institution', which has a wider cultural or historical status.

While the implications of this view are not considered further in the rest of the manuscript, unpublished material suggests that Merleau-Ponty took his reflections on dialogue to directly result in a new account of intentionality. Notes associated with *The Prose of the World* define '[s]peech as autonomous intentionality', and claim that '[s]peech is constitutional contact' (BNF Ms. Vol. III 186/1; 185r). Expression in dialogue demonstrates the need to define 'speech as the constitution of a *style* of the speaker and the listener', and leads to the recognition of a 'gestalt' form that instantiates itself in communication (207r/1). Like the claims above, these remarks indicate that intentionality in speech is of a different order than that of perception, and that intentional directedness is facilitated by the structure of dialogue itself, here likened to a *Gestalt* form (or 'figure'). Dialogical exchanges establish their own structures of directedness. As Merleau-Ponty understands the reciprocity of speech, 'everything that I do, I make [my partner] do, and everything he does, he makes me do' (PW n.1 19–20/29).

The descriptions above showed that dialogue establishes a structure in which subject and object roles are in principle reversible. This has important implications for intentionality, insofar as it points towards a view of directedness on which objects (listeners) can take on the role of subjects (speakers). Alternatively, it shows that a theory of intentionality must also accommodate the possibility that the objects of a perceiver's gaze or a speaker's expressions can determine intentional directedness as much as vision or speech themselves. Dialogue reveals this by showing how a spontaneous 'auto-organisation of the given' enables us to follow and respond to the guidance of subjects who will in turn be directed by us. In other words, intentionality cannot be a uni-directional relation that originates in subjects and moves out towards objects or the world. Objects are also sources of intentional direction. These observations lead Merleau-Ponty to define 'intentional transgression, the coupling [*l'accouplement*] by language', as 'a reciprocity of speaking and listening' (BNF Ms. Vol. III 192r). Dialogue offers a prime example of intentional transgression and encroachment.

As Emmanuel de Saint Aubert argues, encroachment was already a focus of Merleau-Ponty's research in the late 1940s. Of particular importance for this work was a protracted reading of Beauvoir, which led Merleau-Ponty to develop a view of encroachment on which subjects can 'pass into' one another, in active and passive modalities.[37] More specifically, Beauvoir's account of encroachment in experiences of freedom and love as described in *Le sang des autres* led Merleau-Ponty to conclude that the concept is central to the theory of expression and embodiment.[38]

This evidence demonstrates that earlier discussions of encroachment (and transgression) undoubtedly laid the groundwork for later research, and became central to Merleau-Ponty's understanding of intersubjectivity. As de Saint Aubert notes, however, insights from these investigations are applied to philosophical concerns falling within a familiar existentialist framework. Conversely, the conclusions drawn from later dialogical versions of encroachment are developed under the auspices of a different model of sense-making, expression and experience. This suggests that encroachment in speech had a special significance for Merleau-Ponty's transition to ontological investigations. That dialogical versions of encroachment are more frequently associated with other novel, proto-ontological tenets further suggest they exercised a decisive influence on the trajectory of his later research. For example, dialogical speech shows that 'language . . . admits of a truth not conditioned by the decisive acts of human beings' (193r/3). Intentionality in language points towards a view of truth that is not analysable solely in terms of a subject's activity. Recall that the goal of articulating a new view of truth is a guiding concern of Merleau-Ponty's ontological projects. Until this point, he held that a subject's intending and perceiving of the world is the ultimate source of truth (PhP lxxx/16–17; PrP 11/43). The phenomenology of dialogue reveals a different ground of truth, and indicates that a non subject-centric analysis is needed to understand it.

This observation suggests an additional consequence of intentional encroachment uniquely connected to speech. Despite his reliance on some Husserlian terminology, Merleau-Ponty thinks his own view of intentional encroachment in speech undermines accounts reliant on a view of 'contemplative consciousness' (BNF Ms. Vol. III 207r/1). The 'intentional transgression of speech' is 'an intention of my phenomenal body, of "another body", [. . .] of my speech and another's speech' unlike that found in Husserl (209r/3).[39] In this vein, he asks: 'Now how do the 2 [subjects] understand one another? *L'Ueberschreiten* or intentional transgression. How to understand this across constitution, *Sinngebung, Auffasung als*? It is impossible'.[40]

While similar criticisms of Husserl are found in the *Phenomenology*, the nascent analysis of intentionality in speech also serves as a necessary corrective to Merleau-Ponty's own earlier positions. These notes sometimes criticise them together with classical phenomenological views. This move marks a significant shift in focus. For example, Merleau-Ponty claims that his study of language discloses a 'consciousness that presupposes language [*le langage*]'; namely, a 'consciousness-unconsciousness that is perception' (BNF Ms. Vol. III 218v). The point is not that we are unaware of intentional directedness while speaking, rather, we could not be directed to meaningful content in dialogue without the help of another speaker. The dialogical relationship enabling this, moreover, is not a result of our deliberate activity. It depends on a quasi-unconscious or tacit form of intentional directedness that originates in a source partially external to us. The very idea of intentional directedness, once analysable in terms of the motor activities of a single subject, has been significantly revised.

These remarks show that attention to dialogue coincides with a profound shift in Merleau-Ponty's view of intentionality, and reveals a broader turn to a different set of philosophical presuppositions. The criticisms above offer earlier versions of rejoinders directed to the *Phenomenology*'s account of intentionality in *Le monde sensible et le monde de l'expression* (1953).[41] Further, the claim that perceptual intentionality presupposes an intentional use of language marks a major departure from the *Phenomenology*, which held that language is a secondary or 'founded' level of meaning dependent on perception.[42] At this stage in his career, language is thought to be as basic as perception. What is more, the nature of intentional directedness in dialogue seems to more successfully meet an original goal of the *Phenomenology*: namely, the undermining of a subjectivist view of intentionality and perception. In his discussion of intentional encroachment in language, Merleau-Ponty claims that 'this is what I wanted to say in showing in the *PhP* that the *Sinngebung* is not ours' (BNF Ms. Vol. III 218v). Instead of 'motricity' or 'ambiguity', the resources for this goal are to be developed with reference to intentional encroachment in dialogue.

Later texts confirm the central influence of dialogical expression on this view of intentionality (VI 203/253, 224/273). Intentionality in speech is thought to have a direct ontological bearing, and discloses the 'common tissue of which we are made'. But it generalises beyond the domain of intersubjective communication, and can purportedly explain the *écart*, 'brute' being, and the concept of '*Ineinander*', a recurring cluster of terms in Merleau-Ponty's later work. This more general, 'ontological' view of intentionality first originates in dialogue: 'the sensible initiates me to the world, as language to the other: by encroachment, *Ueberschreiten*' (218/267).

3. THE EXPLICIT ONTOLOGICAL IMPLICATIONS OF DIALOGUE

By anticipating views of intentionality, activity and passivity, reversibility and perceptual narcissism, the evidence above testifies to the implicit ontological import of Merleau-Ponty's phenomenology of dialogue. Recall that in remarks in Brussels in 1951, he unequivocally identified the phenomenology of language as a foundational domain that should inform all other areas of philosophy. Texts above confirm that he was already aware of its broader consequences, and that his analysis of dialogue played a particularly crucial role in motivating this conclusion: 'The experience of living language has sufficiently convinced us that it has a metaphysical significance' (PW 38–39/54–55). In fact, language is identified as a privileged mode or 'vehicle' for the experience of truth, an all-important ontological topic (129/180–81). His published work from this period claims that language is no mere regional problem (S 88/142), that speech has an ontological bearing of its own (86/140), that the phenomenology of language teaches us 'a new conception of the being of language', and that 'language is much more like a sort of being than a means' (43/69).

These conclusions suggest that Merleau-Ponty was already shifting to different accounts of truth and meaning during the writing of *The Prose of the World*.[43] He claims that his analyses of speech attempt 'to awaken a carnal relation [*rapport charnel*] to the world and the other', and that they disclose 'our first insertion into the world and into the true [*le vrai*]' (PW 139/193). The idea of a 'carnal relation', a recurring concept in later texts, refers to a general structure obtaining in experience, which guides perception, language and thought, and which is eventually associated with the flesh.[44] Guided by this structure, 'as speaking subjects we *continue*, we resume the same effort, older than us, upon which we are grafted [*entés*] to one another, which is the manifestation, the becoming of truth [*le devenir de la vérité*]' (144/200). Put differently, dialogue grants subjects access to a domain of truth that is not merely produced by a particular linguistic exchange, or sustained by the intentional activities of subjects (it 'cannot be assigned a place') (141/196–97).

In addition to the rejection of a 'face-to-face' analysis of dialogue, this claim is also motivated by the broader structure of meaning-formation and truth revealed by a study of intersubjective language use. Merleau-Ponty claims that this structure is instantiated in dialogue without being limited to it. The study of dialogue shows that '[t]he foundation of truth', which ontology will investigate, is clarified by a focus on the transformations of meaning and the genesis of sense at work in linguistic expression. Speech is a particularly good domain for this investigation because it exemplifies a view of meaning-transformation that 'cannot be grasped in terms of contemplation', or using philosophical and phenomenological concepts traditionally employed in investigations of meaning, truth and being (144/200). The limits of these concepts, which all rely too heavily on subject-centric analyses, are demonstrated by a study of dialogue.

These texts also indicate a shift in the focus of Merleau-Ponty's attention; namely, toward 'being' or 'meaning'. Both terms are discussed in the *Phenomenology*. But dialogical experience reveals a structure of meaning-formation that unfolds across a number of different perspectives, in active and passive modalities. This cannot be accounted for with a focus on the pre-personal or motor intentional activity of a single subject. A note associated with *The Prose of the World* claims that

> it is in language and only by way of language that one can understand how [speaking is listening] consciousnesses exchange their roles, and how a being for many is constituted [*comment se constitue un être à plusieurs*], because one understands there how speaking is listening and listening is speaking. From the perspective of consciousness, this is not thinkable. (BNF Ms. Vol. III, 197r)[45]

In addition to confirming the central analytical role of intersubjectivity, this remark also signals the increasing importance of language. A study of language use in speech discloses a new kind of entity, formed at the intersection of multiple perspectives. The tenets discussed above (in sections 2.1 to 2.3) together explain how meanings in language use are gradually formed by the multi-directional participation of speakers and listeners. As I noted, a reversal of speakers' positions, intentional roles, and of activity and passivity, allows one subject's interventions to be taken up and completed by others. Together with the self-critical remarks discussed above (see section 2.3), this text also marks a departure from the *Phenomenology*'s claim that a subject's perception of the world is the ultimate *explanans* of meaning, truth and being. Even if speech is an embodied activity, it already points beyond the *Phenomenology*'s conceptual framework: 'The body announces, by its own magic, a much greater wonder [*merveille*] that is accomplished by speech' (224). This evaluation marks the decreased importance of direct descriptions of embodiment. As we will see in part 3, in no sense does Merleau-Ponty abandon his interest in embodiment, or his commitment that any account of perception must be informed by it. But embodiment is no longer thought to undergird the analytical framework that should direct an interpretation of experience.

What is more, Merleau-Ponty increasingly emphasises the importance of 'the intersubjective thing' (S 173/282). In one of his earliest statements of plans for ontological research, he identifies the need to shift analytical focus to a non-subject–centric, 'lateral', 'divergent' or 'bi-directional genesis' of meaning (IP 133/178). As I showed above, an entity whose meaning is generated intersubjectively is at the heart of ontological analysis. But it cannot be adequately understood using the terms of *Phenomenology* (136/182). Unsurprisingly, this claim follows his research into dialogue, which suggests that intersubjective meaning-constitution unfolds in ways that a subject-centric analysis cannot take account of. An attempt to analyse this sort of entity is a stable and recurring goal across the various thematic pursuits of Merleau-Ponty's later work, which attempts, at bottom, to understand how objects can 'have another sense than that which we are in a position to recognise in them' (VI 94/127). Whatever their more local aims might be, the concepts of 'reversibility', 'dimensionality', 'brute' being, the '*écart*' and 'the flesh' are deployed to probe this intersubjective domain of meaning.

4. ONTOLOGICAL EXPRESSION IN THE MAKING

At this point, I would like to take stock of some conclusions licensed by the considerations above. In stressing the importance of dialogue, I have left open, for the moment, how best to understand the deeper meaning of the terms 'sense', 'truth' or 'being'. Except for the constraint that any account of these terms must recognise the important role of intersubjectivity, one could accept the basic conclusions of the reconstruction above and entertain a range of different conceptual influences or definitions of Merleau-Ponty's ontology. Dialogue certainly motivated a shift in focus to intersubjectivity. But thus far, we have reason to conclude that this research anticipates later concepts only in outline. The influence of philosophers from Hegel to Sartre, of literary critics, writers, of the philosophy of history and nature, and more, remains to be specified. More will need to be said to understand the key claims of Merleau-Ponty's later thought: but the centrality of intersubjectivity and sense will be basic to any analysis of its substantive commitments.

It is already clear, however, that language plays a key role in the genesis and development of Merleau-Ponty's ontology, whatever its deeper commitments might be. This influence is acknowledged throughout his later writings. For example, he claims that language is 'in a sense everything' and is a 'special domain' for ontology (VI 155/201, 117/154–55).[46] While the extant sections of *The Visible and the Invisible* do not contain sections or chapters devoted to detailed analyses of language, the evidence above helps to clarify some of the motivations behind these remarks. Merleau-Ponty attaches ontological weight to language because his enquiries into a particular use of language in dialogue served as an early testing ground for his subsequent ontological research.[47] This conclusion will come into further relief with the help of the analyses undertaken in part 3.

In addition, the account of dialogue suggests that Merleau-Ponty's later work is in no way an 'abandonment' of earlier projects.[48] Even if there are significant differences between the basic aims of the *Phenomenology* and *The Visible and the Invisible*, the clear development of concepts implicit in research from the early 1950s suggests that this view must be reconsidered. Of course, the incipient nature of these inquiries does not justify the view that he either maintains or unpacks largely formulated conclusions or 'theses'.[49] As I noted, many other influences intervene between this research and his final projects. Still, the reading I have offered in this chapter allows us to recognise a range of influences, while observing an underlying continuity of focus. A concern with the topics of intersubjectivity, sense and truth remains constant throughout the developments in Merleau-Ponty's ontological research, which testifies to the catalytic role of dialogue for the trajectory of his later thought.

As will become clear in chapter 7, together with his exploration of literary expression, the expressive characteristics of intersubjective language use led Merleau-Ponty to formulate a new understanding of linguistic signification. This new view of expression will eventually become a core feature of his positive view of ontology. His study of dialogical expression demonstrated that dialogue has the 'power to say in total more than it says word by word, to precede itself, whether in launching the other toward what I know and what they have not yet understood, or in carrying myself toward what I will understand' (PW 131/182–83). Much like the account of first-order expression we encountered in chapter 2, linguistic gestures in dialogue produce meanings by availing themselves of an intentional structure that may not be clear to us or to our interlocutors, but which nevertheless successfully accomplishes our initially vague expressive intentions, and manages to share them with others.

On the basis of his observations of dialogue, Merleau-Ponty draws an additional conclusion, which dovetails with his criticisms of formal languages, and with some of his observations about indirect literary expression. Dialogue teaches us that:

> That which masks the living relation between speaking subjects, is that the *statement* [l'énoncé] or the *indicative* [l'indicatif] is always taken to be the model of speech. One does so because one believes that beyond statements, there is only confused stammering [*balbutiements*] and unreason [*déraison*]. This is to forget all the tacit, unformulated, and un-thematised that figures in the statements of science, which contributes to determining its meaning [*sens*] and which gives to the science of tomorrow its field of investigation. (144/200–201)

Together with the conclusions discussed in chapter 4, this provides more evidence in favour of the view that the success of formal modes of expression in no way rules out the plausibility of informal or inexact ones. But Merleau-Ponty takes these findings to directly lead to another important conclusion. The remark above suggests that a 'tacit' or 'un-thematised' mode of expression underwrites scientific enquiry. In other words, the study of dialogue provides more reason to think that an indirect form of expression is in some sense more basic than a categorical one. In unpublished notes, he suggests that these characteristics might apply to language *tout court*, and not only to the indirect forms of expression found in literature or dialogue: 'one must understand that the mode of language is not the indicative, the statement [*l'énoncé*], verification [*la constatation*], the thesis. All language of this sort is enveloped [*est enveloppé*] in a different language, which is [a language] of invocation' (BNF Ms. Vol. III 207v). Dialogical expression realises just this 'invocative' mode of expression, teaches us about its deeper structure and philosophical characteristics and licenses us to accord greater priority to indirect or inexact modes of expression.

This is a controversial claim, to which one could plausibly object that even a search for 'mere' facts or empirical findings could yield conclusions that we did not expect. As we saw in chapter 4, this indeterminacy remains a feature of scientific enquiry (even if it is often unacknowledged or suppressed). Of course, Merleau-Ponty need not deny this. Even if we might want to temper its supposedly universal scope, the claim above does not chiefly concern this point. Instead, these findings are aimed at laying the groundwork for a new view of phenomenological expression. A plan for *The Prose of the World* announces an intention to develop a view of language that will bring together the following features:

Prose of the World –
> against a poetry of transcendence
> against prose
> for a poetry of speech [*pour poésie de parole*]. (222r)[50]

The rationale for this division is explained in a subsequent note: 'One should not oppose to a poetry of transcendence, a conception of prose as absolute transparency. It is necessary to oppose to deliberate poetry [. . .] an involuntary or implicit poetry which is language itself, and which by consequence emerges toward the truth without quitting its inherence' (236r–v).[51] Together with accounts of literary language advanced by Valéry and Proust, observations from dialogical speech offer resources with which to formulate a non-formal interpretation of expression. This interpretation will privilege the creative and allusive possibilities of expression, without surrendering a link to truth and to the evidence of perception. To be sure, Merleau-Ponty has a different view of 'truth' in mind than what standardly figures in scientific, philosophical or formal expression. In chapter 4 we saw that he suggests that formal expression is more partial than it is false, and that for this reason it must make way for a non-literal and more literary (but not wholly poetic) approach to expression. A hybrid account of expression, which includes literal and creative features, is better positioned to capture the sense of experience, which he increasingly thinks cannot be adequately stated using traditional categorical resources.

Unlike in earlier texts, in this period he draws increasingly general conclusions from observations about dialogical expression. In addition to remarks about the 'metaphysical' significance of speech, he takes his research from the early 1950s to have deep and direct methodological and conceptual implications for phenomenology and for its broader goals. The following passage from a contemporaneous article nicely describes the transformations at work in his understanding of the phenomenological project:

> Now if it is really the peculiar office of phenomenology to approach language in this way, phenomenology is no longer the synthetic determination of all possible languages. Reflection is no longer the return to a pre-empirical subject which holds the keys to the world; it no longer circumambulates its present object and possesses its constitutive parts. Reflection must become aware of its object in a con-

tact or frequenting which at the outset exceeds its power of comprehension. The philosopher is first and foremost the one who realises that he is situated in language, that he *is speaking*; and phenomenological reflection can no longer be limited to a completely lucid enumeration of the 'conditions without which' there would be no language. It must show why there is speech – the paradox of a subject turned toward the future who speaks and understands – [. . .] Reflection is no longer the passage to a different order which reabsorbs the order of present things. (S 104–5/169–70)

As this remark suggests, analyses of dialogue and lived language use play an important role in Merleau-Ponty's understanding of reflection and the basic goals of phenomenology. If reflection unfolds in language (a position he continues to hold), and if linguistic expression, in general, exhibits the sort of tacit or unthematic features encountered in dialogue, then the phenomenological disclosure of sense is subject to the same trials and tribulations characteristic of everyday language use. In fact, these conditions continue to exercise an important influence on supposedly higher-order or 'pure' reflective activity: any description of an object must also attend to how it deploys language, and it must be keenly aware of the theoretical constraints imposed by language use (and by the special constraints imposed by a particular natural or technical language). The passage above finds Merleau-Ponty openly accepting a consequence that remained merely implicit in the *Phenomenology*'s account of the *cogito*: that the phenomenological field is an expressive field. Put differently, phenomenological description is now identified as a linguistic undertaking of a special kind. And it 'does not possess the truth about language and the world from the start, but is rather the recuperation and first formulation of a *Logos* scattered out in our world and our life and bound to their concrete structures' (105/170). In part 3, I offer an interpretation of how this 'recuperation' might be understood.

NOTES

1. For influential studies see Madison 1981, Dillon 1988, Dastur 2000, Barbaras 2004, de Saint Aubert 2004, 2005.

2. Françoise Dastur has highlighted the importance of Husserl's account of double-sensations in *Ideas II* for the concepts of 'flesh' and *'chiasma'* (Dastur 2000, 38–42; see also Moran 2010, 138, and Richir 1998).

3. See Alloa 2009, Kearney 2013, Stawarska 2013. For a phenomenological reading of Saussure inspired by Merleau-Ponty see Stawarska 2015.

4. For the former, see Dillon 1988, 174; for the latter, see Madison 1981, 231–32; see also Butler 2005.

5. See Lawlor 1999, Robert 2005, but cf. Noble 2014, 222–28, Barbaras 2004, 305.

6. MSME 118, 203–4; VI 9/24, 133–34/173–74, 146/187–88; BNF Ms. Vol. VI 172/13, 174v/18.

7. VI 146–47/189–90. See also VI 153/198, 125/164, 138/179, 155/201; cf. 221–22/271; NC 202.

8. For example, see VI 206/256, 213–14/263–64, 224/273, 233/282.

9. Contrast, for example, NC 123–24 with HLP 51/63.

10. See Morris 2010 for the connection between sense and ontology, and Jean Hyppolite's 1946 remarks on the *Phenomenology*'s implicit ontology of sense (PrP 39/97–99).

11. See, for example, a project from 1958, entitled '*Être et sens*', *ou*: '*La Généalogie du vrai*' (2/1; 18r/1). As its title suggests, this project connects the topic of sense with 'truth', 'being' and 'ontology' (4/2; 4v/3; 5v/5; 11r; 18r/1). Here, ontology is defined as the 'recognition of this link between beings [. . .], of being (or *Weltlichkeit*) as meaning [*sens*]' (16/F). Merleau-Ponty claims that ontological questions can be answered only by clarifying the 'problematic' of 'vertical sense'. Another project, entitled *La nature ou le monde de silence*, also pursued this goal (see 'La nature ou le monde de silence, Pages d'introduction', in de Saint Aubert 2008, 44–53; cf. BNF Ms. Vol. VI 23–66, 67–146; see also 147 ff., 245/27). In this work, nature is understood as brute being (BNF Ms. Vol. VI 98). A study of nature is instructive for ontology because nature admits of a mode of conception and a 'sense of meaning' incompatible with 'a philosophy of the subject' (49r/1). This investigation, Merleau-Ponty claimed, could yield non-subjectivist categories from which to develop an ontology. Even if only a subset of its goals track the eventual structure of *The Visible and the Invisible*, the *Être et Monde* project (VI 198/248) also aimed to 'reformulate our notion of being (and subject)', and to develop an understanding of '"vertical", "savage" or "brute" Being' (BNF Ms. Vol. VI 188).

12. A published reference to the work occurs at least as early as 1947 (SNS 94 n.13/188 n.1). *The Visible* contains three notes outlining this project, all dating from January 1959 (VI 165/217, 166/218, 168/219–20). See also unpublished references (from January 1959: BNF Ms. Vol. VIII 273; February 1959: 255/75a; and an undated remark 308/86a).

13. 'Lateral' is an important term used to describe intentionality, meaning and ontology in Merleau-Ponty's later work. See CPP 453; MSME 205; PW 142/197; IP 61/103; VI 78/108, 102/137, 125/164, 143/186.

14. See self-critical remarks in MSME about the *Phenomenology*'s reliance on classical, subject-centric categories (45–46).

15. Barbaras 2004, 14–17/33–36.

16. See Bonan 2001, chapter 5, on the importance of intersubjectivity in Merleau-Ponty's ontology.

17. For earlier versions of similar claims, see descriptions of perceptual consciousness (MSME 45–51), and the claim that the problem of intersubjectivity stands at the limit of an analysis of perception (53).

18. See PhP 370/412, the 1947 course Communication et Langage (Silverman 1979, 95–107), and analyses of dialogue in *Child Psychology and Pedagogy*.

19. See Landes 2013, 135. See also Robert 2005, who claims that dialogue offers a 'first sketch of the idea of *flesh*', without further developing this observation (151–56).

20. Landes 2013, 135.

21. See, for example, Landes 2013, 134; Bonan 2001 §17, 252, 342; Thierry 1987, 69–81; Stawarska 2013; Kearney 2013.

22. As I noted in chapter 4, Saussure certainly paves the way for a study of speech (PW 22–23/33), though Merleau-Ponty also credits this to Husserl and Pos (25/37). See chapter 4 for more on Merleau-Ponty's reading of Saussure and possible Saussurean influences on his thought.

23. For the former, see VI 139/181, 141/183, 249/297; for the latter, see VI 133–35/173–76, 144/187. See Hughes 2017 for a good overview of the concept of reversibility.

24. See, for example, PhP 189/224, 192/227; S 86/140, 95/156.

25. Despite these similarities, he also makes observations that are not congenial to his later account of intentional directedness. He sometimes suggests that a dialogical partner is a spectator 'copied from me' (135/187), that my perceptual field remains the privileged frame of reference (136/188), and that 'I *identify* myself with the person speaking before me' (18/28). By contrast, the accounts of reversibility and narcissism maintain a difference between subject and object, even if they stress their co-dependence. Still, if we look beyond some of the more local aims in this text, it is clear that this analysis provides an incipient account of the basic structure of both reversibility and narcissism.

26. See Hughes 2013; Morris and Maclaren 2015; Carbone 2004, 1–14.

27. See Casey 1984.

28. See Vallier 2005, 112–13.

29. See Husserl 1970, 368–69. Merleau-Ponty adopts a similar view (S 59/95).

30. PhP lxxxii/18, 441/480, 453/492.

31. See S 165/269 ff. See also VI 173/224–25, 238–39/287–88, 244/293. Cf. Butler 2005, 181; Dillon 1988, 85.

32. I provide a more detailed account of Merleau-Ponty's later view of intentionality in chapter 6, section 2.2.

33. For the former, see VI 200/250, 203/253, 248/297; for the latter, VI 218/267, 238–39/287–88.

34. See de Saint Aubert 2013, 157, for a list of passages where Merleau-Ponty links transgression and encroachment.

35. See Husserl 1970 §36 for more on this concept.

36. See de Saint Aubert 2004.

37. de Saint Aubert 2004, 64, 62, 81–82.

38. Ibid., 66; see also 72 passim.

39. See de Saint Aubert 2013, 153–61 for differences between these two accounts.

40. Instead of relying on Husserl's concept of *Paarung*, Merleau-Ponty invokes his own view of linguistic 'intentional transgression' (S 94/153).

41. See claims arguing for the need to move beyond a subject-centric account, towards a view of perceptual intentionality as 'imperception' (MSME 48–51). See also VI 189–90/240–41, 243/291–93.

42. See PhP 131/162–63, 414/454, 425/465.

43. Some remarks even identify *L'origine de la vérité* and *La prose du monde*, suggesting that they were connected or identical projects (BNF Ms. Vol. III 189, 218r, 237; VIII 115/2). See also remarks from the time of his candidature to the Collège de France, which claim that an enquiry into truth and intersubjectivity is required by his current research: 'The philosophical foundations of these essays are still to be rigorously elaborated. I am now working on two books dealing with a theory of truth' (PrP 6–7/41–42).

44. See VI 83–84/114, 208/258, 269/317.

45. Noble 2014, 225 notes that this description is similar to those associated with the concept of '*Ineinander*', but does not explore the connection with dialogue.

46. See VI 102/136–37, 117 n.1/154, 118/156, 126/165, 201/252.

47. Even in his philosophy of nature, the formative role of language is clear. While his 1959 to 1960 course The Concept of Nature claims that 'the ontology of Nature [is] the way toward ontology', and that 'the concept of Nature is always the expression of an ontology – and its privileged expression', he still

indicates that this research was only possible after investigations in the philosophy of language (N 204/265): 'this program' (viz. an ontology nature) 'took us several years; language' (220/282).

48. This view was first expressed by Claude Lefort (PW i/xi, ix–xi/xvii–xviii).

49. Cf. Dillon 1988.

50. Merleau-Ponty's intention to merge poetry and speech (or prose) resembles a demand articulated by Schlegel in *Athenaeum* Fragment 116. However, Merleau-Ponty develops this in a different direction, and I am not aware of any evidence suggesting that he was influenced by Schlegel's account of poetry.

51. See PW 147/204 for a published reference to 'involuntary poetry'.

Part III

6

LANGUAGE AND WORLD

In chapter 2, I argued that according to *Phenomenology of Perception*, empirical or first-order linguistic expression has a tripartite structure and articulates the meaning of lived experience. That account showed that Merleau-Ponty is chiefly interested in understanding lived language use. Language use articulates a subject's perspective in a distinctive gestural 'style'. But under certain conditions, expression can also transform our view of the world. This possibility was typically reserved for 'authentic' modes of aesthetic expression. In authentic expression, artists reinterpret linguistic norms and generate novel possibilities for understanding experience. Authentic expression typically has a broader cultural value, but as I suggested in chapter 3, some claims in the *Phenomenology* also pointed to the conclusion that phenomenology itself realises a version of authentic expression. They brushed up against some of the more modest, descriptive goals that Merleau-Ponty claimed phenomenology must pursue.

As this chapter will attempt to show, Merleau-Ponty's later reflections on empirical expression develop the hitherto restricted claim that linguistic expression can transform the meaning of the world and subjects' experience. His later writings accord a greater world-forming role to expression at the empirical level. Unlike in the *Phenomenology*, which also claimed that expression gives voice to experience, Merleau-Ponty now holds that expressive operations modulate the 'being' of the world, and not only the perspective of a subject who happens to find herself in it. This does not mean that everyday expression is necessarily aesthetic, artistic or authentic (the latter term rarely appears in his later writings). Instead, it suggests that language plays a central role in securing the intelligibility, coherence and meaning of experience, one hitherto reserved for perception.

In chapter 1, I argued that the goal of understanding the consciousness-world relation is already present in Merleau-Ponty's first systematic writings. In *Structure*, his account of this relation rested on an incipient view of the role that language plays in unfolding the meaning of 'structure'. But even if higher-order behavioural structures and human consciousness are ultimately clarified by appeal to 'expressive' activities, *Structure* did not consider the possibility that language intervened in perceptual structure at the first-order level. Perception was identified as our primary access point to the world. Subsequent writings also stop short of drawing this inference, despite Merleau-Ponty's increasing interest in and recognition of the philosophical importance of language. As we saw in chapter 3, Merleau-Ponty's premises entail that phenomenological description transforms the meaning of lived experience, and that perception cannot be unproblematically construed as a sufficient phenomenological foundation. Nevertheless, he maintained the distinction between the 'tacit' and 'spoken' *cogito*, affirming the priority of the former.

Renewed attention to psychological, literary, formal and phenomenological theories of expression in the early to mid-1950s motivate a shift in this position. As we saw in chapters 4 and 5, insights into creative modes of expression in literature, together with new discoveries connected to studies of dialogue, led Merleau-Ponty to sharpen his focus on the inventive and constructive power of language. New findings suggested that language is no mere medium for the expression of a more fundamental category of meaning. Instead, Merleau-Ponty was led to conclude that language co-constitutes the meaning of experience. This view is a defining feature of his later thought.

This chapter will reconstruct and unpack the basic concepts and assumptions underlying the view that language co-constitutes experience. I first review potential influences on this position (section 1). I then consider Merleau-Ponty's view that meaning can be understood as 'cohesion' or 'coherence' (section 2). This important position is informed by a set of new concepts that emerge in his later writings, including *'l'écart'*, the 'flesh', 'reversibility', 'latent' intentionality and 'institution'. These terms are the basic building blocks of Merleau-Ponty's later reflections on world, 'being', experience, and meaning, and they jointly lay the groundwork for his later account of the perception-language relation. On his account, perception and language (and by extension, thought) are intertwined (section 3.1). While he argued in previous texts that all thought unfolds in language, he now claims that perceptual experience is also mediated by linguistic meaning, which is 'instituted' or 'inheres' in the spatio-temporal field (section 3.2). We perceive objects as determinate and meaningful unities because we possess linguistic concepts associated with them. Perceptual meaning does not depend only on perceptual givens. Background linguistic meanings help to secure the coherence, familiarity and seamlessness of our everyday frequenting of the perceptual world; with another set of linguistic concepts, the world would appear differently. Linguistic meaning lends experience a degree of intelligibility that perception is unable to achieve on its own.

Language also plays a more active role in forming experience, which unfolds at two levels (section 3.3). First, expression brings out perceptual meanings that would otherwise remain unsaid. This contributes something essential to experience, and Merleau-Ponty construes linguistic expression as a realisation or completion of perception. Second, a natural language offers specific possibilities for naming and ordering the objects of experience. At this level, language forms experience by allowing it to appear and to be expressed under a certain guise. Different natural languages offer distinct possibilities for ordering experience, and Merleau-Ponty thinks these different perspectives jointly constitute the meaning of the world. This account may motivate worries about relativism, about the extent to which experience or the world really have a cohesive meaning at all, and about how one might substantiate its basic claims; I conclude the chapter by briefly considering them (section 4).

Before considering possible influences on Merleau-Ponty's increased interest in the role that language plays in everyday experience, I would first like to address potential worries about the decision to consider his later view of empirical expression on its own. Some readers might doubt that he intends to develop an account of empirical expression at all. Assuming that he does, it might seem mistaken to consider this account separately from remarks about the transcendental or 'ontological' dimension of language, given that he denies (or at least does not strictly observe) the empirical/transcendental distinction.

Merleau-Ponty's later texts offer some analyses of non-philosophical modes of language use. For ease of presentation, and to identify continuities with earlier writings, I use the term 'empirical' to characterise such accounts. I think it is clear from the textual evidence that Merleau-Ponty offers descriptions of language in this vein, and that these descriptions modify some earlier assumptions about empirical expression. While he certainly does not observe the distinction as clearly as Kant or Husserl, he still accepts that we must pose different kinds of questions about everyday and philosophical modes of language use.[1] To be sure, he stresses that these two domains are continuous, to an arguably greater degree than before. However, unless one is prepared to accept that Merleau-Ponty wholly collapses the distinction between everyday and reflective or ontological engagements, it should be unproblematic to concede that he has some account of non-ontological modes of expression. The evidence considered in this chapter suggests that the first claim is difficult to maintain. Further, the incomplete state of *The Visible* requires that we carefully sort textual evidence and philosophical analyses pertaining to separate modalities of language use.[2]

1. PHILOSOPHICAL PREDECESSORS AND POTENTIAL INFLUENCES

It will be helpful to first consider potential influences on Merleau-Ponty's view that language plays a formative role in experience. This will also serve to identify the broad outlines of Merleau-Ponty's approach to the language-perception relation in his later work. The claims below may strike some readers as quite proximate to positions advanced by his German philosophical predecessors, and it is plausible that he may have adopted some of them. To begin with a more recent example, in the *Tractatus* Wittgenstein claims that 'the limits of my language mean the limits of my world'.[3] In later writings, he holds that facts about language use shape historically determined 'forms of life', which support a particular *Weltanschauung* and a 'picture' of what makes for a philosophical problem.[4] The evidence below suggests that Merleau-

Ponty would agree with both claims. In the hermeneutical tradition, Heidegger and Gadamer advance similar views.[5] More recently, Charles Taylor has defended a 'constitutive' view of language, on which language shapes the world instead of merely processing bits of information contained in it.[6] Taylor's view is influenced by Merleau-Ponty's early work, which Taylor argues is continuous with the German Romantic tradition, especially Herder, Humboldt and Hamann. Taylor contends that like these thinkers, for Merleau-Ponty language use presupposes an irreducible sense of intrinsic rightness (that *this* word can be used to express *that* idea), supported by a form of life that cannot be explained by appeal to cognitive processes or reductive accounts of meaning.[7]

Various remarks on Herder, von Humboldt, Heidegger and Cassirer from the late 1930s until the end of his career leave little doubt that Merleau-Ponty encountered and entertained versions of the claim that language shapes experience and the meaning of the world. However, textual evidence does not suggest that these sources are decisive for his own version of this claim. For example, he seems to have not been particularly sympathetic to Wittgenstein's *Tractatus*.[8] His engagement with von Humboldt and Cassirer is more extensive, but his remarks about these thinkers, and the structure of his account of the language-world relation, do not suggest they exercised a decisive influence. His reading of Heidegger is a different matter, and will be considered in greater detail in later sections and in chapter 7.

1.1 Humboldt's '*innere Sprachform*'

The key concept from Humboldt's philosophy of language that Merleau-Ponty returns to is the '*innere Sprachform*' or the 'inner language form'. The inner language form underwrites linguistic expression and includes semantic content and grammatical rules.[9] It is present in each natural language in a different modality, and reflects geographical, cultural and historical differences. By maintaining a sensitivity to the features that make a natural language unique, Humboldt suggests that a particular people, culture or nation generate a distinctive worldview based on a given language form.

Merleau-Ponty does not usually cite a specific text from Humboldt when invoking this concept.[10] It makes an appearance as early as 1949, in one of Merleau-Ponty's lecture courses at the Sorbonne. He accepts Humboldt's claims that '[each] language has its manner of expressing different relations like time or space', and that the *innere Sprachform* 'is the totality of processes and expression that are produced when we are on the point of expressing our thought or understanding the other's thought'. This concept testifies to the 'junction of pure thought and language', 'which differs according to how we speak or write, how we address ourselves or others. [. . .] It is this space of thought in language, non-explicitly, that constitutes *style*' (CPP 48–49). Here, the *innere Sprachform* is used to explain how linguistic expression allows subjects to develop a broader worldview. Members of a given culture grasp objects, problems or concepts with the help of their linguistic resources. Recall that Merleau-Ponty makes a similar point when developing his account of rationality in *Phenomenology*, and in his account of 'institution'. Put simply, we can think just those thoughts that are supported by our linguistic resources. Merleau-Ponty also holds that the '"*innere Sprachform*" is a mental landscape common to all the members of a linguistic community and through which it is possible to coexist with one another in the cultural milieu' (CPP 50). As we will see below, these claims are also made in Merleau-Ponty's later writings, and they take on a deep philosophical importance.

In a rare direct reference published during his lifetime (1953), Merleau-Ponty invokes Humboldt to explain spoken expression. Referring again to the *innere Sprachform*, he claims that

> The words and turns of phrase needed to bring my significative intention to expression recommend themselves to me, when I am speaking, only by what Humboldt called *innere Sprachform* (and our contemporaries call *Wortbegriff*), that is, only by a certain style of speaking from which they arise and according to which they are organised without my having to represent them to myself. (S 88/143)

While this further clarifies empirical expression, the appeal to Humboldt does not seem to add much to Merleau-Ponty's existing non-cognitive account of linguistic style. At best, Humboldt's theory can be seen as a precursor to the *Phenomenology*'s account, but one that, as we saw in chapters 2 and 3, Merleau-Ponty did not avail himself of. He occasionally interprets the *innere Sprachform* in very specific terms, noting that it varies from person to person, much like the *Phenomenology*'s account of gestural style (e.g., he claims that the difference between chatty and reticent people can be explained by differences in their respective *inneren Sprachformen*).

In The Problem of Speech, a nontrivial shift in Merleau-Ponty's interest in the *innere Sprachform* can be detected. He invokes the term less frequently to describe first-personal linguistic style.[11] It still captures the idea that language is 'plastic' and that it responds to different expressive needs (BNF Ms. Vol. XII 40/28v). The *innere Sprachform* can also help us better understand the 'thickness' (*épaisseur*) or ambiguity in language, showcased in intersubjective expression, for example. But the concept also suggests that 'all language is a global share [*portion*] of a world and must be studied in this totality'. Empirical expression not only articulates a subject's particular stance, but also connects her to the world.

Although Merleau-Ponty referred, in earlier texts, to Humboldt's view of the world-forming role of language, that he increasingly stresses it in later work suggests a renewed interest in the broader constructive possibilities of expression. Largely following Goldstein's interpretation of Humboldt in *Language and Language Disturbances*, Merleau-Ponty stresses that language guides our view of the world, and that it is inseparable from worldly structures (84v).[12] In the mid-1950s, he distinguishes these deeper constructive possibilities from instrumental or mundane uses of language: 'Humboldt has expressed this function that underlies constituted language [*le langage constitué*] and thought, this relation to the world that is to be grasped in each language [*langue*] or each individual'. Even if Merleau-Ponty agrees with Humboldt that different languages individuate distinctive relations to the world, the account below reveals that Merleau-Ponty's eventual reading of the language-world relation does not draw this conclusion using Humboldt's premises.

1.2 Cassirer, Language and Representation

In addition to Humboldt, Merleau-Ponty was also familiar with Cassirer's reflections on the world-forming role of language. In a discussion of the 'fit' between consciousness and world in *Structure*, he refers to Cassirer when making the following highly suggestive remark about the language-world relation:

> If language did not encounter some predisposition for the act of speech in the child who hears speaking, it would remain for him a sonorous phenomenon among others for a long time; it would have no power over the mosaic of sensations possessed by infantile consciousness; one could not understand how it could play the guiding role which psychologists agree in granting to it in the constitution of the perceived world. (SB 169/183–84)

This remark draws familiar conclusions: linguistic expression is integrated with other expressive capacities, and it helps us navigate the world. It is noteworthy chiefly because it identifies the world-forming capacity of language so early in Merleau-Ponty's career. However, as we will see below, he does not return to this specific version of the claim when eventually developing his own view of how perception is informed by language.

The citation in the final sentence above is also significant. It traces the 'psychological' view that language has a guiding role in perception to a 1934 French translation of Cassirer's 'Die Sprache und der Aufbau der Gegenstandwelt' (1932). This article develops Cassirer's account of the world-forming role of language, and suggests a proximity to some of Humboldt's views.[13] The article also contains multiple references to empirical literature (also found in *Philosophy of Symbolic Forms*) that Merleau-Ponty would eventually avail himself of in *Phenomenology*.[14] Cassirer's article is the source for Merleau-Ponty's claim above about language use in children, and for the related point that language guides perceptual experience. Indeed, in this article, Cassirer makes two claims that Merleau-Ponty subsequently accepts. Cassirer holds that language is 'the means of the formation of objects'.[15] And he claims that 'lived experiences' are 'lodged with the development of language', and can organise the 'manifold' of representations.[16] Both claims entail that elementary perceptual experience is guided by linguistic usage, and that language forms the structure of experience.

Despite agreeing in principle, a close look reveals that Merleau-Ponty is not guided by the specific versions of these claims when he develops his own view. A key difference concerns Cassirer's reliance on the category of 'representation'. For Cassirer, advanced forms of representation presuppose specific and historically variant linguistic supports, which enable representations of a determinate kind. Anticipating an insight adopted in *Structure*, he contends that more objective forms of representation depend on a deeper subjective meaning-making capacity. Developmental psychology will succeed insofar as it takes direction from this basic insight. For Merleau-Ponty, however, 'representation' is an inadequate category for understanding linguistic and perceptual meaning, and for specifying the relations obtaining between them. If the former can influence the latter, this occurs through some other means. For this reason, Merleau-Ponty does not appeal to Cassirer when advancing his version of the world-forming role of language, even if he also accepts that it has such a role.

As with his readings of other figures in the history of philosophy, we must tread carefully when evaluating Merleau-Ponty's interpretation of Cassirer and von Humboldt. He uses these thinkers selectively, filters their claims through his own phenomenological lens, and (in the case of Humboldt) often relies on secondary readings. Indeed, it is not always clear how much of Merleau-Ponty's own views are being read into these thinkers. A more important consideration weighs against the suggestion that Merleau-Ponty relies on Cassirer or Humboldt when articulating his own view. A basic limitation of these accounts concerns their evaluation of the all-important perception-language relation, which is fundamental in Merleau-Ponty's account of how language shapes experience and the world. Humboldt generally overlooks it, and Cassirer approaches it through a theoretical framework that Merleau-Ponty finds wanting.

2. MEANING AS COHESION

Merleau-Ponty's distinctive interpretation of the world-forming capacity of language unfolds within the context of a broader theory of meaning, which I will call 'meaning as cohesion'. A set of new concepts make up its basic constituent parts. In the early sections of *The Visible and the Invisible*, and in associated research and lecture notes, Merleau-Ponty identifies the analysis and interpretation of meaning (*le sens*) as a guiding concern of his later projects:

> Our point of departure shall not be *being is, nothingness is not* – not even: *being is all there is* – these are formula of totalising thought, of a high-altitude thought [*d'une pensée de survol*] – but: there is being, there is a world, there is *something*; in the strong sense in which the Greek speaks of τὸ λέγειν, there is cohesion [*cohésion*], there is meaning [*sens*]. (VI 88/119)

For Merleau-Ponty, it is uncontroversial that our experience has some sense to it, and that it meaningfully hangs together. One way to express this point is to say that our experience has an integrated, unified or cohesive meaning. Accordingly, the passage above links the concepts of 'meaning' and 'cohesion'. (The term *'cohésion'* can also mean 'coherence'. This translation sometimes better captures the sense of the text, and I will use it in such cases.) Meaning can also be understood as cohesion because, despite the different standpoints from which we experience the world (which depend, for example, on physical abilities, geographical location, culture, gender, language and more), there is an integrated core of sense that underlies and under some conditions can even unify diverse perspectives. Our perspectives are ours, but we share a world in common with others. For Merleau-Ponty, the conditions for sense-making are intersubjective. In principle, we can observe fundamental points of contact between different perspectives. Meaning coheres across these perspectives.

Different perspectives do not converge only in the perceptual realm. Subjective intentions also intersect at the level of 'ideal' meaning, which Merleau-Ponty often refers to using the term *'signification'*. As we saw in chapter 4, his incipient account of metaphysics held that metaphysical consciousness investigates the world's intelligible or 'rational principle' (or 'Logos'), and that this structure unifies perceptual and higher-order cultural meanings. Though distinct, different views of a material object might share intentional elements. As Merleau-Ponty now argues, this presupposes shared background conditions (e.g., a given conceptual scheme or set of definitions). The view of meaning as cohesion also aims to detail these ideal conceptual conditions. This suggests that Merleau-Ponty's approach to meaning has become more holistic. A focus on perceptual or ideal conditions on their own will prove insufficient. This holistic approach to the analysis of meaning can be better understood by disentangling and defining some later concepts that show how meaning coheres: they include the '*écart*', 'flesh', 'reversibility', 'narcissism' and 'institution'.

2.1 The '*Écart*'

As I argued in part 2, Merleau-Ponty's research in the mid-1950s led him to conclude that key philosophical concepts must be defined with reference to intersubjectivity. Famously, Husserl's early theory of perception contends that material objects have infinitely many profiles that are in principle perceptible by numerically different perceivers. This anticipates his own interest in intersubjectivity, which subsequent phenomenologists took seriously. Merleau-Ponty adopts this perceptual claim and develops it in two new directions. This bears on how we should interpret '*l'écart*', an important and recurring concept in his later writings.

First, Merleau-Ponty widens the scope of Husserl's claim. Any object or 'being' at all is mediated by multiple perspectives (this includes 'being' itself; that is, the sum total of perceived and ideal meanings). In the 1959 article 'The Philosopher and His Shadow', Merleau-Ponty claims that the 'solipsist thing', or the object as seen by a single subject, is not primarily what Husserl (or phenomenology) is ultimately interested in understanding (S 173/282, 171/279). The paradigmatic object of phenomenological enquiry, and not only of perceptual experience, is an intersubjective entity.

Second, Merleau-Ponty elevates Husserl's claim to a guiding methodological principle: phenomenological analysis must be advanced by taking account of the perspectives of multiple perceivers (and not only those that a single subject could possibly occupy). Intersubjective analyses take direction from 'the miraculous multiplication of perceptible being, which gives the same things the power to be things for more than one perceiver' (S 16/30; VI 8/23). Phenomenological descriptions and concepts can be developed only by taking account of multiple perspectives. On this assumption, an explanation of perception, space and time, or material objects must be structured in a way that is not *ipso facto* indexed to a single perspective; instead, it must be in principle open to others.

While these claims are familiar, they are strengthened by the introduction of an important technical term, coupled with some nontrivial philosophical shifts in Merleau-Ponty's approach to the analysis of experience. While he retains an emphasis on visual phenomena, he also modifies the *Phenomenology*'s account of perception (VI 83/113–14). One important shift concerns the claim that perception is characterised by a 'distance', 'divergence' or 'difference'.[17] As he claims, 'The sensible order is *being at a distance* [à distance]' (S 167/273). The claim that there is a distance or divergence between perceiver and perceived was a feature of his earlier work (see for example, PhP 45/68, 247/285). This was typically understood in a spatial vein: subject and object are separated by a spatial distance. In later work, objects are thought to stand at a distance from perceivers because their meaning is fundamentally opaque, and because it resists comprehensive or satisfactory clarification. Earlier observations about spatial or temporal distance, and about the 'ambiguity' of perception, are now supplemented by claims to the effect that given the plurality of perspectives from which a perceptual (or ideal) object may be engaged, a stable definition of the object remains elusive. Divergence characterises perceptual meaning because different subjects could, in principle, engage objects in fundamentally dissimilar ways. The full range of meanings associated with a given object or experience cannot be exhaustively detailed by appeal to its presence to a single subject.

This understanding of the '*écart*' is consonant with the view that meaning is located at the intersection of numerically distinct perspectives ('meaning as cohesion'). Other textual evidence also supports an intersubjective reading of the '*écart*'. A text from September 1958 claims that his later ontology takes direction from the idea that philosophical analysis must integrate multiple viewpoints (past, present and future) of experience and being. It is opposed to 'the idea that this world is the only possible [one]' (BNF Ms. Vol. VIII 141/6b).[18] While the *Phenomenology* took intersubjective concerns seriously, it did not identify intersubjectivity as a basic orientation point of phenomenological analysis. By contrast, the phenomenological fact of perspectival pluralism is now approached primarily from an intersubjective point of view:

> My perceived world and the half-disclosed things before me have in their thickness what it takes to supply more than one sensible subject with 'states of consciousness'; they have the right to many other witnesses besides me. When a behaviour is sketched out in this world which already goes beyond me, this is but one more dimension in primordial being, which comprises them all. (S 170/277)

To claim that a 'distance' characterises perception, then, also means that a given perspective on a particular object cannot be privileged without qualification. Different viewpoints together comprise what Merleau-Ponty calls 'being', the sum of possible (and not only actual) perspectives on the world. The features of objects I cannot fully grasp might be better comprehended by others. This suggests that subjective experience of an object or the world can be better understood by taking an intersubjective perspective. As Merleau-Ponty claims elsewhere, 'Being [is] no longer being *before me*, but surrounding me [*m'entourant*], and in a sense traversing me, and my vision of Being [does not form] itself from elsewhere, but from the midst of Being' (VI 114/151). This deeper sense of 'distance' or 'divergence' makes frequent appearances in his later writings.

I noted earlier that the concept of 'divergence' was linked to Merleau-Ponty's view of meaning.[19] This continues in *The Visible*, which claims that perception

> is constantly enshrouded by those mists we call the sensible world or history, the *one* [l'on] of corporeal life and the *one* of human life, present and past, as a pell-mell ensemble of bodies and minds [*esprits*], promiscuity of faces, words, actions, with, between them all, that cohesion which cannot be denied them since they are all differences, extreme variants [*écarts*] of the same thing. (VI 84/115)

This text modifies Merleau-Ponty's view of the 'anonymity' or ('one') of perception, a claim once used to describe the pre-personal dimensions of perceptual experience. The term now expresses the idea that perceptual meaning is not the property of any particular subject. A subject's perspective is but one node in a broader network of worldly meaning. Perceptual anonymity is no longer invoked solely to describe the tacit nature of perceptual experience (though this feature persists). While we might approach numerically identical experiences or objects from different first-personal perspectives, our diverging views of the former are linked and open onto an underlying core of meaning. Claims about perceptual divergence, then, do not preclude the convergence of perspectives. Following the passage above, divergence can be taken in a perceptual vein: the *écart* is the range or distribution of differences between perceivers' construals of a given object. Despite the different intentions that engage a particular object, different views pick out a cohesive core (which cannot be reduced to purely material properties). Below, I consider a key non-perceptual condition that underlies these experiences of meaning-cohesion.

A look at Merleau-Ponty's later reflections on intentionality will also help to disambiguate his view of meaning as cohesion. He invokes the concepts of 'flesh', 'reversibility' and 'narcissism' to account for our directedness to the world. Together with the concept of 'institution', which explains how past (and 'ideal') meanings are integrated in the present, these concepts identify additional conditions for sense-making.

2.2 'Latent' Intentionality ('Flesh', 'Reversibility' and 'Narcissism')

In Merleau-Ponty's later work, the concept of the *écart* is sometimes paired with 'the flesh' (*la chair*). This term is billed as an original and necessary supplement to the history of Western philosophy. Despite pre-Socratic echoes, Merleau-Ponty alleges that the tradition lacks a name for the particular relation he has in mind (140/182). For

> [t]he flesh is not matter, is not mind, is not substance. To designate it, we should need the old term 'element', in the sense it was used to speak of water, air, earth, and fire, that is, in the sense of a *general thing*, midway between the spatio-temporal individual and the idea, a sort of incarnate principle that brings a style of being wherever there is a fragment of being. The flesh is in this sense an 'element' of Being. (VI 139/182)

According to this text, an individual object, space and time, and importantly, our relation to the world, is structured according to the flesh. The flesh is at once general and particular. This suggests (despite the name) that it is not material.[20] Its generality consists in a certain 'style' (or form) that instantiates itself in experience. In this restricted sense, the flesh makes meaningful experience possible, though Merleau-Ponty does not suggest that this should be read along the lines of transcendental conditions of possibility.

Despite the enigmatic descriptions associated with the term, a closer look at the opening sections of the last complete chapter of *The Visible* suggests a familiar motivation for deploying it. Undoubtedly, 'the flesh' is used in a range of contexts, any one of which may be privileged in an attempt at definition.[21] As I will read it, the concept of flesh describes the intentional relation between perceiver and perceived, or between subject, object and world (140/182). The latter terms, however, miss something fundamental about subjective intentional contact with things, others and the self, and should be replaced by what Merleau-Ponty takes to be a more adequate philosophical vocabulary. Still, evidence suggests that the term attempts to answer a classical phenomenological problem: namely, how subjects are directed to objects. To explain this link, Merleau-Ponty does not invoke classical terms like 'noema' or 'intentional pole'. Instead, he claims that perceivers are directed to 'things' or 'elements' (218/267), sometimes also called 'rays of the world' (114/151, 218/267, 240/288–89, 265/313). Despite shifts in terminology, the intentional role of the flesh comes through. Here it will suffice to review some of its intentional features, and note their connection to language.[22]

The flesh supports an intentional relation to objects because, as a basic 'element' underlying possible objects or experiences, it is present in both sides of the intentional relation: 'my body is made of the same flesh as the world (it is a perceived), and moreover that this flesh of my body is shared by the world, the world reflects it, encroaches upon it and it encroaches upon the world' (248/297). This suggests (without using the term) that the flesh constitutes 'subject' and 'object'. Further, it occupies two (or more) terms in a relation of intentional 'encroachment' or 'transgression', two terms we first encountered in chapter 5. If 'a body – world relationship is recognised', then it becomes clear that my flesh is somehow present in the world and vice versa (136 n.2/177). This basic structure is evidenced in different modalities of intentional experience, including that between thinking and its objects.

In later writings, familiar terms like 'encroachment', 'latency', 'reversibility' and 'narcissism' are used to work out this relation. In various texts, Merleau-Ponty announces his desire to develop an account of 'latent intentionality' (VI 173/224–25, 238–39/287–88, 244/293). Most basically, this view of intentionality accords a greater degree of passivity to the subject than can be found in Husserl's early or classical view (or in its variants, like that advanced by Gurwitsch). On this view, subjects are open to and directed by perceptual objects to a greater degree than in the *Phenomenology*. This is the deeper sense of intentional 'latency' that Merleau-Ponty thinks an account of directedness to objects should privilege (one that, despite his own contributions, ultimately originates in the later Husserl).

A key aim of this account of intentionality is to capture our everyday feeling of proximity to objects, and to describe it in a nonintellectualist manner (one consistent with actual experiences of intentional directedness). According to Merleau-Ponty, when directed to objects, we do not experience ourselves actively determining or forming their meaning. Perception is instead characterised by a sense of familiarity with empirical givens. We can usually successful name what we see, and can seamlessly identify the basic features or characteristics of an experience, without having previously investigated it or subjected it to analytical scrutiny. It seems as if objects or visual fields offer their meaning to us, and that our gaze successfully picks them out because it is guided by them. Intentional directedness makes us feel of a kind with the objects we are directed to (143–44/186).

These observations are partly captured using the concept of 'encroachment'. We observe that objects and the world itself solicits subjects, and that this process generates meaningful experiences. This suggests that a classical picture of subject-object roles, on which the former determine the latter, should be replaced by a view on which subject and object 'encroach' on one another. The structures we locate in objects seem (according to the phenomena) to exercise as much influence in forming the intentional relation as the intentions originating in us. This does not mean that we should embrace a 'myth of the given' or put faith in a return to the 'immediate' (99/133, 122/160).

Rather, as we saw in chapter 5, the concept of encroachment can helpfully describe a relation on which subject and object occupy equally important intentional and semantic roles. That the term 'encroachment' succeeds in capturing this intentional relation confirms that Merleau-Ponty continues to profit from his research into dialogue.

Intentionality can also be described using the terms 'narcissism' and 'reversibility', two concepts closely related to 'encroachment'. In my analysis of dialogue, I argued that attention to dialogical expression leads Merleau-Ponty to articulate early versions of both concepts. When applied to experience, the claim that perception is narcissistic can be understood as a consequence of the view that subject and object codetermine the intentional relation (or, in the earlier case, that they codetermine the meaning of conversation). The meaning of perception also depends on conditions originating in the subject; namely, the assumptions subjects rely on when frequenting the world. For example, these background conditions have it that I see a small, bear-shaped felt object as a toy rather than a precious object (assumptions about what a 'toy' looks like and about material value separate the former from the latter). Concepts (which are linguistic unities, for Merleau-Ponty) are an essential part of these background conditions. As I will suggest below, perceptual narcissism has a linguistic version.

Like 'encroachment', the concept of 'reversibility' also highlights the tight connection between subjects and objects (135–36/175). Sense modalities like sight, touch and taste are, in principle, reversible with their objects (the seen, the touched, the tasted) because both can fulfil roles traditionally designated by subject and object. Experiences in which we feel our vision, touch, and more directed by an ostensibly passive or inert object reveal that intentionality is a bidirectional relation, not one that flows unidirectionally from subject to object. The qualitative character of perception is formed in the encounter between subject and object. As we saw above, this relation is also present in other important dimensions of experience, like embodied activity and passivity.

These tenets, which further develop the claim that 'divergence' (*l'écart*) characterises experience, comprise Merleau-Ponty's updated, 'ontological' account of intentionality. The distance in perception enables contact or 'proximity' with objects and is also the condition that allows objects to guide our gaze (135/176, 213/263). The proximity he has in mind is not that of classical phenomenological 'apprehension'

(*Auffassung*) (he maintains that it is not 'frontal'). Instead, it allows for a plurality of possible perspectives, which mitigates the sufficiency of a single subject's grasp of sense at a given time. Thus far, the terms used to detail intentional experience and the cohesion of meaning have been read in a descriptive register. They commit us to assuming their existence at the moment a subject confronts her world, but do not have an extra-subjective status. Thus far, they do not point to further 'ontological' posits; that is, claims about the structure of reality absent our sense-making activities (below, 'institution' refers to meanings that transcend our current perspectives, but which were nevertheless intended by past subjects). I will return to this point in chapter 7.

For now, an important connection between intentionality and language can be observed. If intentionality has the structure described above, then it seems untenable to hold that perceptual meaning founds linguistic meaning. If intentional relations are reversible and require equal contributions from subject and object, and if background conceptual commitments (which are language-like) determine intentional content, then a reversibility also obtains between a subject's grasp of linguistic meaning and the objects she intends. More fundamentally, Merleau-Ponty's earlier distinction between linguistic and non-linguistic elements of intentional experience is put under stress. Reformulating the relations of priority between perception and language is required by his new and distinctive take on how language structures experience. The claim that meaning is 'instituted' also supports this shift.

2.3 'Institution'

The view that meaning is 'instituted' is widely seen as an important development in Merleau-Ponty's later work. Like many other later claims, it refines existing commitments (in this case, his earlier account of sedimentation and ideal meaning or *signification* is refigured). The move to emphasise instituted meaning is sometimes thought to rival the phenomenological theory of meaning constitution; Merleau-Ponty sometimes suggests as much (IP 165). But his account of institution only rules out a narrow, intellectualist view of constitution.[23] If constitution is understood more fundamentally as the process of meaning-formation that explains how objects or experiences come to have a sense, then there is no tension between the two terms.[24] Evidence from later texts suggests that Merleau-Ponty is not averse to this more basic meaning of constitution (IP 102/136; S 173/282; VI 216/266, 249/297).

The concept of institution is examined in depth in a 1954 Collège de France course. A full review of the course is not possible here, but one of its more important conclusions is that 'sedimented' meaning (*la signification*) is not divorced from occurrent perceptual experience.[25] In fact, the very idea of purely sedimented meaning is put under stress by new analyses of expression that emphasise a continuity between cultural, historical, linguistic and perceptual meaning. These analyses suggest that sedimented meanings are located in and accessed through first-personal perceptual experience (earlier accounts of sedimentation did not directly address the question of how sedimented meanings are accessed, though they presupposed that subjects have direct contact with abstract meaning) (IP 48/87, 53/93; see also HLP 49/60, 53/64).[26] Merleau-Ponty does not collapse the distinction between *sens* and *signification*, but he suggests that perception makes contact with significations that are not founded solely on perceptual meanings (VI 171/223).

To understand how institution makes experience coherent, consider the important claim that an institution is 'the establishment of a dimension' (IP 25/61). This remark links concerns about institution with the philosophy of time. As in Husserl's account, the concept of institution presupposes an account of time-constitution and temporality, and a few words about time and institution will help us better understand Merleau-Ponty's renewed interest in the concept. In his later work, he claims that time is 'dimensional'. This view is thought to move away from Husserl's early view of time-consciousness (the version Merleau-Ponty was familiar with). The *Phenomenology* developed an account of embodied and lived time, but still endorsed the basics of Husserl's account. It held that time has a tripartite articulated structure, which consists in retentions of the past, impressions of the present and protentions or expectations of the future (PhP 442–44/481–83). This structure is 'transcendent'; that is, forward-looking or progressive. Even backwardly referring processes like recollection or memory are understood to produce a new temporal object (the memory of the past in the present). Temporal experience always presupposes a past, which it integrates into the present; but the relation between the different layers of time is ultimately progressive.

This model of temporality was presupposed in post-*Phenomenology* writings, and Merleau-Ponty's definition of institution continued to reflect basic Husserlian commitments. In *The Prose of the World*, for instance, the term '*Stiftung*' was used to describe the 'unlimited fecundity' of each present, which can persist 'universally' (PW 68/96). Each present can, in principle, be reaccessed thanks to the underlying retentional continuity of time, which extends into the future. Claims like this suggested that despite some inevitable (though seemingly minor) modifications, institution fundamentally preserves the meaning of the past. Still, even in these texts, it is unclear if Merleau-Ponty wants to stress the modificatory or the preservative character of institution. Some of his remarks during this period remind us of claims from the *Phenomenology* that subjects can access instituted meanings or memories 'precisely as they were'; that is, without significant modifications (PhP 446/485).[27] He claims, for example, that past moments can 'perpetually come to life again' (PW 68/96).

By invoking the concept of 'dimensionality', in his middle and later writings Merleau-Ponty increasingly stresses the transformative possibilities of institution, which were less prominent in earlier discussions. This moves him somewhat further away from some Husserlian assumptions influencing his earlier account.[28] The experience of the temporal present, as evidenced by experiences of memory and forgetting, does not suggest that the past is accessed by way of a sequence of prior memories. Even if we deliberately try to recall some past event, the experience of remembering suggests that past and present are connected by discontinuous references. Time is better understood as dimensional because it is characterised by relations that extend in a diverse plurality of directions. The present opens onto the past (and future) in a manner that cannot be individuated by a linear time-series. According to Merleau-Ponty, temporality

> contains an intentional reference which is not only from the past to the factual, empirical present, but also and inversely from the factual present to a dimensional present or *Welt* or Being, where the past is 'simultaneous' with the present in the narrow sense. This *reciprocal* intentional reference marks the limit of the intentional analytic: the point where it becomes a philosophy of transcendence. (VI 243–44/292)

The deeper sense of transcendence in time is one of intertwining reference. Time transcends itself, and the (helpful but ultimately insufficient) boundaries of a linear analysis, because time flows in multiple directions. Temporal experience suggests that time is not bound by a time-series. To return to the case of memory, Merleau-Ponty observes that we often recover a forgotten event or object (in part or whole) through some engagement or activity in the present, which does not bear a relation to the past that is immediately clear to us. For example, I might remember the name of a childhood friend while engaging in some activity I shared with that friend. My friend's name might elude me if I were asked to recall it on the spot, at some other time. Nevertheless, the name is preserved in my memory, but it is accessed indirectly. When I eventually recall the name, I do so while engaged in some activity here and now. Even recollection, which is the active attempt to revive the past, presupposes this mode of access to past experience (evidence about past events or objects is often confused, and the connections between moments of the past and present are often disordered, even as we try to specify them). This account is offered as a description of what Merleau-Ponty thinks is our typical experience of time. Influenced by Proust, he suggests that temporal experience mixes active and passive elements, and connects past, present and future through interweaving and indirect references.

While it highlights the complexity of temporal relations, this account still suggests that present, past and future are closely bound up with one another. Merleau-Ponty makes this point by claiming that present and past are 'simultaneous': current engagements could immediately recall some past, and divisions between moments of time seem artificial. Past and present implicitly contain and refer to one another: my acquaintance's name is latent but is unlocked by some activity in the present; it needs the right sort of engagement for it to be accessed. This approach to temporality recalls the relation of mutual codetermination encountered above.[29] Time admits of a similar characterisation: 'time' and 'space' have a 'carnal' (*charnelle*) quality, a term often associated with 'the flesh' (IP 195/254). The claim that time is instituted holds that there is a 'coupling' relation between past and present.

As I suggested, this understanding of temporal preservation attempts to explain how we access and transform past (or 'instituted') meanings. An institution endows experience with 'durable dimensions' that can be taken up, modified and related to other moments of time (IP 77/125). Indeed, each moment of the present and past is characterised by 'generality': it can, in principle, intersect with and be developed in different directions (HLP 45/54).

The model of institution is significant not only because it supports the new view of temporality Merleau-Ponty wants to develop, but also because it helps him describe empirical objects and experience itself. Like the spatial and temporal conditions that support our contact with them, material objects can also be understood as 'dimensions' (VI 218/267, 247/296, 260/308). That objects have a dimensional quality means that they too are bearers of instituted meaning. This suggests that instituted meaning is present in the empirical and phenomenal domain, not only in the abstract or ideal realm of *signification*. Merleau-Ponty suggests this when he claims that instituted meaning is also accessed through perception (IP 195–98/254–56). This points to another reading of the claim that present and past are 'simultaneous'. It suggests that subjects' everyday perceptual experiences are connected to a rich network of linguistic, historical and cultural sense, and that language use is informed by instituted meanings through a perceptual and not merely an abstract avenue (294; VI 176/227).

This marks an important change in Merleau-Ponty's view of the relation between language, perception and meaning. If the structure of intentionality is such that objects are, in principle, reversible with subjects, if material objects are informed by or refer to linguistic meaning, and if the coherence of experience depends on these conditions, then language will play a nontrivial, world-forming role at the first-order level. The founded character of linguistic meaning and the theoretical posit of the 'tacit' *cogito* are no longer tenable: in experience, language is as important as perception.

3. ARTICULATING THE WORLD

Like Cassirer, Humboldt or Wittgenstein, Merleau-Ponty argues that language structures our experience. But by stressing the intimate connection between language and perception, he offers a distinctive interpretation of how one relates to the other. More pointedly than these and other thinkers who have argued for the world-forming role of language, Merleau-Ponty attempts to locate and detail the influence of language at the first-personal level of conscious experience. The concepts considered above have prepared us to understand his view that thought, language and perception are 'intertwined', and that perceptual meaning is informed by background linguistic conditions. Linguistic competence makes experience coherent; by articulating it, language use also shapes and transforms the world.

That Merleau-Ponty holds these positions is suggested by his descriptions of language use and by the new concepts that emerge in his later writings. As above, I will try to unpack some of his more challenging remarks about the language-perception relation, so as to better nail down his later understanding of empirical expression. Accordingly, the analyses below have a reconstructive character, and attempt to highlight links between sometimes incipiently formulated claims and seemingly disparate texts.

That everyday language use expresses experience is a familiar position; but the view that modulations in expression also shape structures of experience is (for Merleau-Ponty) a novel claim. This requires that he reject two tenets central to the *Phenomenology*'s account of empirical expression: the 'tacit *cogito*' and the 'founded' status of linguistic meaning. The 'tacit *cogito*' only shows that language use is not 'impossible', while failing to show how it is possible (VI 176/227). The distinction between the 'silent' perceptual subject and the 'spoken' subject of expression merely 'posed a problem'; namely, that of how one relates to the other.

To better understand how Merleau-Ponty defines the contours of the language-perception relation in his later work, I would like to recall some conclusions from his analysis of 'institution'. In a lecture course on Husserl's 'Origin of Geometry', he claims that Husserl's view of instituted sense requires that world and language are 'interwoven' (*verflochten*) (HLP 41/50). Husserl's approach to institution reveals that there is 'a *Vor-Sprache*, a down-side or "other side" of language, an *Ur-sprung* of language' (43/53). Merleau-Ponty takes this to mean that linguistic meanings are located in the world. The 'other side' of language, or 'pre-language', is coextensive with the perceived spatio-temporal world. This does not mean, however, that the meaning of objects in experience is a mere 'product' of language, nor that it is reducible to linguistic units, that is, to propositions ('things said') or merely verbal labels (VI 96–97/130; 108/142).[30]

The claim that language and perception are intertwined or interwoven will be made more precise below. It will be helpful to first consider what this position rules out. Merleau-Ponty is not suggesting that instituted meaning is sufficient to define intentionality, material objects, space, time and more. More importantly, this claim rules out the view that language is 'founded' on perception. As I noted above, the traditional model of institution (as *Fundierung* or *fondement*) has been supplemented by a view that emphasises the transformative possibilities of instituted meaning. Merleau-Ponty's estimation of the inadequacies of his earlier view of institution have been noted.[31] He still claims that perception (or 'brute' 'imperception') is silent (VI 268/316), that 'the perceived world is primordial language (mute), *i.e.* where signifiers and signifieds are not detached from one another' (BNF Ms. Vol. III 246v/30), and occasionally notes that 'thing' and 'world' are a 'text' (VI 36/57). However, these claims (especially the latter) no longer have the same force. The view that instituted linguistic meaning is intertwined with the world and with perception entails that linguistic expression does not translate perceptual meaning into a linguistic register (VI 213/263). The relation between linguistic and perceptual meaning is not one of a copy to its original (S 42–43/69–70). Language is not founded on perception; language does not 'say' what perception 'really means'.

While the *Phenomenology* argued that perceptual *sens* and ideal *signification* are part and parcel of expression, it did not go so far as to claim that *signification* is accessed in perceptual experience. This later position is evidenced in comments asserting a continuity between *sens* (which is visible or perceived) and *signification* (which is invisible or ideal). For example, Merleau-Ponty notes that there is an invisible of the visible (VI 151/196), or that the visible always refers to the invisible (215–16/265; 235/284; BNF Ms. Vol. VIII 338/7).

In light of tenets like 'reversibility', this new approach to the language-perception relation challenges the claim that the subject of perceptual experience is a tacit *cogito*. Recall that this concept expressed an assumption consistent with the account of 'founding'; namely, that the subject of pre-predicative experience accesses the most fundamental layer of meaning, which subsequently supports expressive and cognitive operations. But if perceptual meaning is co-present with linguistic meaning, then perception must avail itself of linguistic supports, which the tacit *cogito* by definition lacks (171/222–23). The claim that linguistic meaning is the other side of perceptual meaning, which is consistent with the reversibility relation that Merleau-Ponty argues obtains between conditions and conditioned, subject and object, and more, rules out the possibility of a tacit or non-linguistic, *cogito*. Perception and language are equally fundamental conditions for experience: the latter is not ontologically or temporally prior to the former.[32]

By rejecting the priority of a non-language-using perceptual subject, Merleau-Ponty appeals to new tenets to explain the coherence and sense of experience. Recall that when expressing the view that meaning is cohesion, he likened cohesion and meaning to 'τo λέγειν' (VI 88/119). The Greek verb λέγω can mean 'to speak', 'to mean', but also 'to order' or 'to gather'. Merleau-Ponty wants to retain these nuances: linguistic expression articulates the meaning of experience, but also forms, orders and makes the world coherent.

3.1 The Intertwining of Speech, Thought and Perception

A fundamental commitment of Merleau-Ponty's later philosophy of language is that expressive and cognitive activity is interwoven or intertwined with perception at the first-order level. This position adopts some elements of his earlier view of gestural expression, and it will be helpful to identify which commitments are retained in later writings. The gestural theory of expression held that thought and speech are closely integrated (see chapter 2). Merleau-Ponty maintains that '[t]hought and speech anticipate one another. . . . [all] thought comes from spoken words and returns to them; every spoken word is born in thoughts and ends up in them' (S 17–18/32–33).[33] Later texts also invoke earlier categories like 'operative' or 'speaking' speech (VI 154/200, 175/227, 202/252; S 18/33). Linguistic understanding or 'interpretation' (which was described earlier using the term 'transcendence') remains important for linguistic expression and understanding. The interpretation of sentences or words at a given time and place, by one or more subjects, is key for linguistic analysis: 'The very idea of a complete statement is inconsistent. We do not understand a statement because it is complete in itself; we say that it is complete or sufficient because we have understood' (S 17–18/32–33).

The few direct descriptions of empirical language use found in Merleau-Ponty's later texts identify important continuities with those advanced until *The Prose of the World*. For example:

> The speaking-understanding relation: the moving oneself perceiving the goal relation, *i.e.*: the goal is not posed, but it is what I am lacking, what marks a certain deflection on the dial of the corporeal schema. Likewise I speak by rejoining such and such a modulation of the linguistic space with the linguistic apparatus – the words bound to their sense as the body to its goal.
>
> I do not perceive any more than I speak – Perception has me as has language – And as it is necessary that all the same *I* be there in order to speak, *I* must be there in order to perceive – But in what sense? As *one* [on] – What is it that, from my side, comes to animate the perceived world and language? (VI 190/241)[34]

Empirical expression continues to be understood as a non-cognitive activity. The first paragraph above paints a picture consistent with earlier descriptions of gestural expression. Expression is a modulation of bodily intentionality or of the 'corporeal schema', and consists in a reorganisation of existing linguistic terms. Further, this process is not explicitly goal-directed. Except in rudimentary cases like small talk, speaking is understood as a spontaneous activity that unites sound and sense through a reorganisation of existing possibilities for linguistic expression (those given by our 'linguistic space'). As before, this presupposes that instituted or 'sedimented' meanings support linguistic expression. Merleau-Ponty concedes that in limited cases, meaning can be clarified by appeal to existing conventions (e.g., in cases of rudimentary language use) (VI 201/252). Still, he has not changed his view that the deeper meaning of linguistic conventions, and of the formal features of language, is only legible in acts of expression: 'language has its thinkable structure', but 'when we speak we do not think about it as the linguist does; we do not even think about it – we think about *what we are saying*' (S 19/33; cf. HLP 52/64; VI 154/200). Conventional and formal features are necessary conditions for language use, but they are insufficient to explain it.[35]

Despite these points of continuity, the text above also hints at important shifts. Most immediately, Merleau-Ponty wonders anew about the subjective conditions necessary for expression and perception. The second paragraph suggests that empirical expression (and perception) depend on conditions outside our control, which seem to guide us. This indicates a departure from an emphasis on (pre-) personal expressive projects, an important part of the gestural account of expression. Even if Merleau-Ponty occasionally invokes the term, gesture is no longer a controlling concept of his analyses of expression (see, e.g., VI 154/200). The project-centric account of gesture emphasised the subject's role in initiating and seeing through expressive attempts, but it also held that linguistic meaning must be analysed by appeal to external conditions. In the end, however, these conditions referred us to other subjects: they detailed how a linguistic project is interpreted by other language-users. The decreased importance of gesture may be read as an implicit self-criticism of this subject-centric focus. In any case, the evaluation that 'gestures can be speech . . . but not all speech is a gesture' is well-supported by the evidence.[36]

The passage above makes a second, related point. The *Phenomenology* used the claim that perception is 'anonymous' to argue against the view that the perceptual subject is defined by its cognitive activities (PhP 86/113, 136/168, 363/405, 476/514–15). Instead, perception is a pre-personal and pre-reflective undertaking. The concept of 'anonymity' is now deployed to argue that linguistic usage is guided by structures that are 'of the world', even if they also populate a subject's phenomenal field. Worldly conditions are as important for expression as any project or impetus originating from a speaker. According to the *Phenomenology*, linguistic expression modulates subjective motor-intentional capacities. As the second paragraph above intimates, subjective contributions in expressive acts are now thought to have a more mitigated role. Using a term that also appeared in *The Prose of the World*, Merleau-Ponty claims that expression takes direction from a '*Vorhabe*' and an implicit 'neo-teleology' (VI 201/252). The non-cognitive pragmatic intention described by the *Phenomenology* does not fully originate in us, even if subjects necessarily execute it. Unlike in the account of linguistic transcendence, expressive goals are guided by the givens of perception, and by structures irreducible to those of subjective activity. The basic assumption that subject and object codetermine one another is once again evidenced in these claims.

3.2 'Inherent' and 'Spoken' Language

Various remarks above have pointed to the view that perceptual objects, and perception itself, is a 'pre-language' (this idea has also been expressed using the terms *Vorhabe* or *Vorsprache*) (VI 126/166). As I will attempt to show in this section, in invoking this and similar terms, Merleau-Ponty aims to show that perceiving subjects are implicitly guided by linguistic or conceptual meanings. The meaning and intelligibility of perceptual objects depends in part on the background condition of instituted linguistic meaning. Merleau-Ponty's premises suggest that if we lacked the name(s) or concept(s) associated with an object, we would not see it in the same way: our perceptual experience would be relevantly different. Perceptual objects have a linguistic ('other') side, which points to specific and determined ways of articulating what we see. Drawing on his account of instituted meaning, Merleau-Ponty's observations lead him to posit that instituted linguistic meaning is bound up with (or inheres in) the perceived spatio-temporal world.[37]

A proper grasp of the 'pre-language' or linguistic 'fore-having' that guides perception is important, not least because the *Phenomenology* ostensibly made a similar claim when it held that perception is 'mute'. This was a consequence of the view that perceptual meaning is ontologically and semantically prior to linguistic meaning. It assumed that mute perception contains only perceptual meaning. With tenets like institution and reversibility in the background, which draw a direct link between instituted and perceptual sense, the 'pre' in perceptual pre-language can be understood differently. Objects point to and suggest specific possibilities for linguistic expression because they are also bearers of linguistic meaning. Objectual 'pre-language' is not ontologically or semantically prior to perception: when objects come before our vision, we make contact with perceptual data that are already invested with linguistic meaning. Perceptual givenness coincides with a limited range of expressive avenues. Before expressing something that we come into perceptual contact with, that we see some determinate perceptual object at all can be explained by our possession of associated concepts.

According to Merleau-Ponty, visual recognition of objects is directly aided by linguistic meanings, which allow us to identify the object before us *as* something in particular.

The basic idea sketched above effectively applies the account of instituted meaning to perception (see section 2.3). The view that material objects offer definite linguistic avenues through which they can be articulated is evidenced by new distinctions in Merleau-Ponty's later writings. The tight connection between perceptual (visible) and linguistic (invisible) meaning allows perception to be described using the Stoic term λόγος ἐνδιάθετος; alternatively, as an 'inner', 'inserted', or 'inherent' *logos* (though Merleau-Ponty modifies the meaning of this term).[38] Inherent language can in turn be distinguished from 'λόγος προφορικός', that is, 'spoken' or 'uttered' *logos* (VI 168–69/220–21; 170/221–22).[39] In my estimation, this distinction is coextensive with those between 'visible' and 'invisible', *sens* and *signification*, and 'vision' and 'speech'. I have singled out the inherent-spoken version of the distinction because it neatly states the relevant difference. However, each dyad points to the same basic relation between language and perception. These distinctions suggest that material objects and experience itself can be interpreted under two aspects. Objects of experience can be understood as nonverbalised cores of meaning that incline towards specific modes of articulation; and they can be understood as the verbalised or articulated counterpart of the former. When I see a glass, I do not see the word 'glass'. But I have no difficulty in articulating what I see. I reach effortlessly for the name and call on it if necessary. Members of my linguistic community can do the same. The distinction above attempts to explain this by positing that my perception of the glass concomitantly gives a semantic unity that has linguistic import. When I see the glass, I also discover the concept that can articulate it. But I do not apply the concept to my perception of the glass, nor do I read it into my experience. The concept or word is already there: that the concept 'glass' comes to mind, rather than some other, leads to the conclusion that linguistic meaning inheres in perception as one of its fundamental enabling conditions. The word is a feature of my world insofar as I belong to a tradition that includes it among its stock of concepts. For Merleau-Ponty, language and perception are two sides of the same coin.

This distinction might seem like a recharacterisation of the long-standing *langue-parole* division. Merleau-Ponty continues to hold that ideal (or instituted) meaning tracks the more formal meanings associated with '*langue*', while expressed meanings are better captured by '*parole*' (VI 118/155). But 'inherent' language is not a paraphrase for *langue*. The former is accessed in perception, unlike the typically abstract *significations* associated with *langue*. 'Inherent' language is the not-yet-verbalised core of meaning associated with a given object. It is the word or set of linguistic units that seamlessly enter your mind whenever you hear a sound, see an object, or find yourself overcome with some sensation or emotion. We do not make contact with meanings of this sort in a reflective or abstract attitude. 'Spoken' language is the verbalised version of hitherto unexpressed pre-linguistic meanings. Alternatively, it is what the latter become once they are expressed. Inherent language comes before, or is 'prior' to spoken language, only because it inclines a subject towards some linguistic expression, without requiring that the latter necessarily takes some specific form. As in Proust's literary descriptions of experience, Merleau-Ponty claims that the perceptual world 'appears as containing everything that will ever be said, and yet [leaves] us to create it (Proust): it is the λόγος ἐνδιάθετος [inherent language] which calls for the λόγος προφορικός [spoken language]' (VI 170/221–22). Experience has its own proper integrity and meaning, which we discover more fully when attempting to articulate it. Experience does not yield a regimented plan for how it might be expressed, but the fact that we find ourselves searching for some terms and not others suggests that a discernible and articulable pre-linguistic meaning is instituted in experience. This picture supports Merleau-Ponty's distinctive interpretation of the claim that vision and thought are 'structured like a language' (VI 126/165).

The suggestion that perception is invested with linguistic meaning, and that concepts help to make it intelligible, is a veritable shift from Merleau-Ponty's emphasis on the *pre*-predicative and *non*-linguistic nature of perceptual experience. Like Husserl, Merleau-Ponty held, in the *Phenomenology*, that phenomenal content yields intuitive evidence from which language-meanings derive. In his later work, he does not want to reduce perceptual meaning to linguistic meaning, or to commit errors he once associated with the Vienna Circle. Rather, his broader aim is to show that background linguistic conditions, and a familiarity with linguistic meaning, play an important role in making experience intelligible and cohesive. Experience remains 'mute' because it does not express itself; for this, speakers are needed. But experience is not 'mute' because it is extra-linguistic or separated from linguistic meaning.

According to Merleau-Ponty, seemingly non-linguistic motor-intentional activities must be informed by linguistic meaning in order to grasp the 'λόγος that pronounces itself silently in each sensible thing, inasmuch as it varies around a certain type of message, which we can have an idea of only through our carnal participation in its sense, only by espousing by our body its manner of "signifying"' (VI 208/258). Objects exercise intentional demands on perceivers because they have a structural logic that perceivers adapt themselves to. We discern or anticipate this structural logic when we see some object. Given the claim above, Merleau-Ponty thinks that perceptual objects ('sensible things') have a meaningful structure that is articulable in a literal sense. We see unified, meaningful entities (e.g., a 'tool', not iron and wood), which present us with concepts that make appearances determinate. Merleau-Ponty's decreased emphasis on subjective activity leads him to describe this process in quasi-dialogical terms, as if perception 'offers' us meanings like an interlocutor. For example, he claims that perception begins an 'effort of articulation' that we take up (127/166). Subjects do not apply linguistic labels to experience or construct the world at will. And yet, we see determinate objects that are taken to be connected to some specific linguistic meanings. We discover and can articulate perceived structure upon reflection.[40] This observation leads him to posit that processes of perceptual recognition presuppose linguistic concepts when grasping empirical objects, and that perceptual structure is not a function of merely perceptual givens.[41]

The distinctions between inherent and spoken language, silence and speech, or visible and invisible may show that experience is articulable, but do they also show that language and perception are co-present prior to its articulation? The final claim might seem like a sort of inference to the best explanation. Merleau-Ponty does not provide detailed arguments or examples to elucidate his basic point, but we can attempt to do so. By returning to the experience of seeing a tree, an example considered in chapter 1, we can better understand the division between inherent and spoken language, and why perception and language might co-constitute experience.

Suppose that you see an oak tree before you. If asked to explain what you see, you would simply report that you see an oak. It would be a stretch to say, for example, that you see a conjunction of matter and secondary properties (e.g., thick branches plus a widely shaped trunk plus the brown, green colours, etc.). Perceptual experiences of meaningful objects like this tree are the bedrock of everyday life. They show that experience is already characterised by a degree of unity and intelligibility. What explains this? On Merleau-Ponty's later view, a combination of instituted linguistic and perceived meanings make possible the seamless perception of something as determinate as an oak tree. You happen to be a member of a linguistic community that includes 'oak' and 'tree' among its concepts, which you have inherited. You are familiar with this concept, and you can see the objects associated with it. Like natural languages, ideal meanings evolve over historical time and are malleable.[42] They animate perception by investing it with a rich layer of cultural, historical and conceptual meaning. They allow perception to be at once determinate and open to further exploration. Perception finds support in language: without a background network of linguistic meaning, our perception of the world would be either inhibited or fundamentally different. We would not see the world in the same way. That subjects do not mechanically apply concepts like 'oak' or 'tree' to visual experience (or associate predicate and subject through judgement) leads Merleau-Ponty to hold that the terms inhere in the world, and that they are legible in perception. This is how one might interpret his claims that the visible is not separate from the invisible, or that ideal meanings are one with the world. To see an object in the full sense, perceivers must presuppose linguistic meanings.

What would one see if one lacked the concepts in question? One would surely have a perceptual experience, but not one of seeking an oak tree. The experience would still be meaningful, but its meaning would be analysed in different terms. The key point is that the relevant difference in these two cases can be explained by each subject's respective background linguistic conditions. The first subject sees an oak tree because her visual field is informed by relevant linguistic meanings. The second subject lacks these 'instituted' or 'inherent' meanings, and fails to see an oak. Unlike the *Phenomenology* occasionally suggested, upon analysis, lived meaning is never reducible to purely perceptual givens.[43] The difference in the two cases would arguably be most pronounced were the two subjects asked to describe their experiences. It seems unlikely that the second subject would report that she perceived an 'oak tree'.

These distinctions and examples aim to show that linguistic and perceptual meaning mutually inform one another. They lead to the conclusion that language is an indispensable condition for meaning-making at the empirical level. They also advance a philosophical view on which language plays an essential role in securing the qualitative character of experience. Another example may offer more evidence for Merleau-Ponty's view that language plays a fundamental role in forming the meaning of perceptual experience. Imagine that you are visiting a museum. During your visit, you come across a long, sharp object. It seems to be some sort of spear, or perhaps an eating or cooking utensil. But as it turns out, the long sharp thing before you is an object of religious worship, endowed with spiritual powers. Needless to say, when you gaze at it, you fail to grasp something fundamental. You misapprehend its function and are unaware of its deeper cultural significance. Neither is perceptible in the object's shape, colour or physical composition. Unaware of these features, you fail to grasp what the object is.

Your experience of seeing the object certainly has some meaning to it: you see what appears to be a spear. But this is not what the subject or community who used it to worship their gods experienced; your qualitative and intentional experience of the object is unlike this. Cases like this are of consequence for our understanding of the language-perception relation. Only if you had some pre-conception of the object and its possible uses could you see it for what it was. This suggests, first, that mere perceptual acquaintance with visual data offers imperfect insights into perceptual experience. Indeed, this and other examples call into question the very tenability of a purely perceptual experience, viz. one that does not rely on some minimal background conceptual commitments. Second, these examples also suggest that background conceptual (viz. linguistic) assumptions help us explain the world and individuate meaningful experiences. In the case above, the visual data we encounter are fundamentally unlike those of the subjects from whose culture the object derives: when called to explain what you see, you would give a fundamentally different account than the subject who used the object for religious worship. Beyond a basic physical or atomic level (insufficient for a rich philosophical account of experience), objects do not bear the same meanings: one plausible explanation for this is that inherent linguistic meanings in the former and the latter case are relevantly different. But if that is the case, these meanings contribute something essential to making objects what they are. They give us access to a world, and make us sensitive to the possible permutations of experience.

Merleau-Ponty's emphasis on visual experiences might suggest that his account is exclusively directed to material objects, or that it can only handle similar cases. Despite somewhat generic remarks about 'things' or 'the world' (which are usually informed by observations directed to material objects perceived in space), he intends to offer a picture that can explain the full range of lived experience, including, for example, our experience of emotions, auditory phenomena, touch and more. In short, he intends this view to apply to any meaningful experience or entity, and to appearance as such.

3.3 Expression and World-Formation

The distinctions and examples above showed that a porous relationship between *sens* and *signification* obtains at the perceptual level. They chiefly focused on nonverbalised experience, in which perceptual recognition of objects is shown to presuppose familiarity with language. However, the distinction between spoken and inherent language also points to the possibility that language can shape experience through more active (i.e., 'spoken') means. Perception opens us to the world; in linguistic expression, its meaning takes shape. Another novelty in Merleau-Ponty's later account of expression is his recognition that empirical language use plays a central role in securing the intelligibility of experience, and allows it to achieve a degree of integration that perception alone is unable to realise. This identifies another level at which empirical expression has a world-forming role.

Consider the following claim:

> We need only take language [*le langage*] too in the living or nascent state, with all its references, those behind it, which connect it to the mute things it interpellates, and those it sends before itself and which make up the world of things said [*choses dites*] – with its

> movement, its subtleties, its reversals, its life, which expresses and multiplies tenfold the life of bare things. Language is a life, is our life and the life of things. (VI 126/165)

In the 'living' or uttered state, language is 'the life of things': it articulates the meaning of objects and of experience itself. For Merleau-Ponty, human language enjoys this role because it is tightly connected to objects and to the spatio-temporal world by structures like reversibility, latent intentionality, and institution. But this passage suggests that everyday expression not only articulates the meaning of objects but also 'multiplies' the 'life of bare things'. Expression gives voice to states of consciousness, feelings, desires or views one might have, but it can also inflect each with new sense. Without linguistic expression, the passage suggests, the meaning of experience would remain incomplete (or 'bare'). This identifies a new role for empirical expression. It is consistent with Merleau-Ponty's earlier observation that language has deep creative power in dialogue. But the remark above, together with other texts, suggest that this view has been developed and applied to empirical expression as such, which is accorded a more liberal role in first-order experience.

I would first like to clarify two points before considering how this more creative aspect of expression might be understood. Merleau-Ponty's account of the creative and world-forming capacity of language is not an endorsement of the view that worldly meaning is a mere product of language. The inherent/spoken language distinction identifies a continuity and interdependence between perception and language; expression articulates a sense given in perception. A note entitled 'Mute Experience and Speech' helps to bring this point out. It discusses 'dimensionality', a concept frequently invoked to express the idea that the world is intersubjectively and historically constituted, and concludes that 'speech is another dimension of the *same-world-Being*' (BNF Ms. Vol. VI 262). Incidentally, this anticipates the 'transformation' that expression brings to perceptual sense; I will return to this below. The note also stresses that the 'visible-invisible dialectic' (i.e., the bidirectional relation between perception and language), 'animates the *silence* of the sensible', and creates 'a meaning [*sens*] that speech will attempt to recover [*rejoindre*] by a second silence, indirect language'.[44] Expression brings out the latent meaning of perception but is not sufficient to create it. What is more, 'Silence opens onto speech (Proust[:] things call for speech)', while 'Speech opens onto silence (to the brute) (locked up in it) (Mallarmé, Valéry')' (BNF Ms. Vol. VI 262r–v). Even if instituted linguistic meaning is a collection of human expressive acts, and evolves over time, it is not produced by some particular subject, either now or in the past. As I suggested above, objects 'call' or incline subjects towards specific modes of expression. But the meaning of these expressions, as this text makes clear, should be understood by referring to the objects themselves, and that goes for instituted sense too.

Second, Merleau-Ponty's claims above and elsewhere that language expresses the structure of the world or 'being' might be read in a Heideggerian vein. For example, he claims that 'it is not we who speak, it is truth that speaks itself at the depths of speech' (VI 185/236); that 'language has us and that it is not we who have language. That it is being that speaks within us and not we who speak of being' (194/244); and that 'things *are said* and *are thought* by a Speech and by a Thought which we do not have but which has us' (S 19/35–36).[45] In a 1958 to 1959 seminar, Merleau-Ponty associates Heidegger with the view that speech 'seizes' or expresses being (NC 125 ff.), claims that 'operative' language states the meaning of being, and that our 'experience of Being' (rather than a logical or formal language) guides this form of expression (132). Merleau-Ponty identifies Heideggerian precursors to the statements above and to the concepts of 'operative' or 'speaking' speech. However, his own claim to the effect that language 'operatively' expresses 'being' is not appropriated or taken from Heidegger. The substantive details of Merleau-Ponty's reading of Heidegger in this seminar (which I cannot consider in detail here) bear this out, but more direct considerations can be adduced in favour of this point.

First, Heidegger's claim that being 'speaks' in language is not offered in the spirit of a description of empirical language use.[46] By contrast, Merleau-Ponty is interested in this dimension of language. This is a nontrivial methodological and philosophical difference, which gives a different sense to the two versions of the claim. Second, as I suggested in chapter 4, Merleau-Ponty praises a range of philosophers and linguists for revealing the inadequacy of formal approaches to language. Heidegger's contributions are certainly of importance, but in this respect they are not wholly original: 'Husserl's analyses foreshadow

Heidegger's thoughts on "the speaking of speech"' (HLP 9/RC 168). If we take Merleau-Ponty at his word, he thinks that the key philosophical merits of Heidegger's account of the 'speaking' of language are anticipated by Husserl, among others. Third, and most importantly, Merleau-Ponty's claim that being 'speaks' is better understood in light of the inherent/spoken language distinction. Perceivers enter into contact with coherent structures of meaning, and in this sense they are directed by 'being' (according to intentional reversibility, objects 'have us'). But perceivers can also express these structures, and do so in different ways. These modes of expression (or 'speech') correspond to the expressive possibilities given by natural language. For Merleau-Ponty, the meanings encountered in everyday life 'speak' through us because we attempt to utter them at a particular time and place. Heidegger's 'Letter on "Humanism"', for instance, indicates that his interest in language is further afield from acts of empirical expression.[47] More broadly, Heidegger might be taken to suggest that the world or experience is not meaningful absent expression in language.[48] In his later writings, Merleau-Ponty argues that language is bound up with material objects, but he maintains that there are 'non-language' meanings. For these reasons, his version of the claim that 'being' 'speaks' is relevantly different from Heidegger's.[49]

Let us return to the claim that language 'multiplies' or transforms the meaning of objects (a view that, insofar as it grants subjects the ability to intervene in the structure of experience or 'being', marks another significant departure from Heidegger). Recall that the shift in Merleau-Ponty's understanding of *Stiftung* led him to privilege its transformative rather than its preservative possibilities (see, e.g., HLP 32/38). And even if creative transformation is not absent from formal or designative modes of expression (e.g., in mathematics, as noted in chapter 4), a significant drawback of these methods is that they miss the deeper transformative power of expression. Merleau-Ponty maintains that 'the error of the semantic philosophies [is] to close up language as if it spoke only of itself: language lives only from silence; everything we cast to the others has germinated in this great mute land which we never leave' (VI 126/165).

The creative and formative possibilities of expression were partially described using the term 'work' in *Structure*, 'transcendence' in the *Phenomenology*, and 'coherent deformation' in *The Prose of the World*.

Merleau-Ponty's later understanding of the formative role of expression builds on and extends these accounts. In a course on Husserl's 'Origin of Geometry', he holds that Husserl 'takes language seriously' insofar as he also 'gives it an ontological function' (HLP 43/52–53). While this position effectively states Merleau-Ponty's own view on the matter, the contrast drawn helps to clarify in what sense language might have an 'ontological' function. Unlike 'the British' and allegedly Wittgenstein, language for Husserl is not a mere 'thing'; that is, an entity with rigidly determined properties.[50] Instead of converting stable *significations* into a verbal form, or predicating true statements of the world, expression highlights overlooked features of experience, and reveals new dimensions of the world (VI 268/316). Underneath its more mundane manifestations, expression admits of a deeper 'conquering, active, [and] creative' power (153/198).

Despite the incomplete state of the text, extant sections of *The Visible*, together with contemporaneous writings, point to two further ways that empirical expression takes on a world- or experience-forming role. First, language brings a 'quasi-natural displacement' to perception because it highlights features of experience that would remain overlooked (235/284). Background linguistic conditions accord an initial coherence to experience, but by converting it into a verbalised or spoken form, we can better understand how and why an object, person or event appears under the guise that it does. Lived experience is complex and multilayered; expression adds something new by unfolding its layers, further specifying their meaning and role in experience. To illustrate how this might work, assume that you make a new acquaintance, with whom your friend is on good terms. Your friend is enthusiastic about this person, but something seems off to you. The acquaintance rubs you the wrong way: a facial gesture seems dismissive, a tone of voice belies arrogance. Your experience with this person inclines you to form negative judgements. Merleau-Ponty accepts that expression has a productive and disclosive power because he assumes that our experience in this and other cases comes into greater relief when it becomes a topic of discourse. By attempting to express just what it was that led us to perceive arrogance in our new acquaintance, the inchoate meaning of the meeting starts to take on a more determinate form. This ampliative power of expression is evidenced in claims to the effect that linguistic expression presents what 'silent' or nonverbalised perception is unable to do on its own (VI 154/199–200; 176/227).⁵¹ When we commit ourselves to expressing what we see, hear or feel, we open ourselves and others to the possibility of attaining a more profound grasp of experience. This is due to the fact that perceptual openness to the world is on its own insufficient to work out the meaning of perceptual modalities, and because the possibility of expressing the initial meaning of experience is anticipated by the instituted character of linguistic meaning. When we think about or discuss our meeting with the acquaintance, a negative facial gesture might begin to seem more neutral, and what we read as a pronounced personal characteristic might be consigned to the periphery of the conditions that make this experience intelligible. Of course, one could also form the opposite view. In either case, the point is that these possible permutations of meaning are implicitly contained in your initial encounter, but must be expressed to show themselves. Expression takes experience as its object, and can unfold new meanings, thereby revealing experience in a new light. It enjoys this role because the initial cohesion of meaning encountered at the perceptual level is semantically underdetermined. Expression transforms the sense of unarticulated intuitive evidence, and in doing so, continues to shape it. (Merleau-Ponty does not suggest that all expression is thereby 'authentic' in the *Phenomenology*'s sense [this term is no longer invoked], even if authentic expression also harboured a similar possibility.)

Language also enjoys a formative influence on experience by shaping our broader attitude towards the world. Recall that Merleau-Ponty claims that speech (or empirical expression) is another 'dimension' of 'Being' or of the world, and amounts to 'being speaking in us' (HLP 44/53). Having moved away from concerns of strict fidelity, and having rejected tenets like the tacit *cogito* and the founded status of linguistic meaning, he now contends that empirical expression shapes the world by establishing possible 'dimensions' of experience. Put differently, language delimits the horizons of sense-making, and it does so by furnishing us with specific kinds of expressive and interpretive resources. A language supports specific subjective stances or perspectives on the world. The sense of transformation as perspective-creation borrows from the logic of meaning transcendence at work in gestural expression, but the view here builds on and extends what *The Prose of the World* called a 'triple resumption', whereby expression takes up and modifies past and present meaning (PW 68/95; see also SB 176/191).

The following remark points to this formative role:

> For the moment we want only to suggest that one can speak neither of a destruction nor of a conservation of silence (and still less of a destruction that conserves or of a realisation that destroys – which is not to solve but to pose the problem). When silent vision falls into speech, and when speech in turn, opening up a field of the nameable and the sayable, inscribes itself in that field, in its place, according to its truth – in short, when it metamorphoses the structures of the visible world and makes itself a gaze of the mind, *intuitus mentis* – this is always in virtue of the same fundamental phenomenon of reversibility which sustains both the mute perception and the speech and which manifests itself by an almost carnal existence of the idea, as well as by a sublimation of the flesh. (VI 154–55/200)

Consistent with remarks above, this passage suggests that empirical language takes up and transforms (or 'metamorphoses') perceptual givens. But the invocation of the word *field* (sometimes used in the *Phenomenology* to describe 'transcendental' functions) suggests that its capacity to form experience extends beyond specific instances. Now Merleau-Ponty claims that this depends on perception: 'All the possibilities of language are already given in [perception]' (155/200). But notice that tenets like institution and reversibility require that we not read this claim as if perceptual meaning explained (or 'founded') linguistic meaning. Above, the passage claims that language has its own 'truth', even if it requires a perceptual basis, and is 'emancipated but not freed from every condition' (153/198; see also 126/165). This clarification helps to show that language has a formative role because it makes possible certain expressive modalities, or ways of expressing perceptual experience. Language-users necessarily appeal to determinate modes of 'naming' or 'saying' what they perceive (and by extension, are unable to access others). These possibilities are given by the terms and concepts of a natural language. Language shapes the 'structures of the visible world' because it specifies the concepts and expressions we presuppose in perception and those we draw on when we think about, interpret and express what we see.

As the passage above makes clear, Merleau-Ponty is no longer concerned to isolate the transformative from the literal dimensions of expression. This indicates that expression has taken on a different function. Expression will always transform perceptual meaning. But that does not estrange subjects from their world, since to 'have' a world is to have a perspective on experience. Natural languages, or systems of empirical expression, provide resources with which to take up just such a perspective: 'Speech is a relation to Being through a being'; namely, the sonorous and silent manifestations of natural language (118/155–56). Language is a fundamental medium through which we come to grips with the world, and thanks to which objects begin to make sense for us. Indeed, at this higher-order level, having access to a natural language furnishes subjects with a 'dimension' or 'opening' (*Eröffnung*) to the world (HLP 44/53). Different natural languages offer distinct resources for articulating experience. Each supports a dimension or view of reality, and accordingly, the 'truth' of language referred to above will vary. For example, some languages have rich vocabularies for describing natural phenomena like snow, wind or the sea; others have special terms for emotions like shame; others gender nouns or pronouns; still others lack gender at all. Users of different languages will accordingly enjoy different possibilities for interpreting the world. Some might simply see 'the sea'; others might name the point at which water reflects light. To adapt a term from Charles Taylor, a language 'figures' a world by 'fitting' words to experience in a non-arbitrary way.[52] Merleau-Ponty reminds us that this process is non-arbitrary because it responds to perception; but this is also due to the fact that perceptual data appear under a guise that can be articulated, and get their sense from it. Language use 'in the living or nascent state' encounters meanings that are not simple corollaries of subjective activity, and which have an integrity that becomes more coherent by being expressed.

4. THE LIMITS OF LANGUAGE AND WORLD

Informed by tenets like 'reversibility' and 'institution', Merleau-Ponty's later view of first-order language use, and of the language-world relation, can be distinguished from similar positions by its focus on perception, and by the claim that language and perception are intertwined. Expression is by no means sufficient for securing the coherence of the world, but it is one of its central conditions. Merleau-Ponty accepts that language plays an implicit and explicit role in forming the meaning of everyday experience. Implicitly, processes of perceptual recognition rely on background linguistic meanings. If we lacked the name or concept, we would not see an object in the same way. Perception opens onto determinate objective unities in large part because we possess a stock of inherited linguistic concepts, which we do not experience as separate from the spatio-temporal world. When experience becomes a subject of discourse, its implicit layers take shape, and their meaning is modified. But the expressive possibilities given by natural languages also support distinct perspectives on experience. We relate to our world through our language. Language forms the world and shapes experience insofar as it helps us take up intentional stances that make both coherent.

These observations develop the earlier claim that 'speech is the vehicle of our movement towards truth' (PW 129/180–81). Merleau-Ponty would go on to note that this understanding of truth is one on which there is 'truth-to-be-made', rather than simply discovered and expressed in propositional form (AD 200/269). Having considered some of his later reflections on language, this idea comes into greater relief. The meaning of experience is ultimately disclosed through an effort of articulation. But because language, thought and perception are intertwined, the meaning of phenomena will also depend on how subjects express them. This effort, which Merleau-Ponty sees as an intersubjective undertaking, will disclose the conditions that secure the coherence of experience, and can also transform them: the coherence of experience is always in the making.

Because Merleau-Ponty's work on his final projects was tragically interrupted, many texts that work out his later approach to expression are characterised by incipient and sometimes imprecise formulations. I have attempted to sketch his general attitude to empirical expression, but some of the details may remain obscure. His inchoate later reflections on language invite many questions and criticisms, and I would like to conclude this chapter by considering some.

Some worries might be occasioned by ambiguities in Merleau-Ponty's formulations, which sometimes make his positions difficult to grasp. For example, he might be criticised for failing to provide enough evidence for the view that language is the 'other side' of perception, that instituted linguistic meaning inheres in experience and in the spatio-temporal realm, or that concepts mediate perceptual experience. I have attempted to make these positions clearer by reading them as theoretical posits designed to explain our experience of the perception-language relation. Still, one might deny that the conceptual framework outlined above actually corresponds to or helpfully describes the experiences in question. Disagreement on this point is of course possible; after all, Merleau-Ponty aims to broaden and not limit the range of possible perspectives on experience. But since the issue boils down to how one should interpret first-personal experience, readers may be of different minds on this point.

As some remarks in the last section indicate, Merleau-Ponty seems hesitant to take a strong position on the extent to which expression invents, transforms or preserves perceptual meaning. It neither 'destroys' nor 'conserves' perception, and once again we are left wondering about its precise role. This leaves him vulnerable to the criticism that his view actually entails that the supposed cohesion of meaning found in experience is the mere whim of language-using subjects (or that he has simply failed to precisely specify the extent to which language forms experience). There is indeed an ambiguity in his position, but even if the details remain unclear, it is safe to say that for him expression is best understood as a response to perceptual openness to the world. We neither invent the meaning of experience nor produce the (perceptual and linguistic) conditions that grant access to it. Language-users inherit and do not wholly invent expressive resources. They have significant leeway in how they articulate their world, but not so much that linguistic expression becomes untethered from perception and from instituted meaning.

For some readers, the view that the qualitative character and meaning of experience depends in large part on linguistic and conceptual traditions might seem too relativistic. For it seems to allow that different language users inhabit different worlds. If users of different natural languages can shape the coherence of perceptual meaning in different ways, in what sense is there *a* world, or *an* object of experience, on this view? What happens when perspectives conflict? How might ensuing disputes (within or across linguistic communities) be adjudicated? The supposedly cohesive character of experience seems to quickly break down.

Merleau-Ponty does not worry much about this set of issues in large part because he thinks that the presence of multiple and potentially irreconcilable perspectives is a (positive) feature of the world. Subjects do, in fact, approach what seems like the same object from different perspectives. One might inhabit the world differently while speaking German, Swahili, Japanese or Spanish, but this need not entail that these perspectives are in principle irreconcilable. The observation that the world (or 'being') is constituted by a plurality of perspectives does not license an 'anything goes' attitude, nor does it force the conclusion that there is no truth, sense or coherence to experience.

The de facto presence of different perspectives is an opportunity for deeper convergence, which Merleau-Ponty thinks is possible. Multiple perspectives can intersect, and his account of intersubjectivity affirms as much. By attempting to articulate our experiences, measuring our differences and entering into dialogue with others, barriers of this sort may be overcome. Intersubjective exchanges may show that one perspective is in touch with elements of experience that another has overlooked. Nothing in Merleau-Ponty's account blocks the judgement that the former is superior to the latter. Such exchanges could also show that diverging stances are both legitimate and well supported. On this score, a Merleau-Pontyean response to the charge of relativism brings him closer to Gadamer. Having drawn significant philosophical conclusions from his account of dialogue, he would accept that linguistic communication is the fundamental medium that discloses the world, and is the avenue through which its divergent perspectives might be reconciled, augmented or challenged.[53] Indeed, more than Wittgenstein, Heidegger, Humboldt or Cassirer, Gadamer's understanding of the language-world relation seems proximate to Merleau-Ponty's. These links strengthen the hermeneutical tenor of Merleau-Ponty's philosophy of language, a characteristic I noted in chapter 2. To be sure, Gadamer reaches similar conclusions with some different premises, but he also holds that there is a basic, lived, bidirectional, co-constitutive relation between language and world. The world is 'only insofar as it comes into language, but language, too, has its real being only in the fact that the world is presented in it'.[54] Language discloses a world because subjects understand it and one another by means of language use.[55] For Gadamer and for Merleau-Ponty, a language establishes a relation to the 'infinity of beings'.[56] On these grounds we may conclude that '[w]hoever has language "has" the world'.

NOTES

1. This methodological distinction is not always observed (see Waktin 2009, chapter 2).

2. Some outlines suggest this division: see VI xxxv–xxxvi/10–11, 165/217, 274/322; BNF Ms. Vol. VI 4v/3, 9, 125, 250.

3. Wittgenstein 2001, 5.6; see also 5.62.

4. Wittgenstein 2009, §§19, 23, 122, 182, 115. For more on the relation between Wittgenstein and Merleau-Ponty, see the essays in Romdenh-Romluc 2007.

5. See Guignon 2013, 96; see also Kerr 1965, 519–20; and Gier 1981, 204–17.

6. See Taylor 2016.

7. Ibid., 130, 139.

8. Merleau-Ponty's knowledge of Wittgenstein seems limited (see *Texts and Dialogues* 66). Evidence suggests he was only familiar with the *Tractatus*. He seems to have read Wittgenstein, like 'the British', as a positivist who treats language as if it were a mere 'thing' (HLP 43/52–53).

9. von Humboldt 2000, 51.

10. Chabrolle-Cerretini and Raynaud note that the term *Sprachform* usually appears as *'Form der Sprachen'* in *Über die Verschiedenheit des menschlichen Sprachbaues* (1827–1829), and as *'innere Sprachform'* in the later *Über die Verschiedenheit des menschlichen Sprachbaues und ihren Einfluss auf die geistige Entwicklung des Menschengeschlechts* (1830–1835) (Chabrolle-Cerretini and Raynaud 2015, 96). Merleau-Ponty does not seem to be sensitive to this difference.

11. In this course, Merleau-Ponty often discusses Saussure in tandem with Humboldt (sometimes critically distinguishing the two, and favouring the former over the latter). As in other works, he argues against finalist, formalist and reductive historicist views of language. In addition to Saussure, Humboldt's views (despite some of his other commitments) contribute to these goals. Still, Merleau-Ponty criticises Humboldt for thinking that the linguistic system must be animated by a subject that stands outside it (BNF Ms. Vol. XII 35).

12. See Goldstein 1948, 32, 92. Merleau-Ponty quotes from Goldstein's interpretation of Humboldt's claim that language view is worldview (BNF Ms. Vol. XII 3/85r).

13. Cassirer 2013, 336/123. Incidentally, this confirms that Merleau-Ponty was already familiar with different versions of the world-forming view of language early in his career.

14. See, for example, Cassirer 2013, 339–41/126–29; 349/137–38; 352–54/141–43. Cassirer is mentioned only twice in the main text of the *Phenomenology* (PhP 53/80, 126/157), but notes to the text are replete with references to *Philosophy of Symbolic Forms*, Volume 3. Some of these references suggest that Merleau-Ponty's understanding of empirical studies of pathology owe much to Cassirer's analyses, especially those of Gelb and Goldstein (in particular, PhP 127/158, 197–98/233, 294/333–34, 356/398, 357/399 suggest a debt to Cassirer 1965, part 2, chapter 6). Other remarks point to more substantive commitments that come closer to Cassirer's account of language and expression (cf. PhP 129/160, 149/184, 187/222, 244/282 and Cassirer 1965, part 1, chapter 1).

15. Cassirer 2013, 339/126.

16. Ibid., 342–43/130. Drawing on themes of his earlier work (which are also discussed in the *Phenomenology*), Cassirer extends this analysis with a look at aphasiacs (see 344–45/131–33).

17. These terms cannot be simply substituted for one another, but the basic point about the 'distance' in perception is made variously throughout Merleau-Ponty's later texts using both *'écart'* and *'distance'*.

18. I am grateful to Franck Robert for sharing his transcription of this material with me.

19. Recall the claim in chapter 5 that meaning (*le sens*) can be defined according to the 'divergence' of the plurality of perspectives that engage an object (IP 136/182).

20. See VI 146/189, 153/198. But cf. remarks to the effect that the fleshly subject and the world it is in contact with 'must be taken at [their] word [*à la lettre*]' (133/173). This complicates any reading of the concept, but the majority of textual evidence points away from a literal (or material) reading of flesh.

21. For a helpful account of this concept see Dastur 2000.

22. For a fuller account see Apostolopoulos 2017.

23. While Merleau-Ponty rejects an intellectualistic view of constitution in the *Phenomenology*, he also uses the term to describe a more fundamental process of meaning-formation (PhP 186/220, 189/223, 221/258, 261/298, 288/326, 370/412, 437/476, 450–51/489–90, 466/504).

24. Cf. Toadvine 2009, 274.

25. For a good overview of this course see Vallier 2005.

26. Merleau-Ponty's account of the development of 'perspective' in Western painting from antiquity to the Renaissance offers a good example of how instituted meaning develops and is modified over time (see IP 42–47/80–86).

27. For similar claims in the *Phenomenology* see PhP 436/475, 438–39/477–80.

28. Merleau-Ponty continues to be influenced by Husserl's account of the *Ablaufsphänomen*, or the recession-impression, which is referred to as '*l'écoulement*' (PhP 243–44/292–93).

29. For more on the dimensional present, see analyses of Proust in IP 197 ff./256 ff. See also Barbaras 2004, 221–26.

30. See also the following claim: 'One can reduce philosophy to a linguistic analysis only by supposing that language has its evidence within itself, that the signification of the word "world" or "thing" presents in principle no difficulty' (VI 96/130).

31. Besmer 2007, 99.

32. Merleau-Ponty still claims, however, that perception (or 'imperception', i.e., a nonintellectual, synthetic or activist view of intentionality) requires that we posit a meaning before 'logic' or speech (VI 168–69/220). This should be taken to mean that perceptual meaning is not reducible to linguistic meaning, and especially not to the contents of *la signification*.

33. See also VI 224/273, and the following unpublished note: 'Language is speech, one speaks in the word' (BNF Ms. Vol. VIII 148/72b). The note goes on to describe the 'thought in the word' according to a dialogical relation, in which a speaker's words call for an interlocutor's response.

34. For another description of empirical language use see the following unpublished remark: 'It is not *we* who perceive in the sense of the *I* that speaks – What exactly is the silent *I*? Being speaks and perceives in us – the perceptual I (the I of primary retention) as distance [*écart*] – as *one* [*on*], anonymous, – first upflow [*surrection*] of *meaning* [*sens*] – meaning of figure-and-ground-corporeal schema of space and time' (BNF Ms. Vol. VIII 168).

35. See claims to the effect that language cannot be reduced to a collection of ideal (or abstract) meanings, 'things said' or 'statements'; that is, to the sort of non–time-bound meanings one might associate with propositions (VI 50/74). Charles Taylor makes a similar observation about third-personal or designative views of expression, which he argues are traceable to Hobbes, Locke and Condillac (Taylor 2016, 112; 132). While Merleau-Ponty agrees that human meanings are 'primary and inescapable', he develops this point in a different direction than that taken in *Phenomenology*. Taylor focuses on that account, and, in particular, on the concept of 'motor intentionality' (ibid., 149).

36. Besmer 2007, 105. For the argument that this choice amounts to a self-criticism, see 99–100, 104.

37. These analyses effectively develop the account of sedimented sense encountered in chapter 2, by showing that meanings handed down in a linguistic tradition can also be accessed outside circumscribed expressive activities. The concept of 'institution' can better capture what Merleau-Ponty has in mind here, and that is partly why 'sedimentation' makes less frequent appearances.

38. For the Stoics, the 'inner' or 'inherent' speech characteristic of rational agents differentiates them from non-rational animals, and finds its outward expression in speech. The two-sided *logos* reveals our link to the world's rational structure. Language expresses this rational principle at the semantic level of the *lekton* (Chiesa 1991). This distinction would later take on a religious dimension, and was used, for example, by Theophilos to distinguish God's *logos* from that realised in his creations. Unlike in these versions, for Merleau-Ponty 'inner' language is not confined to the soul or mind.

39. This distinction is also explored in Merleau-Ponty's final course on nature (N 212/274). The course notes identify 'inherent' language with nature (or perception), 'on which the Logos of language relies'. Merleau-Ponty also claims here that the 'origin of language is mythic', and that there is 'always a language before language, which is perception' (219/262). These remarks suggest that human language originates in nature, that instituted sense is also natural (the final remark refers to the 'institution of Nature'), and even indicate a reemergence of the foundation relation between perception and language. As I have argued, Merleau-Ponty no longer holds the latter view. Still, there is no reason to deny a continuity between nature and institution; indeed, Merleau-Ponty's premises suggest that these terms are interdependent. However, on his considered view, the meaning of human language cannot be understood in naturalistic terms (recall that this possibility was addressed and rejected already in the *Phenomenology*). The formulation above reflects Merleau-Ponty's longstanding goal of eliminating artificial conceptual divisions between nature and culture. The meaning of the suggestion that language could have a mythic origin becomes clearer a few pages later, when Merleau-Ponty describes the predicament we confront when attempting to analyse language; namely, one in which it resists reduction to convention, already presupposes a familiarity with expressive and communicative norms, refers implicitly to a broader totality of expressive operations, and can thereby appear 'quasi-natural' or mythical (226–27/289–91). However, the 'naturalisation' of language is in turn explained in terms of 'sedimentation': the facility of expression supported by institution makes it appear as if language has an unknown, natural or even mythical source. Merleau-Ponty indicates the exploratory character of these claims when he holds that relations between the visible and the invisible, or between the 'logos of the visible world and the logos of ideality, will be studied (*The Visible and the Invisible*)'; this suggests that these relations have yet to be fully

explored, and that a more worked-out account of the nature-language relation remains to be specified (227/291). This does not, of course, rule out the possibility that Merleau-Ponty has an inconsistent account of the nature-institution-language relation, but in light of the evidence considered here and in chapter 7, the remarks about language in the *Nature* course are likely the exception and not the rule.

40. Madison makes a similar point: 'The silent logos which is to be recovered cannot be grasped in its silence; to be recuperated, it must be *transformed* into a spoken Logos' (1981, 141). Like other commentators, however, Madison assumes that this process of transformation unfolds at the explicitly philosophical, ontological or transcendental level. See also Andrieu 1993, 59.

41. Priest claims that for Merleau-Ponty 'linguistic preconceptions categorise the way the world appears to a language user', but he concludes that the 'I can' of bodily intentionality and being-in-the-world are more fundamental (1998, 174). Priest helpfully calls attention to the tight connection between world, perception and language. As I am attempting to show, for Merleau-Ponty intentionality is directly informed by linguistic commitments, such that it is not possible to draw a clear distinction between linguistic and 'non-linguistic reality', or identify a strict priority between perception and language (ibid., 175). Priest is certainly right that Merleau-Ponty does not think mere linguistic analysis is sufficient. By contrast, however, attending to language use tells us something fundamental about the world.

42. Recall the account of 'sedimentation' in chapter 3, which assumes that conceptual content evolves across historical time.

43. Even in cases where subjects lack the ability to use language in whole or in part (for example, infancy, language disorders, mutism, etc.), they are nevertheless members of a world in which linguistic meaning is instituted. Linguistic meaning is indirectly available to these subjects; for example, through gesture, sign or symbol, in the form of written text, or through some other external support (e.g., with help from other language-using subjects).

44. As this note suggests, in Merleau-Ponty's later work, the term 'indirect language' refers to a wider range of expressive operations.

45. On this point see also NC 133–35; VI 274/322; BNF Ms. Vol. VIII 181.

46. See, for example, Heidegger 1971, 190 ff., in which Heidegger claims that the 'language' he is interested in is not what we typically associate with human speakers.

47. See Heidegger 1998, 248–49; 253–54.

48. See Dillon 1988, 239.

49. For a development of this claim that is closer to what Merleau-Ponty has in mind, see Gadamer 2004, 458–59 ff.

50. Merleau-Ponty was likely unaware of some Wittgensteinian claims about the language-world relation that he would agree with (e.g., that linguistic assumptions prefigure our understanding of the meaning and limits of philosophical reflection and experience; see Wittgenstein 2009 §19, §23, §47, §115, §122, §182, §241; Wittgenstein 1972 §94, §162).

51. For an ostensibly similar claim, see Dillon: 'Experience expresses itself in language and the language that speaks is the voice of things' (1988, 214). A basic difference lies in the fact that for Dillon, Merleau-Ponty continues to hold that language is founded on perceptual *sens* (209, 212–13). As I have argued, Merleau-Ponty's account of institution, reversibility and latent intentionality suggests that perceptual sense is already informed by linguistic meaning, which undercuts a founding relation, and inclines towards a different reading of the claim that language expresses perceptual meaning.

52. Taylor 2016, 130; 139.

53. Gadamer 2004, 443. Incidentally, this response might also lead one to wonder about possible connections to Levinas. Like Levinas, Merleau-Ponty finds an 'ontological' valence in language, and he is especially interested in the intersubjective dimensions of language use. Despite these similarities, Levinas argues that like his philosophical predecessors, Merleau-Ponty offers a 'theoretical' account of the other because he succumbs to the temptation to privilege vision and consciousness. He also claims that Merleau-Ponty misunderstands the nature of expression because he fails to consider intersubjective experience as a genuine address to the other (see Levinas 1990a, 1990b for these criticisms). As I attempted to show in chapters 2 and 5, Merleau-Ponty's gestural account of expression rejects representationalist and consciousness-centric explanations of linguistic expression. He would gladly concede that dialogical expression is guided by conversational partners. Dialogue is a productive site for phenomenological exploration because it is an exemplar of an experience whose intentional structure cannot be understood in mentalistic terms. In this sense, it offers a paradigmatic case of the attitude Levinas claims is needed for a genuine intersubjective address. The mere fact that Merleau-Ponty offers a perceptual account of intersubjective linguistic experience need not license the conclusion that he reduces the other (for responses to Levinas's criticisms see Marratto 2017 and Reynolds 2002).

54. Gadamer 2004, 440.

55. Ibid., 441–43.

56. Ibid., 449.

7

ONTOLOGY AND LANGUAGE

The Visible and the Invisible claims that it is necessary to bring the results of *Phenomenology of Perception* and related texts 'to ontological explicitation [*explicitation*]' (VI 183/234; see also BNF Ms. Vol. VIII 183). Merleau-Ponty's earlier writings did not ignore their potential ontological import, but observations like this suggest his later writings engage different themes (see, e.g., SB 144/156; PhP lxxxiii/19, 419/459, 431/470). Given his choice of terminology, it might seem that whereas the *Phenomenology* and related texts ultimately aim to describe conscious experience, later writings pursue more discernibly metaphysical or speculative goals. This assumption is reflected in some readings of Merleau-Ponty's later ontology.[1] An influential line of argument contends that while Merleau-Ponty's ontology is the 'fulfilment' of his phenomenology, it overcomes the subject-centric limitations of the latter, thereby permitting a more direct engagement with the question of the meaning of 'being'.[2]

This chapter explores Merleau-Ponty's ontology in light of his later philosophy of language. I argue that if its linguistic dimensions are taken seriously, his ontology can be understood as an expressive project, whose fundamental goal is to describe the meaning of the perceptual world and subjective experience. With respect to its basic aims, ontology is continuous with phenomenology. However, ontology places a greater emphasis on conceptual invention and creative expression. Merleau-Ponty overcomes the tension between description and creation by developing a hybrid mode of philosophical language that is both creative and descriptive. Accordingly, ontology is more sensitive to challenges associated with language and philosophical expression than the transcendental version of phenomenology we encountered in chapter 3.

In his ontological projects, Merleau-Ponty is mainly interested in what it means for something to exist, not if it does, or which 'category of being' it belongs to (VI 96/129). For him, 'being' ultimately refers to 'meaning' (*le sens*). This is not a metaphysical enterprise in the traditional sense (for example, an enquiry into first causes, an inventory of substances or categories), and it is somewhat unlike modern and contemporary metaphysical projects. It is consistent with the view of 'metaphysics' considered in chapter 4, on which a metaphysics explores the underlying assumptions or conditions that make experience coherent. Accordingly, Merleau-Ponty's ontology aims to identify and describe the conditions that make sense and sense-making possible, where these are understood in an intersubjective and historical context. Any account of 'being' is at bottom an account of 'meaning' and how it is formed. The latter is given to subjects on the basis of both perceptual and linguistic conditions. Merleau-Ponty assumes that an accounting of these conditions will profit from an understanding of how they might differ or be construed otherwise. In this sense, ontology does admit of some speculative or counter-factual investigations. As I will try to show, however, for him the scope of ontological research remains firmly wedded to the lived, phenomenal, spatio-temporal domain. Instead of a positively metaphysical project, his ontology is 'negative' and 'indirect' (VI 179/230–31).[3] He claims that 'One cannot make a direct ontology' because he thinks that the basic premises, concepts or building blocks of ontology depend on prior descriptive work (and not because meaning must be predicated of objects negatively, as if ontology were akin to negative theology). Accordingly, he aims to develop an 'ontology from within'; namely, a set of philosophical concepts and categories that are informed by a sophisticated description of lived experience (237/286).

In some of its basic details, this project is broadly consistent with the ontologies of his earlier phenomenological predecessors, insofar as they too are interested in detailing the meaning of experience and the world. He appeals to concepts like 'flesh', 'reversibility' or 'interrogation' in order to identify structural features of experience and the world, and to specify the reflective methodology needed for ontological explorations. On this score, he follows the spirit of Husserl, the early Heidegger and

Sartre. But while he profits from his phenomenological predecessors, Merleau-Ponty does not accept, as Husserl, Sartre or Heidegger did, that ontology will develop fixed philosophical categories (e.g., the a priori categories of formal ontology, the 'existentialia' of fundamental ontology or the dual categories of the 'For Itself' and the 'In Itself'). Terms like 'flesh' are thought to correspond to the structure of the world and intentional experience, but on the whole, ontology invents concepts whose extension and content can be reinterpreted.[4] In later courses and writings, Merleau-Ponty frequently complains that 'traditional' ontology is too rigid. His ontology is a recapitulative enterprise: its 'descriptions' and 'articulations' of experience require continual refinement (BNF VIII Ms. Vol. 177/16b; see also 178/13b). Ontology amounts to a study of the world's 'intelligibility' and is a 'pre-objective use of the concept' (222/4).[5] As I have argued, in his later writings Merleau-Ponty contends that perception and language jointly secure the coherence of experience. The conditions for the intelligibility of experience vary, and conceptual categories must reflect this. Given its linguistic presuppositions, ontology does not amount to a systematic account of the fundamental categories of being, which enjoy a priori, formal validity. Instead, ontology begins by reflecting on the givens of experience, invents concepts that promise to describe it, and revises them accordingly.

As in the *Phenomenology*, Merleau-Ponty assumes that a sophisticated account of reflection is needed to meet his philosophical goals. Accordingly, I begin the chapter with a look at his later account of 'hyper-reflection' (section 1). This account is consistent with his earlier view of reflection, but it is also billed as an improvement. As I suggest, a key advantage over the earlier account is that hyper-reflection is more sensitive to the limits that philosophical language imposes on reflective activity. Ontological reflection maintains an openness to the meaning of experience by adopting an 'interrogative' attitude (section 2). These two tenets jointly support a view of ontological expression that attempts to marry description with creation. Merleau-Ponty's later view of meaning holds that meaning cannot be accessed through direct description alone; a more creative and indirect mode of expression is needed to unfold it (section 3). These characteristics give ontological investigation a dialectical character: to describe the structure of conscious experience, ontological investigations require that we continuously measure descriptions against intuitive evidence, and accordingly revise our view of each (section 4). Consistent with his estimation of the limitations of reflection and the importance of creative descriptions, Merleau-Ponty also contends that ontology needs new concepts: existing conceptual resources, he thinks, are too rigidly defined, and limit our view of the phenomena. Accordingly, he concludes that concept invention is an important ontological task (section 5).[6] The new concepts he invents in his later texts reflect this assumption. Some serve the role of phenomenological 'essences', a concept that he reinterprets and adapts to the needs of his own ontological research (section 6). Terms like 'flesh' and 'reversibility' offer essential insights into experience by detailing its structure or making it explicit, and importantly, they show us how it could be otherwise; the latter is especially valuable for investigations of an ontological scope. This reading, I suggest, can help us make sense of the strong conclusions Merleau-Ponty draws about the philosophical importance of language in his later thought (section 7).

1. 'HYPER-REFLECTION'

In chapter 5 I argued that the goal of offering an intersubjective account of sense motivates Merleau-Ponty's early ontological research. *The Visible* contends that an enquiry into 'being' will study 'the sense of sense [*le sens du sens*]' (VI 107/143). To understand 'the meaning [*le sens*] of the world's being', it is necessary to rethink concepts like 'being', 'world', 'consciousness' and 'representation' (6/21). Extant definitions of these traditional philosophical concepts cannot be presupposed. In this section, I suggest that this basic requirement circumscribes the subject-matter of Merleau-Ponty's ontology and influences his account of 'hyper-reflection' (*surréflexion*), one of its basic tools.

Before considering this in greater detail, note that most of the guiding philosophical concepts noted above implicate the first-personal standpoint: 'being' or 'world' is (or fails to be) 'represented' to 'consciousness', and 'meaning' is perceived by a subject (or by a plurality of subjects). Visual or perceptual intuition remains a *fil conducteur* for philosophy, and by extension for ontology. In his early sketches of ontological research, Merleau-Ponty announces his intention to undertake 'an ontology of the perceived world' (IP 133/178).[7] The perceived is not a 'residue' of consciousness, but it is necessary to begin with perceptual evidence. Ontology takes direction from the assumption that there is sense prior to reflection, a structure or field of vision, and that sense is divergence between perspectives (136/182). This observation also serves as a first defence against the charge that the interpretation of ontology on offer in this chapter reduces the meaning of perception to language.[8]

Ontology unfolds by means of careful reflection on meanings given in experience. The *Phenomenology*'s criticisms of intellectualism, further developed in *Le monde sensible et le monde de l'expression*, require that we reject the idea that 'the relation between thought and its object, between the *cogito* and the *cogitatum*', offers 'the whole nor even the essential of our commerce with the world' (VI 35/56). Reflection must be situated within a 'more muted relationship with the world', which recognises that the 'initiation into the world upon which it rests . . . is always already accomplished when the reflective return intervenes'.[9]

In a note from September 1959 entitled 'The Problem of Analysis', Merleau-Ponty announces his intention to capture the 'unreflected within myself'. The latter refers to meanings given in experience that subsequently become objects of philosophical thematisation. The unreflected is the site of our 'openness' to the world, a characteristic of perception frequently stressed in later writings. As we saw in chapter 6, openness to the world cannot but avail itself of historical, conceptual and linguistic presuppositions, and is defined as 'intentional transgression' (or '*ueberschreiten* by definition'). The note clarifies that unreflected perception is

> the common tissue of which we are made. Wild Being. And the perception of this perception (the phenomenological 'reflection') is the inventory of this originating exit [*sortie*] whose documents we carry in ourselves, of this *Ineinander* that awakens to itself, it is the usage of the *immer wieder* which is the sensible, the carnal itself [. . .], hence reflection is not an identification with oneself (thought of seeing or of feeling) but non-difference with self. . . .
>
> The essential is to describe the vertical or wild Being as that pre-spiritual milieu without which nothing is thinkable, not even the spirit, and by which we pass into one another, and ourselves into ourselves in order to have our own time. It is philosophy alone that

gives it – Philosophy is the study of the *Vorhabe* of Being, a *Vorhabe* that is not *knowledge* [connaissance], to be sure, that is wanting with regard to knowledge, to operation, but that envelops them as Being envelops beings. (203–4/253–54)

This text outlines a number of central topics in Merleau-Ponty's ontology. To anticipate some results below, the claim that an understanding of perception requires an appeal to the *immer wieder* suggests that some account of phenomenological essences may prove necessary for ontological work (for Husserl, reiteration is characteristic of intuitive variation). This remark also suggests that reflection is continuous with lived experience, or with the empirical: fundamentally, reflection aims to 'describe' the being of the world, which requires a return to experience. This assumption, in turn, presupposes that the 'transcendental' (or the 'ontological') and 'empirical' (or the 'sensible') are 'intertwined':

> There is a preparation for phenomenology in the natural attitude. By reiterating its own initiatives, the natural attitude seesaws in phenomenology. The natural attitude by itself surpasses itself in phenomenology – and for that reason it does not surpass itself. Reciprocally, the transcendental attitude is still and despite everything 'natural' (*natürlich*). There is a truth of the natural attitude. (S 164/267)

This remark is offered in the spirit of an interpretation of Husserl, but it reflects Merleau-Ponty's positive view.[10] Despite invoking the term 'transcendental', Merleau-Ponty does not aim to secure transcendental 'conditions of possibility' in the classical sense (VI 177/229). These descriptions and concepts are not wholly 'purified' from experience. Experience can only be understood by returning to perception, and this requires revision of existing concepts, descriptions and explanatory conditions. This approach to the empirical-transcendental distinction was first articulated in the *Phenomenology* (see chapter 3).

The problem of what was earlier called 'idealisation' (the possibility that description misconstrues or distorts lived experience) is also a fundamental concern in *The Visible*. However, the methodological implications of a sensitivity to idealisation are further radicalised. Merleau-Ponty goes as far as to claim that '[it] is to experience therefore that the ultimate ontological power belongs, and the essences, the necessities of essence, logical or internal possibility, solid and incontestable as they may be under the gaze of the mind [*l'esprit*], in the end only have their force and eloquence because all my thoughts and those of others are caught up in the fabric of one sole Being' (110/146). Experience is identified as an ultimate arbiter of higher-order reflections. Reflection always 'emerges within occurrent [*actuel*] experience surrounded by actual experiences, by the actual world, by actual Being, which is the ground of predicative Being'. This estimation accords a priority to experience, and in this sense, it is ostensibly proximate to the *Phenomenology*'s account of the priority of the pre-predicative. However, as we saw in chapter 6, this priority cannot be maintained: experience is already invested with conceptual presuppositions. Even if 'the perceptual life of my body . . . sustains and guarantees perceptual explicitation [*explicitation*]' undertaken in reflection, the latter requires a heightened attention to assumptions that support or inhibit our grasp of experience. This is also motivated by Merleau-Ponty's realisation that reflection itself presents its own proper obstacles to this goal. The *Phenomenology* called attention to the fact that reflection can change the structure of experience, and even if this seemed to necessarily follow from reflective activity, it sometimes suggested that reflection can, in principle, fully recover pre-predictive meaning.

The concept of 'hyper-reflection' (*surréflexion*) is billed as a necessary addition to Merleau-Ponty's existing account of reflection: 'We are catching sight of the necessity of another operation besides the conversion to reflection, more fundamental than it, of a sort of hyper-reflection [*surréflexion*] that would also take itself and the changes it introduces into the spectacle into account' (38/59–60). In chapter 3, I argued that requirements to the effect that reflection employ a 'phenomenology of phenomenology', or that it recursively scrutinises its results, were aimed at investing reflection with critical resources. Still, that discussion indicated that Merleau-Ponty was not aware of the full implications of this requirement: he maintained the possibility that reflection can capture sense 'just as it is'. Moreover, he was not fully sensitive to the challenges posed by his understanding of 'authentic' phenomenological expression.

Like his earlier account, hyper-reflection attempts to maintain the integrity of the 'brute thing and brute perception', viz. sense as it is given in the natural attitude (38/60). But it is also keenly aware that assumptions about the 'subject', 'mind' or 'consciousness' (or 'dimensionality' or 'flesh') can implant a false sense of security that perceptual structures have been exhaustively disclosed. Even sophisticated versions of philosophical reflection foreclose the adoption of a theoretical attitude that could yield a richer (or alternative) account of sense (73–74/102–3). Hyper-reflection attempts to hold fast to this observation, and to elevate it to a guiding methodological principle: 'hyper-reflection ... would then become, not a superior degree at the ultimate level of philosophy, but philosophy itself' (46/69). This mode of enquiry aims 'to make evident the divergence between the eidetic invariants and the effective functioning and to invite us to bring the experience itself forth from its obstinate silence'. Merleau-Ponty assumes from the outset that the products of reflection (in this case, essences or 'eidetic invariants') will always depart from their objects, to a greater or lesser degree. Any attempt at philosophical disclosure requires that we revisit experience, and this entails that descriptions will be subjected to critical scrutiny.

As in the *Phenomenology*, Fink continues to influence Merleau-Ponty's understanding of reflection. In an oblique reference, he notes that 'classical' philosophies of reflection ignore 'the twofold problem of the genesis of the existent world and the genesis of the idealisation performed by reflection' (46/69).[11] As is well known, Fink argues that the genesis or origin of the world is a central issue in Husserl's thought.[12] For Merleau-Ponty 'the *problem of the world*' encompasses both problems. The genesis of the world (i.e., the constitution of its meaning) can only be understood by studying the genesis of reflection, since the latter transforms the former. Despite reservations about other tenets of Husserl's thought, Merleau-Ponty thinks Husserl is keenly aware of this requirement. That reflection often becomes an 'after-the-fact' idealisation, 'which is not that wherein the world is formed', was 'brought frankly into the open' by Husserl's claim that 'every transcendental reduction is also an eidetic reduction' (45/68–69). Essences allow reflecting subjects to 'cease being one with the concrete flux of ... life in order to retrace the total bearing and principal articulations of the world upon which it opens'. This serves as a helpful reminder that Merleau-Ponty does not surrender the goal of developing a sophisticated approach to constitution (and to the reduction), and that Husserl's philosophy cannot be straightforwardly identified as yet another deficient model of reflection.[13]

Hyper-reflection's advantage over classical models of reflection rests on a seldom acknowledged condition. Hyper-reflective methods should be favoured because they are more sensitive to the transformations philosophical language brings to objects thematised by reflection. In the first instance, philosophical language must be carefully scrutinised; in the second, the meaning of natural-language terms that figure in descriptions must be reformulated. To undertake hyper-reflection's 'act of recovery' (a necessary precondition for ontology), extant concepts and natural-language meanings cannot be presupposed as adequate. Reflection requires a 'perhaps difficult effort that uses the significations of words to express, beyond themselves, our mute contact with the things, when they are not yet things said' (38/60). To do so, it is necessary to study our embodied perceptual contact with the world. But Merleau-Ponty signals that embodiment is no longer his central term of analysis – '[o]ur corporeality: do not place it at the centre as I did in the *Ph.P.* [I]n one sense, it is nothing but the hinge of a world, its gravity is nothing but that of the world' (BNF Ms. Vol. VI 222v). This shift coincides with a greater emphasis on the importance of language. Hyper-reflection 'must seek in the world itself the secret of our perceptual bond with it', but to do so, it must 'use words not according to their pre-established signification, but *in order to state* [pour dire] this prelogical bond' (VI 38/60). This entails that reflection is held to a linguistic and not merely a perceptual criterion. Its precise character remains to be specified, but it is already clear that reflection has chances of success only if the current meaning of natural-language terms it uses is reformulated. Alternatively, it requires that words and concepts are extended beyond their current semantic boundaries.

This observation indicates that Merleau-Ponty has brought insights from his study of creative modes of expression to bear on his account of philosophical reflection (see chapter 4). The deeper linguistic character of hyper-reflection leads him to conclude that ontology 'must interrogate the world, it must enter into the forest of references that our interrogation arouses in it, it must make it say, finally, what in its silence *it wants to say*' (38–39/60). The central conceptual and methodological role that language plays in reflection is clearly stated: '[by] considering language one would best see how one is and is not to return to the things themselves' (125/164). Hyper-reflection is therefore a *conditio sine qua non* for ontology. Attention to linguistic meaning suggests that, as for the 'transcendental' descriptions of the *Phenomenology*, language is central for the ontological enterprise.[14] As I suggest below, a fundamental task of ontology is to formulate a mode of expression, and an accompanying set of philosophical concepts, that can articulate the meaning of experience and the 'things themselves'.

2. 'INTERROGATION'

When directed to objects, hyper-reflection adopts an 'interrogative' mode of enquiry. Recall that in his research in the early 1950s, Merleau-Ponty was led to conclude that an 'invocative' attitude was most appropriate for understanding the structure of meaning-formation at work in dialogue. In texts of that period, he drew a distinction between categorical or 'thetic' and non-indicative modes of expression. The latter were better positioned to interpret and understand sense as it is expressed in lived speech, which often implies or suggests its contents without directly stating them. As we saw, this required a more indirect mode of expression and linguistic interpretation.

Basic insights from this dialogical approach to expression are now applied to our encounter with the world and the objects in it. Similarly, an open-ended, questioning or interrogative attitude is also needed for philosophical research. Like an interlocutor, Merleau-Ponty contends that the meaning of 'being' (or sense) is 'latent' or 'dissimulated' (VI 101/135). While 'ambiguity' was a characteristic of perception already in *Structure*, Merleau-Ponty now thinks that sense cannot be clarified using terms that define it directly (e.g., the intentional 'arc', 'motor intentionality', etc.). Instead, ontology must adopt a more 'indirect' method of analysis. I will discuss this point in greater detail below; for now, note that ontology is 'indirect' partly because it takes up an interrogative attitude. The latter is 'an original manner of aiming for [*viser*] something, as it were a *question-knowing* [question-savoir], which by principle no statement or "answer" can go beyond and which perhaps therefore is the proper mode of our relationship with Being, as though it were the mute or reticent interlocutor of our questions' (129/168–69).

The analogy with an interlocutor helps to disambiguate in what sense being is 'reticent' or dissimulated. As in exchanges with a dialogical partner, we are often unable to put our finger on the meaning of what we see or hear before us. Like a conversation, perceptual sense often leaves a remainder: upon reflection, it might support a different conclusion (recall the claim in chapter 6 that the structure of perceptual experience supports differing and divergent interpretations). A more guarded mode of enquiry (and by extension, of expression), or a 'question-knowing', is therefore salutary. Knowing the perceived world is still the goal, as the passage suggests, but the disclosure of lived meaning cannot proceed by stating the meaning of an object or by specifying the subject-object relation in terms that exclude possible alternatives. For perceptual objects admit of new or different construals, and it makes little sense to describe them using terms that suggest otherwise.

In addition to the peculiar characteristics of the perceived world, whose basic features were reviewed in chapter 6, section 2, the considerations motivating the adoption of a hyper-reflective model also require a more interrogative approach. The questions characteristic of an interrogative mode of reflection

> call not for the exhibiting of some thing said which would put an end to them, but for the disclosure of a Being that is not posited because it has no need to be, because it is silently behind all our affirmations, negations, and even behind all formulated questions, not that it is a matter of forgetting them in its silence, not that it is a matter of imprisoning it in our chatter [*bavardage*], but because philosophy is the reconversion of silence and speech into one another: 'It is the experience . . . still mute which we are concerned with leading to the pure expression of its own meaning'. (129/168–69)

This suggests that 'interrogation' characterises a reflective attitude and its mode of expression (reflection is discursive, which is to say that it unfolds in language). To formulate reflective insights in propositional or categorical form (i.e., as a 'thing said') limits their possible meanings. By contrast, an 'interrogative' mode of expression will formulate the meaning of an object in a more open and semantically underdetermined manner. The final remark above, which refers to Husserl's *Cartesian Meditations*, indicates that the description of 'mute' experience remains a fundamental goal.[15] Hyper-reflection attempts to achieve this without precluding alternative interpretations of experience or sense. At the attitudinal level, an interrogative mode of enquiry translates into a willingness to question (and reject) extant formulations of sense, while continuing the 'reconversion of silence and speech into one another'. This attitude promises to yield determinate insights about subjectivity or meaning (e.g., the subject as 'flesh'), but philosophy 'remains a question' that continually 'interrogates the world and the thing'. The disclosure of experience remains partial, since the objects disclosed could take on a different meaning given different conditions. Accordingly, hyper-reflection 'revives, repeats, or imitates their crystallisation before us. For this crystallisation which is partly given to us ready-made is in other respects never terminated, and thereby we can see how the world comes about' (100/134).

Consistent with other texts, the passage above suggests that the interrogative character of ontological investigations is evidenced in the formulation (or 'expression') of research questions, concepts and descriptions. This applies in the first order to reflection:

> It is characteristic of philosophical interrogation [*l'interrogation philosophique*] that it return upon itself, that it ask itself also what it is to question and what it is to answer. This question to the second power, one raised, cannot be effaced. Henceforth nothing can continue as if there had never been a question. The forgetting of the question, the return to the positive would not be possible unless interrogation was a simple absence of meaning. (120/158)

This confirms that hyper-reflection demands a careful attention to objects as they are experienced and higher-order methodological meditations. It also suggests a key point on which Merleau-Ponty is in agreement with Heidegger. In *Being and Time*, Heidegger argues that the formulation of research questions is of utmost importance.[16] The foundational assumptions that go into the definition of a given problem can disclose or occlude it. This insight is evidenced in Merleau-Ponty's reflections on Heidegger and the contemporary state of philosophy in his 1958 to 1959 course *La philosophie aujhourd'hui*. He concludes there that the problem of language (*langage*) or speech (*parole*) is 'cardinal' in philosophy (NC 122). Heidegger's view that ontological questioning cannot be formulated in a way that assumes that being is a 'mere thing' (*Sache*), with rigidly defined properties, is an important motivation for this conclusion.[17]

In this course, Merleau-Ponty formulates an important insight that clarifies how he understands ontological 'interrogation'. Following Heidegger's *Introduction to Metaphysics*, he holds that 'the essence of being is "intertwined" [*entrelacée*] with the essence of speech'. This is of consequence for the initial questions posed about perception, and for the terms we avail ourselves of in asking them. It entails that the disclosure of 'being' depends in large part on the philosophical language used to describe it. Philosophical language is 'the seizure [*la saisie*] of being'. For example, if entities are described chiefly by appeal to terms like 'extension' or 'matter', then they will be defined as bearers of properties, substances or 'mere things' (like Heidegger, Merleau-Ponty thinks this results in a 'degradation' [*une déchéance*] that blocks a richer approach to experience). On these grounds, Merleau-Ponty concludes that language is no mere regional philosophical concern (122–23; see also VI 126/165). This observation directly informs his account of the interrogative attitude. On this mode of enquiry, philosophical questions must be formulated in a way that does not overdetermine possible answers to the question of how meaning coheres. Other approaches lead us into the 'trap' (*piège*) of thinking that philosophical language does not co-determine our accounts of experience.

Not all formulations of ontological research questions lead us astray, however: there is a mode of expression (or λόγος) that can adequately capture the relation between being (*Sein*) and beings (*Seiende*) – that is, between the meaning of entities and the higher-order structures that make meaning coherent (NC 123). To find an adequate mode of expression, however, philosophical language must itself be examined or 'interrogated'. Merleau-Ponty is explicit about this: a 'reflection' (or *Besinnung*) on speech is tantamount to the 'disclosure of being' (NC 124). If language and world are intertwined, reflection on philosophical expression is a precondition for correctly interpreting the meaning of experience. As I argued in chapter 6, first-order perceptual experience presupposes background linguistic commitments (and some degree of linguistic competence), which shape the meaning of the perceived world. This account of the language-world relation is isomorphic to the reflective or philosophical domain. Merleau-Ponty claims that the 'nonexplicitated' linguistic horizon operative in philosophical reflection 'co-determines' the meaning of perception. That means that an ontology will also shape the meaning of experience and the world. Merleau-Ponty's approach to the language-world relation at the philosophical level is consistent with his approach to detailing everyday experience. For that reason, he maintains the strong claim that 'every philosophy is language and nonetheless consists in rediscovering silence' (VI 213/263; cf. NC 148).

In an unpublished note (likely from fall 1958), Merleau-Ponty claims that 'interrogative ontology' can be understood as a 'vision of the frame nature-man-being'. The visual focus is unsurprising; but consistent with the claim above, he notes that the meaning of visual data *'depends* on what will be said further on about language' (BNF Ms. Vol. VIII 165). And he also claims (following the broadly circular model of explanation first gestured to in the *Phenomenology*) that 'this ontology depends on what will be said further on about things, life, φύσις'. However, unlike reflections on language, these areas of research do not transform the meaning of the perceptual world. By contrast, reflections on nature presuppose language. And as this note suggests, Merleau-Ponty does not want to follow Heidegger's approach to ontology all the way, even if he is undeniably influenced by the broader conclusions of Heidegger's formal-indicative approach to ontological questioning.[18] He ultimately criticises Heidegger's approach to ontology, just as he criticises Sartre's (see also 174/19c). As we will see below, his understanding of how philosophical expression should go about expressing the meaning of experience serves to explain some relevant and important points of disagreement.

3. CREATIVE DESCRIPTION

Having clarified the concepts of 'hyper-reflection' and 'interrogation', I will now show how these tenets inform the distinctive approach to philosophical expression that Merleau-Ponty attempts to develop in his later writings. Like the interrogative attitude that informs it, hyper-reflection is designed to support a sophisticated description of perception. The claim that Merleau-Ponty's later work adheres to this or other classical phenomenological goals has been called into question.[19] This negative evaluation may find some support for other classical phenomenological tenets, but it does not apply to the topic of phenomenological description. The goal of offering an *explicitation* or description of experience (e.g., of the 'cohesion' and 'intertwining' of space-time) is repeatedly identified in later texts (VI 117/155).[20] Hyper-reflection is sensitive to the idealisations it brings to experience, but this does not undercut its descriptive goals: '[b]etween thought [*la pensée*] or fixation of essences, which is the aerial view [*survol*], and life, which is inherence in the world or vision, a divergence [*un écart*] reappears, which forbids thought to project itself in advance in experience and invites it to recommence description from closer up' (87/118–19). The project of phenomenological description must be refined, not abandoned.

While Merleau-Ponty does not surrender the goal of describing the perceived world, he does not accept that mere description is sufficient: 'If philosophy is to appropriate to itself and to understand this initial openness upon the world which does not exclude a possible occultation, it cannot be content with describing it' (28/48). He is sensitive to the transformations reflection brings to experience, and concludes that must be supplemented. For phenomenology to claim that it offers a faithful account of experience, critical scrutiny or revision of descriptions is also required. At the same time, because 'language is not necessarily deceptive, truth is not coincidence, nor mute' (125/164). Phenomenological description is not strengthened by drawing an identity between its contents and the purportedly pre-descriptive, pre-predicative, or 'mute' meaning of experience. Description promises to disclose the structures of experience, but it cannot do so either as a categorical or literal mode of expression ('coincidence'), nor as a mere means for articulating the ostensibly pre-theoretical meaning of perception.

Instead, description must be paired with creation. For 'the manifest meaning of each word' is less important than 'the lateral relations' that emerge in the process of philosophical articulation. Already in the *Phenomenology*, the term 'lateral' was used to designate modes of constitution that do not privilege activity or synthesis. In part 2 we saw that Merleau-Ponty applies this term to distinctive modes of literary and dialogical speech. Lateral (or 'indirect') expression is more suggestive, implicative, allusive, and in the case of literature, creative (though it still expresses a content subject to interpretation by others). In his ontological projects, Merleau-Ponty avails himself of terms once used to characterise expression in Proust, Valéry and other writers. He also claims to follow Heidegger in seeking a space between 'created speech' [*parole créée*] and 'received speech' [*parole reçue*] (NC 123). While one might wonder if Heidegger invoked a similar distinction, the dichotomy tracks Merleau-Ponty's longstanding division between 'speaking' speech (*parole parlante*) and 'spoken' speech (*parole parlée*), which also surfaces in *The Visible*, though less frequently (VI 126/165, 175/227). The use of these terms to describe philosophical expression indicates that creative expression plays an important role in ontology.

In fact, evidence suggests that linguistic or expressive creation is a necessary condition of the ontology Merleau-Ponty attempts to develop. Progress in ontological research requires an exploration of linguistic conventions, and must avail itself of its own distinct linguistic inventions: 'Being . . . *requires creation of us* for us to experience it'. Merleau-Ponty is explicit about the need to infuse description with creative resources: '[p]hilosophy, precisely as "Being speaking within us", expression of mute experience by itself, is creation' (VI 197/247–48).

What kind of creative expression is needed to describe the structure of experience? Some attention to Merleau-Ponty's own mode of philosophical expression may indicate an answer. It is sometimes suggested that the unique idiom and terms populating his later texts are metaphors.[21] According to this view, terms like 'flesh' or 'chiasma' amount to an 'ontological poetics' predicated on invention, such that 'the language of metaphor is the language of flesh'.[22] This estimation is partly motivated by the view that formal or literal modes of expression are philosophically inadequate, which Merleau-Ponty agrees with. This makes it more plausible that he would embrace a metaphorical form of expression. He would also be attracted to metaphor because a fundamental goal of his later ontology is to give voice to meanings that are difficult to capture, or which evade formulation in a cut-and-dry manner. Metaphorical modes of expression seem well suited for this task.

Undoubtedly, there are recurring metaphorical elements in ontological modes of expression. Like metaphor, 'operative' expression is indirect. Merleau-Ponty does not shy away from using allusive and often poetic diction, and he is explicit that terms like 'the flesh' are inventions of language (139–40/181–82). If one follows Ricoeur in *La métaphore vive* in holding that metaphorical expression is 'inventive' in the 'twofold sense of both discovery and creation', Merleau-Ponty's own style of philosophical expression might appear more proximate to a metaphorical mode of expression.[23]

However, the final point should give us pause. The view of metaphor just sketched is admittedly weak. On such a view, it seems uncontroversial to hold that philosophical expression is 'metaphorical', since at bottom it amounts to a 'transfer' of meaning from the unthematised, pre-expressive domain to an expressive one. Such a procedure is necessarily inventive or creative. But readers who detect metaphorical elements in Merleau-Ponty's later thought surely have something more robust in mind. (On the previous view, any number of non-literal modes of signification could plausibly count as metaphorical.)

A more robust metaphorical reading, which contends that Merleau-Ponty's chosen mode of expression (or the one he is attempting to develop) is a symbolic mode of purely literary or poetic creation, is complicated by his own implicit and explicit hesitations on this matter. While it is somewhat indeterminate, textual evidence on the whole speaks against a stronger metaphorical reading. The example of 'the flesh' is instructive. One text states that claims to the effect that subject and world are 'flesh' 'must be taken at [their] word [*à la lettre*]' (133/ 173). If that is right, then 'flesh' is material and tangible, and the term is not used metaphorically. However, Merleau-Ponty also claims that there is a flesh of language and ideality, neither of which is tangible or material (153/198). The claim that 'the flesh we are speaking of is not matter' seems to confirm this (146/189).

The latter remarks suggest that the concept of 'flesh' cannot be simply read in a literal sense (a view supported by other uses of the term). That opens up the possibility of a symbolic or metaphorical reading. Consistent with this interpretation, Merleau-Ponty occasionally suggests that metaphor is a helpful category with which to understand the term (125/164, 138/179, 155/201). However, he also claims that the category of metaphor is inadequate for characterising the relations between the visible and the invisible (and by extension, the concepts used to describe them): 'There is no *metaphor* between the visible and the invisible' (VI 221–22/271; see also NC 202). More broadly, a view of 'Philosophy as creation (*Gebilde*), resting on itself – that cannot be the final truth' (VI 174/225). Similarly, an approach to expression on which it is defined as pure creation or poetic invention – that is, one consistent with expression as metaphor – is 'both abstract and insufficient'.

Even if his later writings are populated with metaphors, the mode of expression he endorses is ultimately not metaphorical. While metaphors like '*chiasma*' or 'house of being' shed light on experience, when a metaphor yields determinate insights into perception, it ceases to be a mere metaphor (BNF Ms. Vol. VIII 352/30). When creative expressions capture something essential about the world, they take on the status of descriptions. They are not 'mere' descriptions, given that they actively transform existing terminology and refigure expressive norms. Instead of holding that ontological signification is metaphorical, it is more apt to characterise this mode of expression as a creative description. Some expressions are allusive and indirect, but this does not prevent them from functioning as descriptions, insofar as they chiefly aim to state the meaning of a phenomenon or object, even if they do so creatively. For Merleau-Ponty, invention serves the goals of transcribing the meaning of experience. It does not direct our attention elsewhere, as a symbol might, but purports to describe meanings genuinely given in perception.

4. DIALECTICAL EXPRESSION

Given the inevitable transformations that language brings to perception, to disclose the meaning of experience, reflecting subjects must continually mediate between perceived sense and its linguistic formulation. This gives the creative descriptions characteristic of ontology a dialectical character. The estimation that expression is dialectical is consistent with some of Merleau-Ponty's explicit remarks about ontological expression. It also coheres with the assumptions that ontology requires an 'interrogative' attitude, and that it is guided by 'hyper-reflection'. And as I will suggest in this section, interpreting expression with a view to its dialectical structure also helps to clarify how description is also creative.

Two important initial considerations point to the dialectical character of ontological expression. By extension, they also count against the view that expression is purely metaphorical or poetic. First, this characterisation accords with Merleau-Ponty's understanding of the transcendental-empirical relation. The porous relationship between experience and expression leads to the conclusion that 'thematisation itself must be understood as a behaviour of a higher degree – the relation between thematisation and behaviour is a dialectical relation: language realises, by breaking the silence, what the silence wished and did not obtain' (VI 176/227). Philosophical reflection is on a continuum with pre-reflective life; the former modifies the latter, and vice versa. Transcendental and empirical are intertwined, which is to say that descriptions given in the first attitude are guided by the second.

Second, this characterisation is consistent with the important observation that expression remains under the jurisdiction of intuitively given meanings. Perception and life itself offer the resources with which to construct an 'ontological landscape' (BNF Ms. Vol. VIII 278/37a).[24] Attempts at explicating experience can go astray, and it is necessary to return to pre-reflective life. When this occurs, reflection is supplemented with new intuitive evidence. As we have seen elsewhere, Merleau-Ponty does not assume that this process ever attains completeness. Further, expression is not pure philosophical creation; it responds to sense as it is given. Hence, expression does not 'come to an end': 'There would be needed a silence that envelops speech anew' (VI 179/230). In turn, 'The meanings which philosophy proposes are the rebus which is to be deciphered by experience proper' (MPR 437).

Merleau-Ponty's account of 'hyperdialectic' can shed light on the dialectical structure of ontological expression. I cannot explore his later understanding of dialectic in detail, but some important features can be noted. Merleau-Ponty sees this account as a necessary improvement to existing treatments of dialectic: 'The only good dialectic is the hyperdialectic' (94/127). Hyper-dialectic is of consequence for ontology: 'hyperdialectic is what one calls ontology, that is to say a philosophy that does not *exit* the circle of being and appearances [*de l'être et des apparences*], of being and beings' (BNF Ms. Vol. VI 61/19).[25] The observation that '[w]e are never wholly one with constitutive genesis [and] barely manage to accompany it for short segments' is naturally paired with a dialectical approach to reflection and experience (S 179/292). Merleau-Ponty's reading of dialectic stresses its genetic and evolutionary features. In his remarks about dialectic, he is often concerned with its implications for reflection (the shared prefix 'hyper-' suggests such a connection). He thinks that dialectical methods should inform philosophy's attempt to understand experience. Against views like Sartre's, which emphasise a single moment of dialectical synthesis (i.e., negation), Merleau-Ponty holds that dialectic is better understood in terms of 'movement'. He rejects the idea that dialectical 'surpassing . . . results in a new positive, a new position' (VI 95/127–28) or a new 'thesis' (175/227).[26] For 'the only surpassings we know are concrete, partial, encumbered with survivals, saddled with deficits'. Dialectical synthesis does not yield conceptual results that could be considered either 'more real' or 'more valid' than their predecessors; while progress is made, insights from earlier stages of experience continue to inform philosophical theorising.

A fruitful approach to dialectic also emphasises its 'circular movement' (VI 35/56, 91/123; BNF Ms. Vol. XIV 52/4–53/5). Already in *Structure*, Merleau-Ponty saw circularity as a defining feature of dialectic. Subsequently, this concept is used to characterise tenets like 'reversibility' or 'flesh' (VI 142–43/185–86), and to describe the methodological *modus operandi* of his later work (177–79/229–31, 199/249). As the *Phenomenology* and other texts showed, circular modes of enquiry are not vicious, chiefly because these models encourage the reinterpretation of experience, which promises to refine and improve descriptions.[27]

Merleau-Ponty also uses elements of his reading of hyper-dialectic to detail subjects' relation to the world or 'being'. A dialectical interpretation of this relation is partly motivated by intersubjective readings of tenets like 'dimensionality' and 'reversibility'. These concepts reveal that sense is variable and indexed to different spatio-temporally individuated perspectives, cultures and historical time. The reversals characteristic of intersubjective experiences of sense-constitution are also nicely captured by a dialectical account, which gives us 'the assurance that things have another sense than that which we are in a position to recognise in them' (VI 94/127). Against 'objective ontology', Merleau-Ponty seeks 'in the world of which we have experience, [an]other being and [an]other sense' (IP 126/169–70). Accordingly, in his early ontological formulations in the mid-1950s, he claims that 'being' has a dialectical structure (79/126). He would go on to note that the 'distance' in being (a term associated with the *écart*, intentionality, and meaning-formation) is a dialectical relation akin to that at work in a conversation (BNF Ms. Vol. VIII 148/72b).[28]

These considerations are brought to bear on Merleau-Ponty's view about the formulation of ontological or philosophical expression. Views of dialectic like those advanced by Kojève or Sartre (to consider two important examples) misconstrue the role of the subject that observes and ultimately expresses the meanings encountered in the dialectical movement of experience (though according to Merleau-Ponty, Hegel did not ignore this).[29] For Merleau-Ponty, the reflecting subject 'always codetermines the meaning of what he says' (VI 90/122). Even if Sartre, for example, does not deny the subject a role in dialectic (the For-Itself is the motor of 'nothingness' and of the negations that transform the given), Merleau-Ponty thinks that the deeper consequences of the subject's role in dialectic have yet to be adequately acknowledged. For him, a distinctive advantage of a hyperdialectical approach is that it identifies a role for the subject in experience without sacrificing the extra-subjective conditions on which the disclosure of sense also depends.

For Merleau-Ponty, dialectical expression is a form of 'mediation'. Expression mediates between perceptually given meanings and descriptive explications. The concept of 'mediation' implicitly and explicitly guides Merleau-Ponty's interpretation of dialectic: phenomenology becomes dialectical by '[taking] into account the mediation of being' (IP 79/126).[30] Mediation refers to the transformation of one term into another, and the uniting of two terms into a third. The new term might at first seem tangentially or weakly connected to what comes before it. But this connection is constitutive for both prior terms, as it is subsequently revealed to observers. For Merleau-Ponty, dialectical mediation offers a 'way to decipher [*déchiffrer*] the being with which we are in contact, the being in the process of manifesting itself, the situational being' (VI 93/125). In a movement of dialectical mediation, subject and object terms do not stand in strict relations of priority. Instead, they co-determine the disclosure of sense. Co-determination or co-constitution is a paradigmatic case of mediation, since a new condition emerges from the mutual interaction of two (or more) terms.

The link between expression, dialectic and mediation is identified by the following text:

> Each statement, in order to be true, must be referred, throughout the whole movement, to the stage from which it arises and has its full meaning only if one takes into account not only what it says expressly but also its place within the whole which constitutes its latent content; thus, he who speaks (and that which he implicitly understands) [*sous-entend*] always codetermines the meaning [*sens*] of what he says, the philosopher is always implicated in the problems he poses, and there is no truth if one does not consider, when appraising any statement [*énoncé*], the presence of the philosopher who states [*qui énonce*]; between manifest content and latent content, there can not only be differences, but contradiction as well; nevertheless this double meaning accords to the statement – as when we want to consider some thing *in itself*, and as a result, concentrating ourselves on it, we come to determine it such as it is *for us*. (90/122)

The broader goal of this difficult passage is to suggest that the meaning of philosophical expressions cannot be divorced from their utterer or origin. Alternatively, the meaning of an expression cannot be identified with its content, nor is it given solely by the object an expression refers to. Any philosophical statement about an object (or 'thing') rests on subjective expressive processes, which must be considered when evaluating the expression, object or meaning in question. These prior subjective conditions are rarely legible in the meaning of an expression (they remain 'latent'), but all philosophical expressions are necessarily animated by some subjective intention. Philosophical expression, then, has a 'double meaning'. It expresses some determinate external content – for example, it makes some point about some object, and can be evaluated in terms of it – but it also reflects internal or subjective meaning-making processes (those that 'interrogate' an object), which play a nontrivial role in fixing and formulating the former. Philosophy attempts to isolate the meaning of an object 'in itself', but it can only do so by considering what it means 'for us'.

A sophisticated account of philosophical expression will mediate between these two poles. The 'true' meaning of some object or statement is not given simply by taking both equally into account. Rather, the point is that the meaning of any object is understood at the reflective level through a movement of dialectical mediation between an object as it appears 'in itself' and the descriptions that hold 'for us'. To ignore the important transformations that reflection brings to its objects increases the chances that explications of experience become detached from their 'ante-predicative context', from which they originate (92/124). When that occurs, '[the] very formulas by which it describes the movement of being are then liable to falsify it'. By contrast, ontological reflection remains aware of this possibility, and becomes 'autocritical': it integrates a self-critical moment into its methodology, which reappraises descriptions in light of experience, and vice versa. This movement persists as long as reflective activity attempts to grasp the meaning of experience, and it gives ontological expression a fundamentally dialectical character.

Merleau-Ponty noted the close connection between language and dialectic in the mid-1950s (BNF Ms. Vol. VI 58/13), and at the time of *The Visible and the Invisible* he concludes that

> we would err as much by defining philosophy as the search for essences as by defining it as fusion with things, and the two errors are not so different. [. . .] They are two positivisms. Whether one installs oneself at the level of statements, which are the proper order of essences, or in the silence of things, whether one trusts in speech absolutely, or whether one distrusts it absolutely – the ignorance of the problem of speech is here the ignoring of all mediation. (VI 127/166)

In rejecting the two initial options, the passage suggests that philosophy is better understood as a mediation between sense and its expressed formulation. Notice that linguistic mediation is defined as a 'problem': a productive tension between the two poles above is sustained in ontological enquiry. Merleau-Ponty contends that the meaning of the world or experience, and the concepts that unfold it, will come to light on the basis of the movement sketched above. Different definitions of philosophy or ontology may be privileged, but whatever their goals might be, they will attempt to identify some fundamental fact about meaning, being or experience. When they do so, they will appeal to some language or other to formulate their insights. Merleau-Ponty contends that traditional accounts of philosophy or ontology overlook the fact that by privileging 'univocal' forms of expression (i.e., ones that sever their link from the reflective movement that produces them), these accounts also foreclose on the possible meaning of experience, being or meaning, thereby limiting their explanatory power. The passage above notes that different philosophical styles (e.g., those relying on propositions, a priori essences, and poetic revelation of the 'silence of things') suffer from this limitation. Merleau-Ponty thinks that philosophy is tasked with expressing experience; but because its meaning is difficult to unfold and could be construed otherwise, philosophy must continually reconsider the plausibility of its expressions in light of the meaning of things.

This understanding of ontological expression offers more reasons to think that ontology is ultimately an expressive enterprise. For Merleau-Ponty, ontology does not claim to offer a definitive, once-and-for-all 'solution'; it is instead a 'veil lifted', which gradually unfolds the meaning of experience, and attempts to marshal the conceptual resources needed to better understand it (199/249). It does not seem that this process has a definitive end point. Ontology does not aim to 'objectify the *Gesagte*', but rather to express perception by creatively describing it (HLP 49/60). If philosophical language 'is to remain dialectical, speech [*parole*] can no longer be statement, *Satz*, it must be thinking speech, without reference to a *Sachverhalt*' (VI 175/227). Ontology must critically probe the transformation of sense into language (and vice versa), and it operates between the poles of creation and description.

In addition to offering more evidence for why ontology cannot rely on categorical modes of expression, the approach to philosophical language sketched above also shows why forms of expression that are purportedly purely creative, poetic or 'silent' fall short. These modes claim to reveal the genuine meaning of things, prior to our interventions. But the perspective from which they are articulated is anything but immaterial to the concrete conclusions they draw about experience. Indeed, the claim that the 'true' structure of reality could be given absent some conceptual scheme seems on this account to be an idealisation: philosophical thematisation and expression will always transform experience and shape the meaning of its objects.

By extension, Merleau-Ponty's dialectical approach to expression further clarifies why he does not endorse a view of language like that offered by the later Heidegger.[31] In essays like 'On the Way to Language' and in the 'Letter on Humanism', Heidegger claims that being 'speaks' through language. Instead of any natural language, when language 'speaks', this is tantamount to the speaking of being itself. The language of poetry, for Heidegger, is *par excellence* the language of being.[32] As we have seen, Merleau-Ponty makes ostensibly similar claims. However, as I suggested in chapter 6, his versions of these claims point to different conclusions. He certainly agrees that ontological language is not coextensive with natural language (a point I return to below), and he takes Heidegger's insights about ontological questioning to heart. However, already during the writing of *The Prose of the World*, he indicates that Heidegger's approach to ontology and language leaves something to be desired (BNF Ms. Vol. III 204v).[33] The account of language and mediation above clarifies these hesitations. It questions the presumption that language faithfully delivers the meaning of the 'silence of things' without relying on subjective contributions. The latter reflects a poor understanding of the constitutive relation between language and world. Heidegger trusts in the 'silence' of poetic speech, through which being speaks, but he overlooks and ignores the ineliminable fact that subjective activity will mediate the disclosure of sense to a greater or lesser extent. On these grounds, Merleau-Ponty criticises Heidegger for placing too much emphasis on passivity in expression (HLP 51/63). There is no purely passive saying of being, or a letting-be in language, if creative and reflective activity is needed to unfold the meaning of experience, and if ontological expression can only articulate the meaning of being by navigating between the givens of sense and the claims of description.

Nevertheless, Merleau-Ponty is careful not to overemphasise the role of the subject (VI 177/229, 274/322). He is in qualified agreement with Heidegger's critique of humanism. Still, recall that already in the *Phenomenology*, he accepts that 'there is no experience without speech', where 'speech' is understood in decidedly human terms (PhP 353/394). In later work, he maintains that '[the things'] eminent being can be understood only by him who enters into perception, and with it keeps in distant-contact with them' (VI 220/269). He seeks to jettison overly intellectualist views of subjectivity, but not to altogether eliminate subjective activity from ontology (43/66; see also 172/223–24, 183/234, 200/250). Merleau-Ponty's approach to the relation between humanism, language and ontology profits from an engagement with Jean Hyppolite, which I cannot consider in detail here.[34] Despite rejecting one interpretation of humanism, Hyppolite accepts that the disclosure of sense requires a view of language that reflects the logic of mediation in Hegel.[35] As I have suggested, Merleau-Ponty endorses a similar position in his account of ontological expression.

5. CONCEPT INVENTION

Thus far, I have argued that for Merleau-Ponty, ontology ultimately attempts to grasp the meaning or sense of experience. To do so, it relies on a reflective methodology, and adopts an 'interrogative' disposition towards its objects. Merleau-Ponty's account of hyper-reflection and interrogation suggest that a successful account of experience requires a reformulation of existing philosophical terminology. This sets a linguistic task for ontology, and also identifies a criterion against which to measure its success (namely, the extent to which it succeeds in refashioning philosophical language such that it can better detail the structures of experience). Ontology marries creation with description, but does not collapse into either term. Instead, it critically and dialectically reconsiders descriptions in light of a reappraisal of experience.

I suggested above that ontological creation is not akin to metaphorical invention. In this section I will attempt to specify its creative characteristics more precisely. Ontology is creative because it invents a new set of concepts or a new philosophical vocabulary. Concept invention serves the goal of description. With a new set of concepts, it becomes in principle possible to explore, interpret and ultimately describe a wider range of lived meanings. This serves the fundamental ontological goal of understanding the varying modalities of sense-constitution. Merleau-Ponty's remarks about the pitfalls of conventional philosophical expression and existing conceptual schemes indicate that, for him, concept invention is a necessary step for describing sense.

Since his early writings, Merleau-Ponty has maintained that language (and especially aesthetic modes of expression) has deep creative possibilities. Ontological language is also creative, and bears some similarities to *parole parlante*, *opérante*, or *originaire*, and *langage indirect*. Despite sharing some of their characteristics, ontological creation is chiefly focused on inventing new philosophical concepts. Its creative modalities serve the goals of phenomenological description, which cannot be said for standard modes of aesthetic expression.

The introduction to *Signs* claims that the subject (or 'I') functions 'by construction' (S 14/28). The sense of 'construction' referred to here, and its implications for ontology, can be understood in light of Merleau-Ponty's later view of perception. Recall that *The Visible* claims that meaning is 'brute': it is given in a more dissimulated form than Merleau-Ponty assumed in earlier texts (VI 102/137). Claims about the brute or 'latent' nature of perception pertain to the appearance of meaning and its plural modes of givenness, which are difficult to detail thoroughly (101/135). Paired with a longstanding principle first articulated in *Structure*, on which 'the properties of the phenomenal field are not expressible in a language that would owe nothing to them', these premises jointly point to the need for a more creative mode of expression (SB 193/208). The object of philosophical reflection ('being' as 'flesh') is 'operative': its meaning is latent and is transformed across different perspectives (VI 251/300). Given the principle above, philosophical language must accordingly adopt a more indirect and creative style when attempting to describe it.

A creative mode of expression is also required by the expressive dearth (as Merleau-Ponty sees it) of existing philosophical concepts.[36] Terms like 'subject' or 'noema' foreclose on descriptions of perceptual meaning and circumscribe access to its possible dimensions (VI 38/60, 73–74/102–3). For example, by defining perceivers as 'subjects' whose 'noeses' engage 'objects' or 'noemata', standard philosophical categories encourage us to analyse perceptual objects as passive recipients of subjective sense-making activities. This strengthens the assumption that subjectivity is the active condition supporting meaningful perceptual experience, and that the contribution of the world or of objects is passive. According to Merleau-Ponty, this picture does not track prereflective experience. This realisation is stymied, however, by a reliance on classical philosophical concepts. For Merleau-Ponty, concepts with rigidly defined semantic borders get ahead of the phenomena and block a fuller appreciation of lived meaning. He concludes that classical philosophical terminology is insufficient for describing the meaning of experience and must be replaced (88/119, 155/201).

The formulation of new philosophical concepts thereby becomes a pressing task:

> Should we even say thing, should we say imaginary or idea, when each thing that exists is further than itself, when each fact can be a dimension, when ideas have their regions? The entire description of our landscape and the lines of our universe, and of our inner monologue, is to be redone. Colours, sounds, and things – like Van Gogh's stars – are the passages [*des foyers*] and radiances [*des rayonnements*] of being. (S 15/28–29)

This text identifies the need to infuse descriptions with new concepts. The manner in which material objects are given, Merleau-Ponty contends, exceeds the boundaries of the term 'thing', which has a limited semantic range. This term evokes criteria of identity and non-identity, properties, subjects and predicates. But objects of experience, as the descriptions in *The Visible* attempt to show, are never mere things. Instead, they open us to a world, remind us of the past, allow us to image a future, and initiate vision on its course. Standard philosophical terminology also falls short of grasping similar experiences of space, time, colour, perception and more. A contemporaneous remark identifies the need to '[r]eplace [the] notions of concept, idea, mind, representation with [the] notions of *dimensions*, articulation, level, hinges, pivots, configuration' (VI 224/273). In addition to the concepts of 'being at [*être à*] . . . , pre-intentional presence and transcendence', it is necessary to reformulate 'the entire vocabulary of psychological analysis: for example memories, passions, feelings' (BNF Ms. Vol. VIII 278/37a). The conceptual substitutions referred to here aim to formulate a new philosophical vocabulary (178/13b).

As other texts demonstrate, the reformulation of philosophical concepts is a defining mark of Merleau-Ponty's ontology. A note from January 1959 entitled 'The Origin of Truth' offers a relatively rare direct definition of ontology. After noting the need to properly study various disciplines (e.g., physics, biology, linguistics, history) and philosophical concepts (e.g., 'subjectivity', 'intersubjectivity' and 'historicity'), Merleau-Ponty claims that after doing so he will

> be in a position to define an ontology and to define philosophy. Ontology would be the elaboration of the notions that have to replace that of transcendental subjectivity, those of subject, object, meaning – the definition of philosophy would involve an elucidation of philosophical expression itself [. . .] an awareness [*une prise de*

conscience], then, of the method used in what precedes 'naively', as though philosophy would confine itself to reflecting what is, as science of pre-science, as expression of what is before expression *and which sustains expression from behind*. (VI 167/219)

This text is clear that ontology develops concepts that will replace classical philosophical terms. This confirms that ontology attempts to answer perennial questions – for example, about 'subject, object, [and] meaning' – by formulating a mode of expression that is more faithful to our experience of the objects designated by these terms. The text notes that a study of philosophical expression is part and parcel of such a project. In other words, deliberate reflection on the philosophy of language, and on philosophical issues pertaining to expression, is a *sine qua non* for ontology. These preconditions will invest ontology with a self-critical attitude needed to study the structure of experience prior to its interrogation (without assuming that it could be fully and transparently detailed).

As the passage above suggests, concept invention can overcome the rigidity of our existing conceptual resources. Ontological invention attempts to develop concepts whose meanings are sufficiently fluid. For Merleau-Ponty, philosophy 'cannot be [a] total and active grasp, [or] intellectual possession' (VI 266/313–14). Ontological concepts are characterised by a degree of semantic porosity. They are specific enough to elucidate some particular experience, but remain open to modification, and to the possibility that the meaning of experience could be construed otherwise. Merleau-Ponty thinks that terms like *flesh* or *chiasma* satisfy these requirements. They identify some intentional and structural conditions of experience, but underdetermine how those conditions are realised at the first-personal level.

Merleau-Ponty is clear that absent new concepts, ontology will be unable to successfully meet its goals.[37] This precondition points to a similarity with literary language: '*What* it says, its *significations*, are not absolutely invisible: it shows by words. Like all literature. It does not install itself in the reverse of the visible: it is on both sides' (VI 266/313–14). Concept invention is a linguistic endeavour, and unfolds between received meanings (the 'invisible' storehouse of instituted meaning or *signification*) and those given in perception. As Merleau-Ponty has maintained since his early writings, concepts are coextensive with linguistic *signification*. Like a novel, whose meanings depend on an elaborated linguistic structure, ontology exhibits the meaning of perception through its linguistic constructs. It is important to specify how far the analogy to literary expression extends.

As I noted in chapter 4, for Merleau-Ponty literary expression is 'indirect' and sometimes allusive. Ontological expression also adopts some features of indirect expression:

> But from this it follows that the words most charged with philosophy are not necessarily those that contain what they say, but rather those that most energetically open upon Being, because they more closely convey the life of the whole and make our habitual evidences vibrate until they disjoin. Hence it is a question whether philosophy as reconquest of brute or wild being can be accomplished by the resources of the eloquent language, or whether it would not be necessary for philosophy to use language in a way that takes from it its power of immediate or direct signification in order to equal it with what it wishes all the same to say. (VI 102–3/137)

Ontology attempts to disclose and study meanings that resist direct and thorough elucidation. These meanings, the passage claims, are best revealed through an indirect mode of expression, viz. one that approaches its object ('Being') in unexpected ways, and which does not directly state that some object 'has' some quality 'p' or 'q' (even if it attempts to show these features by means of creative descriptions). In practice, this indirect mode of expression is evidenced in Merleau-Ponty's claims that things are 'dimensions', or that experience is a contact of 'flesh' with 'flesh'. These modes of expression disrupt existing assumptions (or 'habitual evidences') about objects or intentional experiences. Merleau-Ponty alleges that ingrained philosophical presuppositions prevent us from properly grasping our 'openness' onto 'being', and from understanding the unthematised link between subject, object and world. By adopting a more unconventional vocabulary, ontology promises to reveal new and unexpected features of lived meaning. Merleau-Ponty doubts that more standard modes of philosophical expression will be sufficient to 'reconquer' lived experience, given their prior assumptions about its intentional structure.

This requirement points to a fundamental continuity between ontological and literary modes of expression. However, Merleau-Ponty stops short of identifying the philosophical and literary versions of indirect expression. Recall that ontological expression dialectically mediates between creation and description, without identifying itself with either term. Purely descriptive or literal modes of expression (i.e., an 'absolutely pure philosophical word'), and wholly literary or poetic ones, are on their own equally untenable (VI 266/313–14). Merleau-Ponty seeks a synthesis between these two terms. To identify philosophical and literary expression would conflict with this assumption.

Instead, concept invention is informed by a reappraisal of sense and of existing concepts. Invention takes direction 'from what the writer sees' (*à partir de ce que l'écrivain voit*) (NC 217). As we saw in chapter 4, some literary writers mirror phenomenology's descriptive practices, but literature differs from the latter since its creative expressions are 'dictated by the structure of vision' (218). Poetry and art 'speak only silently', whereas philosophy is 'the exhibition [*démonstration*] of this speaking silence' (HLP 49/60). When Merleau-Ponty claims that 'there is . . . a manner of making the things themselves speak', he attempts to strike a balance between description and creation, so that concept invention may track the appearance of sense. He identifies ontological expression with 'a language of which [we] would not be the organiser, words [we] would not assemble, that would combine through [us] by virtue of a natural intertwining of their meaning' (VI 125/164). Passages like this attempt to carve out a mitigated role for creative subjective activity, while noting that indirect expression is still guided by intuitive evidence. The ontological version of indirect and operative expression attempts to faithfully express perceptual meaning in a language that accords with it (VI 6/2). Some of its terms seem like poetic inventions (e.g., 'rays' or 'vortex'), but '[c]oncepts for a philosopher are only nets for catching sense' (HLP 57/64).

I considered some of Merleau-Ponty's own conceptual inventions earlier in this chapter, but a look at an example can help to further clarify his approach to concept-creation. In a note from May 1960, after claiming that all knowledge is found in the '*Logos* of the visible world' and its 'double ontological ground', he claims that in sensible experience

> the subject-object distinction, noesis-noema, makes no sense since we do not yet have *acts* and *Erlebnisse*. [. . .] Just as here there is no noesis and noema, but body and thing (the flesh which 'knows' flesh, the network of anonymous body-things transcendence) – by passing

> to the Ego and to its *Erzeugungen*, there is no noesis and noema, there is the simultaneous genesis of Speech and Meaning (without a relation of priority) as the *control* of mute flux. Speech (which is, vertically, the foundation of all my empirical acts and words, as the *Welt* of all of my perceptions as well as of the Perceiveds) is not, any more than space or time, a concept, it is a Figurative. (MPR 439; BNF Ms. Vol. VIII 345/14)

Despite obvious interpretive challenges, it seems that Merleau-Ponty is attempting to describe perceptual experience without relying on classical phenomenological concepts (e.g., 'act', 'noesis' or 'noema'). If we attend to experience, it is difficult to find something like an 'act' at work. Of course, this term approximates subjects' engagement with objects, but Merleau-Ponty maintains that it is more compelling to describe this relation as one of 'flesh' 'knowing' 'flesh'. The term 'flesh' allegedly better captures the seamlessness of our experience of the body-world or subject-object relation. And the choice to put the word 'knows' in scare quotes suggests that the proximity between subject and object in everyday experience is comparable but not identifiable with the familiarity that obtains between knower and object known. These creative formulations may in fact fail to do more justice to experience than terms like 'act' or 'noesis'. But in any case, the deeper point is that they signal an attempt to develop a new vocabulary with which to describe sense and experience. The extent to which they succeed, or how one might judge their success, is open to interpretation (I return to this issue in section 7).[38]

Consistent with the broadly dialectical approach sketched above, this text also indicates how new concepts might be formulated in ontological expression (or 'Speech'). The language characteristic of ontology is 'Figurative' because it constructs new linguistic forms or 'figures' out of existing expressive and conceptual resources.[39] To do so, one must attend to how meanings encountered in perception incline us to take this or that view, and what concepts one marshals when doing so. By attempting to articulate it in novel ways (e.g., by deploying a term like 'flesh' or 'knowledge' to describe objects or relations typically analysed in different terms), perceptual experience might be understood in a new light. Merleau-Ponty contrasts this 'figurative' capacity with the more traditional clarificatory power of concepts because he thinks the former promises to more thoroughly transform our view of experience than the latter. Furnished with a new set of concepts, subjects can return to and see the world anew. This now familiar estimation of the relation between perception and language finds additional support in claims to the effect that philosophical language is on a continuum with the 'non-thematised *Lebenswelt*' (VI 170/222). The insights philosophy discloses 'will in their turn be sedimented, "taken back" by the *Lebenswelt*, will be comprehended by it rather than they comprehend it'. Concept invention is a dialectical process, which 'does not prevent philosophy from having value, from being something else than and more than the simple partial product of the *Lebenswelt*, enclosed in a language that leads us on. Between the *Lebenswelt* as universal Being and philosophy as a furthermost product of the world, there is no rivalry or antinomy: it is philosophy that discloses it'.[40]

Readers of Merleau-Ponty's later work confront some enigmatic formulations that sometimes defy intelligibility. I have suggested that these newfangled terms are conceptual inventions designed to facilitate the description of experience. Merleau-Ponty resorts to them because he thinks that our experience of sense or 'being' can be better described by more open-ended, non-standard philosophical terminology. This interpretation suggests that terms like 'flesh' or 'chiasma' attempt first and foremost to capture the appearance of meaning. Since they are the building blocks of Merleau-Ponty's later ontology, this also suggests that, for him, the scope and subject-matter of ontology is delimited by conscious experience.

6. LANGUAGE AND ESSENCE

In the previous section I claimed that concept-invention is necessary for the goals of Merleau-Ponty's later philosophical projects. In this section I suggest that, if certain conditions are satisfied, the conceptual inventions or 'figures' described above fulfil basic functions associated with phenomenological 'essences'. The *Phenomenology* hinted that essences may be needed to understand experience (PhP lxxxviii/15). That text argued that essences are linguistic products, and that they maintain a connection to the empirical (lxxix/16). These two assumptions are retained in Merleau-Ponty's later thought. Commentators have argued that he is uninterested in developing an account of essence, or that such an account is inconsistent with some basic premises that he accepts. However, I will suggest that a sufficiently reformulated account of essence is not inconsistent with the basic philosophical outlook considered in this chapter. For Merleau-Ponty, essences are conceptual inventions used to unfold and describe meanings that remain latent and are difficult to grasp. On this reading, they play a positive role in the ontology he attempts to develop in his later work. A renewed appreciation of the links between ideality and sensibility leads him to a new understanding of the fact-essence relation. Some of the concepts that ontology invents become interpretive touchstones that do a good job of articulating the intelligible structure of experience and succeed in helping us describe the coherence of meaning. These figures of language are neither a priori nor necessary; they derive their explanatory power from their sensitivity to experience and its possible permutations.

Before considering the details of this account, I would first like to address two challenges to the suggestion that Merleau-Ponty would be interested in offering an account of essence. First, this seems to run up against textual evidence. He sometimes contends that phenomenological essences are just the sort of classical philosophical commitment that should be rejected.[41] Second, some commentators have argued that the spirit of Merleau-Ponty's work is incompatible with an appeal to essences. It has been argued that insofar as he rejects the need to employ the phenomenological reduction (which Husserl assumed is needed for the imaginary intuitive variation that discloses essences), he also rejects the project of detailing the essential structures of intentional experience.[42]

I cannot consider this issue in detail here, but there are good textual grounds to conclude that Merleau-Ponty aims to reinterpret and not reject the reduction.[43] And as with other classical philosophical concepts (e.g., 'intentionality', 'constitution', 'ontology', 'dialectic', 'being', 'subject'), his considered view of phenomenological essences cannot be understood by focussing only on his negative remarks. Many of his dismissive remarks about essences could be traced to Husserl. In particular, he targets the claims that essences are supra-temporal, a priori, and have a fixed structure. Nevertheless, Merleau-Ponty offers extended, positive accounts of essence.[44] He rejects some features of Husserl's view, but takes his own account to be broadly consistent with Husserl's underlying motivation for developing an account of essence, namely, the goal of identifying invariant structural wholes that can explain the modalities of intentional experience and its objects.[45] Essences are necessary for the same reason that general concepts are: the meaning and structure of experience cannot be understood solely by appealing to particulars. General terms are needed to understand particular experiences or 'facts'; otherwise, experiences refer only to other experiences, and something resembling an explanation of experience becomes unattainable. Indeed, Merleau-Ponty contends that particular experiences exemplify larger, more general structures (e.g., the intentional character of a particular experience corresponds to features described by the 'flesh'). The latter help us understand the former, and importantly, offers a window into how experience could take on different meanings for us or for others.

Merleau-Ponty's interest in the possible 'dimensions' of experience, or in 'the miraculous multiplication of perceptible being', leads him to stress what he sees as the in-principle incompleteness of eidetic variation (S 16/30):

> It is nonetheless clear that Husserl himself never obtained a single *Wesenschau* that he did not subsequently take up again and rework, not to disown it, but in order to make it say what at first it had not quite said. Thus it would be naïve to seek solidity in a heaven of ideas or in a *ground* [fond] of meaning [*sens*]: it is neither above nor beneath the appearances, but at their joints; it is the tie that secretly connects an experience to its variants. (VI 116/153)

Leaving aside possible Husserlian reservations, this reading suggests that for Merleau-Ponty, an essence can be understood as a kind of node that organises experience, or a prism that helps us understand its possible variations or extensions. Instead of relying on necessity or apodicticity to develop his account, Merleau-Ponty stresses that essences are chiefly beings of possibility (by contrast, in his account of essence Husserl is often concerned with 'impossibility'; that is, with the conditions under which an object loses its sense as something of a determinate kind, or its identity criteria). By varying occurrent experience, essences offer insights into possible meanings that point beyond the given. Merleau-Ponty thinks that by interpreting occurrent experience in light of its possible variations, an essence allows us to approach it anew, and this promises to help us understand it better.[46] The role of essences in ontology, then, is quite proximate to the fundamental import of the concept of 'dimensionality'.

For Merleau-Ponty, essences are 'explicitations [*explicitations*] of an experience' (NC 66). An essence explains some lived phenomenon at a higher, more abstract level of generality. But it is not so general that it is divorced from 'facts' or lived experiences: essences are 'ungraspable outside of the fact or outside of existence' (VI 51/62). An essence is an 'inner framework' that is 'not above the sensible world' but 'in its depth, its thickness' (220/269). By applying a general term to a particular experience, an essence gives us a 'fact' (an object or experience) 'considered in all its implications' (174/226). For example, we might account for our directedness to objects by appeal to 'reversibility'. Reversibility refers to a relational and structural feature of intentionality that only shows itself in experience, but which is not wholly indexed to particular experiences of reversible intentional relations. Reversibility is an essential feature of intentionality. It is a general structure that transcends specific intentional experiences, but explains them by helping us imagine how some particular instance of subject-object relations could be otherwise, and how its enabling conditions of possibility could be transformed.

Even if essences are not, for Merleau-Ponty, supra-temporal or supra-empirical, not all features of essences are modifiable. The essence of a table would in all cases point to a material being extended in space. Merleau-Ponty's broader point is that concepts lose explanatory power if they are defined solely in a priori, atemporal terms. This motivates his reformulation of the fact-essence relation: 'If we were to re-examine the antithesis of fact and essence, we would be able on the contrary to redefine the essence in a way that would give us access to it, because it would be not beyond but at the heart of that coiling up [*l' enroulement*] of experience over experience which . . . [constitutes] the difficulty' (113/149). The fact-essence relation, like that between transcendental and empirical, is one of mutual dependence. The empirical domain of facts clarifies the ideal realm of essences, and vice versa. In the case of the table, a broader set of considerations must be taken into account when formulating its essence. These might include historical or cultural features associated with this particular table. To refer only to material characteristics would shed insufficient light on the object, since its meaning in the empirical domain (what it is) depends on its owners, origins, uses and more; none of which are adequately captured by a definition that relies solely on the necessary and sufficient conditions of a table, in general.

By focusing attention on the core features of an experience, and how these could be construed otherwise, an essence reveals its possible permutations or 'configurations' (HLP 51/62). This characterisation is consistent with the 'figuring' capacity of ontological language discussed above. The ideal status of essences also suggests a tight connection to language. Merleau-Ponty clearly draws this link: 'There is no eidetic variation without *speech*' (VI 236/285; see also 115/152).[47] Like other ontological concepts, essences are products of reflection and therefore of expression: 'In this labour of experience on experience which is the carnal context of the essence, it is necessary to draw attention particularly to the labour of speech' (117 n.1/154).[48] The linguistic nature of essences leads Merleau-Ponty to interpret 'the apprehension of the essence as a difference between words [*écart des paroles*]'. By collecting the core features of an experience, we can better measure the differences between our experiences, those of others, and those that remain mere conceptual possibilities. An essence is a linguistic invention developed in reflection and formed at the juncture of these differences; its meaning lies somewhere between the actual and the possible.

Like the concepts discussed above, essences are products of 'operative' modes of expression. Merleau-Ponty's revisionary account of essences presupposes his account of indirect language:

> In a philosophy that takes into consideration the operative world [*le monde opérant*], functioning, present, and coherent, as it is, the essence is no stumbling block: it has its place there as an operative, functioning, essence. No longer are there essences above us, like positive objects, offered to a spiritual eye; but there is an essence beneath us, a common nervure of the signifying and the signified, adherence in and reversibility of one another. . . . As the world is behind my body, the operative essence is behind operative speech [*la parole opérante*] also, speech that possesses signification [*la signification*] less than it is possessed by it, that does not speak *of it*, but speaks *it*, or speaks *according* to it, or lets it speak and be spoken within me, breaks through my present. (118/156)

This text makes clear that essences are inventions of operative expression (see also 47–48/69, 153/198). Their semantically open and context-dependent character, and their adaptable structure, are characteristics shared by ontological expression, and further suggest that essences are open to modification to a significant degree. To explain a table, an essence must account not only for its having a top or a leg, but also for the significance that this table takes on for a particular person, family, culture, and more. The latter make the table what it is but are not necessarily associated with its ideal meaning; but Merleau-Ponty contends that an essence's amphibious status, located between the ideal and sensible, allows philosophically relevant meanings from the empirical domain to be integrated and their dimensions explored. The passage also indicates that the dialectical approach to concept-formation applies to essences: essences are formed at the juncture of the sensible and the ideal domains and are understood in relation to both. This approach to the formulation and employment of essences is consistent with tenets like 'hyper-reflection' and the 'interrogative' attitude needed for ontology.[49]

Merleau-Ponty's remarks about essences are fragmentary and incomplete, and present a challenge for anyone seeking to understand them in greater detail. One instructive example provides additional evidence for how essences are formulated and how they explicate experience. For him, Proust offers one of the best accounts of the visible-invisible relation, and by extension, of essence, which is an 'invisible' entity used to explain the visible. Merleau-Ponty claims that the *'petite phrase'*, five notes from a fictional sonata composed by Vinteuil and variously described throughout *In Search of Lost Time*, is an ideal, essential entity (VI 149/193 ff.).[50] The little phrase is an aesthetic artefact, whose general form and notation remains unchanged. Still, the piece can take on different sonorous forms in the spatio-temporal world, which means that it can appear in a range of different lived experiences. It serves as a guide for Swann to interpret his desires, hopes and regrets at different periods of his life. Hearing the phrase elicits hope and desire in the early stages of Swann's relationship with Odette. After their relationship has ended, the piece triggers feelings of resignation. The *petite phrase* has a general form, but this does not prevent it from elucidating a range of particular experiences and factical conditions (VI 153/198). In the novel, the musical idea is a key that helps Swann understand his experience: when he hears it, new layers of the past come to light, and new meanings are discovered. Consistent with the remarks above, Merleau-Ponty claims that Proust's form of indirect expression supports the essential status of this musical idea.[51] The *petite phrase* refers to a piece of music that can be played and heard by characters in the novel, but for us it is first and foremost a literary invention, and this testifies to the disclosive possibilities of language and ideality. Instead of a conceptual abstraction, essences like the musical idea 'restore the lived world' and disclose its possible 'preconceptual' or pre-predicative meaning (BNF Ms. Vol. XII 1/122r).

Only if a narrow definition of an essence is adopted will it seem that Merleau-Ponty is opposed to the project of using essences to elucidate experience. If an essence is defined as an 'explicitation' or 'articulation' of experience and its possible permutations, there is good reason to think that it plays a positive role in his ontology. Essences are necessary insofar as sense-constitution is plural, intersubjective and unfolds under varying conditions (BNF Ms. Vol. VI 209r-v). This approach to essences 'does not entirely disengage its essences from the world; it maintains them under the jurisdiction of the facts, which can tomorrow call for another elaboration' (VI 108/142). As the dialectical and hyper-reflective tenets guiding ontological research require, essential structures remain incomplete and must be continually refined: there is 'progress toward essence, but never a total explicitation; [an] essence is always a "figure"' (BNF Ms. Vol. XII 1/91r; see also VI 178/229–30). Like the phenomenological reduction, essences are formulated for the sake of seeing anew some experience that we *already* have contact with, not for rigidly circumscribing its meaning in the name of a contrived conceptual clarity (47–48/69).[52]

Merleau-Ponty does not provide a criterion to identify the concepts that could or should count as essences, nor does he consider possible questions that may arise about his account – for example, about the identity criteria of essences. His account of essences remains a work in progress. However, I have suggested that the strong linguistic commitments of his ontology lead him to endorse the view that essences play an important role in the disclosure of experience. The lexical or 'verbal' nature of essences, and their capacity to refigure 'facts', move subjects beyond the limited framework of a single grasp of some state, object or event, which is necessary for clarifying the possible dimensions of experience (VI 174/226). Essences give ontology a necessary degree of generality, and their linguistic character allows other subjects to use, modify and evaluate their persuasiveness in detailing experience and the cohesion of meaning. Terms like 'flesh' or 'reversibility' seem to be the kind of concepts that could count as essences: they are by definition general, open to modification, known with reference to particulars, and construe intentional experience in a way that is allegedly more appropriate to the phenomena than that offered by classical philosophical terminology.

7. PHILOSOPHY AS 'OPERATIVE LANGUAGE'

I have suggested that Merleau-Ponty's ontology can be understood as an expressive, descriptive project. In their basic goals, ontology and phenomenology are of a piece. A view of 'philosophy as interrogation' is fundamentally a 'disposition' and an attitude for 'showing how the world is articulated starting from a zero of being . . . at the joints, where the multiple *entries* of the world cross' (VI 260/308). However, ontology and phenomenology are not simply substitutable terms: ontology is distinguished from the nominally 'transcendental' account of phenomenology considered in chapter 3 by a greater need for conceptual creation, by a willingness to develop and employ new concepts in descriptions and by its attempt to overcome the tension between description and linguistic invention. Consistent with the *Phenomenology*'s claim that '[e]xperience anticipates a philosophy and philosophy is but an elucidated experience' (PhP 65/91), ontology attempts to offer a new take on perceptual openness to the world, and a new view of how meaning coheres in experience. Unlike in his earlier definitions of phenomenology, however, Merleau-Ponty contends that to deliver on these goals, ontology must attend in greater detail to its philosophy of language. Basic ontological preconditions like hyper-reflection and the interrogative attitude suggest that before offering any positive proposals about experience, important issues surrounding philosophical expression must first be considered, and define the subsequent trajectory of ontological enquiry.

This interpretation can account for some strong claims that Merleau-Ponty makes about the philosophical role of language in his later work. Consider, for example, a remark in which he seemingly draws an identity between a distinctive view of expression and the business of philosophy itself:

> In a sense the whole of philosophy, as Husserl says, consists in restoring a power to signify, a birth of meaning, or a wild meaning, an expression of experience by experience. And in a sense, as Valéry said, language is everything, since it is the voice of no one, since it is the very voice of the things, the waves, and the forests. (VI 155/201)

Merleau-Ponty hesitates to fully identify language with philosophy in this passage because he argues that experience is co-constituted by linguistic and perceptual conditions. Despite this qualification, in light of the interpretation developed in this chapter, the claim that philosophy is the expression of experience concedes that accounts of experience, intentionality or world are only possible given nontrivial linguistic preconditions, and that they require protracted methodological and conceptual reflections on language in order to successfully meet their goals. More strongly, it entails that whatever its conclusions, the project of describing experience is first and foremost a linguistic undertaking, and that its linguistic presuppositions are anything but immaterial. For Merleau-Ponty, philosophical concepts and categories do not come ready-made; the concepts that could explain experience must be invented, and their relation to it must be established, which is to say, expressed.

By attending to 'the speaking word' or the non-objectifying 'operative language' characteristic of ontology, Merleau-Ponty rejects the claim that 'the problem of language is . . . only regional'. Instead, if language

> brings to the surface all the deep-rooted relations of the lived experience wherein it takes form, and which is the language of life and of action but also that of literature and of poetry – then this *logos* is an absolutely universal theme, it is the theme of philosophy. Philosophy itself is language, rests on language; [. . .] philosophy is an operative language, that language that can be known only from within, through

its exercise, is open upon the things, called forth by the voices of silence, and continues an effort of articulation which is the Being of every being. (126–27/166)

During the writing of *The Visible*, Merleau-Ponty openly embraces the view that philosophy is ultimately an effort of articulation. Versions of this claim have implicitly guided his research since *Structure*. Experience is meaningful prior to philosophical interrogation, but its meaning is made animate through description. Philosophical problems, objects and questions become thematic when they are formulated and expressed in language. One could, of course, dismiss this as a trivially true precondition; Merleau-Ponty takes it seriously. He concludes that the formulation of a problem, concept, or description shapes and transforms the object it refers to, and makes the object what it is: 'Language . . . is our life and the life of things' (126/165). Philosophical language must accordingly be interrogated and reconstituted so as to better meet the goal of capturing the meaning of experience without reducing it to a merely subjective invention. His methodological sensitivities lead him to conclude that this attempt will remain imperfect and incomplete, which entails that the project of describing experience must continue in a critical-reflective spirit.

This predicament delimits the scope of philosophical claims, but it does not make a satisfactory account of experience unattainable. Instead,

> because he has experienced within himself the need to speak, the birth of speech as bubbling up at the bottom of his mute experience, the philosopher knows better than anyone that what is lived is lived-spoken [*vécu-parlé*], that, born at this depth, language is not a mask over Being, but – if one knows how to grasp it with all its roots and all its foliation – the most valuable witness to Being, that it does not interrupt an immediation that would be perfect without it, that vision itself, thought itself, are, as has been said, 'structured as a language', are articulation before the letter, apparition of something where there was nothing or something else. (126/165)

Merleau-Ponty has argued that language and perception co-constitute experience, and that at the reflective level, lived meanings can be studied when they are expressed. As this passage suggests, the latter is possible provided subjects can appeal to a philosophical vocabulary sufficiently sensitive to how meaning shows itself. That entails that phenomenology's basic goals can be realised only by attending carefully to the philosophy of language. Absent these conditions, lived experience cannot (the passage suggests) be properly understood. Philosophical reflections on language, then, have a privileged place in phenomenology.

While Merleau-Ponty's estimation of the philosophical weight of language is clear, some problems remain unresolved. For example, the longstanding question about the extent to which reflection transforms experience remains open. Merleau-Ponty seems to worry less about this in his later work, because he argues that the 'real', a perceptual object, or the world itself is only ever given at the intersection of multiple perspectives. Above I suggested that he construes this relation as a response to perceptual givens that are subsequently worked out by reflecting subjects; but readers with more realist inclinations may see this as a covert or convoluted way of privileging subject-centric conditions.

Potentially more worrisome is the apparent tension between the non-systematic or open-ended character of his later thought, and the seemingly strong normativity guiding his view of what modes of expression can best express experience. He maintains that philosophical systems amount to human artefacts akin to art (VI 102/136–37). This assumption is consistent with the *Phenomenology*'s claim that phenomenology 'founds itself' (PhP lxxxv/21). Even if ontology attempts to capture the meaning of experience, this does not lead to a stable philosophical ground. On the definition of 'being' (or sense) developed in Merleau-Ponty's later work, the phenomenal field lacks finality and completeness (BNF Ms. Vol. VIII 239/18).[53] Ontology remains an incomplete enterprise, and its tenets can be further refined. Philosophy, he thinks, reflects our experience, and like experience, its truths are never ultimate (NC 86–87; 144). Progress can be made, but no definitive, once-and-for-all solutions to the 'problem' of consciousness, world or nature are forthcoming.

However, Merleau-Ponty is strongly committed to the view that formal or purely poetic modes of expression are inadequate for his philosophical goals. His choice to develop a hybrid philosophical language with definite characteristics suggests a strong view about how experience is best described. An underlying normative criterion about what 'proper' ontological expression looks like pervades his later texts. Ontology is not so open that one could revise his view, for example, about the relative merits or drawbacks of formal, propositional, categorical, or poetic expression. Despite offering some hints, Merleau-Ponty does not clearly identify the norm guiding these assumptions (I leave aside more formal prescriptions to the effect that the linguistic description of an object must genuinely reflect its qualitative character and perceived structure). Nor does he describe in detail how one might properly formulate an adequate mode of expression, or how one might know that one is getting it right. He simply notes that an adequate mode of philosophical expression is 'given with words for those who have ears to hear' (VI 155/201). However, to suggest that these questions will be resolved by attending sufficiently and radically to sense, experience or being begs the question and merely restates the problem. On the whole, a basic ambiguity concerning the normative and open-ended characteristics of his later ontology remains. His indecisiveness on this point might leave him vulnerable to the accusation that the criteria guiding his later approach to language and perception are circular or inconsistent. Given his remarks elsewhere, he could argue that such tensions animate and do not condemn the philosophical attitude he was attempting to develop in his later work, and that the criteria and norms that must guide descriptions of experience can be known only after the effort of articulating its meaning is underway.

NOTES

1. Dillon argues that whereas Merleau-Ponty rejects 'traditional metaphysics', his positive ontological contributions are nevertheless consistent with a revised metaphysics (1988, 243). This understanding of metaphysics seems broadly consistent with that sketched in chapter 4. However, Dillon also draws an identity between the terms 'Gestalt' and 'phenomenon', and claims that the Gestalt has an 'ontological primacy' as 'the basic unit of the perceptual world', which turns out on his reading to be 'the world itself' (1988, 80–81). Despite defining ontology as 'the search for the logos or meaning of things', Dillon concludes that the implicit Gestalt ontology of *Phenomenology* that he argues is developed in Merleau-Ponty's later writings can be worked out in terms of more fundamental structures (4). Haar argues that Merleau-Ponty moves from

a 'regional' to a 'universal' ontology of 'Being', which he reads as the 'dimension of dimensions' (1999, 20–21). Derrida also offers a thicker reading of his ontology (2005, 186–88; 196–97). Other commentators have found points of continuity with more metaphysically inclined thinkers like Bergson (see, e.g., Al-Saji 2007) and Deleuze (see, e.g., Lawlor 1998, which also considers the *Phenomenology*, and Lawlor 1999).

2. For this interpretation, see Barbaras 2004, 77–78. For Barbaras, 'being' is accessed through 'interrogation', that is, philosophical questioning (2004, 87). 'Being' can be understood as phenomenality, and is a unity that appears in different forms (2004, 316). Ontology can accordingly be understood as a description of being (2004, 312–13). At this level, this approach to Merleau-Ponty's ontology is proximate to that developed in this chapter. However, Barbaras's rich reading of Merleau-Ponty contends that ontology is a necessary improvement to phenomenology, and that his analyses of expression are a ground, but not the substance of the former. By contrast, I suggest that ontology and phenomenology are coextensive, but I contend that the former amounts chiefly to a linguistic – that is, expressive – project. Barbaras's distinction between 'Being' and the 'being' (or subject) who 'interrogates' phenomenality (88 ff.), as well as the suggestion that there is a 'belonging to Being' (126), invite further questions about his reading of being, ontology and phenomenality, insofar as these remarks are consistent with the positing of a deeper, extra-subjective structure that transcends the bounds of sense or experience.

3. Note, however, that Merleau-Ponty does not adopt Sartre's understanding of 'negative ontology', which he thinks amounts to a 'bad dialectic' (BNF Ms. Vol. VIII 226/7, 255).

4. See Madison 1981, 234.

5. As this last formulation helps to make clear, the point is not that Merleau-Ponty harbours no metaphysical presuppositions, nor that he makes no metaphysical claims. For example, he holds that there is a 'metaphysical structure of our flesh' (OE 33/359). Rather, my suggestion is that his ontology will be misunderstood if it is associated with more standard metaphysical interpretations of the term. Expressive conditions are basic to Merleau-Ponty's ontology, and any metaphysical claims (e.g., that language is intertwined with vision, or that the 'subject' is 'flesh') will avail themselves of expressive-linguistic resources.

6. There is an important historical dimension to Merleau-Ponty's ontological research, which I cannot explore in this chapter. Merleau-Ponty's reflections on ontology profit from a protracted and careful study of existing ontological proposals, including but not limited to its Cartesian, Kantian, Heideggerian or Sartrean variants. His engagement with the ontology of the Western tradition is also evidenced by his study of historical-critical work by contempo-

rary historians of philosophy (e.g., Gouhier, Gueroult, or Hyppolite). A historical study of ontology has the benefit of showing how an overly 'objective' approach to ontology may be uprooted (VI 165/217, 231/280). Many of the concepts explored in this chapter owe their genesis to Merleau-Ponty's historical investigations. Given the scope of this study, however, and in order to detail connections with issues considered in previous chapters, my presentation of his ontology will analyse concepts largely internal to his texts, and will not discuss their historical dimension in any detail. This point also applies to interpretations of ontology developed by Merleau-Ponty's phenomenological and philosophical predecessors.

7. See also BNF Ms. Vol. VIII 176 for the claim that ontology should be developed on the basis of perception.

8. See N 40/64.

9. The view echoes Fink's claim that a 'secondary enworlding' is required if phenomenological reflection is to adequately communicate and understand its results (Fink 1995, 110).

10. For a sympathetic take on his reading of Husserl, see Zahavi 2002.

11. For more on genesis see VI 12/27–28, 14/30, 58–61/84–88, 102/136, 136/177.

12. See Fink 1970, 97–98.

13. On this point, see Richir, who argues that the last chapter of *The Visible* takes up central problems of constitution (Richir 1993a, 73). Merleau-Ponty notes that Husserl's view of reflection is unlike other 'classical' accounts: 'In recognising that every reflection is eidetic and, as such, leaves untouched the problem of our unreflected being and that of the world, Husserl simply agrees to take up the problem which the reflective attitude ordinarily avoids – the discordance between its initial situation and its ends' (VI 46/70).

14. On the continuity between ontology and phenomenology, see Barbaras 2004, 68–78.

15. Husserl 1960, 38–39.

16. On the necessity of properly posing questions in philosophy see Heidegger 1962, ¶¶1–2. See Jean-François Courtine's discussion of this issue (2007, 247 ff.). Courtine notes that Heidegger's account faces a challenge (indicated by Tugendhat) about the extent to which his formulation of the question of being presupposes commitments that are relative to a natural language (see especially 256 ff.). As I suggest, this issue does not confront Merleau-Ponty's work in quite the same way.

17. For a stronger interpretation of Merleau-Ponty's debt to Heidegger, see Lawlor, who claims that '[e]veryone knows that, under Heidegger's influence, Merleau-Ponty moves from a phenomenology of perception to an ontology of the visible and the invisible, an ontology which revolves around interrogation or the question' (1999, 234).

18. According to Dahlstrom, for Heidegger ontological definitions are not 'given in principle', but are instead formal – that is, they must be supplemented by intuitively given content (1994, 781–82). On this reading, *Being and Time* does not attempt to understand any given 'fact' but instead offers 'an indication of a way of approaching what "to be": means', even if, in the end, Heidegger thinks this has some determinate meaning (782; 785). For Dahlstrom, this approach requires that a philosopher change standard modes of interpreting the meaning of philosophical terms, an assumption that Merleau-Ponty would also agree with (786).

19. Imbert, for example, claims that the vocabulary associated with transcendental phenomenology largely disappears from his later writings (1998, 74–75; 77). Imbert 2005 recognises the influence of literary expression on Merleau-Ponty's later ontology (2005, 38), but nevertheless argues that he distances himself from phenomenological concerns (57, 60).

20. See, for example, VI 52/76, 77/107, 203–4/253–54; BNF Ms. Vol. VI 163, 166, 183; BNF Ms. Vol. VIII 165, 245 (cf. 148/72b).

21. See Sellheim 2012 and Vanzago 2005. See also Gill 1991 for a study of Merleau-Ponty and metaphor. Gill mainly focuses on specific metaphors that are found in some of Merleau-Ponty's texts, and argues that Merleau-Ponty sees philosophy itself 'as a metaphoric activity' (1991, 140). However, even if Merleau-Ponty uses various metaphors in his writings, this is insufficient evidence for this strong evaluation, nor can it shed light on the more specific question of whether he would be prepared to identify philosophical expression as such with metaphorical expression.

22. See, for example, Sellheim 2012, 267–70.

23. Ricoeur 1977, 361–62; see also 114.

24. See also Watkin 2009, 62–63.

25. See also the claim that the central problem of *The Visible and the Invisible* 'is the same as that of dialectic and Marxism'; namely, the 'problem of *openness* [de l'ouverture]' (BNF Ms. Vol. VI 266/54a).

26. Earlier remarks anticipate this claim: see BNF Ms. Vol. VIII 154/26b on the need to reject standard definitions of dialectic, and Vol. VI 255 on the inadequacy of a view on which dialectic becomes 'thesis'.

27. See BNF Ms. Vol. XIV 6 for the claim that dialectical circularity is neither 'subjectivist' nor 'arbitrary'.

28. See also 161, 359/27; BNF Ms. Vol. VI 21, 57v/12, 262.

29. See, for example, the preface to *Phenomenology of Spirit* (Hegel 1977, ¶63). Though I cannot consider this issue in detail here, Merleau-Ponty's return to Hegel in the mid-1950s in lectures at the Collège de France is of central importance for understanding the deeper motivations behind this account of dialectic. It unfolds in the context of earlier French interpretations of Hegel by figures like Boutroux, Brunschvicg, Wahl, Kojève and Hyppolite (see Baugh 2003, chapters 1–3 and Gutting 2011, chapter 2, for relevant background).

30. For an earlier indication of the importance of mediation, see the *Phenomenology*'s evaluation that Sartre's For-Itself and In-Itself cannot be opposed 'without any mediation' (PhP 479/517).

31. For this view, see Lawlor 1999, 244, who claims that Merleau-Ponty was directly guided by Heidegger's 'direct ontology' (see also 236, 242). On this point cf. Barbaras 2004, 305 and Madison 1981, 232–35.

32. Heidegger 1971, 196–97.

33. For more on this point, see Noble 2014, 222–28.

34. See Apostolopoulos 2018b. Merleau-Ponty and Hyppolite first met during their student years at the ENS and remained close friends until Merleau-Ponty's death in 1961. References to Hyppolite are found throughout Merleau-Ponty's work (recall their exchange during Merleau-Ponty's public defence of his doctoral work in *The Primacy of Perception*; for some early references see SB 244/175n.1, 'Hegel's Existentialism' and 'Concerning Marxism' [SNS 120/241]). Hyppolite's *Logic and Existence* contains an important reference to Merleau-Ponty (Hyppolite 1953/1998 24–25/29). His article 'The Human Situation in Hegelian Phenomenology' also approvingly quotes Merleau-Ponty (Hyppolite 1968 162/181). Hyppolite also wrote three interpretive essays on Merleau-Ponty after his death (Hyppolite 1971, 687–758). It is likely that Merleau-Ponty's decision to offer a class on dialectic in 1956 was partly motivated by the recent publication of Hyppolite's *Logic and Existence*. Notes from 1955 to 1956 show that this text influenced his ontological research, still titled 'The Origin of Truth'. In one note Merleau-Ponty writes, '*à propos* of Hyppolite *Logic and Existence*', 'before describing the world as a world-spoken [*monde parlé*], describe the world as a world lived by the body, make sense appear as a relief, coherent deformation, corporeal sense'. This familiar phenomenological commitment, through which 'pre-languagely sense' [*Le sens pré-langagier*] is transformed, is subsequently linked to a view of a properly phenomenological absolute, which finds support in Hyppolite's reading of Hegel, and its emphasis on mediation, language and expression. In Merleau-Ponty's words: 'I happily admit a *logos* and a philosophical dialectic that is not a simple effect of the dialectic truth-[actuality?]. My theory of language and subjectivity is altogether beyond the philosophy of "consciousness" – But all the same I

keep from *phenomenology* the idea that being does not appear except at a distance and viewed from a perspective' (BNF Ms. Vol VI 127/[73?]). Another note suggests that Hyppolite's interpretation of Hegel's philosophy of language did not go unnoticed by Merleau-Ponty, who was attempting to navigate a middle ground between aesthetic and purely philosophical expression in research for 'The Origin of Truth': 'The centre of this research is evidently language [*le langage*]: for language is at the same time the ether of literature and the residue of the *logos* (Hyppolite), being that says itself' (128).

35. See Hyppolite 1997 24/28. See Lawlor 2002, 89, for more on Hyppolite, mediation and language.

36. See remarks on Hegel in 'Philosophy and Non-Philosophy Since Hegel' (NC 282; Silverman 1988, 15).

37. Phenomenological interest in creation is not limited to Merleau-Ponty. In addition to Husserl's praise of invention in *Ideas I*, see this remark from Fink's *Sixth Cartesian Meditation*: 'the constitutive *sense-bestowings* that transcendentally underlie . . . mundane *sense-elements* cannot be exhibited in an immediate way in the being-context of ongoing world constitution, which of course is given by the reduction and by it is made a possible theme for intuitive analyses. It is evident instead that, in order to gain any understanding at all, we have to "*construct*"' (1995 62/70).

38. For other descriptions (e.g., of colour perception), see VI 132 ff./172 ff., 113–14/150–51.

39. For more on this point see the claim in 'The Philosopher and His Shadow' that objects have a 'configurational meaning' that is not indicated by their 'theoretical meaning' (S 181/294).

40. In an interview, Merleau-Ponty claims that philosophy is a tentative verbal expression of what is not ordinarily expressed (see Noble 2014, 242–43).

41. See, for example, VI 107–12/142–49, 114–17/150–55, 121–22/159–60, 127–28/166–67, 186/237, and unpublished remarks to the effect that essences are idealisations of our primary contact with the world (BNF Ms. Vol. VIII 141/30b), that it is necessary to move beyond the fact/essence distinction, or that terms like 'essence', 'existence', 'signification' and 'variation' are abstractions (331/18).

42. Carman and Hansen 2005, 8–10.

43. See Smith 2005. See references to the 'reductions' that *The Visible* would undertake (VI 178–79/230–31). An unpublished note holds that 'My method is generalised phenomenological reduction . . . *i.e.* also applied to the Psyche as much as to "consciousness" and to *Auffassungen* and *Sinngebungen*' (BNF Ms. Vol. VI 241/19).

44. To consider only a few: 'The eidetic variation, therefore, does not make me pass to an order of separated essences, to a logical possible, the invariant that it gives me is a structural invariant, a Being in infrastructure which in the last analysis has its *Erfüllung* only in the *Weltthesis* of this world' (VI 229/278). See also the claims that Merleau-Ponty wants to embrace a verbal essence closer to a Gestalt structure (BNF Ms. Vol. VIII 174/19c), and that essences never result in 'total explicitation', because an 'essence is always [a] "figure" [*figure*]' (BNF Ms. Vol. XII 91).

45. While Husserl claims, for example, that perception or physical objects admit of essential characterisation at higher levels of generality, he also holds that 'eidetic concreta', such as those pertaining to determinate qualitative experiences, are often vague and cannot be fixed precisely (see Husserl 2014, §75). This latter dimension of Husserlian essences is more proximate to Merleau-Ponty's philosophical intentions.

46. Compare this with an earlier comment: 'The eidetic method is that of a phenomenological positivism grounding the possible upon the real' (PhP lxxxi/17).

47. See also the claim that 'Essences are *Etwases* at the level of speech' (VI 174/226).

48. See NC 392 for more on the 'carnal' quality of essences.

49. On this point cf. Barbaras, who claims that essences are 'inadequate to the being of interrogation' because a 'philosophy of essence' presupposes a 'position . . . which comes from beyond Being' (2004, 98). Barbaras marshals a passage where Merleau-Ponty claims that modes of thought reliant on essences are positivistic (VI 127/169). This remark refers to a naïve account of essence whose central flaw is the assumption that essences are a sufficient condition for understanding perception.

50. I explore Proust's influence on Merleau-Ponty's account of essence in more detail in Apostolopoulos 2018a.

51. For discussion of how indirect expression supports the formulation of essences see NC 190, 193, 217, 392; VI 149–53/194–98; BNF Ms. Vol. XII 8/107; 12/112; 113/1.

52. For a different take on the role of the reduction see Barbaras 2004, 105.

53. Marc Richir has also called attention to the 'unfinished' nature of Merleau-Ponty's ontology (1993a, 68), which he claims leads to a view of ontology as 'universal dimensionality' (78).

CONCLUSION

I have argued that from his first mature writings and until the end of his career, Merleau-Ponty remains keenly interested in how philosophical language can best articulate the sense of experience. His early reflections on embodiment and empirical science, like his later ontological projects, are informed by and return to a core set of language-related issues. Different texts from across Merleau-Ponty's career develop philosophically rich observations about everyday expression and language use, offer fruitful insights into the expressive possibilities of philosophical language, and highlight the important role that linguistic descriptions play in phenomenological research. By studying the trajectory of Merleau-Ponty's philosophical development, it becomes clear that many of his most celebrated philosophical contributions owe their origins to reflections on language.

Interpreters of Merleau-Ponty are confronted by the inevitable fact that his sudden death interrupted projects that may have taken a different course. His final texts do not provide a definitive version of the philosophical intention animating *The Visible and the Invisible*. This fact controls the reception of post-*Phenomenology* texts, and, in particular, their standing in relation to his first projects. While it is conceivable that he could have revised his view about the philosophical importance of language, given the state of the textual evidence, this possibility seems unlikely. As I have attempted to show, his estimation of the philosophical importance of language only increases. The version of his thought we are left with allows us to conclude that, in his eyes, phenomenology is chiefly an expressive project, tasked with creatively describing the meaning of phenomena. The philosophical insights issuing from phenomenological research do not enjoy unconditional a priori validity, and they are not construed as products of transcendental reflection (at least not according to the term's typical philosophical connotations). Instead, phenomenological descriptions are the results of inventive expressive activity, are revisable, obtained given certain intersubjective and historical conditions, and remain proximate to what Merleau-Ponty sees as the structures of conscious experience and intentional life.

This interpretation demonstrates that, from the perspective of his philosophy of language, there is significant continuity in Merleau-Ponty's thought. Instead of arguing that his thought is continuous because he maintains an interest in the same themes or objects, more sophisticated interpretive approaches that defend this view typically contend that his later work develops arguments, concepts or 'theses' implicit in his early work.[1] On such approaches, his early and later texts are thought to be continuous because the latter work out the latent implications of the former. This basic picture tracks one way in which Merleau-Ponty's later work follows from his first projects, but this study points to another way of interpreting this continuity.

In part 1, I argued that Merleau-Ponty's early attempts at a systematic formulation of phenomenology indicate the special importance of language for the project. Given the explicit primacy accorded to perception, the important role that language plays in phenomenological reflection does not enjoy the status of a guiding presupposition in *Structure* or in the *Phenomenology*. However, as I argued, its philosophical weight is nevertheless identified (and is sometimes recognised explicitly). This leads to a tension between two competing interpretations of phenomenology; namely, one on which it is a direct and faithful description of perception, and another on which it necessarily transforms but nevertheless manages to present perceptual meaning.

As I attempted to show in parts 2 and 3, this tension is resolved through continued engagement with regional problems in the philosophy of language in the late 1940s and through the 1950s. This research leads Merleau-Ponty to stress the systematic and methodological importance of language more sharply than he had in *Structure* or in the *Phenomenology*. His attention to the inventive dimensions of expression helps him identify the tension that characterised his earlier approach to phenomenology. An attempt to negotiate a solution to this tension subsequently defines the trajectory and goals of his later thought. Insofar as his earlier work is animated by challenges that it cannot resolve given its philosophical presuppositions, his later formulation of phenomenology might be seen as more consistent. And insofar as he is already, in principle, committed to a language-centric view of phenomenology that he did not defend in practice in the *Phenomenology*, his later work could on these grounds be seen as an improvement.

On the face of it, Merleau-Ponty's interest in the philosophy of language is not as pronounced as his interests, for example, in embodiment, perception or empirical psychology. However, unlike philosophical *foci* that make more limited appearances (e.g., in addition to those just noted, linguistics, aesthetics, the philosophy of nature, studies of specific figures in the history of philosophy), detailed studies of language-related topics are found throughout his career. In all of his major philosophical works, Merleau-Ponty probes the problem-domain of language. His interest in other lines of enquiry fluctuates, but interest in the philosophy of language remains constant, takes on different forms, and is only strengthened as his thought develops.

Given these results, Merleau-Ponty's philosophy of language emerges as a conceptual anchor linking the various periods and thematic interests of his thought: it guides a veritably organic philosophical development. This hypothesis is borne out by evidence from areas of research that do not directly engage language-related issues. By focusing on the structure, limits and evolution of claims native to his philosophy of language, we get a better sense of the philosophical motivations behind other developments in his *oeuvre*. But if it serves as a helpful guide in this respect, this area becomes a central philosophical pivot orienting his early, middle and later projects. Across varying and sometimes diverging domains of research, Merleau-Ponty remains keenly interested in the deeper methodological implications of the attempt to articulate phenomenological observations. Its other goals notwithstanding, phenomenology is the current of thought whose methodological reflections demonstrate that philosophical insights accrue only after an effort of articulation. The realisation that this effort is an ineliminable condition of thinking itself leads him to the conclusion that the philosophy of language must also be a conceptual guide in the attempt to unfold the meaning of experience.

By taking Merleau-Ponty's engagement with the philosophy and phenomenology of language as an interpretive guide, readers can observe the idiosyncrasies of distinct periods of his philosophical development, while also recognising that different thematic pursuits are permeated by an interest in their deeper linguistic conditions of possibility. While ostensibly regional questions in the phenomenology of language are often first approached on their own terms, their broader importance for phenomenology quickly emerges. Instead of anachronistically identifying later versions of incipiently formulated positions, or assuming that Merleau-Ponty was more aware of the limits of his work at any given stage than can be plausibly detected from the texts themselves, the interpretation on offer allows us to measure the difference between the various periods of his career by attending to the modifications and transformations in his philosophy of language. In doing so, this study offers an extended argument in defence of the hypothesis that the philosophy of language is the philosophical fulcrum connecting his early and late research.

In addition to shedding more light on Merleau-Ponty's philosophical development, his reflections on the phenomenology of language are also of consequence for the phenomenological enterprise. Most immediately, his account of the perception-language relation testifies to the tight link between intuitive and linguistic meaning. Merleau-Ponty's analyses of experience offer one interpretation on which intuition is mediated by language. This puts the (phenomenological) assumption that there is a purely pre-predicative or pre-linguistic domain of perceptual experience under stress. If Merleau-Ponty is right, then together with this long-standing commitment, the prevailing phenomenological definition of the 'phenomenon' might also be in need of revision. Merleau-Ponty's account of the language-world relation shows that phenomenological disclosure is directed to a world of objects or phenomena that are already informed by linguistic and conceptual meaning. When accounting for phenomena, phenomenology must also account for the linguistic or conceptual conditions that make the experience of an articulated world of objects possible and coherent.

In pursuing this thread, Merleau-Ponty develops a philosophically rich account of how language shapes experience. His approach to this problem is distinctive for emphasising the continuity and interdependence of perception and language, and for using conceptual resources that are not typically appealed to in earlier versions of the claim that language shapes the meaning of the world (e.g., those found in German Romanticism, or in the phenomenological or analytic linguistic turn). He certainly profits from Heidegger and Fink, for example, but his take on ontological expression and phenomenological methodology, and especially his account of how elementary perceptual structures are shaped by linguistic meaning at the empirical level, contribute something new to phenomenological reflections on language, and highlight dimensions of language use that earlier thinkers in the tradition did not address.

These contributions also indirectly touch on long-standing metaphysical and epistemological themes in phenomenology. Since its inception, phenomenology has been associated with a number of metaphysical positions. Husserl's early metaphysical neutrality eventually gave way to a brand of transcendental idealism that traces its roots to Kant. Phenomenological realists from Munich to Göttingen rejected this move, and phenomenological realism subsequently emerged as a viable stance within phenomenology. Subsequent research on the history of phenomenology has motivated realist and idealist interpretations of Husserl, Heidegger and other phenomenologists.

Merleau-Ponty was never comfortable with labels like 'realism' or 'idealism', and attempted to demonstrate the limits of naïve readings of both terms. However, his major texts and philosophical contributions can sustain realist and idealist readings, in both metaphysical and epistemological variants. These diverging readings are supported by the richness of his texts and by the fecund concepts they develop. Depending on one's inclinations, this could be seen as a virtue or a vice. But if we take Merleau-Ponty at his word about his desire to strike a middle course between classical realism and idealism, a focus on his philosophy of language suggests one way in which he could be seen to move beyond the limitations of these traditional categories.

As we have seen, Merleau-Ponty retains talk of the 'real' or 'being'. But he also argues that these terms are not in any important philosophical sense 'extra-subjective', since both are worked out with reference to the first-personal perspective. He freely invokes the term *ontology* while developing a nonstandard interpretation of the term, which cannot be easily assimilated with extant metaphysical or phenomenological interpretations. A detailed account of the metaphysical and epistemological import of these terms is not possible here. However, from the perspective of his reflections on the language-world relation, the evidence seems to point to the conclusion that he occupies a hybrid position, irreducible to the usual options. For him, subjects encounter a coherent world, which is meaningful prior to thematisation. The conditions supporting the cohesion of meaning are not extra-subjective, as in standard realist accounts. As he argues in his later writings, linguistic, historical and cultural meanings always work their way into perceptual structures. That is to say that human meaning-making activity (in the past and present) fundamentally shapes how the world appears to us. But this subjective conditioning is not that of a constitutive act or a judgement, nor is it construed along lines associated with more traditional idealistic approaches. For on their own, subjective conditions are also insufficient to explain perception or the world; there is a sense to experience that transcends the merely subjective perspective. Despite the importance of human meaning-making activities, lived meaning is no mere effect or product of expressive or cognitive activity.

On Merleau-Ponty's account, the structure of reality is formed at the intersection of subject and world or object. Neither world (or object) nor subject are metaphysically or epistemologically primary, especially if these terms are approached in isolation from one another. Our intentional relatedness to the world forms us *qua* subject, and in turn gives the world its extra-subjective character. That neither subject- nor object-centric conditions are sufficient to account for the relation in which both emerge as the fundamental terms of intentional experience might suggest that this relation is itself fundamental. In lived experience, categories like 'subject' and 'object', 'real' and 'ideal', and 'occurrent' and 'historical' intersect; meaning takes shape or becomes coherent when these terms confront and enter into relations with one another. This suggests that for Merleau-Ponty, these concepts are better understood in a relation vein, and that one way to overcome traditional accounts of subject-object or subject-world relations is to privilege the middle term, assert its irreducibility, and redefine 'subject', 'real', 'meaning' or 'world' relationally.

This raises a deeper question as to the metaphysical status of the relation itself. To explore this issue would take us beyond the scope of the present study. Indeed, that Merleau-Ponty's considered account of the perception-language relation has led us to this problem indicates the conceptual limits of an interpretation of his thought that takes its cue and orientation from his reflections on language. For the purposes of this study, however, the broader philosophical import of his argument for the tight connection between perception and language is that it leads him to a position interestingly distinct from existing accounts of the subject-world relation and their associated metaphysical and epistemological assumptions.

Merleau-Ponty's estimation of the importance of language for phenomenology also paves the way for a response to a challenge formulated by Derrida. In the introduction to his translation of Husserl's 'Origin of Geometry', Derrida offers an interpretation of Husserl that also calls the very tenability of phenomenology into question. While directed to Husserl, it has wider implications.

Derrida focusses on two key phenomenological commitments: the tripartite account of the temporal structure of the living present, and the basic assumption that the ultimate criterion of objectivity is intuitive givenness, where the latter is understood in a visual sense. The first assumption is typically thought to support the second: the structure of the living present makes possible an accounting of sense in terms of intuitive evidence. According to Derrida, given these basic commitments, it turns out that phenomenology cannot live up to its own criteria. The living present, located between retentions and protentions, never manifests itself in intuition. The phenomenological 'absolute', which allows for the study of the givenness of objects and experience itself, lies outside the evidentiary boundaries privileged by phenomenology. In Derrida's words,

> Phenomenology cannot be reflected in a phenomenology of phenomenology, and its *Logos* can never appear as such, can never be given in a philosophy of seeing, but (like all Speech) can only be heard or understood through the visible. The *Endstiftung* of phenomenology (phenomenology's ultimate critical legitimation: *i.e.*, what its sense, value, and right tell us about it), then, never directly measures up to a phenomenology.[2]

In short, phenomenology is unable to justify, ground or legitimate itself according to its own criteria. The ultimate ground of phenomenological justification never shows itself.

That the legitimating ground favoured by a philosophical discipline does not itself live up to the criterion it sets for its objects might be seen as fatal weakness. Even if it is not seen as fatal, it might suggest either that another standard of truth or objectivity is needed, or that the standard phenomenology provided is inadequate. At the very least, this observation points to a basic limitation in the phenomenological project.

Derrida's criticism is motivated by a broadly visual interpretation of phenomena, intuition and givenness. He takes this to be justified by Husserl's texts and by the subsequent historical trajectory of phenomenology. In one sense, he is right that on such a reading, phenomenology's justificatory ground cannot be given in a 'phenomenology of phenomenology'. However, Merleau-Ponty's estimation of the tight relationship between language and consciousness, as I have reconstructed it, suggests a possible response to this line of criticism. Derrida also claims that phenomenology is a kind of speech (*parole*), and this fecund observation may be used to advance another understanding of phenomenology's justificatory ground. Following Merleau-Ponty, there is reason to believe that the 'phenomenon' is not a purely visual entity. There is also reason to believe that visual intuition cannot be separated from linguistic meaning. More importantly, the reflective processes that disclose phenomena do not refer us to purely intuitive or visual evidence alone. Phenomenology 'shows' through its descriptions. Doubtless, phenomenological disclosure attempts to decode meaningful appearances. But as Merleau-Ponty demonstrates, appearances are always co-constituted by language. The meaning of appearance, in fact, can only be understood phenomenologically when it is expressed in language. Phenomenology is not, then, legitimated exclusively by a 'philosophy of seeing'; that is, by the evidence of visual intuition. For the latter comes to light in description, or after an effort of expression and articulation.

As Merleau-Ponty demonstrates, the phenomenological 'absolute', like other legitimating phenomenological conditions, has normative import once it is articulated. The legitimacy or persuasiveness of phenomenological descriptions of consciousness, world or meaning must be measured not only by the intuitive evidence that they marshal, but also by how they proceed to articulate it. Derrida is right that phenomenology's *logos* is not given in a visual sense. But that does not condemn the enterprise, since phenomenology also answers to a linguistic standard. Phenomenology can turn its own philosophical descriptions into objects of critical scrutiny. Indeed, Merleau-Ponty contends that it must do so if phenomenology is to be considered a viable philosophical position. Methodologically sensitive, critical descriptions are the precondition that makes the manifestation of intuitive evidence possible. Phenomenological insights are formulated, refined and revised by subjects engaged in the task of describing the structures of conscious experience. The grounds and norms legislating this dimension of phenomenological philosophy fall within the purview of a phenomenological philosophy of language, even while they continue to work out the meaning of intuition. By overlooking this deeper linguistic condition, the challenge above gains more traction. However, Merleau-Ponty shows us how we might take it to heart and develop another, more fertile understanding of phenomenological justification.

In this respect, Merleau-Ponty develops a line of thought incipiently formulated in Husserl's *Logical Investigations*, on which phenomenology is a communal undertaking. While Husserl did not surrender the possibility that phenomenology could be absolutely grounded, he worried about how its results might be communicated to others and understood by a broader philosophical community.[3] This problem chiefly concerns how the unnatural, theoretical language of phenomenology can be intelligibly translated into natural language terms. The challenge stems from the fact that only those familiar with the 'unnatural attitude of reflection' are in a good position to judge the success, failure or limits of phenomenological insights. Husserl took this to mean that a group of researchers must develop and refine phenomenology's trajectory, goals and results. Merleau-Ponty agrees that phenomenology is an intersubjective undertaking, but he stresses that this entails that it is also an expressive one. For him, an intersubjective and historicised approach to objectivity or normativity is most compatible with phenomenology's basic philosophical aims. An appeal to a common and shared linguistic ground, or one that is in principle possible, is a precondition of such an approach. This understanding of the phenomenological research project promises to generate philosophical insights that do justice to experience, and it can pursue this goal without replicating the one-sidedness and partial failures of standard realist and idealist approaches (as he understands them).

With a hybrid set of philosophical commitments in hand, Merleau-Ponty articulates a nuanced and modest account of phenomenology's basic aims. Instead of aiming to secure permanent and unshaken foundations, phenomenology is a nonreductive, open-ended, and descriptive enterprise. It holds fast to our lived experience of the world and invents concepts that shed light on and describe the intentional structures of consciousness that make experience possible. Phenomenological concepts and descriptions remain under the jurisdiction of experience, and their normative import depends on the extent to which they successfully disclose it; given the structure of experience, this standard remains loosely defined and open-ended. Phenomenological descriptions are formulated and refined through a continuing reflection on self, other and world, and with an eye to the possible dimensions of experience. For Merleau-Ponty, reality or the cohesion of meaning is formed at the intersection of subject and object, manifests itself differently across different perspectives, and is known in pre-theoretical experience and as a philosophical theme. Phenomenology is the philosophical discipline that attempts to articulate the birth of meaning across the various modalities of consciousness. This basic picture sketches the philosophical itinerary of a phenomenology that gives as much primacy to its *logos* as it does to *phenomena*.

NOTES

1. Dillon 1988, 85–86. See also Madison 1981.
2. Derrida 1978, 141.
3. Husserl 2001, introduction §3.

BIBLIOGRAPHY

I. WORKS BY MERLEAU-PONTY

Published Works

Merleau-Ponty, Maurice. 1948. *Sens et Non-Sens*. Paris: Nagel.
———. 1953. *Éloge de la philosophie. Leçon inaugurale faite au Collège de France le jeudi 15 janvier 1953*. Paris: Gallimard.
———. 1955. *Les Aventures de la dialectique*. Paris: Gallimard.
———. 1960. *Signes*. Paris: Gallimard.
———. 1964a. *Signs*. Translated by Richard C. McCleary. Evanston, IL: Northwestern University Press.
———. 1964b. *The Primacy of Perception*. Edited by James Edie. Evanston, IL: Northwestern University Press.
———. 1964c. *Sense and Non-Sense*. Translated by Hubert L. Dreyfus and Patricia Allen Dreyfus. Evanston, IL: Northwestern University Press.
———. 1964d. *L'Œil et l'Esprit*. Paris: Gallimard.
———. 1967a. *La Structure du comportement*. Paris: Presses Universitaires de France.
———. 1967b. *The Structure of Behaviour*. Translated by Alden Fisher. Boston: Beacon Press.
———. 1968. *The Visible and the Invisible*. Translated by Alphonso Lingis. Evanston, IL: Northwestern University Press.
———. 1969. *La Prose du monde*. Texte établi par Claude Lefort. Paris: Éditions Gallimard.
———. 1973a. *The Prose of the World*. Edited by Claude Lefort, Translated by John O'Neill. Evanston, IL: Northwestern University Press.
———. 1973b. *Adventures of the Dialectic*. Translated by Joseph Bien. Evanston, IL: Northwestern University Press.
———. 1979. *Le visible et l'invisible*. Texte établi par Claude Lefort. Paris: Gallimard.
———. 1988. *Merleau-Ponty à la Sorbonne: résumé de cours, 1949–1952*. Dijon-Quetigny: Cynara.
———. 1995. *La nature: Notes, cours de Collège de France*. Paris: Éditions du Seuil.
———. 1996a. *Notes des cours au Collège de France, 1958–1959 et 1960–1961*. Texte établi par Stéphanie Ménasé. Paris: Gallimard.
———. 1996b. *Le primat de la perception et ses conséquences philosophiques*. Lagrasse: Verdier.

———. 1998. *Merleau-Ponty: Notes de cours sur L'Origine de la géométrie de Husserl suivi de Recherches sur la phénoménologie de Merleau-Ponty*. Sous la direction de R. Barbaras. Paris: Presses universitaires de France.
———. 2001a. *Husserl at the Limits of Phenomenology*. Edited by Leonard Lawlor with Bettina Bergo. Evanston, IL: Northwestern University Press.
———. 2001b. *Psychologie et pedagogie de l'enfant: Cours de Sorbonne 1949–1952*. Lagrasse: Verdier.
———. 2001c. *Parcours deux. 1951–1961*. Lagrasse: Verdier.
———. 2003a. *Nature: Course Notes from the Collège de France*. Translated by Robert Vallier. Evanston, IL: Northwestern University Press.
———. 2003b. *L'Institution-La passivité: Notes de cours au Collège de France (1954–1955)*. Paris: Bellin.
———. 2005. *Phénoménologie de la perception*. Paris: Gallimard.
———. 2010a. *Institution and Passivity: Course Notes from the Collège de France (1954–1955)*. Translated by Leonard Lawlor and Heith Massey. Evanston, IL: Northwestern University Press.
———. 2010b. *Child Psychology and Pedagogy: The Sorbonne Lectures 1949–1952*. Translated by Talia Welsh. Evanston, IL: Northwestern University Press.
———. 2011. *Le monde sensible et le monde de l'expression. Cours au Collége de France, Notes 1953*. Texte établi et annoté par Emmanuel de Saint Aubert et Stefan Kristensen. Genève: MetisPresses.
———. 2012. *Phenomenology of Perception*. Translated by Donald A. Landes. New York: Routledge.
———. 2013. *Recherches sur l'usage littéraire du langage: Cours au Collège de France. Notes, 1953*. Texte établi par Benedetta Zaccarello et Emmanuel de Saint Aubert. Genève: MetisPresses.
Toadvine, Ted, and Lawlor, Leonard, eds. 2007. *The Merleau-Ponty Reader*. Evanston, IL: Northwestern University Press.

Unpublished Works

Merleau-Ponty, Maurice. Bibliothèque Nationale de France, Department of Manuscripts. NAF 26986. Manuscript Volume III: *La prose du monde*.
———. Bibliothèque Nationale de France, Department of Manuscripts. NAF 26989. Manuscript Volume VI: *Projets de 1958–Projet «Être et monde»*.
———. Bibliothèque Nationale de France, Department of Manuscripts. NAF 26991. Manuscript Volume VIII.1: *Notes de travail*.
———. Bibliothèque Nationale de France, Department of Manuscripts. NAF 26991. Manuscript Volume VIII.2: *Notes de travail*. Transcription by Franck Robert.
———. Bibliothèque Nationale de France, Department of Manuscripts. NAF 26995. Manuscript Volume XII: *Collège de France, 1953–1954. Cours du jeudi, Le Problème de la parole; cours du lundi, Matériaux pour une théorie de l'histoire. Préparation*. Transcription by Stefan Kristensen.

2. WORKS BY OTHER AUTHORS

Al-Saji, Alia. 2007. 'The Temporality of Life: Merleau-Ponty, Bergson, and the Immemorial Past'. *The Southern Journal of Philosophy* 45: 177–206.
Alloa, Emmanuel. 2009. 'La chair comme diacritique incarné'. *Chiasmi International* 11: 249–62.
Andrieu, Bernard. 1993. 'Le langage entre chair et corps'. In *Maurice Merleau-Ponty: le philosophe et son langage*, edited by François Heidsieck, 21–60. Paris: Vrin.

Apostolopoulos, Dimitris. 2017. 'Intentionality, Constitution, and Merleau-Ponty's Concept of "the Flesh"'. *European Journal of Philosophy*, 25.3: 677–99.
———. 2018a. 'The Systematic Import of Merleau-Ponty's Philosophy of Literature'. *Journal of the British Society for Phenomenology*, 49.1: 1–17.
———. 2018b. 'Sense, Language, and Ontology in Merleau-Ponty and Hyppolite'. *Research in Phenomenology*, 48.1: 92–118.
Austin, J. L. 1962. *How to Do Things with Words*. Oxford: Clarendon Press.
Baldwin, Thomas. 2007. 'Speaking and Spoken Speech'. In *Reading Merleau-Ponty*, edited by Thomas Baldwin, 87–103. Oxon: Routledge.
Barbaras, Renaud. 2004. *The Being of the Phenomenon: Merleau-Ponty's Ontology*. Translated by Ted Toadvine and Leonard Lawlor. Bloomington: Indiana University Press.
Baugh, Bruce. 2003. *French Hegel: From Surrealism to Postmodernism*. New York: Routledge.
de Beauvoir, Simone. 1989. 'Merleau-Ponty and Pseudo-Sartreanism'. *International Studies in Philosophy*, 21.3: 3–48.
Behnke, Elizabeth. 2002. 'Merleau-Ponty's Ontological Reading of Constitution in Phénoménologie de la perception'. In *Merleau-Ponty's Reading of Husserl*, edited by Ted Toadvine and Lester Embree, 31–50. Dordrecht: Springer.
Beneviste, Émile. 1971. *Problems in General Linguistics*. Translated by Mary Elizabeth Meek. Miami: University of Miami Press.
Besmer, Kirk M. 2007. *Merleau-Ponty's Phenomenology: The Problem of Ideal Objects*. London: Continuum.
Bimbenet, Étienne. 2004. *Nature et humanité: le problème anthropologique dans l'oeuvre de Merleau-Ponty*. Paris: Vrin.
Bonan, Ronald. 2001. *La dimension commune: Le problème de l'intersubjectivité dans la philosophie de Merleau-Ponty*. Volume 1. Paris: L'Harmattan.
Brunschvicg, Léon. 1905. *L'idéalisme contemporain*. Paris: F. Alcan.
Bruzina, Ronald. 2002. 'Eugen Fink and Maurice Merleau-Ponty: The Philosophical Lineage in Phenomenology'. In *Merleau-Ponty's Reading of Husserl*, edited by Ted Toadvine, 173–200. Dordrecht: Springer.
———. 2004. *Edmund Husserl and Eugen Fink: Beginnings and Ends in Phenomenology*. New Haven, CT: Yale University Press.
Burch, Robert. 1993. 'On the Topic of Art and Truth: Merleau-Ponty, Heidegger, and the Transcendental Turn'. In *The Merleau-Ponty Aesthetics Reader: Philosophy and Painting*, edited by Galen Johnson, 348–70. Evanston, IL: Northwestern University Press.
Butler, Judith. 2005. 'Merleau-Ponty and the Touch of Malebranche'. In *The Cambridge Companion to Merleau-Ponty*, edited by Taylor Carman and Mark B. N. Hansen, 181–205. Cambridge: Cambridge University Press.
Carbone, Mauro. 1993. 'La dicibilité du monde: La période intermédiaire de la pensée de Merleau-Ponty à partir de Saussure'. In *Maurice Merleau-Ponty: le philosophe et son langage*, edited by François Heidsieck, 83–99. Paris: Vrin.
———. 2004. *The Thinking of the Sensible: Merleau-Ponty's A-Philosophy*. Evanston, IL: Northwestern University Press.
Carman, Taylor, and Hansen, Mark B. N. 2005. 'Introduction'. In *The Cambridge Companion to Merleau-Ponty*, edited by Taylor Carman and Mark B. N. Hansen, 1–25. Cambridge: Cambridge University Press.
Casey, Edward S. 1984. 'Habitual Memory and Body Memory in Merleau-Ponty'. *Man and World* 17: 279–97.
Cassirer, Ernst. 1953. *The Philosophy of Symbolic Forms. Volume I: Language*. Translated by Ralph Mannheim. New Haven, CT: Yale University Press.
———. 1965. *The Philosophy of Symbolic Forms. Volume III: The Phenomenology of Knowledge*. Translated by Ralph Mannheim. New Haven, CT: Yale University Press.
———. 2013. *The Warburg Years. Essays on Language, Art, Myth, and Technology*. Translated by S. G. Lofts and A. Calcagno. New Haven, CT: Yale University Press.
Cavaillès, Jean. 1997. *Sur la logique et la théorie de la science*. Paris: Vrin.

Chabrolle-Cerretini, Anne-Marie, and Raynaud, Savina. 2015. 'Humboldt's innere Sprachform: Its Contribution to the Lexicographical Description of Language Diversity'. *Language and History*, 58.2: 95–110.

Chiesa, M. Curzio. 1991. 'Le problème du langage intérieur chez les Stoïciens'. *Revue internationale de philosophie*, 45.178 (3): 301–21.

Courtine, Jean-François. 2007. *La cause de la phénoménologie*. Paris: Presses Universitaires de France.

Crow, Christine M. 1982. *Paul Valéry and the Poetry of Voice*. Cambridge: Cambridge University Press.

Crowell, Steven Galt. 2002. 'Authentic Thinking and Phenomenological Method'. *New Yearbook for Phenomenology and Phenomenological Philosophy*, 2: 23–37.

Crowther, Paul. 1982. 'Merleau-Ponty: Perception into Art'. *British Journal of Aesthetics*, 22.2: 138–49.

Cuffari, Elena. 2012. 'Gestural Sense-Making: Hand Gestures as Intersubjective Linguistic Enactments'. *Phenomenology and the Cognitive Sciences*, 11.4: 599–622.

Dahlstrom, Dan O. 1994. 'Heidegger's Method: Philosophical Concepts as Formal Indications'. *The Review of Metaphysics*, 47.4: 775–95.

Dastur, Françoise. 2000. 'World, Flesh, Vision'. In *Chiasms: Merleau-Ponty's Notion of Flesh*, edited by Fred Evans and Leonard Lawlor, 23–50. Albany, NY: SUNY Press.

———. 2001. *Chair et langage: Essais sur Merleau-Ponty*. La Versanne: Encre Marine.

Davidson, Donald. 1984. 'Truth and Meaning'. In *Inquires into Truth and Interpretation*, 17–36. Oxford: Oxford University Press.

Depraz, Nathalie. 1998. 'Selon quels critères peut-on définir une écriture phénoménologique'? In *Merleau-Ponty et le Littéraire*, edited by Nicolas Castin and Anne Simon. Paris: Presses de l'École normale supérieure.

Derrida, Jacques. 1978. *Edmund Husserl's Origin of Geometry: An Introduction*. Translated by John P. Leavey. Lincoln: University of Nebraska Press.

———. 2005. *On Touching – Jean-Luc Nancy*. Translated by Christine Irizarry. Palo Alto, CA: Stanford University Press.

Dillon, M. C. 1988. *Merleau-Ponty's Ontology*. Bloomington: Indiana University Press.

Dodd, James. 2006. *Crisis and Reflection: An Essay on Husserl's Crisis of the European Sciences*. Dordrecht: Springer.

Dreyfus, Hubert L. 2005. 'Merleau-Ponty and Recent Cognitive Science'. In *The Cambridge Companion to Merleau-Ponty*, edited by Taylor Carman and Mark B. N. Hansen, 129–50. Cambridge: Cambridge University Press.

———. 2007. 'Reply to Romdenh-Romluc'. In *Reading Merleau-Ponty*, edited by Thomas Baldwin, 59–69. Oxon: Routledge.

Dreyfus, Hubert, and Charles Taylor. 2015. *Retrieving Realism*. Cambridge, MA: Harvard University Press.

Edie, James M. 1980. 'The Meaning and Development of Merleau-Ponty's Concept of Structure'. *Research in Phenomenology*, 10.1: 39–57.

———. 1987. *Merleau-Ponty's Philosophy of Language: Structuralism and Dialectics*. Pittsburgh: Center for Advanced Research in Phenomenology.

Fink, Eugen. 1970. 'The Phenomenological Philosophy of Edmund Husserl and Contemporary Criticism'. In *The Phenomenology of Husserl: Selected Critical Readings*, edited by R. O. Elveton. Chicago: Quadrangle Books.

———. 1981. 'The Problem of the Phenomenology of Edmund Husserl'. In *A priori and World*, edited by William McKenna, Robert M. Harlan, and Laurence E. Winters, 21–55. The Hague: Springer.

———. 1995. *Sixth Cartesian Meditation: The Idea of a Transcendental Theory of Method*. With annotations by Edmund Husserl. Translated with an introduction by Ronald Bruzina. Indianapolis: Indiana University Press.

Fontaine-de Visscher, Luce. 1974. *Phénomène ou structure? Essai sur le langage chez Merleau-Ponty*. Brussels: Facultés universitaires Saint-Louis.

Fóti, Véronique, ed. 1996. *Merleau-Ponty: Difference, Materiality, Painting*. New Jersey: Humanities Press.

———. 2013. *Tracing Expression in Merleau-Ponty. Aesthetics, Philosophy of Biology, and Ontology*. Evanston, IL: Northwestern University Press.
Gadamer, Hans-Georg. 2004. *Truth and Method*. Translated by Joel Weinsheimer and Donald G. Marshall. New York: Continuum.
Gallagher, Shaun. 1992. 'Introduction: The Hermeneutics of Ambiguity'. In *Merleau-Ponty, Hermeneutics and Postmodernism*, edited by Thomas W. Busch and Shaun Gallagher, 3–12. Albany, NY: SUNY Press.
Gardner, Sebastian. 2015. 'Merleau-Ponty's Transcendental Theory of Perception'. In *The Transcendental Turn*, edited by Sebastian Gardner and Matthew Grist, 294–323. Oxford: Oxford University Press.
———. 2017. 'Merleau-Ponty's Phenomenology in the Light of Kant's Third *Critique* and Schelling's *Real-Idealismus*'. *Continental Philosophy Review*, 50.1: 5–25.
Gelb, Adhémar, and Goldstein, Kurt. 1920. 'Über den Einfluß vollstandigen Verlustes des optischen Vorstellungsvermögens auf das tactile Erkennen'. In *Psychologische Analyse hirnpathologischer Fälle auf Grund von Untersuchungen Hirnverletzer*, Volume 1, edited by Adhémar Gelb and Kurt Goldstein, 157–250. Leipzig: J. A. Barth.
Gendlin, Eugene T., and Spiegelberg, Herbert. 1964. 'The Structure of Behaviour'. *Modern Schoolman*, 42.1: 87–97.
Geraets, Theodore F. 1971. *Vers une nouvelle philosophie transcendantale: La genèse de la philosophie de Maurice Merleau-Ponty jusqu'à la Phénoménologie de la perception*. The Hague: Springer.
Gier, Nicholas F. 1981. *Wittgenstein and Phenomenology*. Albany: State University of New York Press.
Gill, Jerry H. 1991. *Merleau-Ponty and Metaphor*. Atlantic Highlands, NJ: Humanities Press.
Goldstein, Kurt. 1923. 'Über die Abhängigkeit der Bewegungen von optischen Vorgängen. Bewegungsstörungen bei Seelenblinden'. *Monatschrift für Psychiatrie und Neurologie – Festschrift Liepmann*, 54.1: 141–94.
———. 1931. 'Über Zeigen und Greifen'. *Nervenarzt* 4: 453–66.
———. 1948. *Language and Language Disturbances: Aphasic Symptom Complexes and Their Significance for Medicine and Theory of Languages*. New York: Grune.
Grene, Marjorie. 1970. 'The Aesthetic Dialogue of Sartre and Merleau-Ponty'. *Journal of the British Society for Phenomenology*, 1.2: 59–72.
Grice, Paul. 1989. *Studies in the Way of Words*. Cambridge, MA: Harvard University Press.
Guignon, Charles. 2013. 'Wittgenstein, Heidegger, and the Question of Phenomenology'. In *Wittgenstein and Heidegger*, edited by David Egan, Stephen Reynolds, and Aaron James Wendland, 82–98. New York: Routledge.
Gutting, Gary. 2001. *French Philosophy in the Twentieth Century*. Cambridge: Cambridge University Press.
———. 2011. *Thinking the Impossible: French Philosophy since 1960*. Oxford: Oxford University Press.
———. 2013. 'French Hegelianism and Anti-Hegelianism in the 1960s'. In *The Impact of Idealism, Volume 1: Philosophy and the Natural Sciences*, edited by Nicholas Boyle, Liz Disley, and Karl Ameriks, 246–71. Cambridge: Cambridge University Press.
Haar, Michel. 1999. *La philosophie française entre phénoménologie et métaphysique*. Paris: Presses Universitaires de France.
Hass, Lawrence. 2008. *Merleau-Ponty's Philosophy*. Bloomington: Indiana University Press.
Hegel, G. W. F. 1969. *Science of Logic*. Translated by A. V. Miller. London: Allen & Unwin.
———. 1977. *Phenomenology of Spirit*. Translated by A. V. Miller. Oxford: Oxford University Press.
———. 2010. *The Science of Logic*. Translated and edited by George di Giovanni. Cambridge: Cambridge University Press.
Heidegger, Martin. 1962. *Being and Time*. Translated by John Macquarrie and Edward Robinson. Oxford: Blackwell.
———. 1971. 'Language'. In *Poetry, Language, and Thought*. Translated by Alfred Hofstadter, 189–210. New York: Harper and Row.

———. 1997. *Plato's Sophist*. Translated by Richard Rojcewicz and André Schuwer. Bloomington: Indiana University Press.

———. 1998. 'Letter on 'Humanism''. In *Pathmarks*, edited by William McNeill, 239–76. Cambridge: Cambridge University Press.

Heidsieck, François, ed. 1993. *Maurice Merleau-Ponty: le philosophe et son langage*. Paris: Vrin.

Hughes, Fiona. 2013. 'A Passivity Prior to Passive and Active: Merleau-Ponty's Re-reading of the Freudian Unconscious and Looking at Lascaux'. *Mind*, 122.486: 419–50.

———. 2017. 'Reversibility and Chiasm: False Equivalents? An Alternative Approach to Understanding Difference in Merleau-Ponty's Late Philosophy'. *British Journal for the History of Philosophy*, 25.2: 356–79.

Husserl, Edmund. 1960. *Cartesian Meditations: An Introduction to Phenomenology*. Translated by Dorion Cairns. The Hague: Martinus Nijhoff.

———. 1969. *Formal and Transcendental Logic*. Translated by Dorion Cairns. The Hague: Martinus Nijhoff.

———. 1970. *The Crisis of the European Sciences and Transcendental Phenomenology*. Translated by David Carr. Evanston, IL: Northwestern University Press.

———. 1973. *Experience and Judgment: Investigations in a Genealogy of Logic*. Revised and edited by Ludwig Landgrebe. Translated by James S. Churchill and Karl Ameriks. London: Routledge.

———. 2001. *Logical Investigations. Volume 1*. Translated by J. N. Findlay. London: Routledge.

———. 2012. *Analyses Concerning Passive and Active Synthesis: Lectures on Transcendental Logic*. Translated by Anthony J. Steinbock. Dordrecht: Kluwer.

———. 2014. *Ideas for a Pure Phenomenology and Phenomenological Philosophy. First Book: General Introduction to Pure Phenomenology*. Translated by Daniel Dahlstrom. Indianapolis: Hackett.

Hyppolite, Jean. 1953. *Logique et existence: Essai sur la logique de Hegel*. Paris: Presses Universitaires de France.

———. 1968. *Studies on Marx and Hegel*. Translated by John O'Neill. New York: Harper and Row.

———. 1971. *Figures de la pensée philosophique. Écrits de Jean Hyppolite (1931–1968), Tome II*. Paris: Presses Universitaires de France.

———. 1997. *Logic and Existence*. Translated by Leonard Lawlor and Amit Sen. Albany, NY: SUNY Press.

Imbert, Claude. 1998. 'L'écrivain, le peintre et le philosophe'. In *Merleau-Ponty et le Littéraire*, edited by Nicolas Castin and Anne Simon, 53–82. Paris: Presses de l'École normale supérieure.

———. 2005. *Maurice Merleau-Ponty*. Paris: Association pour la diffusion de la pensée française.

Inkpin, Andrew. 2016. *Disclosing the World: On the Phenomenology of Language*. Cambridge, MA: MIT Press.

———. 2017. 'Was Merleau-Ponty a "Transcendental" Phenomenologist'? *Continental Philosophy Review*, 50.1: 27–47.

Jensen, Rasmus Thybo. 2009. 'Motor Intentionality and the Case of Schneider'. *Phenomenology and the Cognitive Sciences*, 8.3: 371–88.

Johnson, Galen, ed. 1993. *The Merleau-Ponty Aesthetics Reader: Philosophy and Painting*. Evanston, IL: Northwestern University Press.

Kaelin, Eugene. 1962. *An Existentialist Aesthetic*. Madison: University of Wisconsin Press.

Kant, Immanuel. 1998. *Critique of Pure Reason*. Translated and edited by Paul Guyer and Allen W. Wood. Cambridge: Cambridge University Press.

———. 2004. *Metaphysical Foundations of Natural Science*. Edited and translated by Michael Friedman. Cambridge: Cambridge University Press.

Kaushik, Rajiv. 2013. 'The Devolution of Language'. In *Art, Language and Figure in Merleau-Ponty: Excursions in Hyper-Dialectic*, 75–96. London: Bloomsbury.

Kearney, Richard. 2013. 'Ecrire la Chair: l'expression diacritique chez Merleau-Ponty'. *Chiasmi International*, 15: 183–98.
Kelly, Sean Dorrance. 2002. 'Merleau–Ponty on the Body'. *Ratio*, 15.4: 376–91.
———. 2005. 'Seeing Things in Merleau-Ponty'. In *The Cambridge Companion to Merleau-Ponty*, edited by Taylor Carman and Mark B. N. Hansen, 74–110. Cambridge: Cambridge University Press.
Kerr, Fergus. 1965. 'Language as Hermeneutic in the Later Wittgenstein'. *Tijdschrift voor Filosofie*, 27.3: 491–520.
Kristensen, Stefan. 2010. *Parole et Subjectivité*. Hildesheim: Georg Olms Verlag.
Lachièze-Rey, Pierre. 1933–1934. 'Réflexions sur l'activité spirituelle constituante'. *Recherches Philosophiques*, 3: 125–47.
———. 1937. 'Utilisation possible du schématisme kantien pour une théorie de la perception'. *Les Études philosophiques*, 11.3/4: 30–34.
———. 1938. *Le moi, le monde et Dieu*. Paris: Boivin.
———. 1950. *L'idéalisme kantien* (2nd Edition). Paris: Vrin.
Lagueux, Maurice. 1965. 'Merleau-Ponty et la Linguistique de Saussure'. *Dialogue*, 4.03: 351–64.
Lambert, Johann Heinrich. 1764. *Neues Organon, oder Gedanken über die Erforschung und Bezeichnung des Wahren und dessen Unterscheidung vom Jrrthum und Schein*. Leipzig: Bey J. Wendler.
Landes, Donald A. 2013. *Merleau-Ponty and the Paradoxes of Expression*. New York: Bloomsbury.
———. 2015. 'Between Sensibility and Understanding: Kant and Merleau-Ponty and the Critique of Reason'. *Journal of Speculative Philosophy*, 29.3: 335–45.
Lawlor, Leonard. 1998. 'The End of Phenomenology: Expressionism in Deleuze and Merleau-Ponty'. *Continental Philosophy Review*, 31: 15–34.
———. 1999. 'The End of Ontology'. *Chiasmi International*, 1: 233–51.
———. 2002. *Derrida and Husserl: The Basic Problem of Phenomenology*. Indianapolis: Indiana University Press.
Levinas, Emmanuel. 1990a. 'Intersubjectivity: Notes on Merleau-Ponty'. In *Ontology and Alterity in Merleau-Ponty*, edited by Galen Johnson and Michael B. Smith, translated by Michael B. Smith, 55–60. Evanston, IL: Northwestern University Press.
———. 1990b. 'Sensibility'. In *Ontology and Alterity in Merleau-Ponty*, edited by Galen Johnson and Michael B. Smith, translated by Michael B. Smith, 60–66. Evanston, IL: Northwestern University Press.
Levine, Stephen K. 1969. 'Merleau-Ponty's Philosophy of Art'. *Man and World*, 2.3: 438–52.
Loidolt, Sophie. 2014. 'Phenomenological Sources, Kantian Borders: An Outline of Transcendental Philosophy as Object-Guided Philosophy'. In *Phenomenology and the Transcendental*, edited by Sara Heinämaa, Mirja Hartimo, and Timo Miettinen, 190–217. New York: Routledge.
Low, Douglas. 2004. 'The Continuing Relevance of the Structure of Behaviour'. *International Philosophical Quarterly*, 44.3: 411–30.
Madison, Gary Brent. 1981. *The Phenomenology of Merleau-Ponty: A Search for the Limits of Consciousness*. Translated by Gary Brent Madison. Athens: Ohio University Press.
Marratto, Scott. 2017. 'Alterity and Expression in Merleau-Ponty: A Response to Levinas'. In *Perception and Its Development in Merleau-Ponty's* Phenomenology of Perception, edited by Kirsten Jacobson and John Russon, 242–50. Toronto: University of Toronto Press.
Masuda, Kazuo. 1993. 'La dette symbolique de la Phénoménologie de la perception'. In *Maurice Merleau-Ponty: le philosophe et son langage*, edited by François Heidsieck, 225–43. Paris: Vrin.
Matherne, Samantha. 2014. 'The Kantian Roots of Merleau-Ponty's Account of Pathology'. *British Journal for the History of Philosophy*, 22.1: 124–49.
———. 2016. 'Kantian Themes in Merleau-Ponty's Theory of Perception'. *Archiv für Geschichte der Philosophie*, 98.2: 193–230.
McDowell, John. 1996. *Mind and World*. Cambridge, MA: Harvard University Press.

Mercury, Jean-Yves. 2000. *L'expressivité chez Merleau-Ponty: Du corps à la peinture*. Paris: L'Harmattan.
Moran, Dermot. 2008. 'Husserl's Transcendental Phenomenology and the Critique of Naturalism'. *Continental Philosophy Review*, 41.4: 401–25.
———. 2010. 'Sartre on Embodiment, Touch, and the "Double Sensation"'. *Philosophy Today*, 54: 135–41.
Morris, David. 2010. 'The Enigma of Reversibility and the Genesis of Sense in Merleau-Ponty'. *Continental Philosophy Review*, 43: 141–65.
Morris, David, and Maclaren, Kym, eds. 2015. *Time, Memory, Institution: Merleau-Ponty's New Ontology of Self*. Athens: Ohio University Press.
Noble, Stephen A. 2011. 'Maurice Merleau-Ponty: Desiderata for an Intellectual Biography'. *Chiasmi International*, 13: 63–112.
———. 2014. *Silence et Langage: Genèse de la phénoménologie de Merleau-Ponty au seuil de l'ontologie*. Leiden: Brill.
O'Neill, John. 1986. 'The Specular Body: Merleau-Ponty and Lacan on Infant Self and Other'. *Synthese*, 66.2: 201–17.
Parain, Brice. 1943. *Recherches sur la nature et les fonctions du langage*. Paris: Gallimard.
Patočka, Jan. 2002. *Plato and Europe*. Translated by Petr Lom. Stanford, CA: Stanford University Press.
Plato. 1997. *Complete Works*. Edited by John M. Cooper and D. S. Hutchinson. Indianapolis: Hackett.
Pollard, Christopher. 2014. 'Is Merleau-Ponty's Position in *Phenomenology of Perception* a New Type of Transcendental Idealism'? *Idealistic Studies*, 44.1: 119–38.
Priest, Stephen. 1998. *Merleau-Ponty*. London: Routledge.
Proust, Marcel. 1998. *In Search of Lost Time: Volume 3: The Guermantes Way*. Translated by C. K. Scott Moncrieff and Terence Kilmartin. New York: Random House.
———. 1999. *In Search of Lost Time: Volume 6: Time Regained*. Translated by C. K. Scott Moncrieff and Terence Kilmartin. New York: Random House.
Reynolds, Jack. 2002. 'Merleau-Ponty, Levinas, and the Alterity of the Other'. *Symposium*, 6.1: 63–78.
Richir, Marc. 1993a. 'The Meaning of Phenomenology in *The Visible and the Invisible*'. *Thesis Eleven*, 36.1: 60–81.
———. 1993b. 'Merleau-Ponty and the Question of Phenomenological Architectonics'. In *Merleau-Ponty in Contemporary Perspective*, edited by Philip Burke and J. van der Veken, 37–50. Dordrecht: Springer.
———. 1998. 'Le sensible dans le rêve'. In *Merleau-Ponty—Notes de cours sur l'Origine de la Géométrie de Husserl – suivi de recherches sur la phénoménologie de Merleau-Ponty*, edited by Renaud Barbaras, 239–54. Paris: Presses Universitaires de France.
Ricoeur, Paul. 1977. *The Rule of Metaphor*. Translated by Robert Czerny with Kathleen McLaughlin and John Costello, SJ. London: Routledge.
Robert, Franck. 2003. 'Proust phénoménologue'? *Bulletin Marcel-Proust*, 53: 139–54.
———. 2005. *Phénoménologie et ontologie. Merleau-Ponty lecteur de Husserl et Heidegger*. Paris: L'Harmattan.
———. 2008. 'Écriture et vérité'. *Revue internationale de philosophie*, 2: 149–66.
Rockmore, Tom. 2011. *Kant and Phenomenology*. Chicago: University of Chicago Press.
Romano, Claude. 2010. *Au coeur de la raison, la phénoménologie*. Paris: Gallimard.
Romdenh-Romluc, Komarine. 2007. 'Merleau-Ponty and the Power to Reckon with the Possible'. In *Reading Merleau-Ponty*, edited by Thomas Baldwin, 44–58. Oxon: Routledge.
Rouse, Joseph. 2005. 'Merleau-Ponty's Existential Concept of Science'. In *The Cambridge Companion to Merleau-Ponty*, edited by Taylor Carman and Mark B. N. Hansen, 265–90. Cambridge: Cambridge University Press.
de Saint Aubert, Emmanuel. 2004. *Du lien des êtres aux éléments de l'être: Merleau-Ponty au tournant des années 1945–1951*. Paris: Vrin.
———. 2005. *Le scénario cartésien: recherches sur la formation et la cohérence de l'intention philosophique de Merleau-Ponty*. Paris: Vrin.

---. 2006. *Vers une ontologie indirecte: sources et enjeux critiques de l'appel à l'ontologie chez Merleau-Ponty*. Paris: Vrin.
---. 2008. *Maurice Merleau-Ponty*. Paris: Hermann.
---. 2013. *Être et Chair I. Du corps au désir : l'habilitation ontologique de la chair*. Paris: Vrin.
Sanders, John T. 1994. 'Merleau-Ponty on Meaning, Materiality, and Structure'. *Journal of the British Society for Phenomenology*, 25.1: 96–100.
Sartre, Jean Paul. 1984. *Being and Nothingness: A Phenomenological Essay on Ontology*. Translated by Hazel E. Barnes. London: Washington Square.
---. 1988. *What Is Literature? And Other Essays*. Translated by Steven Ungar. Cambridge, MA: Harvard University Press.
de Saussure, Ferdinand. 2006. *Writings in General Linguistics*. Edited by Simon Bouquet and Rudolf Engler. Oxford: Oxford University Press.
Scheler, Max. 1970. *The Nature of Sympathy*. Translated by Peter Heath. Hamden: Archon.
Schenck, David. 1984. 'Meaning and/or Materiality: Merleau-Ponty's Notions of Structure'. *Journal of the British Society for Phenomenology*, 15.1: 34–50.
Schilder, Paul. 2013. *Das Körperschema: Ein Beitrag zur Lehre vom Bewusstsein des Eigenen Körpers*. Dordrecht: Springer-Verlag.
Sellheim, Berndt. 2010. 'Metaphor and Flesh – Poetic Necessity in Merleau-Ponty'. *Journal of the British Society for Phenomenology*, 41.3: 261–73.
Silverman, Hugh J. 1979. 'Merleau-Ponty on Language and Communication (1947–1948)'. *Research in Phenomenology*, 9.1: 168–81.
---. 1980. 'Merleau-Ponty and the Interrogation of Language'. *Research in Phenomenology*, 10.1: 122–41.
---, ed. 1988. *Philosophy and Non-Philosophy Since Merleau-Ponty*. New York: Routledge.
Simon, Anne. 1998. 'Proust et l'architecture du visible'. In *Merleau-Ponty et le Littéraire*, edited by Nicolas Castin and Anne Simon, 105–16. Paris: Presses de l'École normale supérieure.
Smith, Joel. 2005. 'Merleau-Ponty and the Phenomenological Reduction'. *Inquiry*, 48.6: 553–71.
Smith, Michael B. 1993. 'Merleau-Ponty's Aesthetics'. In *The Merleau-Ponty Aesthetics Reader: Philosophy and Painting*, edited by Galen Johnson, 192–211. Evanston, IL: Northwestern University Press.
Smyth, Bryan. 2011. 'The Meontic and the Militant: On Merleau-Ponty's Relation to Fink'. *International Journal of Philosophical Studies*, 19.5: 669–99.
Sokolowski, Robert. 1964. *The Formation of Husserl's Concept of Constitution*. The Hague: Martinus Nijhoff.
Stawarska, Beata. 2013. 'Uncanny Errors, Productive Contresens. Merleau-Ponty's Phenomenological Appropriation of Ferdinand de Saussure's General Linguistics'. *Chiasmi International*, 15: 151–65.
---. 2015. *Saussure's Philosophy of Language as Phenomenology: Undoing the Doctrine of the Course in General Linguistics*. New York: Oxford University Press.
Taylor, Charles. 1978. 'The Validity of Transcendental Arguments'. *Proceedings of the Aristotelian Society* 79: 151–65.
---. 1985. *Human Agency and Language. Philosophical Papers 1*. Cambridge: Cambridge University Press.
---. 2016. *The Language Animal: The Full Shape of the Human Linguistic Capacity*. Cambridge, MA: Harvard University Press.
Thierry, Yves. 1987. *Du Corps Parlant*. Paris: Ousia.
Thompson, Evan. 2007. *Mind in Life*. Cambridge, MA: Harvard University Press.
Tieszen, Richard. 1984. 'Mathematical Intuition and Husserl's Philosophy'. *Noûs*, 18.3: 395–421.
Toadvine, Ted. 2009. *Merleau-Ponty's Philosophy of Nature*. Evanston, IL: Northwestern University Press.

Tugendhat, Ernst. 1982. *Traditional and Analytic Philosophy: Lectures on the Philosophy of Language*. Cambridge: Cambridge University Press.

Valéry, Paul. 1944. *Tel Quel*. Paris: Gallimard.

Vallier, Robert. 2005. 'Institution: The Significance of Merleau-Ponty's 1954 Course at the Collège de France'. *Chiasmi International*, 7: 281–302.

Vanzago, Luca. 2005. 'Presenting the Unpresentable: The Metaphor in Merleau-Ponty's Last Writings'. *Southern Journal of Philosophy*, 43.3: 463–74.

von Humboldt, Wilhelm. 2000. *On Language. On the Diversity of Human Language Construction and Its Influence on the Mental Development of the Human Species*. Edited by Michael Losonsky. Translated by Peter Heath. Cambridge: Cambridge University Press.

de Waelhens, Alphonse. 1967. *Une philosophie de l'ambiguïté: l'existentialisme de Maurice Merleau-Ponty*. Louvain: Publications universitaires.

Waldenfels, Bernhard. 1980. 'Perception and Structure in Merleau-Ponty'. *Research in Phenomenology*, 10.1: 21–38.

Watkin, Christopher. 2009. *Phenomenology or Deconstruction? The Question of Ontology in Maurice Merleau-Ponty, Paul Ricoeur, and Jean-Luc Nancy*. Edinburgh: Edinburgh University Press.

Watson, Stephen. 2009a. *In the Shadow of Phenomenology: Writings after Merleau-Ponty I*. London: Continuum.

———. 2009b. *Phenomenology, Institution and History: Writings after Merleau-Ponty II*. London: Continuum.

———. 2016. '"Philosophy Is Also an Architecture of Signs": On Merleau-Ponty and Cavaillès'. *Research in Phenomenology*, 46.1: 35–53.

Weiss, Gail. 1998. 'Body Image Intercourse: A Corporeal Dialogue between Merleau-Ponty and Schilder'. In *Merleau-Ponty, Interiority and Exteriority, Psychic Life and the World*, edited by Dorothea Olkowski and James Morley, 121–43. Albany, NY: SUNY Press.

Welsh, Talia. 2013. *The Child as Natural Phenomenologist: Primal and Primary Experience in Merleau-Ponty's Psychology*. Evanston, IL: Northwestern University Press.

Wilkerson, William. 2010. 'Time and Ambiguity: Reassessing Merleau-Ponty on Sartrean Freedom'. *Journal of the History of Philosophy*, 48.2: 207–34.

Wittgenstein, Ludwig. 1972. *On Certainty*. Edited by G. E. M. Anscombe and G. H. von Wright. Translated by Denis Paul and G. E. M. Anscombe. New York: Harper and Row.

———. 2001. *Tractatus Logico-Philosophicus*. Translated by D. F. Pears and B. F. McGuinness. London: Routledge.

———. 2009. *Philosophical Investigations*. Edited and Translated by P. M. S. Hacker and Joachim Schulte. Oxford: Wiley-Blackwell.

Zaccarello, Bendetta. 2012. 'La doute de Valéry: pensée, existence, écriture dans les *Recherches sur l'usage littéraire du langage*'. In *Du sensible à l'oeuvre. Esthétiques de Merleau- Ponty'*, edited by Emmanuel Alloa and Adnan Jdey, 161–84. Bruxelles: La lettre volée.

———. 2013. 'Avant-propos'. In *Recherches sur l'usage littéraire du langage: Cours au Collège de France. Notes, 1953*. Texte établi par Benedetta Zaccarello et Emmanuel de Saint Aubert, 9–52. Genève: MetisPresses.

Zahavi, Dan. 2002. 'Merleau-Ponty's Reading of Husserl: A Reappraisal'. In *Merleau-Ponty's Reading of Husserl*, edited by Ted Toadvine and Lester Embree, 3–29. Dordrecht: Kluwer.

INDEX

INDEX NOMINUM

Austin, J. L., 46

de Beauvoir, Simone, 60, 68n38, 150n13, 171
Berkeley, George, 32
Bréhier, Émile, 77, 137
Brunschvicg, Léon, 105n2, 106n8, 284n29

Cassirer, Ernst, 35, 50, 65n4, 67n28, 67n30, 194–195, 230, 232n14
Cavaillès, Jean, 125, 150n4
Cézanne, Paul, 63, 139–140, 151n16
Claudel, Paul, 150n13

de Condillac, Étienne Bonnot, 66n18, 233n35
Davidson, Donald, 66n20
Derrida, Jacques, 110n48, 280n1, 293–294
Descartes, René, 72–73, 84, 106n7

Frege, Gottlob, 46
Fink, Eugen, 2, 35, 37n21, 73–74, 76, 79, 101–102, 107n17, 110n49, 244, 282n9, 285n37, 291

Gelb, Adhéhmar, 19–21, 41, 42, 232n14
Gide, André, 150n13

Goldstein, Kurt, 19–21, 36n8, 41–42, 193, 231n12, 232n14
Grice, Paul, 67n29
Guillaume, Gustave, 127, 128, 129
Gurwitsch, Aron, 202

Hamann, Johan Georg, 190
Hegel, G. W. F., 34, 94, 257, 261, 284n29, 284n34, 285n36
Heidegger, Martin, 2, 3–4, 11n6, 47, 56, 57, 67n34, 101, 148, 154, 190–191, 222–223, 235n46, 238, 248–249, 250, 251, 260–261, 283n17, 290
Herder, Johann Gottfried, 190–191
von Humboldt, Wilhelm, 3, 190–191, 191–193, 194, 195, 231n11
Husserl, Edmund, 2, 25, 36n10, 36n12, 46, 47, 66n23–66n24, 74–76, 78, 80, 81, 84, 88–89, 97, 100–101, 107n21, 109n39, 128, 133–134, 148, 154, 157, 163, 169, 172, 197, 202, 205, 209, 222, 224, 233n28, 239, 244, 247, 270–271, 277, 282n13, 286n45, 291, 295
Hyppolite, Jean, 111n67, 261, 284n29, 284n34

Jakobson, Roman, 127, 128

Kant, Immanuel, 10, 10n1, 32, 36n8, 73, 74–76, 78, 81, 94, 106n4, 107n21, 109n39, 291

Koffka, Kurt, 129
Kojève, Alexandre, 257, 284n29

Lachièze-Rey, Pierre, 72–73, 106n13, 106n14, 109n39
Levinas, Emmanuel, 236n53

Malraux, André, 66n26, 141, 151n16

Parain, Brice, 109n46, 125, 150n4
Péguy, Charles, 118
Plato, 10n1
Pos, Hendrik, 134
Proust, Marcel, 8, 58, 144–147, 148, 152n26, 207, 216, 221, 251, 274

Ricoeur, Paul, 252

Sartre, Jean-Paul, 2, 59–61, 62, 67n28, 109n47, 151n14, 151n23, 238, 250, 257, 281n3
de Saussure, Ferdinand, 8, 66n16, 67n28, 67n34, 127–136, 150n6, 150n8, 154, 159, 231n11
Scheler, Max, 68n35, 128
Schlegel, Friedrich, 184n50
Schneider, 20, 39–40, 40–46, 53, 65n6, 83, 105n3
Simon, Claude, 150n13
Stendhal, 142, 145

Tarski, Alfred, 46
Taylor, Charles, 51, 78, 191, 227

Valéry, Paul, 8, 63, 116, 142–144, 145, 151n22, 152n25, 222, 251, 277

Watson, J. B., 36n3
Wittgenstein, Ludwig, 48, 190–191, 208, 223–224, 230, 231n8, 236n50

INDEX RERUM

activity, 9, 153, 165–168, 207

behaviour, 6, 16–18, 20, 28–29, 36n3, 48, 87, 129, 254

cogito, 72–73, 84–85, 91, 94, 180, 241; spoken (*le cogito parlée*), 83–84, 84–86, 91, 92, 188; tacit (*le cogito tacite*), 83, 89, 90–91, 96, 98, 188, 208, 209, 210–211
'coherent deformation', 66n26, 141, 151n17, 223, 284n34
cohesion (or coherence), 9, 108n25, 117, 155, 187, 196–197, 198, 199, 200, 208, 211, 224–225, 227–228, 249, 250–251, 273, 275, 292
concepts, 22–24, 31, 44, 83, 84–85, 88–89, 215, 216–217, 218, 245, 260, 262, 263–266, 267, 274
constitution, 4, 29, 36n7, 58, 65n6, 71, 73, 80, 83, 97, 100, 108n31, 110n49, 145, 156–157, 157–158, 170, 188, 204, 221, 223, 227, 232n23, 244, 256–257, 282n13, 292, 296
convention, 22, 47, 53, 57, 66n27, 67n28, 122, 123, 136, 212

description, 4, 7, 21–22, 26, 34, 37n19, 75–76, 80–81, 91, 96–100, 103, 108n23, 144–147, 180, 237, 247, 250–252, 254, 262, 267–269, 277, 285n38, 287, 294
diacritic, 131, 132, 134–135
dialectic, 16, 221, 254–255, 257, 261, 268–269, 274, 283n25, 284n29, 284n34; hyper-dialectic, 255–258
dialogue, 8, 67n29, 131, 138, 159–164, 166–168, 182n25, 236n53
dimensionality, 121, 142, 199, 205, 206–208, 221, 225, 226–227, 233n29

l'écart, 8–9, 155, 158, 162, 197–200, 232n17, 250, 256, 273

embodiment, 41, 43, 48, 49–50, 55–56, 59–60, 73–74, 76, 111n67, 159, 165–166, 167, 171, 175, 201–202, 212, 217, 243, 245, 268
empirical, 64n1, 73, 81, 83, 100, 242, 254–255, 272
empiricism, 49, 71, 88, 106n4
enactivism, 37n14
encroachment (*l' empiétement*), 8, 169–173, 183n34, 201, 202

INDEX

essence, 23, 94, 241–242, 242–243, 259, 269–275, 285n41, 286n44, 286n45, 286n50, 286n51
explanation, 75–76, 78, 80, 94, 97, 107n21, 108n23, 270–271, 272–273
expression, 4, 7, 31, 39, 49–50, 92, 103, 115, 116, 119, 140, 153, 177, 220, 237, 284n34, 285n40; authentic, 7, 57–59, 61–64, 67n34, 97–98, 110n56, 126, 138, 187–188, 224, 243; in children, 61, 117, 127–129, 194; creative, 9, 57, 85, 98, 103, 126, 143, 179, 221, 223, 226, 237, 245–246, 250–252, 253, 260, 263, 267–269, 285n37, 287; empirical, 7, 9, 46–53, 57, 64n1, 100, 189–190, 212, 220–221; formal, 8, 64, 120–126, 135, 137, 150n4, 150n5, 177–178, 179, 222, 279; indirect, 8, 103, 137, 139, 142–144, 147, 148–150, 177–178, 221, 235n44, 246–247, 251–252, 263, 266–267, 273–274, 286n51; literary, 58, 97, 140, 142, 143, 146–147, 148–149, 265–266, 284n34; ontological, 189–190, 223, 236n53, 249–250, 251–252, 258–260, 260–261, 261, 262, 266, 274; 'operative', 139, 211–212, 222, 262, 273–274, 277; phenomenological, 35, 85–86, 98, 100–103, 147–149, 178, 247, 250–252, 264, 277, 287, 296; transcendental, 2, 7, 64n1, 82–83, 90–92, 97–98, 100, 101–102, 107n21, 110n56, 189, 276

flesh, 162, 169, 181n2, 200–201, 207, 232n20, 253
form, 6, 16–19, 58–59
founding, 7, 17, 44–45, 87–92, 93–94, 124, 204, 208, 209, 210
freedom, 7, 59–63, 92

genesis, 78, 79–80, 80–81, 108n26–108n27, 244, 255, 282n11
gesture, 46, 49–52, 54–56, 58, 63, 167, 177, 213

idealism, 31–33, 73, 94, 109n39, 291
ideality, 25, 35, 84, 89, 95, 196–197, 204, 208, 218, 234n39, 253, 269–270, 272–273, 274

'inherent' language, 215–220, 220, 221, 223, 228, 234n38, 234n39
Innere Sprachform, 191–193
institution, 133, 204–208, 209–210, 214, 218, 234n37
intellectualism, 49, 72–73, 94, 106n8, 109n46, 261
intention, 49–51, 52, 55, 63, 66n23, 66n24, 192, 212, 213
intentionality, 1, 24, 26, 41–42, 44, 73, 107n17, 153, 163–164, 169, 170, 171–173, 182n13, 182n25, 183n41, 200–204, 206
interpretation, 43, 53–56, 63, 67n28, 91, 211–212, 225, 227, 262
interrogation., 238–239, 245–250, 274, 276, 278, 282n16
intersubjectivity, 54–55, 128, 144, 147, 152n25, 153, 156, 158, 161, 196, 197–199, 236n53, 256, 295
intuition, 2, 4, 11n6, 45, 55, 71, 88–89, 92, 106n14, 110n48, 125, 150, 150n5, 216, 224, 240–241, 255, 290, 293–295

linguistics, 8, 121, 127–133, 135
literature, 8, 58, 116, 137–139, 140–149, 150n13, 265, 267, 277

mathematics, 110n48, 121, 123–124, 125, 126, 150n3, 150n4
meaning, 1, 4, 18, 20–24, 25, 28–29, 32, 35, 39, 45, 46, 48, 49, 50–51, 54–55, 63–64, 66n24, 66n27, 67n28, 67n29, 75, 78, 87, 88, 93, 98, 117–118, 153, 155, 157, 174–175, 175, 188, 196, 204, 204–205, 211, 225, 232n19, 238–239, 240–241, 246, 258, 263, 264, 267, 274, 276–277, 292, 296. *See also* 'sense'; 'signification'
metaphor, 252–254, 283n21, 283n23
metaphysics, 8, 115–116, 116–120, 120–121, 147, 173, 237–238, 280n1, 281n5, 291–292

narcissism, 8, 152n25, 153, 161, 162–164, 203
natural attitude, 2, 25, 36n10, 242
naturalism, 40, 57, 66n18, 67n30, 234n39
nature, 15, 181n11, 183n47, 234n39, 250

ontology, 8, 9, 88, 102, 102–103, 119, 155, 156, 159, 171, 173, 174, 176, 181n10, 181n11, 181n12, 190, 196, 198, 237–239, 240–241, 242, 245–246, 249–250, 252, 255, 259, 264–265, 275, 276, 279, 280n1, 281n2, 281n6, 284n34, 291

painting, 117, 139–142, 151n15, 151n16
passivity, 9, 153, 158, 163, 165–168, 202, 207, 260–261
perception, 2, 5, 30, 44–45, 53, 86–89, 92, 93–94, 110n57, 124, 156–157, 162, 163–164, 188, 198, 199, 202, 204, 242–243, 246–247, 263, 267; 'intertwining' with language, 209, 209–210, 211–214, 227–228, 249, 267; relation to language, 26, 30–31, 35, 39, 43–46, 47, 50–51, 87–89, 90–91, 100, 209–211, 214–219, 218–219, 220, 224, 226, 233n32, 234n39, 249–250, 268–269, 278, 290
pragmatics, 39, 46, 48, 50
psychoanalysis, 163
psychology, 65n3, 129, 194; gestalt psychology, 19–21, 127, 286n44

rationality, 7, 73–74, 76–77, 86, 108n24, 115, 117–118, 119, 132–133, 144, 147, 196–197
realism, 18–19, 24–25, 71, 291
reduction, 2, 25, 36n12, 100–102, 111n67, 270–271, 285n43
reflection, 4, 44, 71, 76, 78–81, 82, 83, 85–86, 89–91, 93, 94–95, 97–98, 100, 106n4, 108n31, 145, 179, 242–243, 282n13; hyper-reflection (*surréflexion*), 243–246, 247–249, 250–251, 255, 258, 274
representation, 49–51, 58, 73, 128, 138, 151n16, 192, 195, 240
reversibility, 8, 152n25, 153, 159, 160, 161–162, 169, 203, 272

science, 8, 16, 40, 121–122, 123, 129, 135. *See also* formal expression
sedimentation, 47–49, 57, 61–62, 65n15, 84, 95, 110n55, 123, 140, 160, 204–205, 212, 234n37, 268

semantics, 39, 46, 50, 97–98, 131
sense (*le sens*), 21–24, 29, 32, 33, 45, 50, 65n11, 75, 77, 88, 92, 98, 108n26, 118, 123, 155–157, 158, 173, 176, 181n10, 181n11, 196, 205, 210, 215, 220, 240, 243–244, 246–247, 256, 267, 284n34
signification (*la signification*), 21–24, 30–31, 32, 33, 34, 43, 43–44, 45, 48, 52, 58, 63, 65n11, 88–89, 196, 204–205, 220, 233n32
situation, 46, 52, 54, 59, 61, 62, 110n57, 165, 179, 257
speech, 29, 46, 47, 49–50, 64n1, 66n16, 93, 119, 121, 129, 130–131, 138, 162, 211, 251–252, 255, 259, 261, 273; '*parole*' vs. '*langue*', 48–49, 66n16, 130–131, 134, 150n6, 216; and silence, 44, 82, 88, 109n46, 143, 152n26, 221–222, 223, 226, 245, 247, 247–248, 249–250, 254–255, 259, 260–261, 267, 277; 'speaking', 44, 47–48, 57, 58, 139, 211, 251–252; 'spoken', 22, 44, 47–49, 215–216, 223, 251–252
structure, 6, 16–19, 27–28, 31

temporality, 61, 92, 205–208, 233n28
thought, 42–44, 49–51, 70, 82, 85, 88, 126, 127, 172, 192, 211, 212, 216, 222, 228, 241
tradition, 84, 89, 95, 140, 160, 215, 234n37
transcendence, 34, 53–54, 57, 60, 63, 166, 205, 207, 223
transcendental, 2, 32, 64n1, 74, 76, 78, 79, 81, 83, 91–92, 98, 109n39, 117–118, 148, 189–190, 201, 238, 242, 244, 254–255, 264, 276
transgression (*la transgression*), 8, 154, 169–173, 183n34, 183n40, 201, 241
truth, 46, 49, 77, 84, 94, 97, 110n50, 119–120, 125, 144, 153, 155–156, 158–159, 171, 173–174, 179, 181n11, 183n43, 226, 228, 251, 279

use, 29, 39, 47–48, 51–52, 53–54, 56, 57–58, 61–62, 66n27, 83, 128, 131, 138, 174–175, 180, 190, 191, 209, 212–213, 220, 222, 226–227, 233n34 world, 16, 24, 32, 41, 57, 58, 62–63, 74, 80, 83, 98, 118, 137, 140–141, 145, 155, 170, 173, 174, 190, 193, 194, 208, 219, 225–226, 229–230, 232n13, 244, 249–250, 282n9, 292

ABOUT THE AUTHOR

Dimitris Apostolopoulos is currently Assistant Professor of Philosophy at Nanyang Technological University. His research focuses on European philosophy, especially phenomenology, and has appeared in venues like the *European Journal of Philosophy*, *British Journal for the History of Philosophy*, *Research in Phenomenology*, and *Journal of the British Society for Phenomenology*.

www.ingramcontent.com/pod-product-compliance
Lightning Source LLC
Chambersburg PA
CBHW050857300426
44111CB00010B/1285